1 MONTH
FREE
READING

at
www.ForgottenBooks.com

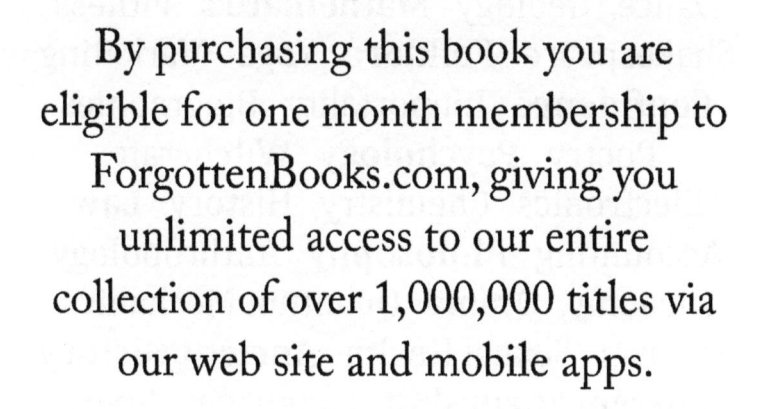

By purchasing this book you are eligible for one month membership to ForgottenBooks.com, giving you unlimited access to our entire collection of over 1,000,000 titles via our web site and mobile apps.

To claim your free month visit: www.forgottenbooks.com/free524635

* Offer is valid for 45 days from date of purchase. Terms and conditions apply.

English
Français
Deutsche
Italiano
Español
Português

www.forgottenbooks.com

Mythology Photography **Fiction**
Fishing Christianity **Art** Cooking
Essays Buddhism Freemasonry
Medicine **Biology** Music **Ancient Egypt** Evolution Carpentry Physics
Dance Geology **Mathematics** Fitness
Shakespeare **Folklore** Yoga Marketing
Confidence Immortality Biographies
Poetry **Psychology** Witchcraft
Electronics Chemistry History **Law**
Accounting **Philosophy** Anthropology
Alchemy Drama Quantum Mechanics
Atheism Sexual Health **Ancient History**
Entrepreneurship Languages Sport
Paleontology Needlework Islam
Metaphysics Investment Archaeology
Parenting Statistics Criminology
Motivational

1,000,000 Books

are available to read at

Forgotten Books

www.ForgottenBooks.com

Read online
Download PDF
Purchase in print

ISBN 978-1-333-59903-4
PIBN 10524635

This book is a reproduction of an important historical work. Forgotten Books uses state-of-the-art technology to digitally reconstruct the work, preserving the original format whilst repairing imperfections present in the aged copy. In rare cases, an imperfection in the original, such as a blemish or missing page, may be replicated in our edition. We do, however, repair the vast majority of imperfections successfully; any imperfections that remain are intentionally left to preserve the state of such historical works.

Forgotten Books is a registered trademark of FB &c Ltd.
Copyright © 2018 FB &c Ltd.
FB &c Ltd, Dalton House, 60 Windsor Avenue, London, SW19 2RR.
Company number 08720141. Registered in England and Wales.

For support please visit www.forgottenbooks.com

BOSTON UNIVERSITY
COLLEGE OF LIBERAL ARTS LIBRARY

Given in Memory of
AUGUSTUS PEABODY LORING, JR.
and
ROSAMOND BOWDITCH LORING
1952

THE SEA TRADER
HIS FRIENDS AND ENEMIES

THE POOL OF LONDON.

From a scarce Line Engraving, kindly lent by Messrs T. H. Parker, Printsellers, 45, Whitcomb Street, London, W.C.

HIS FRIENDS AND ENEMIES

BY

DAVID HANNAY

AUTHOR OF "A HISTORY OF THE ROYAL NAVY"

ILLUSTRATED

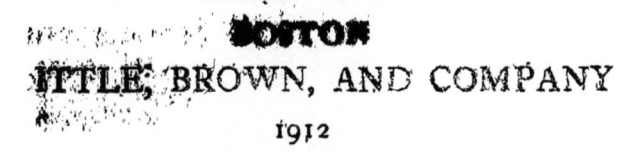

BOSTON
LITTLE, BROWN, AND COMPANY
1912

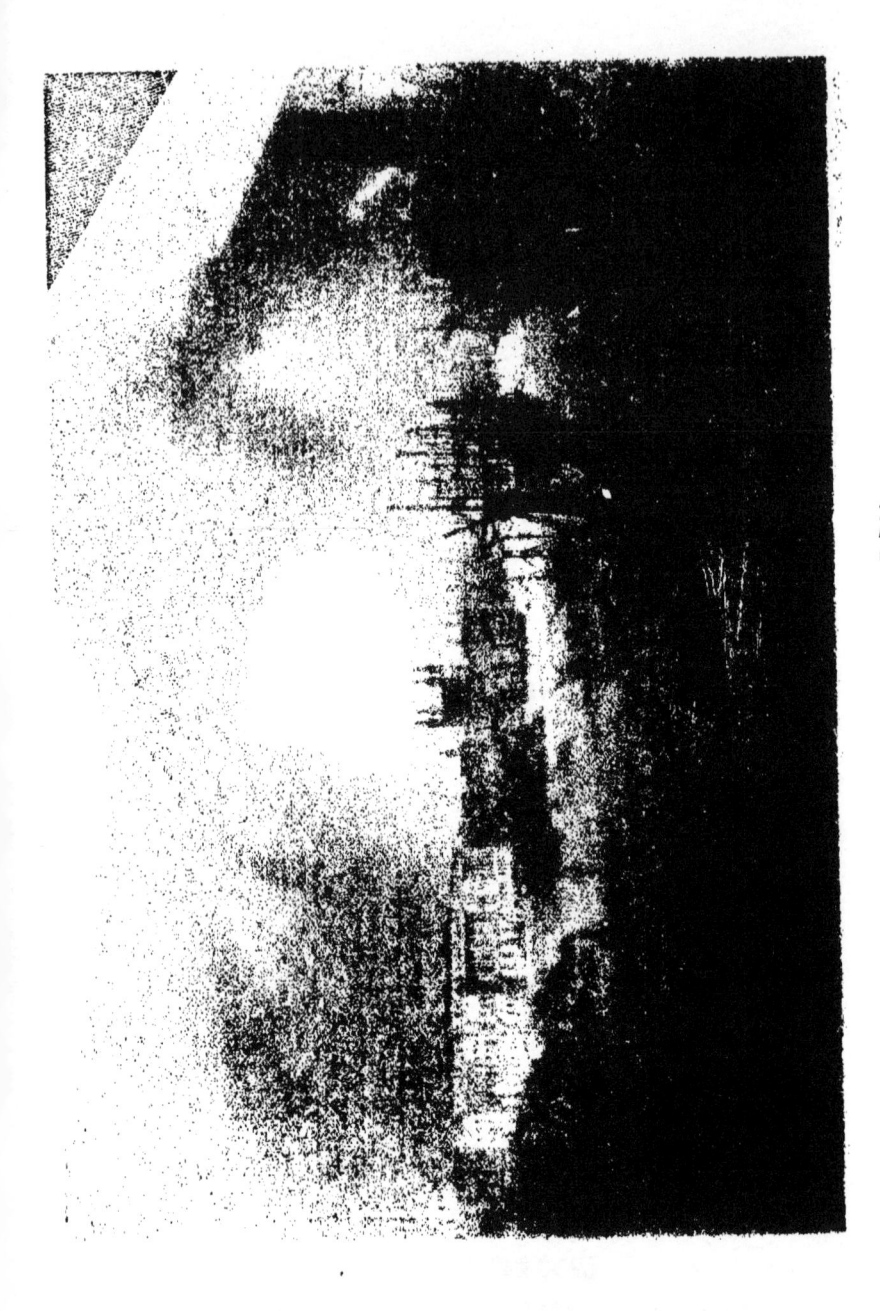

THE POOL OF LONDON.

From a Line Engraving. by Messrs I. H. Trasselers, 45, Whitcomb London, W.C.

HIS FRIENDS AND ENEMIES

BY

DAVID HANNAY

AUTHOR OF "A HISTORY OF THE ROYAL NAVY"

ILLUSTRATED

BOSTON
LITTLE, BROWN, AND COMPANY
1912

" We be three poor mariners
  Newly come from the seas ;
  We spend our lives in jeopardy,
  While others live at ease.
  Shall we go dance the round, the round ?
  Shall we go dance the round ?
  And he that is a bully boy
  Come pledge me on this ground.

" We care not for those martial men
  That do our states disdain,
  But we care for the merchant men
  Who do our states maintain.
  To them we dance this round around,
  To them we dance this round,
  And he that is a bully boy
  Come pledge me on this ground."

(From Deuteromelia, 1609; in " Lyrics from Elizabethan Song-Books." A. H. Bullen, 1887.)

PREFACE

THIS book is not submitted to the favourable attention of the reader as being a formal history of sea-borne commerce. Still less does it pretend to be exhaustive. It aims at no more than at giving a general survey, illustrated by leading examples, of the conditions in which the trade of the world has been conducted at sea. Nothing would have been easier than to multiply examples of some aspects of the life. For instance, whole chapters might have been devoted to stories of shipwreck. But those tales have been frequently and well told. Or, again, it was only necessary to take the Calendar of State Papers for America and the West Indies, in order to find material for three or four chapters full of the doings of pirates. But they would also have been full of sheer repetition. Moreover, it would falsify the picture if I were to give so much prominence to the mere law-breaker and outlaw, who, after all, was the exception. There is too much " exception " in my book as it is, and I can only plead that this is not my fault. We hear a great deal of the fortunes of the sailor when he was robbing, or was being robbed, when he was subject to ill-treatment, or was calling the attention of mankind to himself by violence. What is very difficult indeed to do is to see him in normal conditions, going upon the sea on his " lawful occasions," and in port. Men did not take the trouble to record what to them were the commonplaces of existence. It is easy enough to find accounts of voyages of the sailors of many nations when their purpose had some element of war. But the peaceful trader sailed and came back in obscurity. When he spoke (and narratives by men who had been plain sailors are not very rare), it was for some other purpose than to give a description of the sailor's life. It was to describe some barbarous country, as in the case of Drury; or to tell his adventures as a privateer, and the story of a felonious attempt to defraud an insurer, as in the case of Bather; or he used his sea-life as a thread on which to string his spiritual experiences, as in the case of John Newton. Why should he tell us how he was engaged, paid, fed, lodged? And yet that is precisely what we should like to know. I must leave the candid critic who may think me worthy of notice to decide whether I have been guilty of unpardonable oversights. That much is lacking I know only too well.

There is even greater difficulty in finding pictorial illustrations of the sailor's life. Portraits of ships are not rare, and are often authentic. Fancy pictures of sailors, shipwrecks, fights with pirates, and so forth, are common enough. But are they evidence? Authentic pictures of the merchant-sailor at his work, or in the forecastle, or in the cabin, must be very rare, if they exist at all. I do not remember to have seen one, and authorities whose knowledge is far beyond mine seem to have been no more fortunate. It is exasperating to be told that a draftsman was carried on the voyage, and to see from the published narrative that he was exclusively employed in drawing harbours, plants, and natives. Frezier's "Voyage to Peru," to quote only one of hundreds of instances, is full of Spanish-American harbours and pictures of Araucans, etc. But it never occurred to him to give us the cabin in which he lived, the quarters of the crew in the forecastle, or the deck of the ship. Why should it? They were his daily bread, the

PREFACE

commonplaces of life, and he did not reflect that the ports and the Araucans would remain, whereas the form and habit of the sea-life of the seventeenth century were transitory, and that posterity might wish to recover them. I have tried to make the illustrations really illustrative, and for such success as I have achieved, have to thank, first, Captain Chas. N. Robinson for his advice and for supplying me with the originals of the drawings of the hold of a slave-ship; and then Messrs. Parker of Whitcomb Street, for kindly lending me the plates, which are severally acknowledged; and I cannot end without thanking Mr. W. Foster, of the India Office, for his kind assistance.

DAVID HANNAY.

CONTENTS

CHAPTER	PAGE
INTRODUCTION	1
I. THE ANCIENT SHIP	11
II. THE SKIPPER AND HIS MEN	26
III. THE WAY OF LIFE	45
IV. SALE, PURCHASE, AND PLUNDER	67
V. THE OPENING OF THE OCEAN ROUTES	89
VI. THE INTRUDERS ON THE EAST	109
VII. IN THE EASTERN SEAS	133
VIII. THE INTRUDERS ON THE WEST	162
IX. THE SPANISH MAIN	199
X. THE PIRATE	234
XI. IMPRESSMENT	265
XII. THE SLAVER	293
XIII. THE SEA TRADER IN WAR-TIME	329
XIV. CONCLUSION	366
INDEX	383

LIST OF ILLUSTRATIONS

	TO FACE PAGE
THE POOL OF LONDON	*Frontispiece*
VENETIAN TRIREME	*page* 12
In text, drawn by E. E. HANNAY.	
EGYPTIAN SHIP	*page* 17
In text, drawn by E. E. HANNAY.	
THE CHINESE JUNK, KEYING	24
MERCHANT SHIP	42
WRECK OF THE "GROSVENOR"	64
MERCHANT SHIP	96
ENGLISH SAILORS	132
MURDER OF INDIAN PRINCE	138
A KORA-KORA	144
CIVILIZING THE NATIVES	160
MERCHANT SHIP	214
BARBARY PIRATES	252
FRENCH SAILORS	270
REEFING TOPSAILS	282
THE HOLD OF A SLAVER (A) (*In text*)	*page* 299
THE HOLD OF A SLAVER (B) (*In text*)	*page* 301
A SLAVE DHOW	*page* 314
In Text, drawn by E. E. HANNAY.	
H.M.S. "PICKLE" DEFEATING NOTORIOUS SLAVER	318
MERCHANT SHIP	352
SHARE IN A PRIVATEER (*In text*)	*page* 361
THE CLIPPER SHIP "DUNCAN DUNBAR"	370

THE SEA TRADER:
HIS FRIENDS AND ENEMIES

INTRODUCTION

"Much learned trifling might be spared if our antiquarians would condescend to reflect that similar manners would naturally be produced by similar situations." In this sentence Gibbon stated, with his usual felicity of language, a rule which is of value to all historians and critics, but is of peculiar worth to whomsoever attempts to deal with the lives and the manners of seafaring men. They have always done their work subject to conditions which are at once masterful and permanent. They sailed in unavoidable obedience to tides and currents, storms, and the lie of the land, in those very remote times sixteen centuries before the Christian era, when the fleet of the Egyptian Queen Hatshepsitu made the voyage to the land of Punt, which is recorded by inscriptions and pictures on the temple of Deir-el-Bahari. The ships which navigate the Red Sea, and all seas to-day, can do no other. The skippers and mariners who sailed for Hatshepsitu, and who brought her fleet back " laden to the uttermost with the wonderful products of the land of Punt," worked and lived in ways dictated to them by the form of their vessels, the means of propulsion on which they depended, and the extent of their power to learn where they were. So do the incomparably greater fleets which nowadays visit or pass " the divine land " of Punt, wherever it may have been. On that point I do not presume to have an opinion. It is enough for my purpose that Punt was to be reached oversea by seafaring men who had to depend on the wind and their muscle as they tugged at the oar, and who were coasters, for neither their ships nor their instruments allowed them to venture on the open sea. Put seamen of any race, and of the best knowledge, into similar vessels, make them go the voyage without a compass to-day, and they would be forced to do precisely what the mariners of Queen Hatshepsitu did thirty-five centuries ago.

Those persons who appear to think that nothing is worth saying unless it is flagrantly in conflict with manifest truth, may perhaps think that I am inviting them " to take a peep into the obvious." It is obvious, as obvious as Gibbon's maxim, that men must at all times have done what the nature of things forces them to do. And yet, like many no less useful self-evident propositions, it has been consistently disregarded, with the result that much learned trifling has been devoted to questioning what need never have been questioned, and to explaining what in reality explains itself. My purpose is not to enforce respect for commonplaces and the obvious, but to justify the course I propose to take while attempting to describe what the life of the sea trader has been at all times and in all seas.

The history of sea-borne commerce is divided into the ages before the opening of the great ocean routes at the close of the fifteenth century, and the very much shorter period which lies between us and the voyages of Columbus, Vasco da Gama, and Magellan. The first was the epoch of the coaster. The second is the epoch of the high seas. It is the difference between *la navigation côtière* and *la navigation hauturière*. I do not, of course, mean that there is a hard impassable line drawn between the ages before and those after the year 1492. Men were already using, and for generations had used, the compass when Columbus sailed. They were also making use of the astrolabe to take the height of the sun and so find their latitude. They were no longer confined wholly to the coast. Without the compass and the astrolabe Columbus would never have dared to steer out to the West. There are parts of the world to this day where trade goes on, even in small details, very much as it was conducted by the seamen of the Middle Ages. In the Malay Archipelago, for instance, the native sea traders have still little cause for departing from the customs of their fathers. But though the two conditions overlap, the fact remains

INTRODUCTION

that, until it had been shown to be possible to sail right across the Atlantic, Pacific, and Indian Oceans, all trade was conducted in what were really coasting voyages, longer or shorter, and all seamen were coasters. Since 1492 this has not been the case, and though the coaster survives, and no doubt will survive, he is no longer the typical seafaring man.

The improvement of the ship herself has been of vital importance. In the ancient world, and till late in the Middle Ages, ships were laid up in winter, for they were not qualified to encounter its storms. The development of the rigging was slow, and it was secret. The sailors were jealous of their " art and mystery." The changes came in little by little, and always in the face of dogged opposition. It is quite certain that when the jibsail, about the middle of the eighteenth century, replaced the old square spritsail, the gain to the handiness of the ship was great, and the resources of the seaman were notably increased. It is equally beyond question that the square spritsail was an absurdity, for as it could not be set fore and aft it was of no use when the ship was close hauled. The mizzen could not be set when the spritsail was furled, lest the ship should be overloaded with canvas at the stern, and so come head to wind. Yet we may be sure that old-fashioned seamen shook their heads at the new-fangled jib.

The old experienced seaman had his way in some countries so effectually that he fixed the type of his ship for centuries. Among the races of more open mind change, if slow, has been continuous. The regular bred sailor of one generation could not rig a ship exactly as she would have been rigged by a sailor fifty years before his time. If the model of the hull of a ship of the year 1800 were to be put into the hands of a veteran who began to serve his time about 1850, and he were asked to rig it, he would turn out something rather better than the original he supposed himself to be engaged in reproducing. He would fit it with davits to hang the boats from, whereas none were used in 1800. The seamen of that year knew a davit, but then it was a species of derrick used for hoisting in weights. He would give her spritsail gaffs, and not what she really carried, a spritsail yard. He would fasten the upper shrouds to a necklace on the lower mast, a thing first done to the scandal of orthodox officers in 1811 by Captain Tarbutt, of the East Indiaman *Apollo*. The rigger of 1800 would have fastened the upper shrouds to catharpin staves, and would have supported the catharpins by Bentinck shrouds. And if the rigger of 1800 had been asked to rig the model of a ship of 1750, he would have girdled his lower masts with iron bands, whereas he ought to have woolded them with rope, and to have trimmed the wooldings with wooden hoops above and below. The invention of steam propulsion, and the use of metal as the material for hulls and rigging alike, have made immense changes in quite recent years. The old art of building wooden ships is dying, and a great vocabulary once familiar to all sailormen is falling into disuse. When a wooden vessel was built for Captain Scott's first voyage to the Antarctic, some difficulty was found in discovering a master-shipwright who could direct the work. There can be few of the younger race of sailors who know what were the *spindle*, or *upper tree*, the two *side trees* with their *heel pieces*, the *side fishes, cheeks, front fish, cant pieces*, and *fillings* of a "made mast." The mast of to-day is a hollow iron tube. The time may come when masts and spars will have disappeared altogether, and such familiar names as topgallant mast or flying jibboom will have become as obsolete as the language of the domestic spinning-wheel.

The immense change wrought by steam and metal has come in our own time, for it was not until the end of the first quarter of the nineteenth century that a marine steam-engine was widely available, just when the threatened exhaustion of the forests and the rise in the price of wood drove shipbuilders and riggers to employ iron. In earlier ages the changes were slow, and were rarely recorded in print, and in accessible places.

I do not undertake to write a history of shipbuilding. My purpose is only to say as much of the nature of the vessel in which he sailed as will make the life of the old sea trader intelligible. Still less is it my ambition to give an historical account of the development of nautical astronomy and of navigation. Yet it is impossible to realize what a sea voyage meant to the men of St. Paul's generation, and during ages before and after him, till we understand what means they had of knowing where they were, and how they were to reach their landfall. Some understanding we must have of the astrolabe and the backstaff, which came before the quadrant, octant, sextant, and chronometer. Then we cannot afford to be wholly ignorant of the " periploi," the " rutters," the " portulane," which were the predecessors of the charts and " Admiralty Pilots and Sailing Directions " of the modern seaman.

Then there is still another set of conditions which must be realized. That ships improved and that knowledge increased was much; but it was even more that security could be obtained. In that respect changes came slowly, and all changes were not for the better. Before its own internal corruptions had opened the door to the inroads of the barbarians, the Roman Empire gave the traders of the Mediterranean a fulness of protection which they were not to enjoy again till the warships of the United States and of Britain and the armies of France had made an end of the Barbary pirates. The history of piracy is intimately bound up with the history of sea-borne commerce till very recent times indeed. For long ages the merchant seaman went at his own risk. So late as two hundred years ago the then greatest maritime powers, Holland, Great Britain, and France, did not even profess to protect their traders in all seas. It was much if they could keep them safe at home in the waters of Europe. In far distant seas the traders had to protect themselves. The State did all that then lay in its power when it allowed traders to organize themselves for their own defence into joint-stock companies, and when it armed them with a handsome charter which authorized them to possess warships, exercise martial law, build forts, hire soldiers, and make treaties at their own expense and risk. Some Governments gave protection in this way largely and effectually. The model was the great United Dutch East India Company, which was the big brother, often the bullying and hectoring big brother, of the Company of the Merchants of London trading to the East Indies.

The history of the merchant seaman is not a history of

the Phœnician and the Greek, of the Genoese, the Dutchman, the Englishman, or the American. It is the history of the seafaring man of whatever date, race, or colour who sailed in a small vessel steering by the land, since he could not steer by the compass ; and then of the seafaring man in a larger and better vessel who, steering by the compass and finding his way by the sun, could leave the land behind and strike across the open seas. When men sailed in weak craft, with clumsy rigging and partly in dependence on their oars, certain consequences inevitably followed. They could not keep the sea in winter. They had need of a large crew, for their sails were such as bred what the North Country English sailor derides as " Scotch seamanship," which is " all stupidity and main strength." Everything had to be done by pulling and hauling, and if the sails did not require a numerous crew, the oars did. When the vessel was small and the crew was large, it follows that there could be little room to give cover to the men, or to store water and provisions. Therefore the voyage must be by short stages from watering-place to watering-place. The voyage itself was by necessity long, and if it could not be finished before the winter months began, the ship had to be laid up abroad till they were over.

For centuries all trade was conducted in these conditions—somewhat modified when the compass became known, but still not altered in essentials. Where these conditions still prevail, oversea trade is so conducted to this day. Now, since similar manners are naturally produced by similar situations, we have only to find a region in which conditions once universal still survive in order to meet with an example of such a voyage as would have been made by Phœnician or Greek before the Christian era, and by the medieval seamen in or out of the Mediterranean. The Malay Archipelago is such a region, and for the voyage we have only to go to the the delightful book of Mr. Wallace, and to the account he gives of his cruise from Macassar to Aru in a prau.

Let us begin with Mr. Wallace's ship. She was of some 70 tons burden, and " shaped something like a Chinese junk." The junk has altered considerably in size at different epochs. If we can believe the medieval traveller, Marco Polo, who tells us nothing manifestly incredible about them, there was a time when the " ships of Manzi," which sailed from Canton to Ceylon, were as large as most Spanish galleons of the sixteenth century. The type has altered but little. The junk of all times, and the European " round ship " built for trade, as the " long ship " was built for war, in antiquity and the Middle Ages, was essentially the same kind of vessel. She was built high at the stern, and was steered by two rudders hung from cross-beams aft. The double rudder was not unknown in European craft, but we will for the present keep to Mr. Wallace's prau. A low poop aft provided the " captain's cabin," with its summary furniture of boxes, mats, and pillows. Between poop and mainmast " was a little thatched house on deck about 4 feet high to the ridge, and one compartment of this forming a cabin 6½ feet long by 5½ feet wide I had all to myself."

The prau was masted in one of the oldest of ways, with tripod masts. " If," says Mr. Wallace, " in an ordinary ship you replace the shrouds and backstays by strong timbers, and take away the mast altogether, you have the arrangements adopted on board a prau." It had been used by Egyptians three thousand years before. The rigging was " a wilderness of yards and spars mostly formed of bamboo. The mainyard, an immense affair nearly 100 feet long, was formed of many pieces of wood and bamboo bound together with rattans in an ingenious manner. The sail carried by this was of an oblong shape, and was hung out of the centre, so that when the short end was hauled down on deck the long end mounted high in the air, making up for the lowness of the mast itself. These vessels make one voyage a year as the wind dictates." They leave Macassar in December or January at the beginning of the west monsoon, and return in July or August with the east monsoon. Mr. Wallace saw the building of the praus on the beach of Kè, and out of the timbers brought down from the mountains. The art of the Malay shipbuilder, who uses no nails, nor any metal, is national and peculiar, or was, if the progress of European industry has killed the native arts since Mr. Wallace visited Kè more than half a century ago. But his methods and the scene of his labours were universal till the other day.

If a seafaring man of the Roman Empire, or of a medieval trading city, northern or southern, or a Spaniard of the sixteenth and seventeenth centuries who followed the " carrera de Indias " (the trade to the West Indies), had come back to life at Macassar, he would have seen nothing to surprise him in the constitution or the ways of the crew of Mr. Wallace's prau. The thirty sailors or so who manned this vessel of 75 tons would have appeared to him a reasonable number. Since that huge yard was to be handled by main strength, fewer would not have served the turn. It would have been the very commonplace of the seafarer's life that everyone of the crew carried a little packet of goods as a trading venture of his own. The officers would be just what he expected to find. At the head was not a sea captain, but the merchant who owned or freighted the ship and directed the voyage. Rome knew him as the " exercitor." He had with him his own people, some, if not all of them, being bondmen—debtors bound by Malay custom, enforced by Dutch colonial law, to work off their obligations by personal service. They took their meals with him, and they, no less than the sailors, had their little trading ventures. Under his general direction as to the course of the voyage, the vessel was commanded by a " juragan," whom the Greeks would have called the " kubernetes," and the Romans the " magister," " nauclerus," or " nauclerius," and later peoples the " padrono," the " pilot," the " skipper," the " sailing master." The habits of the Malay crew were as medieval as they well could be. " Our crew," says Mr. Wallace, " though numerous enough for a vessel of 700 instead of one of 70 tons, have it very much their own way, and there seems to be seldom more than a dozen at work at a time. When anything important is to be done, however, all start up willingly enough ; but then all think themselves at liberty to give their opinion, and half a dozen voices are heard giving orders, and there is such a shrieking and confusion that it seems wonderful anything gets done at all."

The men of antiquity would have been quite at home in that fair on the beach at Debbo, where Mr. Wallace's prau's crew ended their outward-bound voyage ; and so would the Spaniards of the " India trade " who went to the yearly markets at Nombre de Dios, or Porto Bello. Debbo was a small mart, but was none the less the faithful picture of the great "staples," or meeting-places, of trade as the old European sea traders knew them. Men crowded together, goods were bartered, and sheds run up while the fair lasted, and then the beach was empty till next year. Least surprising of all to the visitor from old days would have been the constant fear of pirates, the hasty armings, the pitiful stories told by plundered mariners, the excursions and alarums, which Mr. Wallace heard of. For centuries they were the daily bread of the sea trader. One feature of the old existence would, indeed, not have been visible. When the ships of Hatshepsitu came back " laden to the uttermost with the wonderful products of the land of Punt," they did not come only with the different " precious woods of the divine land, and with heaps of the resin of incense, and fresh incense-trees, with ebony (objects) of ivory set in pure gold from the land of the Aarnu, with sweet woods, Keshit wood, with alum incense, holy resin and paint for the eyes, with dog-headed apes, with long-tailed monkeys and greyhounds, with leopard-skins," but also with " *natives of the country, together with their children.*' The uplifted scribe who drew the inscription at Deir-el-Bahari rises into enthusiasm as he completes the list. "Never," he cries, "was the like brought to any King of Egypt since the world stands." He was thinking of the amount, not of the constitution of the cargo. The like of those " natives of the country, together with their children," had come to Kings of Egypt before the days of Hatshepsitu, and were to come to many purchasers till the reign of Queen Victoria and humanity. Whatever else may have altered in the course of centuries, the value of the slave as an article of commerce was never overlooked. When the trade of Europe was at its lowest in the evil days at the close of the Carolingian dynasty, the Jews of Verdun and traders of Ragusa could make handsome profits by purchasing prisoners of war, or children of starving parents in Central Europe, and exporting them to fill the harems and recruit the slave-guards of the Khalifs of Cordoba. When that omission is made good, the voyage of the prau from Macassar may supply us with a useful sketch-map of the country we have to cross. Mr. Wallace's narrative points the way to the natural divisions of our subject, and suggests the guiding questions : (1) What were the ships of the ages of the coasters ? (2) How was the crew organized, paid, and disciplined ? (3) What were the methods of navigation, and the seamanship—a far more obscure point ? (4) The ways of life in these vessels, the methods of trade and the cargoes? (5) The enemies who preyed upon all such as went upon the sea upon their lawful occasions ?

CHAPTER I

THE ANCIENT SHIP

I AM in the happy position of one who can approach his subject, not wholly without fear, but with a comparatively light heart. It is no part of my humble task to inquire into the unsolved, and too probably never-to-be-solved, mystery—what was the disposition of the oars in a many-banked ancient galley? Classical scholars who read scholiasts and poets in a confiding spirit, who take the burlesque use of a Greek phrase which answered coarsely to our " wipe your boots upon somebody " in the literal sense, and who quote a Spanish priest of the fifth century as an authority for the war galleys of the battle of Actium, come to one set of conclusions. Some of them construct models. But seamen and shipbuilders reject their conclusions and their models as absurd. We possess a bas-relief of a middle section of an Athenian trireme. The original is in Athens; there is a plaster cast in the École des Beaux Arts in Paris, and many drawings and photographs have been taken. The drawings and photographs are commonly touched up. Visitors who look at the original see what they are disposed to see on its rather battered surface. To some it proves that the oars come through ports rising one above the other. To others it clearly shows that the oars issue from one row of ports in sets of three, and that the Athenian trireme was simply the well-known and perfectly intelligible Venetian trireme of the light oar " remo zenzile " of one man to each oar, and three oars to the bench. As each fallible man thinks so the clock tinks.

Happily, we can leave the many-banked galleys of antiquity in peace, for whatever else they were, they were warships, and not cargo vessels. But we may stay for a moment by the *trireme de tre reme e de tre uomini per banco*, for it helps us to make a distinction. Observe that the Venetians made experiments. They built boats of four oars and four men to a bench—quadriremes, and of five oars and five men to a bench—quinqueremes. Then they gradually came to set the three, four, or five men to pull at the same sweep, "scaloccio," and still called the galleys triremes, quadriremes, and quinqueremes, though there were no longer

VENETIAN TRIREME.

sets of oars, but only tiers of rowers. So the same name stood for very different things. The word "frigate," which began by being the name of a rowboat, ended, before it disappeared altogether, by being the name of an iron armourclad screw steamer of 6,000 tons displacement, carrying 9-inch guns in a central battery. Putting aside modifications in detail, let us see what were the characteristics of the Venetian trireme, which we select here as the typical example of the galley.

She was a long, narrow, and shallow craft. Her length was about eight times her beam, and her depth below the water-line was little more than a quarter of her beam. A 120-foot trireme would have 16 feet of beam, and a draft of some 4 feet. Looking on her deck from above you see that she has a small forecastle and poop. The two are connected by a central gangway. She has an oblong superstructure, by name a " palamante," which is supported by the sides, and transverse beams fore and aft. It projects at its fore and after ends from the sides of the galley, is surrounded by a light bulwark, and has gangways fore and aft at its outside edges. There are masts which carry lateen sails, but we will leave them aside as of secondary consequence. The essential fact concerning the galley—be it trireme, or more or less than trireme—be it " a remo zenzile " or " a scaloccio "—is that the chief motive power is given by the rowers, whose oars rest on the palamante below the bulwarks. As we look down, what we see is the central gangway between poop and forecastle and the benches of the rowers. These benches are not thwarts set at right angles to the gangway, whose proper name, by the way, is the " cursia." They are " bancos " seats set at a slope from the gangway to the side, placed, in fact, *en échelon,* so as to make an obtuse angle aft with the line of the cursia. The innermost, which also is nearest the stern, is the highest. The other two slope slightly away from the stern, and down to the side. In the galley of one man to the oar, each rower is so placed that his oar goes sufficiently clear of the man between him and the side to allow all rowing together without confusion, when all are good rowers. The Greeks would have called the inside man, who of necessity pulls the heaviest oar, the " thranites," and the outside man who pulls the smallest,, the " thalamites." There are twenty, or perhaps twenty-three, sets of three rowers to each side. The oars of each set come out at the same port. There are thole pins for the middle and the upper oar.*

* I repeat that I have no intention of losing time over the venerable trireme dispute, which is a contention between those who think they know things because they know words, and those who know the things, but are not supposed to be capable of understanding those words. Yet I am well assured that, if the shade of one of those

Now, here is a vessel of which we can assert with absolute confidence that she cannot have carried water for the two hundred men or so—rowers, deck-hands, marines, servants, and officers—who constituted her crew for more than a very few days, nor dry provisions sufficient to last any considerable time. It would be absurd to assume that she could have carried bulky goods. Gold or incense she might carry from one watering-place to another, but horses, slaves, timber, or grain in large quantities, she could not have carried. She was a fighting vessel, and not a trading vessel. Apart from the obligation to find fresh water, the galley was limited by the absolute necessity for giving rest to the rowers. She could not go day and night unless she carried a double crew, a thing to be done only when a message had to be carried in urgent haste, and then for no long distance. The size of the crew imposed limitations on the galleys of antiquity and the Middle Ages alike. What trade was done was carried in craft of another type.

Plausible speculation surveying with extensive view the blank mists of extreme antiquity has made guesses at the origin of the ship. A floating log, a nautilus, a water-fowl, have been credited with the honour of having first shown man how he could transport himself across the water in a hollow vessel. It has been supposed that the original of the constructed ship with sides, a stem, and stern, was a coracle, a framework on which hides were stretched. It is the strength of such guesses as these that they cannot be proved to be unfounded, and their weakness that they are wholly incapable of being shown to be accurate. The coracle, which is a product of skilled workmanship, must needs have been the fruit of a long development, progressing through ages for which we have no evidence. When we first

---

rowers of Phormio's squadron who carried their oars across the Isthmus of Corinth at a crisis in the Peloponnesian War were to have the model of a Venetian trireme of one man to each oar and three to each bench, which was made by Admiral Luigi Fincati, and also the model of a quinquereme, which the illustrious Graser made for the Berlin Museum, put before him, he would have no hesitation in saying which was most like the " triêrês " he himself had served in. I may add that it would be good to see the face of Aristophanes when someone explained to him the use made by literal pedantry of a certain line in the "Frogs."

find records of a real ship, it was already a developed instrument of trade or war, and this was inevitable, for records belong to times of advanced civilization.

Mr. Villiers Stuart, in his " Nile Gleanings," reproduces a silhouette of an Egyptian vessel. He assigns her to the Third Dynasty, which flourished about 4400 B.C., and the drawing is taken from the tomb of Ka Khont Khut at Kau-el-Kebir. Now, the dates of archæologists are subjects to dispute, and the work of Egyptian artists was done according to rigid conventions. We are not bound to accept the ship from the tomb of Ka Khont Khut as being exactly of the date given us by Mr. Villiers Stuart. Yet she was assuredly built many centuries before Christ. Then the Egyptian, when painting or engraving on stone, represented all men, animals, and things by sharp outlines, profiles, and flat surfaces. He did not foreshorten, nor did he give perspective. He was indifferent to proportion, and was wont to mark the relative importance of the persons by size. The great people were drawn colossal, and the little ones ran in and out between their legs. His pictures, therefore, are to be taken subject to inventory. It is fortunate that the conventional signs of the draughtsman can be corrected, at least occasionally, by the records of the scribes who drafted the inscriptions. When the due allowances are made, the ship from Kau-el-Kebir can be received as a trustworthy testimony to the shape and qualities of the earliest craft as to which we have anything deserving to be called evidence.

She was already a complete ship, designed for the navigation of the Nile, but perfectly capable of making a coasting voyage. Her two ends are similar in shape, being both sharp. She has a deck, and on it a deck-house, the cabin, perhaps, of the overbearing person armed with what has much the appearance of a cat-o'-nine-tails, who towers over the humble crew. She can be rowed or paddled, but she has a two-legged mast, which is unshipped. As the portrait is a silhouette, we cannot tell from it what proportion her beam held to her length. But there is evidence for the relation of length to beam in Egyptian ships.

Una, servant of the Pharaoh Men-en-Ra of the Sixth Dynasty, whose faithful services are recorded on his tomb, went up the Nile to seek stone for the sarcophagus of his master, and also building material. He took with him " six broad vessels, three tow-boats, three rafts, and one ship manned with warriors." The ship manned with warriors is a very early example of convoy. A distinction is implied between her and the " six broad vessels," but the line is drawn very sharply between them and the rafts. We are fairly entitled to conclude that they were the trading vessels, cargo boats, *naves onerariæ*, ships of burden, and round ships of the Egyptians. It is recorded on the tomb of Anna, an official of the age of Hatshepsitu, that a ship was built for such duties as those performed by Una, of 120 royal cubits by 40, which, if the royal cubit is taken as 20·12 inches, would be in round figures 200 by 69 feet. Here we have a proportion which will be found prevailing till it was beaten out by the competition of the " Yankee clippers "—the length is three times the beam. I venture to assume that Anna gave the total length, including the rake of bow and stern, and not the length of the keel only. As the projection of the hull at bow and stern, technically called the " rake," was very marked in Egyptian vessels, the keel would be from one-half to two-thirds the total length. The observation applies to the trading vessels of European peoples till quite recent times. Perhaps we go too far in speaking of the keel of these Egyptian vessels. They have much the look of flat-bottomed punts, and so in all probability the mere river craft were. The ships of Hatshepsitu must have been something more. Yet they had this much in common with the river boats that they were meant to be rowed, and had but one mast placed amidships, and rigged to carry a single square sail or course.

With the ships carved on the tomb at Deir-el-Bahari we come to what was to be the type of trading ship for many centuries and among all peoples. Put this picture of one of Queen Hatshepsitu's fleet beside a drawing of the Norse ship found at Gokstad, or the Bayeux tapestry, or the seals of medieval cities, or pictures in illuminated books, or on such ancient maps as that of Grazioso Benincasa of Ancona.

THE ANCIENT SHIP

A glance will show that they are all alike in essentials. They differ only in details, which might be altered without affecting their intrinsic character. The comparison must be made with some critical attention. We must allow, for instance, for the fact that a picture of a ship on a coin or seal would tend to conform to the circular shape of the metal it was stamped on. Ancient artists were indifferent to proportion, or had other ideas than ours as to how proportion was to be indicated, and what elements of the picture ought to be prominent. But these allowances are easily made. Ships on medieval seals have the air of having been squeezed from both ends. They rest on the surface of the water, and do not swim in it. They have flying platforms

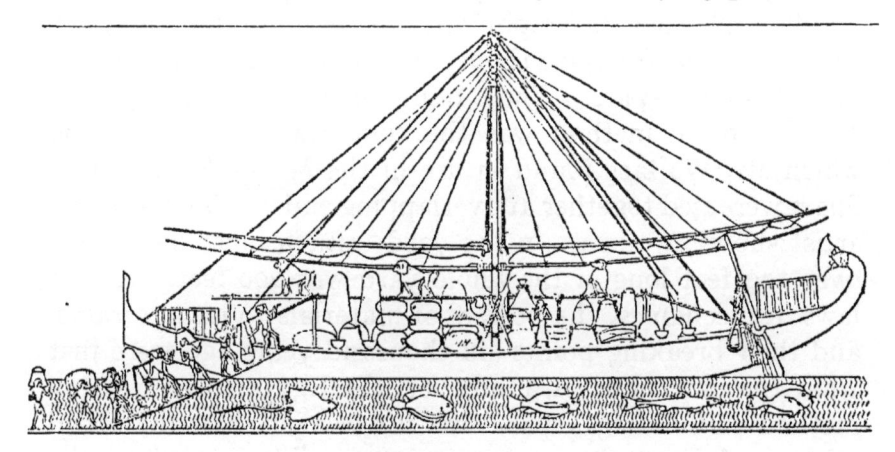

EGYPTIAN SHIP.

at bow and stern to serve as fore and after castles. Put these vessels in the water, make their length take a proportion to their height which will allow them to possess a reasonable margin of stability, remove the platforms from bow and stern, and you have the ships which sailed for the Egyptian Queen who was the sister and spouse of Thotmes II., and to all seeming a very notable, managing woman.

When we have done this, a good deal remains to do. There is, to begin with, the question of size. We cannot believe that the vessels of Deir-el-Bahari were of the proportions of the craft built by Anna to carry the great obelisk down the Nile. She must have been flat-bottomed, for if the depth of her hold bore a ship's proportion to her beam, she would have drawn 25 feet or more, and she would have been of more than 3,000 tons burden. Neither can we accept her length as a possible standard for the Deir-el-Bahari vessels. Observe that their yards are very nearly equal to their total length. Now, if we accept the artist's proportions, one of two things must be true: either these vessels were of much less than 200 feet long, or their yards were nearly 100 feet longer than the mainyard of a 110-gun ship of 1830, and 120 feet or so longer than the mainyard of a 1,300-ton merchant ship of that year, which were respectively 102 and 86 feet long. Note, too, that the mainyard of the 110-gun ship was 24 inches, and that of the 1,300-ton merchant ship 21 inches in diameter at the middle. Neither the shipbuilders of the Egyptian lady, nor those of King George III. attempted to make their yards out of single spars. They built them of several pieces. The Egyptian method was the comparatively artless one which Mr. Wallace found in use in the Malay Archipelago. Spars were tied together at overlapping ends. The Egyptian artist shows two spars in the yard. Each must have been over 100 feet long, if the whole yard was 200 feet. As the laws of mechanics, the powers of materials to resist strains, and their breaking points six thousand years ago were just what they are now, as, moreover, the Egyptian and Malay method of building a yard was far weaker than the artful scheme of European and American builders in 1830, the girth of the spars used in the ancient world cannot possibly have been less than it was in the modern. The Egyptian ship carried a species of Chinese lug, with a yard at the foot as well as the top of the sail. Two made yards of 200 feet or a little less long, and of not less than 24 inches in diameter at the thickest part, would have represented a mass of unhappy and unsupportable proportions. The "immense" yard of the Malay prau was nearly 100 feet long, and was made of many pieces. That is as much as we can allow to the Deir-el-Bahari ships. The prau was of 75 tons, and we may be fairly confident that the Egyptian ships were not much longer.*

* But perhaps the draftsman employed at Deir-el-Bahari was careless of proportion and of realism as we understand it. There

If we cannot place entire confidence in the pictures of the outward and visible shape of ancient ships (for what has been said here of Egyptian carvings on tombs applies equally to paintings on Greek vases, and the designs on Roman coins), still less can we feel sure as to what was the internal construction—the skeleton of keel, ribs, and beams. Egyptian boats of 33 feet long, 7 to 8 feet wide, and 2½ to 3 feet deep have been found in the tombs of the Pharaohs of the Twelfth Dynasty at Dashur. They answer exactly to the description given by Herodotus of the river boats of his time. They were undertakers' boats used to carry the mummy of the Pharaoh to his tomb, but, though stripped of all fittings not necessary for that purpose, they were no doubt identical with the standard river craft. There are no ribs, and the boat holds together by the neat fitting of her planks of acacia wood and their trenails. It is quite possible that the larger craft used in the Red Sea trade were not very unlike these Nile boats in the principles of their construction. To obtain some conception of how they were built we cannot do better than turn to the account given by Mr. Wallace of the Malay shipwright work he witnessed at Kê. These praus are built, as it were, from the outside inwards. A " foundation piece, broad in the middle and rising considerably at the two ends," is the basis. A " skin " of planks, neatly cut to fit, and held by trenails, is then adjusted to the foundation piece, and the whole is bound together by seats in the smaller and beams in the larger craft, and by ribs of a single piece of wood, cut to fit the already shaped side. These vessels sail the length and breadth of the Malay Archipelago. It is, indeed, a lady's sea, but it is not therefore exempt from sudden and passionate squalls. On the other hand, it is to be observed that Herodotus remarks on the absence of ribs in the Nile boats as a peculiarity. He does not say that seagoing vessels were so constructed. There is no reason to believe that Greek, Roman, or medieval ships were built otherwise

---

is every probability that he was, and that he exaggerated the length of the spars in the interest of his " composition," and to secure a harmonious balance of line. And if that is so, we cannot ask him to give us what he never meant to give.

than from the keel, or that the sides were formed in any other than the modern way—by bolting the planks to a framework of ribs. As good as nothing is known with certainty of details of the ancient shipbuilders' art. We can form only a general idea of the products of their skill and the strength of their construction.

One thing is patent from the pictures of Deir-el-Bahari. It is that these vessels were extremely liable to " hog "— that is to say, to bend upwards in the middle and drop at the ends. Apart from the fact that a ship which is hogged is on the way to break her back, this distortion of her lines reduces her speed and spoils her handiness. Hogging was a standing vice of all ships till the end of the eighteenth century, and was difficult to guard against. The French builders of the eighteenth century endeavoured to cure it by the use of oblique iron binders and other devices. Sir Robert Seppings, Master-Shipwright at Chatham after 1804, fought it by filling the spaces between the frames with timber, and adding longitudinal beams throughout. The ancient builders adopted another device, which has, however, been used in modern times. They had to face the fact that, while a ship is strongly held together from side to side by the beams connecting one to the other, she is kept in shape from end to end only by the outside planking and inner lining, the ceiling or foot wailing, which was laid on the beams below longitudinally. Even when the art of shipbuilding had notably improved, the longitudinal support given by the planking was insufficient, and it was a known fact that the majority of vessels were more or less hogged after two or three years of service. The weaker the framework, the more marked would be the tendency of the ends to drop. The Egyptian builders met it by the use of a truss, or " swifter." In the Deir-el-Bahari ships we see a strong cable carried directly from stem to stern inside, and supported by upright beams, with a fork at the top. We hear of a cable called a " hypozoma " by the Greeks, and a " tormentum " by the Romans, used to hold the vessel together longitudinally. It has been supposed that the hypozoma and tormentum were fastened on the sides, where they would have tended to strengthen the vessel, and would have been useful fenders. There can be no reasonable doubt that they were trusses, used inboard to strengthen the ships longitudinally, as in the Egyptian ships, for exactly the same reason, and on the identical principle of the fore-and-aft bands of iron used in American river steamers.

The moral is that the ancient ship was weak. By ancient I mean all ships till the close of the Middle Ages, for they were all the same thing. There is, I repeat, no essential difference between the Deir-el-Bahari ship, the corn ship on the brasses of the Emperor Commodus, the ships of the seals of Poole and Dover, and the Benincasa Map. There were differences in detail. The original method of steering was by an oar, or two or three oars, at the stern. It was the way which would naturally occur to men who began on a river. A boat is best steered by an oar on a river and among shallows, for the same reason that an oar is more useful in a whale boat than a rudder. It brings the boat round quickly. Paddles slung to the side in front of the stern post, and worked by a tiller, replaced the oar. Late, very late, in the history of the ship the rudder prevailed over the paddle, but never completely. The "trabacolo" of the Adriatic is steered by a paddle to this day, and so is the Malay prau. A small mast, stepped well forward, and carrying a small square sail—the forerunner of the spritsail of quite recent times—was added to the main central mast with its great square sail. We are not risking a hazardous guess if we conclude that these vessels were as a rule built on the formula used by the Basque builders of the fifteenth century—three, two, ace. The keel was twice the beam, and three times the height. The total length, including the rake fore and aft, was equal to the keel and beam.

Now, there is one thing of which we can be certain. It is that the men who navigated such vessels were subject to the perils of the sea to an extent of which the happier modern seaman has no conception. These ships must have pitched abominably, and therefore must have been subject to a strain they were ill qualified to bear. Then the leverage of the great mast and sail in the centre must have been destructive. We can readily believe that in favourable conditions they could make fair progress. A Roman vessel of the time of Trajan, when fresh from port and clean, could sail from Sicily to Alexandria in the west trade-wind of the Mediterranean summer, and on the easterly surface current of the African coast, in six or seven days, at the rate of 6 or 7 knots an hour. But when she had to make the return voyage against the wind, her inability to sail nearer to it than seven points—the nearest she could lie—made her progress very slow. If she met with bad weather, she had little resource save to seek harbour. We have one excellent record of an ancient trading voyage in the Acts of the Apostles. The ship of Alexandria, in which St. Paul was carried as a prisoner, was probably one of the best class of vessels of her time. Yet we see that she was ruined by a spell of bad weather, which would have seemed a very small matter to men who had rounded the Cape, or worked through the storms of the Straits of Magellan. She was obviously helpless except in fine weather, and with the wind behind her. No wonder that shipwrecks were common even though the seamen of the Old World avoided the sea in winter.

From the fact that the ships of the Old World were weak it follows that they were small. Feebleness of construction would be aggravated by size, which would entail more severe strain. We hear it is true of large ships, but never on what can be accepted as satisfactory evidence. The colossal vessels built for Sicilian tyrants and Greek Kings of Egypt, if they ever existed, were mere house boats for harbour and river use. It does occasionally strike the plain man that classical scholars do not sufficiently allow for the tendency of manuscripts to become corrupt as they pass through the hands of successive copyists, and of men to exaggerate and to lie! We are told that the ship of Alexandria in which St. Paul was wrecked carried 275 passengers. Therefore it is presumed that she must have been a vessel of considerable size. But, in the first place, scholars have been found to maintain that the number ought to be seventy-five. The testimony, therefore, is not unquestioned. But nobody who knows how human beings were packed into ships for eighteen centuries after the time of St. Paul will allow that even the 275 persons alleged to have been wrecked in his ship imply a large vessel. In the reign of George I. two privateers of in all 580 tons, the *Duke*, and *Duchess*, of Bristol, left England for a voyage to the South Sea. They carried so many men (225) that they could not accommodate the whole of the watch below at one time. It was found necessary to make tent houses on the upper deck to give them cover. During the revolutionary and Napoleonic wars, British soldiers, with the women " on the strength " and their children, were put into transports of from 150 to 200 tons, without regard, not only to convenience, but to decency and health, in such numbers that many of them were compelled to sleep on the open deck. Examples might be multiplied indefinitely. We are told that the ship in which Josephus was wrecked carried 600 persons, but is the number certain ? And if it is, are we bound to believe that the ship was of as much as 400 tons ? We hear of a Saracen ship taken by Crusaders, which carried 1,500 fighting men in addition to her crew, and we can believe that story if we are prepared to swallow the portentous numbers habitually given by medieval writers. There is in existence a piece of Greek humorous writing, by name the " Ship or the Wishes," attributed, apparently, on insufficient authority, to Lucian, a writer of the second century A.D. It professes to give a description of a large corn-carrying vessel from Alexandria, which was driven by bad weather into the harbour of Athens. Her measurements, according to the author, were 180 by 50 feet, and her depth was $43\frac{1}{2}$ feet, or nearly equal to her beam. The depth has excited the doubts of commentators, who would, perhaps, have done well by doubting from the first whether it was safe to take the words of an avowedly ironic sketch in their literal meaning. Moreover, this corn ship, which was, we are told, as long and as broad as a three-decker of the eighteenth century, had at the most the one big mast, and the small mast forward of the corn ship on the coins of Commodus. What must have been the size of her mainsail if it was to be of use to her bulk, and the size and weight of her mainyard, and the tackle, and what the number of men required to handle them ?

There were, indeed, very big ships on the sea in the Middle

Ages if all tales be true—viz., " The Ships of Manzi that sail upon the Indian Seas." Manzi was China, and the authorities are Marco Polo, the Venetian, and the Arab or Moor, Ibn Batuta. Marco Polo has much to say of the ships of Manzi which is of interest. Being a citizen of the most famous maritime city of the Middle Ages, and as he was addressing his countrymen, who were not to be bamboozled on such a subject, he speaks of matters which told them something. The ships of Manzi were built of fir, and had one deck, with fifty or sixty cabins. The cabins were the deck-house of the Malay prau writ large ; as for their number, did Marco Polo give it, or did the amanuensis, to whom he dictated his story when they were both prisoners of war in Genoa, understand him aright, or have we to thank a copyist ? These ships which sailed upon the Indian Seas were built with double planking, fastened with iron bolts, and caulked in and out with a mixture of lime, chopped hemp, and wood oil. It was, says Sir Henry Yule, who warrants the mixture as good, the poisonous oil of nuts of the *Elceococca Kerrucora*. The ships had four masts, a vast improvement on the one of the European model. The hold was divided by bulkheads into watertight compartments. They were repaired by adding fresh planking, and they carried from 5,000 to 6,000 baskets of pepper. Their crew was from 200 to 300 men. The five ships with which Drake started on his voyage round the world amounted in all to 275 tons, and they carried 169 men. The Chinese of the thirteenth century did not, we may be sure, pack less close than the Englishmen of the sixteenth. So the vessel in which Marco Polo made his tedious voyage, with the daughter of the Great Khan from Canton to the Persian Gulf, was just a big junk, much such a vessel as the *Keying*, which sailed from Canton by the Cape of Good Hope to Gravesend in 477 days, and arrived on March 28th, 1848.

Marco Polo says the ships of Manzi had once been bigger, and if we are to believe his successor in Eastern travel, Ibn Batuta, they became much bigger once again. He certainly travelled in the East, and he saw shipbuilding at Canton which bears an obvious likeness to the art as Mr. Wallace saw it practised at Kè. But what is to be done with a

THE CHINESE JUNK, KEYING (CAPTAIN KELLETT)

The first junk tea to

if all tales be true—viz., "The Ships of Manzi that sail upon the Indian Seas." Manzi was China, and the authorities are Marco Polo, the Venetian, and the Arab or Moor, Ibn Batuta. Marco Polo has much to say of the ships of Manzi which is of interest. Being a citizen of the most famous maritime city of the Middle Ages, and as he was addressing his countrymen, who were not to be bamboozled on such a subject, he speaks of matters which told them something. The ships of Manzi were built of fir, and had one deck, with fifty or sixty cabins. The cabins were the deck-house of the Malay prau writ large; as for their number, did Marco Polo give it, or did the amanuensis, to whom he dictated his story when they were both prisoners of war in Genoa, understand him aright, or have we to thank a copyist? These ships which sailed upon the Indian Seas were built with double planking, fastened with iron bolts, and caulked in and out with a mixture of lime, chopped hemp, and wood oil. It was, says Sir Henry Yule, who warrants the mixture as good, the poisonous oil of nuts of the *Elceococca Kerrucora*. The ships had four masts, a vast improvement on the one of the European model. The hold was divided by bulkheads into watertight compartments. They were repaired by adding fresh planking, and they carried from 5,000 to 6,000 baskets of pepper. Their crew was from 200 to 300 men. The five ships with which Drake started on his voyage round the world amounted in all to 275 tons, and they carried 169 men. The Chinese of the thirteenth century did not, we may be sure, pack less close than the Englishmen of the sixteenth. So the vessel in which Marco Polo made his tedious voyage, with the daughter of the Great Khan from Canton to the Persian Gulf, was just a big junk, much such a vessel as the *Keying*, which sailed from Canton by the Cape of Good Hope to Gravesend in 477 days, and arrived on March 28th, 1848.

Marco Polo says the ships of Manzi had once been bigger, and if we are to believe his successor in Eastern travel, Ibn Batuta, they became much bigger once again. He certainly travelled in the East, and he saw shipbuilding at Canton which bears an obvious likeness to the art as Mr. Wallace saw it practised at Kè. But what is to be done with a

THE CHINESE JUNK, KEYING (CAPTAIN KELLETT).

THE FIRST JUNK THAT EVER ROUNDED THE CAPE OF GOOD HOPE, AS SHE APPEARED OFF GRAVESEND, 28TH MARCH, 1848, 477 DAYS FROM CANTON.

From a scarce Aquatint kindly lent by Messrs. T. H. Parker, Printsellers, 45, Whitcomb Street, London, W.C

traveller who tells us that the Chinese first made the sides, then connected them by beams ("slabs" is the word in the translation), and then "apply the bottom planking." He also says that "the timbers projecting from the sides towards the water serve the crew for going down to wash, and for other needs, and to these projecting timbers are attached the oars, which are like masts in size, and need from ten to fifteen men to ply each of them." When Ibn Batuta will have us to understand that these ships carried 600 sailors and 400 marines, we are really entitled to remember that he was a most amusing and attractive, but also most romancing and unscrupulous, scamp, who looked out for wonders, and wrote to amuse his countrymen who loved to hear of wonders.

In short, we hear of great ships in the ancient and medieval world. We never see them. The brasses of a Roman Emperor, struck to commemorate his own merits as a purveyor of corn in time of dearth, show a vessel which must needs have been small. We hear of large vessels built by Norse Kings, but the Viking ship, dug out of the mound at Gokstad, is 77 feet 11 inches long, by 16 feet 7 inches in the beam, and her depth is 5 feet 9 inches. And she was built for war and piracy. In the thirteenth century, St. Louis, King of France, bought vessels from the Venetians and Genoese for war and transport. The Venetian vessel was 70 feet on the keel, and 110 feet long from figure-head to taffrail. The Genoese were smaller. The larger of all these craft was not of greater bulk than the caravel of Columbus, which was of 233 tons, or the vessels in which Vasco da Gama made the first voyage to India by the Cape. Nobody has estimated the Portuguese ships at more than 300 tons, and many have put them far lower. Is it credible that King Emmanuel would have sent his envoy on a voyage on which, as he justly believed, the fortune of his kingdom depended, in ships inferior to the best he could obtain?

CHAPTER II

THE SKIPPER AND HIS MEN

When Mr. Ashburner undertook to illustrate the Rhodian Law, he made use of the medieval codes. The document is itself medieval and Byzantine, though it bears the name of an ancient Greek Republic which produced a maritime code. Late as it is, it gives us pretty nearly all we know of the life of the seamen of the ancient world. We have probably not lost much by the disappearance of earlier sources of information. We may be confident that the life partially revealed in the Rhodian Law, and in the Laws, Judgments, and Roll of Oleron, or other codes of Wisby and elsewhere, was very much what it had been in the time of the Carthaginian, the Greek, and the Roman. These codes, so called, do not satisfy the modern standard for a body of laws. They are not, or not uniformly, orders given by the State, and enforced by penalties. They are collections of customs, and of the findings of the " good men " of some trading centre, who were asked: What is the right thing to do in this or that case? What ought to be done with a person who has acted thus? What said the wisdom of our fathers touching such matters as these?

The model of many of them, and the typical example of them all, is the collection known as the " Laws of Oleron." The Island of Oleron, on the west coast of France, belonged to the great feudal Duchy of Guyenne. It was a central meeting-place, an exchange and mart, a winter harbour, for the men concerned in the main western European sea-borne commerce of the early Middle Ages—the wine-trade. Wine is always the typical cargo with which the code deals. Here men of various races and allegiances met and argued the question. Here the aged and experienced men were called in to give counsel and say what the wisdom of their fathers had decided, and what was thought right in the old days before them. Scholars do not know to whom belongs the credit of having collected the decisions of the good men, the "prud'hommes." By some it has been attributed to that Eleanor, Alienor, or Elnor, who was Duchess of Acquitaine, the unfaithful wife of Louis VII. of France, and then, when he had put her away, the very exacting, rebellious, and unmanageable wife of Henry II., Plantagenet, King of England. Little good can be said of that lady. Whether she did it, or another, or whether the collection was made for convenience' sake and by the necessities of the case, the Laws of Oleron do represent the "good uses and customs of the sea" in Western medieval Europe. They were followed at Wisby in Gothland, once the great trading centre of the Baltic, and adopted by Alfonso X., the Wise, of Castile, in the thirteenth century. Other and corresponding collections were made in the Mediterranean at Trani, at Amalfi, and in the Catalan "Consolato del Mare." All were liable to indulge in sentiments and moral exhortation. The famous Consolato del Mare is insufferably verbose. Something of the Roman Law filtered into them, and here as elsewhere "similar manners" were bred by "similar situations." Be their merits what they may, they, by virtue at times of that mere garrulity, and their habit of quoting a leading, even if imaginary, example of conduct, do show what the customs were, what the life was.

A simple string of questions imposes itself on the inquirer. Who owned the ship? Who managed the trading business of the voyage? Who commanded the ship on the voyage? What powers had he? Who commanded under him? Who were the mariners? How were they recruited, paid, punished, and what rights had they?

The shipowner was not unknown to antiquity, and became known again to the Middle Ages, towards their close, in his modern form as a capitalist who lived ashore, and made money out of his vessels. The Dominus Navis, the Senyor de Nau of the Consolato, the Lord of the Ship, was a known person, and was distinct from the shipper of the cargo and the sailing master, yet it appears to be doubtful whether the Lord of the Ship was her owner, or the person who had jurisdiction at the port to which she belonged. The capitalist shipowner in the modern sense was probably preceded by, and he certainly coexisted with, another quite modern form of ownership, the single ship Company. The Consolato del Mare, in its talkative, motherly way, draws a lively picture of a stirring Catalan, who is persuaded that there is money in shipowning, and who runs about persuading his friends to take shares in a vessel he is going to build, if he can get the money together. " It often happens " says the Consolato, " that a person takes a share in a ship or vessel from the great friendship which he has for the man who wishes to build the ship or vessel more than from any hope of gain which he expects to make of it."

Whether sole possessor, or shareholder, the capitalist of ancient days had little control over his property when once it had sailed from port. Means of communication were at the best few and erratic. Generally there were none. The real power fell to the person who was called in Latin an " exercitor," and in other tongues the " merchant." He took over the vessel and sailed her. " He " was not infrequently replaced by " they." Single ship companies were formed for the voyage, as well as for the building of the ship. The merchants went on the voyage themselves, and when they did not also do the work of the sailing-master, they exercised the control which in after times was entrusted to the supercargo of an English or Dutch Indiaman. They decided to what port she was to go, and what cargo she was to ship. Obviously it was the easiest thing in the world for the " exercitor," or merchant, to be sailing-master also, and the combination of the functions was a plain economy. The Byzantine Greeks had a noble name for the man of double function. They called him a " nauclerokubernetes " (merchant-master). Observe that " naucleros " stands for merchant, and " kubernetes " for master. In later times the sailorman aspect of the merchant-master swallowed the commercial. " Naucleros " became in Latin " nauclerus," skipper or master, and in due course the " nochiero," " notxer," " nauxer," " naucher," or the Italians, French, and Catalans. To return to Mr. Wallace's prau for a moment. The captain or merchant with whom he sailed was a " naucleros " in the earlier sense, and the " juragan " was his " pistikos," or " kubernetes." The name of " kubernetes " was not unknown to our English forefathers. The fleet of Richard the Lion-hearted wintered in Sicily on its way to the Holy Land. Sicily was then the centre of the maritime life of the Mediterranean, the meeting-place of the Norman and Italian, Greek and Arab. Through the Sicilians we heard of the Kubernetes. A translation of the name " Gubernator " was used by us as the alternative to " Justiciarius," for a commander of the King's vessels. In Sicily, too, we heard of the Arab " Emir-al-Bahr," who was to be known to all men before very long as the Admiral.

When the merchants forming the "single voyage company" sailed together, they might choose one of their own number as skipper, and then he was known as the " patronus," the " patron," the " padrone " of the Spanish or Italian fishing-boat or coaster of to-day. The title has come down in the world. When Felix Faber went as a pilgrim to the Holy Land in 1480-1484, the skippers of the Venetian galleys, which were the " greyhounds " of the time, were called the " padrone."

Let us drop the merchant for the present, and apply ourselves to the skipper. The Inquisition of Queenbro', taken in the forty-ninth year of the reign of Edward III., 1376, giving the reason why the master was entitled to a double share of a prize, says that he was " of greater charges and greater estate "—*i.e.*, rank, than any other man in the vessel. We can believe it, but the standard of comparison was modest. M. Charles de la Roncière, historian of the French Navy, has published in the fifty-eighth volume of the " Bibliothèque de l'École des Chartes," a document which introduces us to the contents of the kits of a ship's company of the thirteenth century. She belonged to Messina, and was named the *Saint Nicholas*. In the year 1297 she was homeward bound from Tripoli with a cargo of hides, camels' skins, buckrams, and Arab cloth, when she was seized at Angosta by one Reniero Grimaldi, a Genoese who served the King of France. The capture was unduly made in time of truce.

When the skipper of the *Saint Nicholas* appealed to the King of France, orders were given to restore her, and an inventory was taken of her goods and the belongings of her crew, composed of a captain, a mate, and twelve men. It shows that the captain had just twice as many shirts and pairs of breeches as any of his crew—that is to say, he had four of each. To be sure, he had a coat lined with rabbit-skins, and one of his pairs of breeches was of silk. He had also a silver whistle, and a leather belt, from which hung his purse and writing materials. Two crossbows were among his belongings. His mate had what appears to have been a kind of hooded boat cloak, green, lined with red " sendal," worn over a Lombard doublet, and the buttons of the doublet were of amber and silver. He had one crossbow. They, no doubt, made dashing figures, but their kit, though it contained other garments than those named here, would have gone into a small kit-bag.

It may have been an accident that the padrone of the *Saint Nicholas* of Messina had exactly twice as many shirts and pairs of breeches as the other members of the ship's company, yet it is to be observed that the proportion of two to one, or thereabouts, obtained in every respect between him and the mariners. The Inquisition of Queenbro' allows a master sailing for the King sixpence a day, and the mariner threepence halfpenny. He had two shares of a prize, and the man one. When profits and tonnages (to which we shall return) were to be divided, the master's share was again two. It would appear that this continued to be his fair allowance in the opinion of the seamen at a very much later period. The pirates who sailed with Avery conceded his right to a double share. But two to one is not the proportion as between master and sailor in the times following the Middle Ages. And the reason for the difference is plain. Unless he was one of the single ship company owning the vessel, or was himself sole owner, or had a share as a merchant in the voyage, the medieval skipper was no more than a foreman.

He had, and could have, no claim to a higher position on the score of his knowledge. That was to come to him with the development of the science of navigation, which began in the fifteenth century. The medieval seaman had no instrument to use. The magnetic needle was known from the twelfth, and perhaps even the eleventh, century, but anyone in the ship could see what it had to tell as well as the skipper. The astronomical, or rather astrological, astrolabe was known in the fourteenth century, but the use of an astrolabe for purposes of navigation dates from the fifteenth century. The instruments were not identical. Before the later fifteenth century the skipper had not necessarily more skill than one of his mariners. And not only so, but he must often have been on no more than an equality with many of the merchants who sailed with him. They had made repeated voyages, and had sometimes worked their passage. They knew the headlands by which the coasting seaman steered, the anchorages, the watering-places. They carried arms, and assisted in the defence of the ship. They were often his equals in his own art, even when they were not his employers.

It follows that the medieval skipper was by no means the man whose word was law. On the contrary, he figures in the Judgments of Oleron and the Consolato as a species of chairman of a debating society. "A ship,' says the Law of Oleron, " lieth in a haven and tarrieth for the freight, and time to depart—the master ought to take council with his fellows, and say, ' Mates, how like ye this weather ?' Some will say, ' It is not good, let it pass.' Others will say, ' The weather is good and fair.' The master ought to agree to the most, or else if the ship perish he is bound to restore the value as it is apprised, if he have wherewithal." The master and men messed together, as we see from such Judgments of the good men of Oleron as these :

" A master hireth his mariners, and ought to keep them peaceably, and offer to be their judge, and if any say that his fellow lieth, having bread and drink at the table, he ought to pay four pence, or if any belieth the master he ought to pay eight pence, and if the master belieth any also to pay eight pence, and if the master smite any of the mariners he ought to abide the first buffet, be it with fist or flat with his hand, but if he smite any more he may defend him."

In the Mediterranean vessels the sailor had also to abide

one buffet, and go behind the second bench for the oarsmen in a galley. If the patron then followed him he could lawfully defend himself. The Judgments of Oleron provide for the case of an assault on the master by one of the men. The sailor is to lose his hand, or pay five shillings—that is to say, about one-half of the wages given for a voyage to Bordeaux.

The crew had a voice in deciding what penalties were to be exacted.

"If variance fall between the master of a ship and the mariners, the master ought to take the towel away that is before the mariner, or ever [*i.e.*, before] he put him out." The expression sounds odd, but the meaning can be guessed with sufficient confidence. The master is first to shut him out of the mess, or "cut the tablecloth before him," and is not to proceed at once to the extreme measure of turning him out of the ship. The judgment goes on, "and if the mariner offer to make amends at the agreement of his mates that be at the table, and the master will not, but putteth him out, the mariner may follow the ship till it come to the right discharge, and ought to have as good wages as if he had gone on the ship, amending the trespass at the verdict of his fellows. And if so be that the master take not in as good a mariner as he, and the ship by chance take harm, the master is bound to restore the ship and goods if he be able."

In practice the authority of the master would depend a good deal on the weight of his fist, his capacity, and character. But we see that he was considered as a kind of first among equals, not as a decided superior. He had to take the counsel of his mates, and though he might disregard it, he did so at his peril. He might jettison cargo against the wish of the merchant to whom it belonged, but he must have the support of at least a third of his crew, who were to swear that the goods were sacrificed to save the body of the ship. There was probably more of the debating society in the vessels of the Mediterranean, manned from the free Italian republics or such towns as Barcelona which were self-governing vassals of a prince, than in the monarchical and feudal West. Yet it was to be found there also.

The master was supported by officers—by his mate, his boatswain, his carpenter, his caulker, if not by others. Of course, when his vessel was pressed by the King, or the Republic, for service in war, there were yet others, and some were of higher "estate" than himself. The knight, or gentleman, put in as commander of the fighting men, who in the Middle Ages were far more numerous than the sailors, was the social and hierarchical superior of the master. He was the captain. The title of captain was not strictly military in origin. "Capitaneus" was applied in the Mediterranean to the merchant skipper, though not often. In the Spanish navy a ship-of-war carried a Capitan de Guerra (of war), who was a soldier, and a Capitan de Mar, a sea-captain, who was a sailorman. When a corps of naval officers was formed, and the functions were combined, the title was Capitan de Mar y Guerra—of sea and war. A pressed or hired ship used for warlike purposes carried a "constable," the predecessor of the modern gunner. He was the sailing master's equal, and the Inquisition of Queenbro' allows him the same salary, sixpence a day.

A merchant ship, when following her own trade, was content with a more modest staff. We hear of an officer who, with the title of clerk, and in the Mediterranean of "scribanus," or "scriba," did the duty of purser. In England little, if any, distinction seems to have been made between them and the mariners. But in the Mediterranean they took share and a half. Suppose, for instance, the ship sailed on the profit-sharing system, as in the case given as an example by Mr. Ashburner, and that she carried a master, four officers, twenty mariners, and four other hands, boys, "grommets" —*i.e.*, ordinary seamen—and what not, whom the Byzantine Greeks classed as "parascharitai," half the profits went to the crew. Their portion was divided into thirty shares. The skipper took two, each officer one and a half, each mariner one, and each of the "parascharitai" a half.

The functions of the Italian "scriba," or "escriva," as he is termed in the languages of the Spanish Peninsula (the Spaniards never could pronounce a word beginning with s and another consonant without putting an *e* before it), are much insisted on in the Mediterranean codes. The

Consolato del Mare, which is generally benign on the subject of punishments, threatens him with horrid penalties if he breaks his oath to deal honestly. He is to suffer nothing less than the loss of his hand, and branding on the forehead. By the nature of the case he keeps the list of the ship's company, and all the accounts, whether of pay and shares, or of goods shipped and discharged. In some of the Italian Republics he was bound to deposit his accounts with the city authorities when the ship returned home. But every vessel was not able to afford a special " scriba." The *Saint Nicholas*, of Messina, carried none. The second padrone, or mate, supplied his place, and was provided with a stamp to mark all goods received.

From what has already been said it will be seen that the body of the crew was by no means neglected in the medieval " good usages and customs of the sea." On the contrary, they were treated as a very important body of men. In the Italian Republics the seamen were naturally of great account. But even in so monarchical and unmaritime a country as the Kingdom of Castile, the Hermandad—that is, the Brotherhood of the seaports of Biscay and Santander, commonly called the " marisma," the nautical guild, was a very important corporation. The King contracted with it for his squadrons, and it negotiated on its own account with English Sovereigns. As the customs of the sea were settled by the " Judgments " of men who, perhaps in all cases, and certainly in many, were, or had been, themselves mariners, the sailor had a fair chance of consideration. There was no doubt a time when the crews of ships trading in the Mediterranean, and even out of it, were largely composed of slaves. Nothing could be more consistent with the prevailing bestiality of the later Roman Empire than that this should have been the case. But when the Northern barbarians had let the air into the Roman world, and had shattered the cruel machinery of oppression and degradation erected by Diocletian and his successors, the door was opened again for the free seaman. He had the sea to himself in the Middle Ages. He might, it is true, be a vassal; but the vassal was not a slave. He was a man bound to render definite service in return for an ascertained benefit conferred on him. It is no doubt notorious that from the later part of the fifteenth century forward the war galleys of all powers which employed that class of vessel were manned by slaves. Free men could no longer be found to endure the life, or not in sufficient numbers. Desperate men did sell themselves to labour in the galleys for a fixed period, and were known to the Italians as " benevoglie " volunteers. But the bulk of the " chiourmes," the " chusmas," the " ciurme," of French, Spanish, and Italian galleys, were criminals, or such political and religious offenders as the State chose to treat as criminals.* In earlier times all rowers were free, though a State was often forced to recruit them among poorer neighbours. This had been the case with Athens, and was no less true of Venice. The city could not have found men out of its own population for its industry, its eight yearly trading convoys ("mudue"), and its war galleys also; so it recruited oarsmen among the Sclavonians of the eastern shore of the Adriatic, and from the Greeks of the Morea, and the islands of the Levant. The Sclavonians were tall, clean, sober, and loyal to their salt. They did not desert. But their health suffered from confinement in the galleys. Moreover, they had not the staying power of the Greeks. These latter were thick-set, incorrigibly dirty, much addicted to drunkenness in harbour, sea lawyers, and unscrupulous in deserting when offended. But they had lived in boats from their boyhood, and had pulled at the oar from the beginning; therefore they did not suffer in health in the galleys, and they could go on pulling long after the Sclavonian had given in. For these merits the Venetian captains forgave them their vices. It was not until the spread of the Turkish power had begun to shut her out from the Eastern Adriatic shores and the islands that Venice fell back on the galley slave.†

* Chiourme, chusma, and ciurma, all come from the Latin *turma*, " a troop or squadron," the tenth part of the " ala," the cavalry wing of the legion. As we never had the vile thing, the English language is not defiled by a name for it.

† It must be understood that when we speak of Greeks of the Middle Ages and modern times, we do not mean men of the same race as the Hellenes of the ancient world. Greece had been nearly depopulated under the blight of the Roman Empire, and was then flooded by Slavonic barbarians from the North. The ancient race survived only in a few fastnesses, such as the rocky peninsula of Maina.

The digression on the rowers is legitimate, as the galley was used in one branch of Venetian trade, the pilgrim traffic to the Levant. But the typical trading vessel was such a craft as the *Saint Nicholas*, of Messina. She might use the oar, or sweep, at a pinch, but she was a sailing ship. Her crew were free sailors. And as she was, so were the other trading ships of ancient times and the Middle Ages. A conscription was levied, in Venice at least, to fill up the crews of the vessels composing the eight yearly trading convoys, but the men so raised were no otherwise slaves than the conscripts of Germany or France.

The men were hired by free contract, and the bargain was clenched by " giving the hand," by the hand-grip of sailor and skipper. They were paid by a share of profits (" ad partem "), or by wages (" ad marineraciam "), or partly by pay and partly by tonnage. This third form, which prevailed in Western Europe, gave the man a fixed wage, and the option of occupying a stipulated space of the ship with a venture of his own, or of hiring it out to a merchant. Long after the system had ceased to be in general use it obtained in the ships of the East India Company, which adhered to it because it gave officers and men an interest in promoting the success of the voyage. The Inquisition of Queenbro' goes at large into the pay and allowances of mariners. For a voyage from the Pool of London to Lisbon a man was entitled to twenty shillings for his tonnage, which was 1 ton. If the destination of his ship was Bayonne, he was to be content with ten shillings. The " tons " were plus his wages, meat, and drink. For a voyage to Bourgneuf Bay, near Noirmoutier, in Brittany, in search of " bay salt," his wages are fixed at five shillings, and his allowance at the value first cost, of three-quarters of salt, for that is what we may understand by " as much as three-quarters did cost at first carriage abated." He may also bring away a bag of half a quarter of salt, if he has a box to stow it in, supposing, that is to say, that the word " pavillon " means a box. For a voyage to Ireland he shall have ten shillings wage, and tonnage, here named " portage," of three dickers (half-scores) of hides. If the voyage is beyond the old Head of Kinsale to the west, or northward of the Tuscar Rock, then he shall have two shillings extra. For a voyage to Sluys, twenty shillings; and each three mariners shall have a " lastwar " (a last of 4,000 pounds) among them. A last of herrings, or rather, the freight of that weight among three, is the addition made to eight shillings and fourpence wages per man for a run to Scone, in Scotland.

There is an air of an " assize of labourers "—*i.e.*, of an attempt to fix wages by authority—about all this. It is, perhaps, doubtful whether the sums were adhered to in practice and in the higgling of the market. When it comes to bargaining, human nature has a wonderful capacity for getting in by the back-door when authority has chosen to close the front. What the effective value of the mariner's pay and allowances was depended on the purchasing power of money in the later thirteenth century, and that is a matter of uncertain estimate. It is not necessary to speculate on the subject here. The point for us is that the crew were paid by a fixed sum, the freight of a certain space or weight, or a chance to speculate on their own account. If the vessel was freighted at different prices, the man was allowed the average.

It was, however, clearly contemplated that he might trade on his own account. "If a ship be arrived to be charged at Bordeaux, or any other place, the master is holden to say to his fellows: ' Mates, will ye freight by yourselves, or be allowed at the freight of the ship?' That is, to be at their own provision. They must answer what they will do; if they take the freight of the ship, they shall have as the ship shall have; and if they will freight by themselves, they ought to freight in such wise that the ship do not tarry." This is the Judgment of Oleron. From the fact that the captain is to make his offer at the destination, and not at the port of departure, it would appear that tonnage was allowed for the homeward voyage only. And this supposition is consistent with the rule that, when a man was to receive a fixed sum for a run to a particular port, he was to be paid one-half before sailing, and the other when he reached the destination. This would leave him nothing to receive for the return voyage, unless that part of his cruise was paid for by his tonnage. His half-pay would be convenient for investment in that case, if he were wise. If not, he spent his money " dipping his nose in the Gascon wine." The vexatious question of advances was familiar to the wise men of Oleron, and they gave their judgment thereon to the effect that, if a sailor asked for part of his money before the date on which it was due, and he had neither bedding nor clothes to serve as security, the master was not bound to give him anything. The bedding was apparently the property of the men. The inventory of the *Saint Nicholas* includes a mattress, sheet, and blanket for each man, with his coarse cloth doublet, and his " jaque." This garment, which we called a " jerkin " or " jack," was a quilted doublet fortified by pieces of metal sewn in. It formed part of his armour. The merchant seaman of old went armed.

The crew of the *Saint Nicholas* were provided with gorgets of iron to protect the neck, helmets, an iron gauntlet for the right hand, and a buckler. We can hardly suppose that these comparatively costly articles were always provided by the sailor himself. Yet the Consolato del Mare expressly states that a man is not to sell his arms while the voyage lasts, which may imply that they were his to dispose of when he was paid off. The customs of the sea were tolerably uniform, and the British, French, Italian, or Flemish seaman had probably the same rights as the Catalan. The armour he wore was not made by a fashionable armourer, and of fine steel. He had to be content with iron " reach-me-downs " made wholesale. The careful seaman of to-day, who keeps his kit-bag well supplied, would in the Middle Ages have seen to it that he had a headpiece, gorget, gauntlet, and buckler.

The sailor had a reason to go provided with defensive armour, because the age believed it was of use. Yet what can have been the good of it ? A man of means who could spend sums equivalent to £100 and upwards on a steel " carapace " might have it made to fit him, and he could buy a padded inner suit to prevent the metal from cutting his flesh. So long as he stood still, the thing was tolerable, and it was gorgeous to look at ; but if he had to exert himself on a warm day, he must have been promptly reduced to a state of clammy exhaustion, wrapped in wet clothes, sopping with perspiration, which was not allowed to evaporate. No wonder the armour-using men were worn out in middle life. An active man in his shirt-sleeves could have walked round an opponent in complete mail. A vigorous blow delivered with an axe, or a quarter-staff for that matter, on the back of his knees would bring the knight in shining armour clad rattling to the ground, and then he was as helpless as a blackbeetle on its back. As for the poor man in the ranks who wore iron " reach-me-downs," and protected his skin by stuffing rags and straw under the edges, he was covered with sores and callosities, and crippled by curvature of the spine. Armour had a certain passive value for a body of men formed in close order. But was not the real explanation of its use to be found in simple cowardice and fear of wounds? Stupid fear! for when the formation was broken, the disordered men were massacred with ease, as at Morgarten, Granson, Moret, Agincourt, Towton, and innumerable other places. The uselessness of armour was demonstrated during the wars of Arragonese and Angevines in Naples and Sicily in the thirteenth century. The Navarrese and Arragonese soldiers, named Almogávares, who wore no armour, and who used the weapons of the Roman soldier—two heavy javelins and a stabbing broadsword—defeated the Angevine chivalry again and again. A French knight accepted the challenge of one of these Spaniards to fight a single combat in the lists. The Almogávar never allowed his lumbering opponent, mounted on his lumbering horse, to get into a position to use his lance. When he had " played the bull " to his own satisfaction, as the " banderillero " does in the ring, he drove his javelin through the Frenchman's mail (for no complete suit of armour could be thick) and killed him on the spot. Yet armour continued to be worn till gunpowder convinced the most thick-headed that it was useless; for great is cowardice, and everything a man has, including all the reasons for living, will he give for his life. To the sailor mail was peculiarly worthless, for not only did it hamper his movements, but if he slipped into the water while trying to board an enemy (and all sea fighting was by boarding till the sixteenth century), it dragged him down.*

The kit of the medieval sailor did not include "oilies." As he figures in old illuminations, he appears dressed in loose trousers and a hooded "jumper." We see the hood drawn over his head and fastened under his chin, like the head-covering of an Esquimaux or Arctic traveller. It was a protection against cold, but must have been useless against wet.

Next to good pay comes good provend, in the opinion of Dugald Dalgetty. When the ship's company went "ad partem," they remained out till they had "made their voyage," as the old sea phrase had it, had gained as much as left profits to divide. Then they came home, and every man took his two shares, share and a half, single share, or half share, as the case might be. But when they went on part fee and part profit, or wholly "ad marineraciam" for wages, the case was not so simple. It might be necessary to go beyond "the port of right discharge" to find a sufficient cargo. In that case extra allowances had to be made. The English, or perhaps even the Western European, custom was to pay the extras by "kenning" and "course." Kenning was a run from one headland to another in sight. Course was from one place to another not in sight—say, from Havre to the Isle of Wight. In the Mediterranean, where the trading season was from March to November, the pay was given in three instalments, on March 1st, June 1st, and September 1st. March 1st for wife and family; June 1st for expenses abroad; September 1st for a small investment on the return voyage.

As touching the provend, it must be confessed that the western men were more concerned with liquor than with meat. There may have been teetotal ships in the Middle Ages, but I have not heard of one. The seaman of the Atlantic and the North had very distinct opinions as to the amount of liquor they were entitled to. If they sailed

* Of course, I do not mean that armour is of no use on a ship. A ship is a floating fort, and the walls of forts should be impenetrable. But forts do not perspire, nor suffer from sores and curvature of the spine. Yet if a projectile could be made capable of going through any armour—what then?

from a country which did not produce wine, they would do without it, but expected an equivalent. The Norman, whose home is a cider land, insisted on two meals because he had no wine; but when he came to a country of vineyards, he looked to have it served out. The Breton sailor had only one meal, but that was because he had wine both going and coming. It was the belief of all the seamen of the West that when they were bringing home a cargo of wine, the merchant was bound to serve out a double ration on all feast-days, which were numerous in old times. The Judgment of Oleron on the point is that there was no such right, but that the merchant was to give what he chose. A merchant who wished for a quiet life and cheerful service would be wise to give the " pot " or " pots " asked for.

The Consolato del Mare, which sometimes abounds in useful details, is tolerably full on the question of rations. The mariners of a decked or seagoing ship were entitled to a ration of fresh meat on Sunday, Tuesday, and Thursday, and on other days to porridge. Fresh meat on three days in the week would have been luxury indeed to the sailor of the long ocean voyages. On every day, " banian " day or not (a " banian " day for the English sailors of modern times was one on which there was no meat ration) the Catalan mariner was entitled to an evening ration of bread, with an accompaniment of cheese, or onions (garlic), sardines, or some other fish. On meat ration days there was wine in the morning, and always wine in the evenings, unless fruit was served out. On a solemn feast the rations were doubled. The ship must be provided with a cook. The word used is servant, but the context shows that a cook was meant.

How were the men in general treated? One must not speak with too much confidence. Judgments of Oleron, tables of Trani, and Consolatos are words on paper, and practice is quite another matter. Friar Felix Faber describes the Supracomito of a Venetian galley, who at that time was a boatswain, as being in the habit of raining blows and curses on all hands. He was feared like the devil ("sicut diabolum"). But this was at the close of the fifteenth century, a brutal time, and in a galley, just when that class of vessel was becoming an acknowledged "hell afloat." The Consolato del Mare condemns the sailor who takes his clothes off, except when the vessel is in a winter harbour, to be ducked—which sounds both dirty and oppressive. Yet on the whole my own impression is that the medieval seaman was better off, and better protected against harsh treatment, than his successor from the sixteenth to the nineteenth century. The Judgments, Rolls, Tables, and Codes contain provision protecting him from arbitrary dismissal. When a man has given his hand to the skipper to ship for a voyage, he is not to be discharged because another comes along and offers to do the work for less. Even if a man turns out to be unsatisfactory, he is entitled to his wages, unless he has fraudulently shipped as a carpenter or caulker. In that case he must take what the master will give him. If a man was killed in defence of the ship, the Italians gave his family the whole amount he would have been entitled to if he had completed the voyage. If he fell sick, he was to be taken care of; and if hurt in the service of the ship, then healed at the ship's expense. When he came to grief by his own fault, he had to take his chance.

"Mariners," so say the Judgments of Oleron, "bind them to their master, and if any go out without leave of the master and drink drunken, and make strife so that any of them be hurt, the master is not bound to cause them to be healed nor to purvey aught for them, but he may well put them out of the ship ... and hire others in their place, and if any cost more than the mariner put out, he ought to pay, if the master finds anything belonging to him." The qualification was judicious. The mariner who goes out without leave, drinks drunken and makes strife, commonly has nothing belonging to him. It is much if he has not stolen part of the ship's fittings to sell for drink. But "if it chance that any mariner be taken with sickness in the ship doing service thereto belonging, the master ought to set him out of the ship, and seek lodgings for him, and ought to find him light, as tallow or candle, and give him a lad of the ship for to take heed of him, or hire a woman to keep him, and ought to purvey him of such meat as is used in the ship, that is,

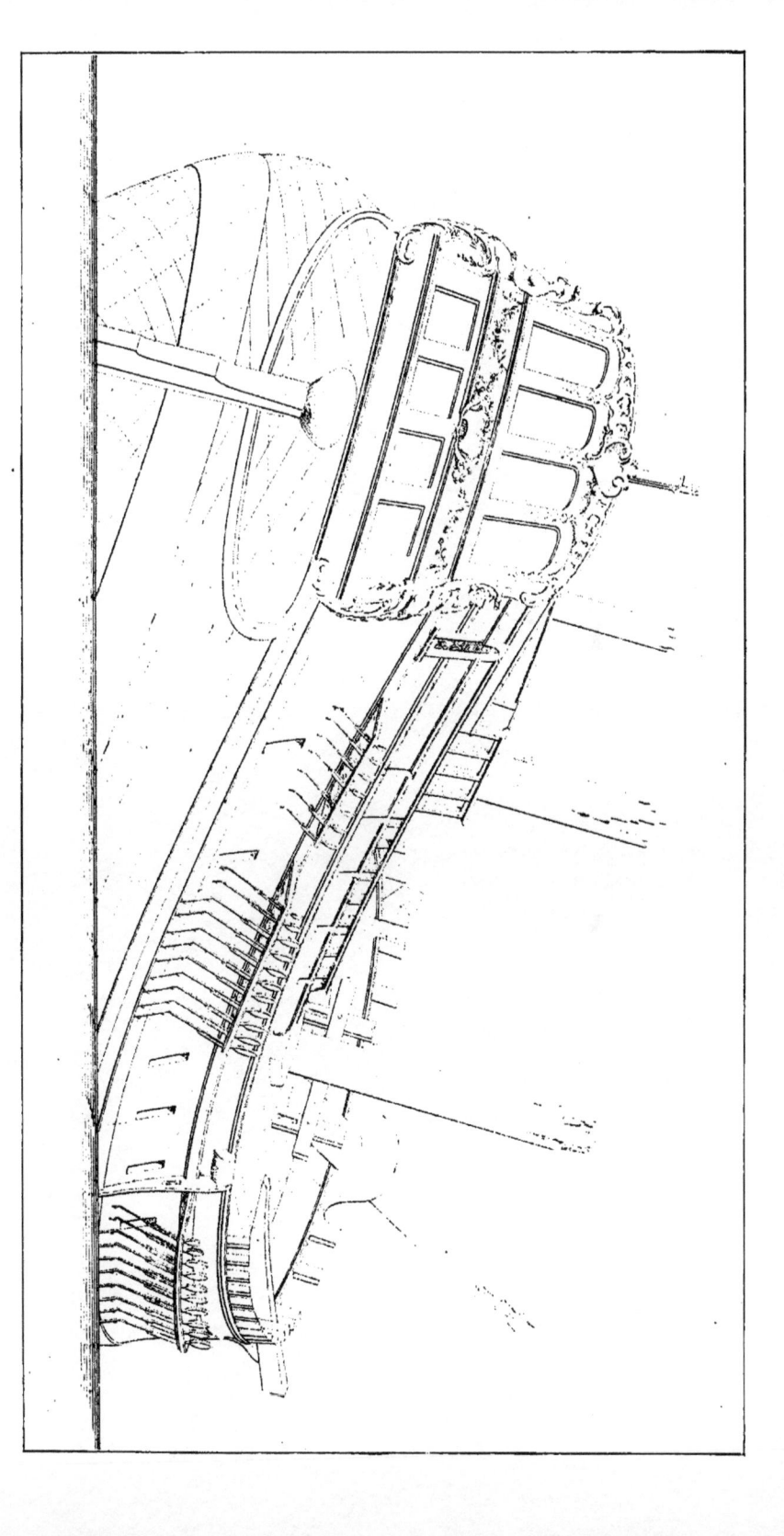

MERCHANT SHIP.
From Chapman's "Architectura Navalis Mercatoria."

To face page 42.

to wit, as much as he took when he was in health, and no more, but if the master will. And if he will have daintier meats, the master is not bound to give him any, save at the cost of the mariner. And if the ship be ready to depart it ought not to tarry for him. And if he recover to have his hire in [on] paying and rebating that the master laid out for him. And if he die, his wife or next kin, or friend, ought to have it for him."

The provision was not lavish, but an eighteenth century sailor would certainly have had no more, and might well have had less.

It is not, however, from such texts only that we may conclude that the medieval sailor was more fortunate than his successor. He came from a small community, and went back to it. The corporate feeling, the guild-brotherhood sentiment, was strong in his time. So was the bond of kinship. The men of Yarmouth or Lübeck, of Venice, Genoa, Barcelona, were not the casual unstable population of a great modern seaport, who drift together no man cares from whence, and float away no man knows or asks whither. The fishermen of Brixham, with their widely distributed interest in the lordship of the manor, form a real representation of the maritime populations of the Middle Ages. The fact that a man could defend himself if a blow was prolonged to a beating was some protection. His right to appeal to the judgment of his mates counted for more. The common table, at which master and men messed, tended to good comradeship. They belonged to the same religion. No obligation to learn even the beggarly rudiments of the science of navigation obstructed his rise to master. He was encouraged to thrive by trading ventures. The order of his day was doomed to pass when knowledge had increased and the ocean routes had been explored, or to survive only locally, as, for instance, in the English coal-trade. Its weak point was that it tended to hand the vessel over to a debating society. When the merchant sailed with his goods, and knew as much as the master, and the master knew no more than his men, who also had their venture on board, there may well have been wrangling at every emergency. None the less, the change, which was inevitable, destroyed good as well as bad. Progress taught the world a great deal, and made it richer; but it broke the old feudal, corporate, and guild bonds of affection and loyalty. The plain seaman was relatively in a better place in the ships of the Middle Ages than he was to be when the mainmast marked a barrier hard to cross, and when it separated the crew into two classes, connected to far too great an extent by the " cash nexus " only.

CHAPTER III

THE WAY OF LIFE

When we know more or less what the functions and the status of seamen of old were, the next questions which occur to us are : How did they direct their course ? How did they live ? The answer to the first is that they sailed by the land, or the trade-winds, until they were supplied with the mariner's compass. Even when they had that instrument they still went much by the land and the trade-winds or monsoons.

The discovery that a needle can be magnetized by being touched by the loadstone at one end, and will then point to the north, was only the first of several steps which were to be taken before a useful compass could be supplied to the seaman. A mariner's compass is composed of a magnetized needle fixed below a compass card on which the points of the horizon are marked. The combined needle and card must then be so placed that they remain steady, however much the ship may pitch or roll. This steadiness in position is indispensable, not only in order that the helmsman may see, but because a fall or a succession of blows will discharge the fluid and render the needle useless. When we remember —what many learned men appear not to understand— that needle, compass card, and steadiness are all equally necessary, then the question whether the Chinese did or did not know of the virtue of the loadstone in remote ages becomes of very little consequence. Allow that they did. Suppose that some Chinaman in " a ship of Manzi " showed the strange thing on the Malabar coast to a seaman who had sailed thither from the Red Sea by the help of the wind of Hippalus—the south-westerly monsoon ;

suppose, further, that his hearer then brought news of it to Europe—we are still centuries away from the mariner's compass. Our very far-off ancestresses, in lake dwellings and tents on the Pamir, knew that a pot will boil over a fire, and that steam will lift a lid, but they were not predecessors of Newcomen and Watt. It must be shown that Chinamen made a mariner's compass. Now, they never have. The Arabs in whose hands was the trade between the Red Sea, or Persian Gulf, and India, call their compass by names they have taken from the Italian " bussolo," the box, which answers to our binnacle. This is tolerably clear evidence as to whence their knowledge of the instrument came to them.

Again, those men of learning of the twelfth century among Europeans who knew of the quality of the magnetized needle could do little to help sailors. A charged needle placed on a straw or reed lying in a basin of water made a mere toy. It would point to the north, but would be of no use in a ship except in a dead calm and a fog. A further step was taken when the needle was balanced on an upright, and placed in a box on which the points, or eight or twelve of them, were marked. On land that might be a tolerably useful compass, but the needle would soon have been discharged of its fluid amid the pitchings and rollings of a vessel in rough weather. Moreover, it would obviously have been necessary to shift the box in order to maintain its correspondence with the needle whenever the course was altered. This alone would render such an arrangement of little value. The steersman cannot be left to guess whether the ship's head is pointing east and by north, or south-east, by mere observation of the needle. He must be able to see the points at once, and this he can do only if the marking remain always in the same relative position to the needle.

Before these markings of the points could be made available it was first obligatory to divide the circle of the horizon on a scheme at once intelligible and universal; and this was long in the doing. The peoples of the Mediterranean from early times divided the circle into eight points, the four cardinals and the four halves. They naturally began counting from the sunrise—the east. The men of the Middle Ages had a religious reason for starting from the same point. In the east lay the Holy Land and the Sepulchre, and from the east the Lord would come in judgment. The Italians named the eight main winds: "levante," the east; "scirocco," south-east; "ostro" or "mezzodi," the south; "libeccio" or "garbanto," south-west; "ponente," west; "maestro," north-west; "tramontana," north; "greco," the north-east. When subdividing these eighths of the circle they said, "Maestro un quarto verso Tramontana"—north-west and a quarter to north—*i.e.*, N.W. and by N.—and so of the other points. An alternative division by twelve was proposed in the ancient world. Charlemagne, who was doubtless told of it by the scholars he favoured, is said to have given names to the twelve winds; "ostroniwint," east; "ostsundroni," east by south; "sundostroni," south-east; "sundroni," south; "sundivestroni," south by west; "westsundroni," south-west; "westroni," west; "westnordroni," north by west; "nordwestroni," north-west; "nordroni," north; "nordostroni," north by east; "ostnordroni," north-east. But the division by twelve was apparently no more than a suggestion of scholars. The natural course was to take the cardinal points and halve them, and halve again. The total of thirty-two finally reached was made up between the seaman of the Mediterranean and the Adriatic, as experience taught them that more was needed than the original eight points.

There may have been no more than that number of points marked on the card when it was first fixed to the needle, when the two were slung in gimbals—*i.e.*, concentric rings having their axles at right angles, and when the mariner's compass was well and truly made. When and by whom the great work was done have been much discussed questions, and probably will continue to be. Everybody has heard the line "*Prima dedit nautis usum magnetis amalphis.*" Amalfi first gave the use of the magnet to sailors. It has been quoted and confuted as if it meant that Amalfi claimed to have discovered the virtue of the magnetic needle; but this is not the necessary meaning. It says, perhaps, only that Amalfi shaped the mariner's compass. As this Southern Italian city lay at the very centre of maritime enterprise in the thirteenth century, there is nothing improbable in the supposition that the claim is well founded. Whether the man who did the work was a Flavio de Gioya of Positano, and whether it was done by the year 1302, are simply questions which can be answered neither in the affirmative nor in the negative, because of lack of evidence.*

The compass in any of its developments is not absolutely necessary to the mariner who wishes to make a long voyage out of sight of land, if he has a trade-wind or monsoon to rely on. The natives of Polynesia make long runs, yet use no compass. Sea traders of the Roman Empire went to the coast of Malabar and came back, and so did the Arabs, before they knew of the compass. In the Mediterranean Roman ships could sail from Sicily to Alexandria in summer without finding it necessary to make the land of Crete or Africa. The Polynesian had the trade-winds, the ancient Red Sea traders the monsoons, and the Mediterranean seamen the westerly summer wind to carry them on. They had only to trim their sails at the proper angle to the unfailing wind, and it carried them towards their destination. In the leisurely old world time was of but moderate consequence, and it mattered little to the sea trader if he did make his landfall fifty miles off his destination, so long as he did not fall to leeward. Even that misfortune fell chiefly on the crew, to whom belonged the back-breaking task of tugging at the sweeps. But going by the wind is possible only when experience has taught you that it listeth to blow for so many months in the same direction. Without that security you are bound in the absence of a compass to sail by the land.

The ancient and medieval seamen had the help of sailing directions; the Greek and Carthaginian " periploi," per-

---

* The development of the mariner's compass has given rise to a whole literature of controversy. Summaries and copious references to authorities will be found in "Die Italienischen Portulane des Mittelatters," by Herr Konrad Kretschmer, Berlin, 1909; and "Die Nautischen Instrumente bis zur Erfindung des Spigelsextanten," of Herr A. Breusing, Bremen, 1890.

ambulations, so to speak, on water ; the Italian " portulane " or harbour-books ; the French and English " routiers " and " rutters." The sailing directions of the pre-Christian world have for the more part reached us only in fragments, or in the form of summaries by historians. This is, for instance, the case with the voyages of Hanno, the Carthaginian, round the north-west shoulder of Africa, and of Pythias, the Greek of Marseilles, to the North of Europe. But the " periplus " which goes under the name of " Scylax of Caryanda " has survived nearly complete. In its present form it is, perhaps, a revised and corrected edition of an earlier work, and is supposed by scholars to belong to the age of Alexander the Great, when the Greeks had scattered their colonies from the Black Sea to Spain, and had need of such books. The scheme of the author was to start from the Pillars of Hercules (Straits of Gibraltar), follow the coast of Europe to the Tanais (the Don), then give the coast of Asia Minor, Syria, and Northern Africa, and so return to the Straits.* To me Scylax appears as a writer who would be of more value to the passenger who wished to know where he was and what he was passing than to the skipper desirous to be told what anchorage he could find, and where he would renew his water-supply. Yet he gives us one valuable piece of nautical information. He measures his distances by the time taken to cover them, in days and nights. One thousand stadia made an average twenty-four hours' run. The exact length of a stadium, or stadion, has been debated, but if we take it to have been a little less than the eighth part of an English mile, it follows that the Greek seamen of the age of Alexander the Great were satisfied if they made on the average about five miles an hour. In favourable conditions, going large in a steady breeze and on a friendly current, they would make more than the average. We may note, for purposes of comparison, that the mean speed obtained by Captain Cook was three knots an hour—three geographical, a little more than three statute, miles. Similar treatises can be traced in summary

* For Scylax and his followers, Byzantine and Italian, I must again refer the reader to " Die Italienischen Portulane des Mittelalters," of Herr Konrad Kretschmer, and to Nordenskiöld's " Periplus."

or fragment for the Black and the Red Seas. We have the remains of a Byzantine " periplus," the so-called " stadiasmos," a name given by a modern editor. It was manifestly composed with the intention to aid the mariner. It is full of such matter as this: " From Heracleion to the city Chersonesos is 130 stadia. There is water (*e.g.*, drinking water to be got), and there is an island with a tower and an anchorage."

The medieval seamen were not inadequately supplied with " Admiralty Pilots and Sailing Directions," the works, not of public departments, but of seamen, or perhaps merchants. Among ourselves they were known as " rutters " — *i.e.*, route-books — and by the Italians as " portulane." In later times a " portulano " came to be the name of a map. Many of these sailing directions still survive in manuscript, but some found their way into print at the close of the Middle Ages. One of these was the " portulano " printed by Bernardo Rizo in Venice in 1490, and quoted by his name. It is a collection of pilotage and sailing instructions for parts of the Mediterranean, and for the west coast of Europe as far north as the banks of Flanders, and is a type of all the rest. Rizo's author gives tables of tides of a rough kind, depths and such pilotage directions as this:

" From Corrubedo to the island of Bayona is twenty-five miles, and as far as the town of Bayona it is thirty-two miles. Cape Finisterre bears N.W. by N. from Bayona island. If you keep that course you will avoid the Lobeiros shoal, which is a bad shoal."*

" The island of Bayona is a good port, and whoever

---

* The island of Bayona, of which the "portulano" speaks, is one of the string lying over against the entry to Vigo Bay, and now generally called Cies and Bayona. The distances are given in "miglia," which Herr Kretschmer calculates to have measured a kilometer and quarter. But the Italians' distances and bearings are approximate, and must be taken subject to accurate measurement, and to the variations and deviations of the compass. Finisterre light is in 42° 53″ N. and 9° 16′ W. of Greenwich—Cabo del Home, the cape on the mainland almost exactly opposite the north end of Cies and Bayona is in 42° 15′ N. and 8° 52″ W. The latitude of Corrubedo is 42° 34′ N. There are several " Lobeiros "—small rocky islands and shoals on the coast. The town of Bayona and its bay lie at the south-west point of Vigo Bay, on the mainland.

wishes to go in holds on till he sees the white sand in the middle of San Esteban, and there is there good anchorage and clean ground on all sides. And from the middle of the said island on the east the Gulf of Redondela [now called Bay of Vigo] runs inland twenty-five or more miles, but no ship ever goes into that gulf for it lies out of [or takes her out of] her road. Bayona [*i.e.*, the town] is a good port, and the entry is wide, and the land is good, and on the north are many little reefs and shoals covered with water which force you to enter by the open passages. Keep to the mainland on the east side and when you are in and opposite the town there is a shoal. Beware of it. Leave it on the right hand, and anchor where you see that the ground is good all round. And within Bayona [the bay not the town] on the S.E. there is a port three miles away, and it is named Seis. There is a river and a place to winter in. Three miles to the west of Bayona [the town this time, not the bay] near the cape about half a mile off are many little reefs and shoals, called the Estelas, and they are very dangerous. Beware of them."

The Italian " portulane " have survived in comparatively large numbers. An example of an English " rutter " may be consulted in Volume LXXIX. of the publications of the Hakluyt Society—the volume which contains Hues "Tractatus de Globis." It is full of such matter as this :

" At the Lands End lieth Raynoldis stone (Rundle or Runnel Stone). A little berth of but twelve fathoms shall lead you all be outen him, and S.S.W. of the Lands End lieth the Gulph. The Longships and Lands End lie N.N.W., and S.S.E. . . . Beware of the hidre [*i.e.*, hidden stones]."

The " rutter " came from the Paston Papers, and is supposed to have belonged to Ambrose Paston, a seaman of the time of Henry VIII.

The northern seamen would not be wholly without sailing directions, but far less is known of them than of the Italian " portulane." Bare statements in Sagas that Iceland or Greenland could be reached in so many days and nights hardly deserve the name. Mr. E. N. Dahlgren, who contributes a chapter to Nordenskiöld's " Periplus " quotes an undoubted Book of Pilotage for the coast of Norway, and some scanty sailing directions for a voyage to the Holy Land from the Danish King Valdemar's " Jordebog "—a Doomsday Book. After the age of the Vikings the Norsemen became timid sailors. They drew on the Italians for knowledge of the coasts south of their own. Little, or even nothing, seems to be known of the sailing directions of Germans and Netherlanders before the sixteenth century.

Written sailing directions and charts complete one another, and it is natural to suppose that they arose together. The ancients may have drawn charts to illustrate their " periploi," but if they did, no example of their work remains. The Italian cities, which set the example to Europe in so many ways, were the leaders in chart making. A claim has, indeed, been put in for the Balearic Islands. In the later Middle Ages their seafaring men were skilful chart makers; but when their condition in earlier times is taken into account, it is incredible that they should have forestalled Venice and Amalfi. The Italian claim is too strong to be set aside. The earliest existing charts were made by them, and there is no excuse for supposing the existence of yet earlier examples for which we have no evidence. The oldest surviving " mariner's card," to use the name which prevailed in England down to the seventeenth century, was drawn in Pisa in the thirteenth century.*

The maps have scales of distances at the sides, and a very individual appearance is given to them by the so-called compass or loxodromic lines.† They are covered by a network of straight lines starting from several central points, and crossing one another at oblique or acute angles. The points are sometimes, usually in the case of the later maps, marked by little compass cards or wind roses. As there is reason to believe that the lines were drawn before the coast

---

* Ancient cartography has been widely studied during the last three-quarters of a century. A bibliography of works on the subject would be long. Those which I have used are: Kretschmer, " Die Italienischen Portulane des Mittelatters "; Fischer (Theobald), " Beiträge zur Geschichte der Erdkande und die Kartographie in Italien im Mittelalter "; Viscount Santarem, " Essai sur l'Histoire de la Cosmographie et de la Cartographie pendant le Moyen Age "; and Nordenskiöld, " Periplus."

† Loxodromic Line: "The line of a ship's course when sailing oblique to the meridian " (Admiral Smyth's " Sailors' Handbook ").

was filled in, they may have served to guide the draftsman. To the seaman they can have been of no practical use. They would not give the true compass bearings, the rhumbs, or loxodromic lines, unless the maps were on Mercator's projection ; but they were on no projection, and were done by course and compass with the help of the sea astrolabe. They were, all things considered, fairly accurate, though the Mediterranean as charted by them has a marked twist to the north at the western end. Accuracy was not, in fact, possible for the early chart makers. Apart from their dead reckoning—the calculation of the days run—and the compass, their only aid was the sea astrolabe. This instrument, an adaptation of the astrologer's astrolabe, was in early times made of wood. The first brass astrolabes were constructed by Regiomontanus, George Müller of Konigsberg, in Franconia, in the fifteenth century.* It was a graduated circle, with a movable index, for taking the altitude of stars and planets. The index was pivoted on a central bar, and had on each end an upright copper plate pierced in the middle. The mariner held the astrolabe up by a ring, and worked the index till the ray of the " star," which might be the sun, shone directly through both holes. Then he noted the angle made by the index and the graduated scale, and so got his latitude, after a fashion. But the epoch of the great ocean voyages had lasted two centuries and a half before the navigator was provided with an instrument which allowed him to find the longitude. He knew well enough how it could be done. Men were perfectly well aware that if the seaman could carry with him a clock which could be trusted to give him the time of his starting-place accurately throughout his voyage, he could fix his longitude. So convinced were they that that way was the best, that experiments in clock making continued throughout the sixteenth century. Robert Hues, author of the learned " Treatise of the Globes," which appeared in its original Latin in 1594, discusses various methods, all " uncertain " and " ticklish," for finding the longitude, and then ends indignantly : " Others have gone other ways to

* For Regiomontanus and his successors, see L. Gallois, "Les Géographes Allemands de la Renaissance."

work, as, namely, by observing the space of the equinoctial hours betwixt the meridians of two places, which they conceive may be taken by the help of sundials or clocks, or hour-glasses, either with water or sand or the like. But all these conceits long since devised having been more strictly and accurately examined, have been disallowed and rejected by all learned men (at least, those of riper judgment) as being altogether unable to perform that which is required of them. But yet for all this there are a kind of trifling imposters that make public sale of these toys or worse, and that with great ostentation and boasting, to the great expense and abuse of some men of good note and quality who were perhaps better stored with money than either learning or judgment. But I shall not stand here to discover the errors and uncertainties of these instruments, only I admonish these men, by the way, that they beware of these fellows, lest when their noses are wiped (as we say) of their money they too late repent them of their ill bought bargains. Away with all such trifling, cheating rascals."

The trifling, cheating rascals were on the right road, but they were not to be vindicated till Harrison produced his first chronometer in 1736. The early Italian chart makers did not confine themselves to the Mediterranean, but went as far in Western and North-Western Europe as the trade of Venice spread, and they added what they learnt from the seamen of the German Hansa. Considering their limited means, they were successful, and it is no reproach to them if the imitations of their charts used in the Mediterranean in the eighteenth century were found to be inaccurate by surveyors armed with far superior instruments. Admiral Smyth* did find that such important points as Cape Matapan were marked miles out of their exact place. None the less, the old charts, with all their indifference to latitude and longitude, served the coasting seaman for centuries, and men trained in that school opened the great ocean routes. It was naturally enough the case that the " portulane " and early " rutters " were brief. The modern " Pilot and

* Rear-Admiral William Henry Smyth charted the Mediterranean 1815-1824. See his " Mediterranean : A Memoir," 1854.

Sailing Directions for the West Coast of France, Spain, and Portugal" devotes many pages to the coast between Corrubedo and Bayona. It gives innumerable details of depths of water, number and shape of rocks, where Rizo's "Portulano" is content to say that the shoal is dangerous and you must beware. The Italian and his English contemporary have nothing to say of longitude and latitude, nor yet of lights, which are carefully specified in modern "pilots." Lighthouses were, indeed, not unknown to the Ancient World and the Middle Ages, but they were few and weak—mere guiding beacons at the entries of ports. The old seamen had nothing to correspond to the light which warns the passing steamer off the dangerous Abrolhos on the coast of Brazil. Still less had he the support and comfort of the long line of guiding beams which show him the way on the admirably lighted coast of France by Ushant. When "making the land" he lay to at night, and by day he went slowly; yet, however cautious he might be, he ran risks unknown to the modern seaman. Take an Admiralty Chart—say, No. 1053, which shows the Spanish coast from Finisterre to Bayona—and note the jagged line of rocky islands, reefs, shoals, and cliffs. Remember that the westerly and south-westerly gales blow for weeks together on the shore, and set up a current which carries ships towards all these perils. Remember, too, that the square courses which constituted the whole spread of sail of ancient and medieval ships were all but useless for the purpose of working to windward, while the sweeps or oars could make no head against the combined force of wind and current, though the crew tugged for their lives till their heartstrings broke. Then it is easy to understand why the Rizo Portulano, which is, on the whole, so summary, yet stops to note the "invernada," the winter harbour at Sies. When they were caught on such a coast, the old seamen made for the nearest winter harbour, and stayed there till the wind abated, or even till the whole season of storms was past.

The seamen of old were no great penmen; therefore we should look in vain for an account of their life from them. We could well spare many bald reports of murderous conflicts between the mariners of England and their rivals of Normandy or the Basque Coast, for one good story of a voyage for wine to Bayonne or Puerto de Santa Maria. It is only when others saw him that we can see the sailor at his work, and such witnesses are few and sparing of detail. Naturally enough, our best authorities are holy men and friars, who wrote legends of miraculous voyages, and went on pilgrimage to the Holy Land. St. Brendan, who is " included in the second rank of Irish saints," may never have sailed to the Paradise of Birds, nor yet have met the iceberg on which Judas Iscariot enjoyed his yearly merciful release from torment ; but the author of his voyage sought verisimilitude. So when he tells us how the saint and his companions " embarked," and " they had a fair wind, and therefore no labour, only to keep the sails properly set ; but after twelve days the wind fell to a dead calm, and they had to labour at the oars until their strength was nearly exhausted," he is taking his verisimilitude from his own experience on some not miraculous voyage. To sail when the wind was favourable, when it was a following wind, and then to labour at the oars till their strength was nearly exhausted, were the two extremes of luck and ill-luck for the old seamen.

Brother Felix Schmid (in Latin, Faber) is a more prosaic person than the author of the voyage of St. Brendan, but we have to thank him for a very lively picture of one side of the sea life of the Middle Ages.* Brother Felix, a very innocent soul, came from Zurich, and was a Dominican at Ulm. He went on his own account to the Holy Land as a pilgrim in 1480, and in 1483 he accompanied the Dean of Mayence, Bernhard von Breidenbach, whose travels are told in a famous book. He had seen the voyage from Venice, and also the Levant, more than most men. The pilgrim traffic to Palestine was the great passenger-carrying business of the Middle Ages, and the galleys of St. Mark

* The " Evagatorium : The Wanderings of Brother Felix Schmid " (Faber) has been published in the original Latin—which is the dog-Latin derided in the " Epistolæ Obscurorum Virorum "—among the publications of the " Bibliothek des Literarischen Vereins in Stuttgart," and edited by C. D. Hassler (1843). An English translation is among the publications of the Palestine Pilgrims' Text Society.

employed in it were the forerunners of the ocean liners of to-day.

The galleys of Venice, in which the pilgrims are carried, Brother Felix tells us, are as like one another as the nests of the swallow. Some, it is true, are biremes and some are triremes. A bireme has two rowers and two oars—an oar per man—on each bench. In the trireme there are three rowers, each pulling his own oar, to the bench; but the general arrangement is the same in both. The galley has masts and sails. A gangway runs fore and aft amidships, and on it the " exhorters," who call the time to the rowers, run up and down. There is a poop aft wherein there are cabins. In front of the poop on the starboard side is the kitchen and the stall for the live stock to be eaten on the voyage. Therefore there are fewer benches on the starboard than on the port side. Wealthy passengers can hire private bunks under the poop cabins. The ordinary pilgrims occupy the hold, which runs the length of the galley from the first-class poop cabins forward. In a trading galley the hold is full of cargo. In a passenger galley it is the pilgrims' common sleeping-place. You go down to it by one hatchway close to the mainmast, and by a ladder of seven steps. It is lighted only by the hatchway—and we may add, that of course it is not ventilated.

Here the pilgrims sleep, their heads towards the side of the galley, their feet towards the gangway amidships. Their boxes fill the gangway. Their mattresses touch one another. When any of the pilgrims come down late they have to climb along the boxes, and tumble over the legs of those who are down and are trying to sleep. Some men will persist in talking noisily, others will keep a candle alight, to the exasperation of the more somnolent. Friar Felix has seen a candle put out and its owner drenched by the reversal of an unnameable vessel—whence bad language, abuse, and blows, rapidly spreading all round till the whole dormitory is in a general hurlyburly, and if the purser were to make his appearance for the purpose of restoring order he would be torn to pieces. If work is in progress above, the cabin resounds with noise. Brother Felix once made a voyage when horses were stalled between the benches on the upper deck. Their endless trampling and pulling at their head-ropes murdered sleep.

Under the deck of the common cabin is the keel, the bilge, full of sand ballast. The pilgrims have access to it, and can put bottles of wine there, or eggs, or anything else they wish to keep cool; but more goes into the ballast than their private stores. Nobles of Venice, who die on the voyage, are buried in the ballast, to be brought home and transferred to the family vault—a disgusting practice, of which there are examples in far later times. And the drainage of the galley—but here Brother Felix goes beyond quotation.

As for meals, there are two a day announced by trumpet. The rich who live aft can eat in their bunks by candlelight. The common ruck of pilgrims must come hurrying to the table laid for them on the poop, for there are never seats enough for all; and if you are late, you must sit among the rowers. Our authority makes no complaint of the food, unless it be that the animals killed for the passengers' table are always those who show every sign of being just about to die a natural death. Private dishes can be provided by the four cooks—for ready-money. Promises to pay are not accepted, for the cooks are impatient and peremptory. Nor can their impatience be wondered at, for they work all four in a small hot space, full of pots, food, and braziers, and the passengers mob the door and bellow for their savoury messes. The state of a ship's cook moved Brother Felix, a kind-hearted man, to commiseration. The pilgrim ship, we gather, was not pious. The passengers amused themselves with cards, and in ways not to be dwelt on. The fact is that pilgrimage was often a cover for travel the very reverse of religious. The "white slave traffic" went on beside such pious persons as Brother Felix, or the aged ladies of honourable birth who made a voyage with him, incurring danger and much discomfort that they might see the Holy Sepulchre before they died. Prayers were held at stated intervals, but in a perfunctory way. Did not Brother Felix himself begin a hopeful sermon, and was he not forced to desist because a man of Belial sat on the bulwarks and moved the congregation to laughter by ribald jests? It may be that the good Dominican, meaning no such thing, helped Erasmus to construct his cruel account of what a pilgrimage meant at the end of the fifteenth century.

And what of the captain and crew? Of them the Friar speaks but incidentally. The padrone, we see, was a great man, with whom the pilgrim contracted for the voyage. The boatswain was a terrible fellow, feared by the crew like the devil ("sicut diabolum"), for he was as free as Mr. Chucks with the rattan. As for the men, we gather, from the silence of the Friar as to any other quarters they had, that they slept under the benches on the upper deck. Punishments, he says, not very consistently, were light—a mere matter of being flogged by the boatswain, who was a "diabolus," or, in extreme cases, marooning. On the whole, Brother Felix seems to have regarded the boatswain and his men alike as an unhallowed race. When detailing all the reasons why the Host must not be consecrated, or elevated, or kept in a monstrance in a ship, he includes among them this: that on any sudden emergency calling for exertions the crew would assuredly pay no respect to priest or Sacrament, but would spill them, altar and all, into the scuppers: He rather implies that they would enjoy the chance.

We must not be ungrateful to the Friar, who tells us so much, if he does not tell us all we should like to know. It would be satisfactory, for example, if he had noted how the work was divided between the oars and the sails. From one passage (which cannot be quoted) it would appear that no use was made of the oars by night. They were hauled in, not unshipped, and the blades were left projecting from the galley's side. It must not be overlooked that the galleys in which the pilgrims made these voyages to Palestine bore the same relation to the ordinary trading ship of the time that the Cunarder or Royal Mail steamer does to the 12-knot tramp now. Brother Felix notes that the space below the deck of the cabin was sharp in the galley, and not wide as it was in "other vessels." The other vessels were the usual round ships of trade. The character of the galley is emphasized by his statement that, when it was used for fighting purposes, a crossbowman was added to the two or three rowers, as the case might be, of each bench. The ship in which Brother Felix was pestered by the trampling of the horses was probably a round one—a mere trader. She must at least have depended on her sailing power, for rowing was impossible when the space between the benches was occupied in that way. Incidentally, the Dominican helps to show us how men were packed together in the ships of the fifteenth century. The galley in which he made his second voyage was a trireme of thirty benches on each side of the central gangway, the "cursia." As this gave three rowers to the bench she carried 180 in all, and the officers, steersmen, cooks, and pilgrims. The total cannot well have been less than 360 persons, all crowded in, on, and about such a centre of infection as the common cabin must have been. No wonder that, though Brother Felix had not often seen men die while a good breeze was blowing, he had known many wither and die in calms. In the stagnant air the food was turned bad, vermin swarmed, men grew torpid, or were exasperated. And yet he was sailing in the best conditions then afforded, and gives no sign of thinking that better could be provided.

In his own age, and for centuries before it, no better was to be found. The galley of Saint Mark, of which he speaks, cannot possibly have been the same sort of craft as a common cargo boat. He does say, indeed, that the space occupied by the pilgrims under the deck of the rowers might be filled by cargo. And so the great steamers which carry passengers to America and the East can load goods in empty cabins when their regular customers fail, but they do so at a loss. Whatever the profits of trade and the freight may have been, a vessel which required 180, or even 120, rowers, and officers, steersmen, and sail-trimmers in addition, can have been no more capable of being run at a profit as a mere cargo boat than are the Cunarders, Royal Mail steamers, and P. and O. liners of to-day. The typical trader must have been much more like the *Saint Nicholas*, whose fortunes have been recorded already.

There is no cause for wonder, nor yet for condemnation, if the crews of such craft appear somewhat timid when compared to modern seamen. The confidence of the sailor has grown with the improvement of the ship. Men who sailed in a tub built on the three, two, one formula, which pitched horribly, built, too, without inner lining or outside sheathing, and therefore dependent on her caulking to keep out the water, provided with sails which were of as good as no use at all, except on a lady's sea and in a fair wind, and compelled to have recourse to the killing toil of the oars in calms or in danger, are not to be blamed if they sought a winter harbour from October to March. By the laws of the Italian Republics no ship was allowed to go to sea before April or after October. The trading convoys ("mudue") of Venice were divided into those which left at Easter, or, when it fell in March, then immediately afterwards, and returned by September, and those which sailed in August and wintered at the port of discharge, returning next summer. It was long before seafaring men quite gave up avoiding the sea in winter. Stout-hearted British naval officers of the seventeenth and early eighteenth centuries held that there was madness in keeping ships out after September. Horace Walpole gleefully asked a correspondent to compare the intrepidity of Hawke, who cruised off Ushant in the winter months, with the timidity of Blake and Cloudesley Shovel, who came back to port in September. He would probably have smirked with assenting leer if anyone had pointed out to him that ships rigged with a spritsail could not cruise on a lee shore as safely as those rigged with a jib. And Hawke's ships had jibs, Blake's and Shovel's had not. By the seventeenth century vessels had been so far improved that the caution of the Middle Ages was no longer necessary for sailing ships. The galleys, which lingered on till the middle of the eighteenth, were always laid up in winter.

So many things reintroduced as entirely new turn out to be old when properly examined that we are not surprised to learn that the Middle Ages had their official load-lines and Plimsoll's mark. They were known at least at Venice, and the line was placed according to the age of the ship. As the ancient seamen did carry cargoes for centuries, we need no persuading to believe that they did not load their ships at random. Use and wont, embodied in laws by the Italian cities, established elementary rules. Ballast must be taken in under the competent supervision of the master or mate, and, once loaded, must not be disturbed. Heavy goods, such as lead, might be used as ballast. In stowing the hold the weightiest goods must be placed lowest of all. The master was to see that the orthodox course was taken. He and his crew were to do the work when there were no stevedores at hand. In the busier ports there were stevedores, and the Middle Ages would not have been the Middle Ages if these craftsmen had not been formed into guilds and brotherhoods, very jealous of infringements of their rights, and prepared to enforce them by violence. The perils of deck cargo made themselves felt as acutely in the thirteenth as in the twentieth century. Therefore it was forbidden to be carried save under close restrictions. Tackle, armour, and rations were allowed on the deck, nor does one see where else they could have been carried. Wood, food, and horses were suffered as deck cargo, and an exception was made in favour of a ship which transferred cargo from another in distress. Fire was a palpable danger, and was guarded against by rules. None were allowed by some codes while the vessel was on her way from one anchorage to another. It is highly probable that this restriction did not apply to the lighting of a pan of charcoal.

Even if the old traders had not had to fear dangers other than those of the sea, men compelled to risk their lives in weak unhandy vessels would have had good reason for preferring to sail in company where help would be at hand. No doubt they did so as far as they could long before the law began to take notice of and to control an established custom. The word " conserva " (a convoy) began to be familiar after the twelfth century—that is to say, when the Crusades had promoted a great development of trade in the Mediterranean. These associations of sea traders were voluntarily made, and might have much of the character of a partnership. The convoy went on common profit and loss. If one of the vessels composing it was wrecked or taken by pirates (a very present peril during many centuries), then the loss was divided among all. It was but just that as the profit was common so should the loss be. The substance of our own Act of 57 George III., " for the better Protection of the Trade of the United Kingdom during the Present Hostilities with France," was to be found in the Laws of Ragusa, the practice of Venice, and the Tables of Amalfi. Convoy was enforced, and a " capitaneus " was appointed to see to it that no skipper departed from the regulations made for the general good.

Our ancestors were not tender, and these old Rolls of Oleron and so forth contain some speaking examples of what they were prepared to do, or at least thought they ought to be allowed to do, to their natural enemies. One of these would be the incompetent or fraudulent pilot. Therefore, saith the Roll of Oleron:

" It is established for a custom of the sea that if a ship is lost by the default of the lodeman [*i.e.*, pilot] the mariners may, if they please, bring the lodeman to the windlass, or any other place, and cut off his head without the mariners being bound to answer before any judge, because the lodeman has committed high treason against his undertaking of the pilotage."

That this was ever law anywhere is hard to believe, but it does very well express the natural sentiments of a sailor towards a defaulting pilot. As much may be said for a good deal we hear about another of the seaman's enemies—the wrecker.

This villain, who is now even more of a memory than the pirate, was once a very real monster; and it is one of the ugly things of the Middle Ages that he was encouraged. The laws which gave the lords of the manor on the coast a right to an interest in wreckage thrown on their land were an obvious incentive to deliberate wrecking, and to the robbery and murder of shipwrecked men. When there was no survivor of a wreck, there was nobody to make trouble. Certain it is that wrecking was a sufficiently flagrant sin to call for violent denunciation in Councils of the Church. In fact, all the authority of the Church and the power of the King were needed to make knights, barons, and smaller fry understand that it was any sin at all. The King, moreover, took his share of wrecks. When we hear of the chivalry of the Middle Ages, and of their superiority to the greedier age of the capitalist, let us remember that the age of chivalry awoke very late, or not at all, to the utter meanness of pillaging shipwrecked men.

What the sailors thought of it they have put on record. Hear Pierre Garcie, *alias* Ferrande, author of the "Grand Routier," and compiler of a late edition of the Laws of Oleron. He is our mouthpiece for whole long generations of infuriated seafaring men.

He begins with the orthodox doctrine as to good behaviour in lords of the manor. If a ship is lost and some of the crew escape, they are to be allowed by the lord of the place to salve the fragments. He who hinders them ought (this is pious opinion) to be excommunicate, and treated as a thief. The lord ought to have the wreck salved, and pay the salvors out of the goods. The residue of a total wreck he ought to keep for a year, and if it is not claimed in that space, " he ought to sell publicly, and to the highest offer, the said things, and from the money received he ought to have prayer made to God for the dead, or to marry poor maids, or to do other works of mercy after reason and conscience. And if the said lord taketh of the things a fourth or other part, he shall incur the malediction of our Mother Holy Church, and the penalties above said without ever having remission if he make not satisfaction. . . . Likewise if a ship be lost by striking against any coast, and chanceth that the crew imagine to escape and save themselves, and come to the bank half drowned, thinking that someone will aid them, but it chanceth that some time in many places there are inhuman felons more cruel than dogs or wolves enraged, the which murder and slay the poor sufferers to obtain their money, or clothes, or other goods, such manner of people the lord of the place ought to seize, and inflict on them justice and punishment, both as regards their persons and their goods, and they ought to be cast into the sea, and plunged in it, until they are half dead, and then they ought to be dragged out, and stoned, and massacred, as would be done to a dog or wolf."

So much for what ought to be, but hear what is :

" Likewise a ship cometh to any place, and would enter into a port or haven, and it sets an ensign to have either a pilot or a boat to tow it within, because the wind or tide is

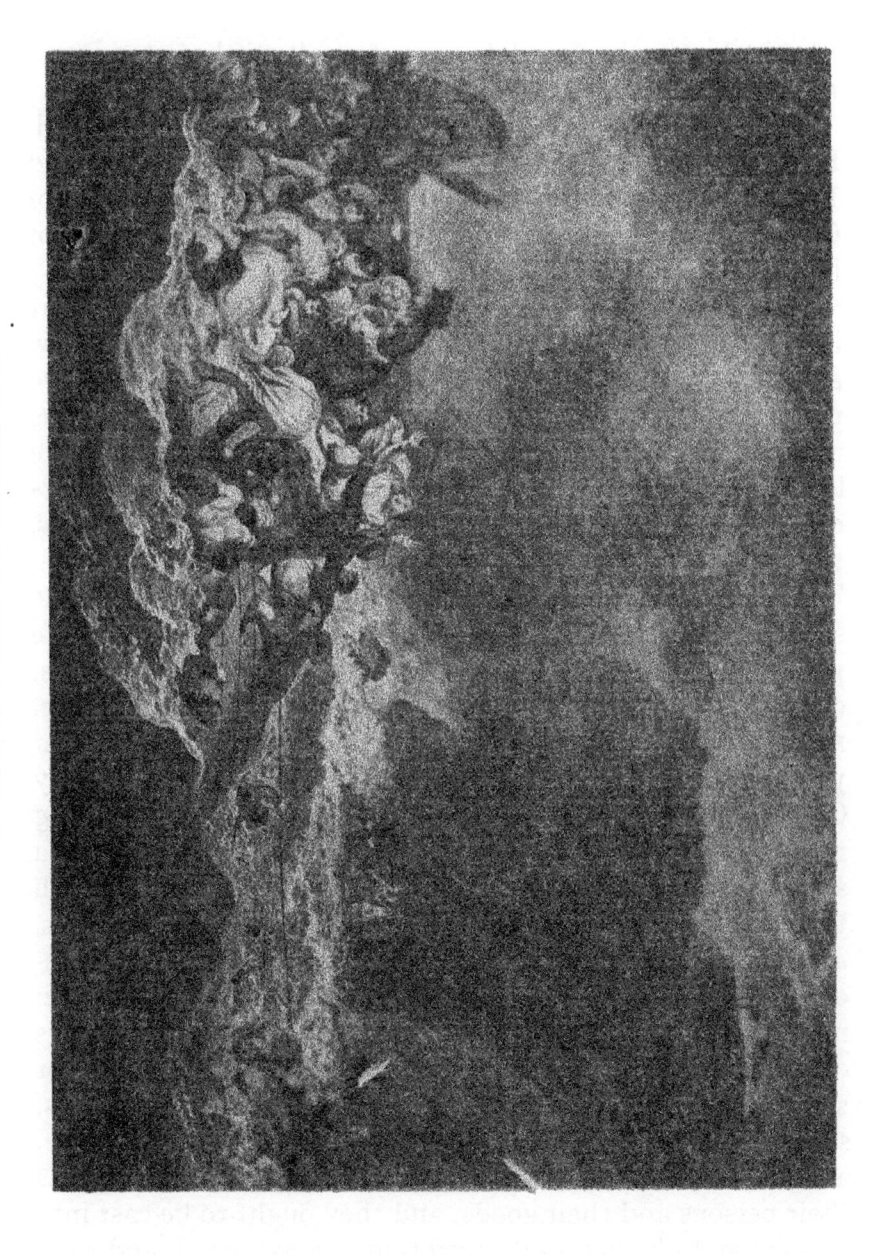

THE WRECK OF THE GROSVENOR,
EAST INDIAMAN, ON THE EASTERN COAST OF AFRICA, AUG. 4, 1782

of chivalry awoke very late or not at all, to the utter meanness of pillaging shipwrecked men.

What the sailors thought of it they have put on record. Hear Pierre Garcie, *alias* Ferraude, author of the " Grand Routier," and compiler of a late edition of the Laws of Oleron. He is our mouthpiece for whole long generations of infuriated seafaring men.

He begins with the orthodox doctrine as to good behaviour in lords of the manor. If a ship is lost and some of the crew escape, they are to be allowed by the lord of the place to salve the fragments. He who hinders them ought (this is pious opinion) to be excommunicate, and treated as a thief. The lord ought to have the wreck salved, and pay the salvors out of the goods. The residue of a total wreck he ought to keep for a year, and if it is not claimed in that space, " he ought to sell publicly, and to the highest offer, the said things, and from the money received he ought to have prayer made to God for the dead, or to marry poor maids, or to do other works of mercy after reason and conscience. And if the said lord taketh of the things a fourth or other part, he shall incur the malediction of our Mother Holy Church, and the penalties above said without ever having remission if he make not satisfaction. . . Likewise if a ship be lost by striking against any coast, and chanceth that the crew imagine to escape and save themselves, and come to the bank half drowned, thinking that someone will aid them, but it chanceth that some time in many places there are inhuman felons more cruel than dogs or wolves enraged, the which murder and slay the poor sufferers to obtain their money, or clothes, or other goods, such manner of people the lord of the place ought to seize, and inflict on them justice and punishment, both as regards their persons and their goods, and they ought to be cast into the sea, and plunged in it, until they are half dead, and then they ought to be dragged out, and stoned, and massacred, as would be done to a dog or wolf."

So much for what ought to be, but hear what is :

" Likewise a ship cometh to any place, and would enter into a port or haven, and it sets an ensign to have either a pilot or a boat to tow it within, because the wind or tide is

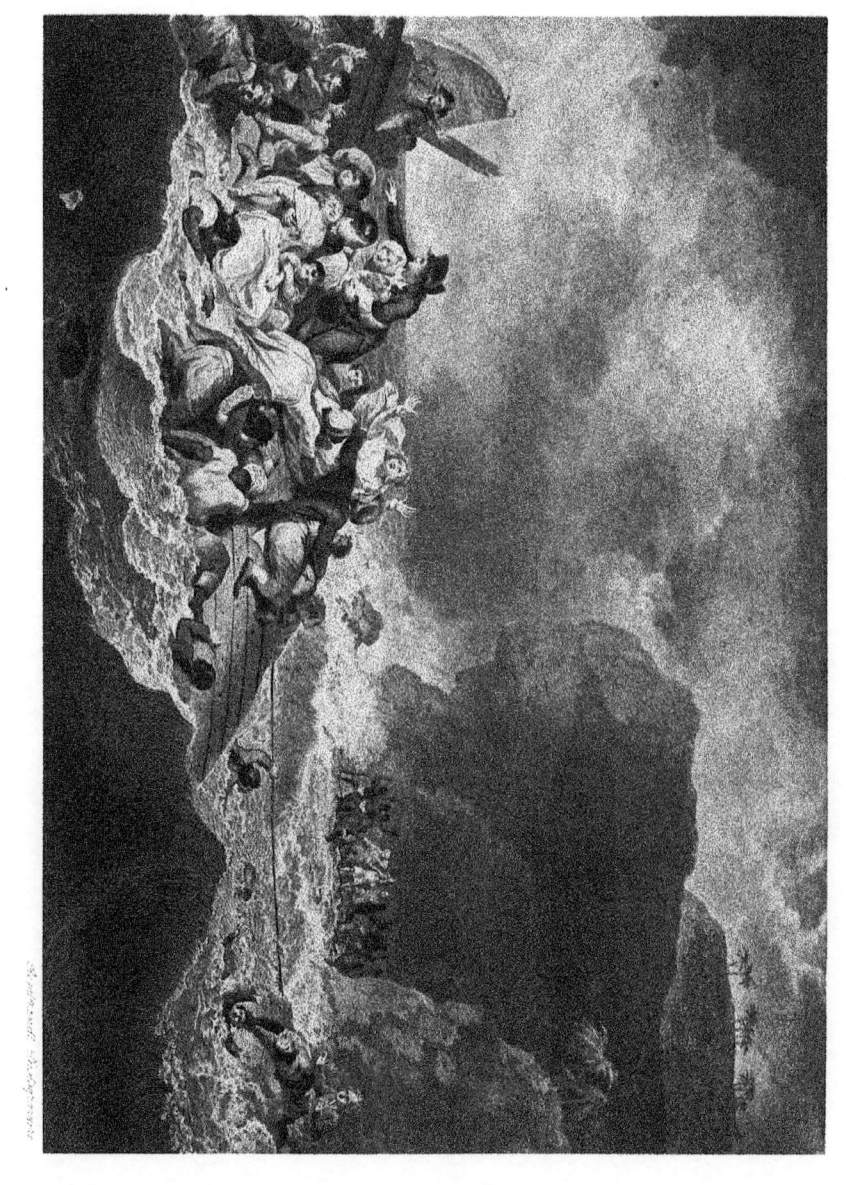

THE WRECK OF THE GROSVENOR,
EAST INDIAMAN, ON THE EASTERN COAST OF AFRICA, AUG. 4, 1782.

contrary. It chanceth that those who go to bring in the said ship have made a bargain for the pilotage or towage, but because in some places the accursed and damnable custom runs without reason that of the ships that are lost the lord of the place taketh a third or a fourth, and the salvors another third or fourth, and the residue the masters or merchants, these things considered, and to be sometimes in the good graces of the lord, and also to have some of the goods of the said ship, like disloyal villains and traitors they guide the said ship on to the rocks wittingly to their knowledge and of certain malice, and cause the said ship and the merchandize to be lost, and feign to succour the poor people. And they are the first to pull to pieces and break up the ship, and to carry off the merchandize, the which is a thing contrary to God and reason. And to be welcome in the house of the lord, they run to tell and announce the poor disaster, and loss of the merchants, and so cometh the lord with his people, and takes his part of the goods adventured, and the salvors the other part, and the residue awaits the merchants. But seeing that this is contrary to the commandment of God omnipotent, notwithstanding any custom or ordinance, it is said and decreed (at the Lateran Council of 1179 to wit) that the lord, the salvors, and others who shall take anything of the said goods, shall be accursed, and excommunicated, and punished as robbers as is above said."

And so the writer goes cursing and propounding punishments almost as ferocious as our own form of execution for high treason in those ages. The false pilots are to be hung on high gibbets, "to serve as a landmark to other vessels that shall come there." The lord who encourages their business is to be tied to a stake in the midst of his house, and burned together with it. Our friend was no sentimentalist, nor even an enemy to wrecking and slaying when properly used. He adds:

"Likewise the things preceding ought to be understood if the ship was not engaged in the practice of pillage, that the crew of her were not pirates or sea rovers, or enemies of our Holy Catholic Faith. For in that case, if they be pirates, pillagers, or sea rovers, or Turks, or others opposed to, and enemies of, our Holy Catholic Faith, everyone may take from such manner of men as from dogs, and may strip them, and despoil them of their goods without any punishment."

Now, all this need not be accepted as a sober statement of what was the law. It is the expression, probably, to judge by the prominence given to our Holy Catholic Faith, worded by some sympathetic priest, of the long-drawn rage and hate of the seafaring man against the longshore villains who profited by his misfortunes. It brings out an ugly side of the Middle Ages. It helps to explain why the sea traders preferred to go in convoys for mutual support. It throws some light on the origin of the sailors' belief that all landsmen were his natural enemies. That it is rhetoric is undeniable. That it is pleonastic at times is obvious. But it was sincere. Pierre Garcie, *alias* Ferrande, who included it all in his "Grand Routier" as "useful and profitable," was a Portuguese seaman in the service of Henry II. of France. He knew very well that it dealt with a foe of old standing who had not been abated in his own time, and the state of things he describes represented an improvement. Time had been when the lord of the place took the whole of a shipwrecked vessel and her cargo. It was a decided advance that he should be limited to a part. Very slowly and by successive steps were "lords of the place" and their people brought to understand that a wreck was not to be treated as a gift sent them by Providence.

CHAPTER IV

SALE, PURCHASE, AND PLUNDER

WHEN the ships of Hatshepsitu reached the Land of Punt, or the Phœnician trader undid his bales and chaffered with the dark Iberians, the scene was assuredly such a one as Mr. Wallace saw on the beach at Debbo. The skippers and sailors looked to the repair of their ships and their own small bargains. The traders landed and opened booths for the display of their goods. Sellers of provisions hurried down to supply their needs. Buyers of their goods came to exchange and to cheapen. The solitary beach and the at other times stagnant town were alive with a stirring crowd. Nor did business occupy all their attention. Pleasure was not absent, nor was piety neglected. The men of the Ancient World were ready enough to discover their own deities under foreign names. The goddess who was Aphrodite to the Greek, Venus to the Roman, and Astarte to the Carthaginian, received, or her priests and priestesses received for her, the prayers and offerings of the seamen of all nations, when her temple stood near an exchange and mart. There was something of the Japanese Koshewara about such a place of worship as the great Temple of Aphrodite, near Trapani. Men came to give thanks for a good voyage, to make offerings for favours to come, and they feasted. The medieval man had one church, and its altars were everywhere. The Italian seaman knew and venerated the shrines of the Levant. He prayed at them, and when occasion served he could carry off their reliques, not without effusion of blood—the head of one saint, the thigh-bone of another, a piece of the Virgin's hood—to add sanctity to his own shrines at home.

Violence was never far away from the life of the Old World. It was even closer at sea than on land. The same man was trader or pirate, as the case might be. The heroes of the Norse sagas are as ready to trade as to fight, or to fight as to trade. Gudrun's lovers, Kjartan and Bolli, go on a trading voyage to Norway, open a booth, and sell their goods. They were also of the stuff of which Vikings were made. The same man might be trader to his friends, and pirate to all others. Sir William Monson, the Admiral of James I. of England, found a precisely similar morality prevailing on the coast of Ireland in the seventeenth century. It is not unknown in the wilder places of the earth to-day. The first renowned seafarer whose biography we possess was own brother to Gunnar or Bolli, to Vasco da Gama or Sir John Hawkins. The reader recognizes the wise Ulysses, whom he may call Odysseus if he wishes to be very Greek. Here, in the words of the most inaccurate, but also the most readable translation of Homer, we see him at work, and we shall see something very similar in the life of Sir John:

> " The wind from Elion to the Cicons shore
> Beneath cold Ismarus our vessels bore.
> We boldly landed on the hostile place
> And sack'd the city and destroyed the race;
> Their wives made captive, their possessions shar'd,
> And every soldier found a like reward.
> I then advis'd to fly: not so the rest,
> Who stayed to revel, and prolong the feast."

But—

> " With early morn the gathered country swarms
> And all the continent is bright with arms,
> Thick as the budding leaves or rising flowers
> O'erspread the land when spring descends in showers,
> All expert soldiers skill'd on foot to dare,
> Or from the bounding courser urge the war.
> Now fortune changes (so the fates ordain);
> Our hour has come to taste our share of pain.
> Close at the ships the bloody fight began.
> Wounded they wound, and man expires on man.
> Long as the morning sun's increasing bright
> O'er heaven's pure azure spread the growing light,
> Promiscuous death the form of war confounds,
> Each adverse battle gored with equal wounds.
> But when his evening wheels o'erhang the main,
> Then conquest crown'd the fierce Ciconyan train.
> Six brave companions from each ship we lost;
> The rest escape in haste and quit the coast.
> With sails outspread, we fly the unequal strife,
> Sad for their loss, but joyful of our life."

Because he feared violence and could use it himself, the sea trader valued the possession of a " strength "—a stronghold for his goods, a storehouse for his plunder. The Phœnician took hold of Cadiz for exactly the same reason that the East India Company was glad to obtain Bombay. It was an island, and therefore defensible. It was near the mainland, and therefore it was accessible to the native who came to sell or to buy. The next best thing to a fortress of your own was a " factory "—a place ceded to you by a native ruler. It was yours to govern and to defend. When the ruler was weak, it was practically a fortified province cut out of his territory. The Steelyard of the Hanseatic traders in London was in character just such a possession as the Genoese suburb, Pera, at Constantinople. The difference was that the Kings of England were stronger than the Emperors at Constantinople, and the English were not so easily bullied as the Greeks. At Bergen, where the League was strong, and the Norwegians, weakened by the century-long emigration of their boldest men, were feeble, the League dictated, and hectored, and enforced a monopoly.

This famous League was the fine flower and model of maritime enterprise in medieval times. It was what the Greek or Italian cities might have been if they had been less bitterly jealous of one another—if Pisa had not achieved the ruin of Amalfi, if Genoa had not shattered Pisa, and had not in its turn been beaten to its knees by Venice. It consisted of a loose confederation, a " Hansa," of German trading cities, inland and maritime. Its political history does not concern us, and is, moreover, obscure. On its commercial side it was very intelligible. First it was a combination of traders to protect themselves, a very natural and innocent purpose in the days of robber knights, who lay in wait for caravans in mountain passes and at the fords of rivers ; of pirates at sea, and of Kings who, when pressed for money (a very common case with them), had no scruple whatever in extorting blackmail, either in brutal simplicity, or under the names of loans and benevolences. Then it was a combination to make use of the strength organized for defence as a means of establishing a tyrannical monopoly.

It has been said of the Hansa, as of the city of Amsterdam,

that it was built upon herrings. The obligation to observe the fasts imposed by the Roman Catholic religion caused fish to be a very important article of diet in the Middle Ages. Whoever had the command of a constant and ample supply could be sure of a steady sale. The maritime cities of the Hansa were in that fortunate position for two reasons. The first, and the more vital, was that till the beginning of the sixteenth century the migration of the herring was to the south of Sweden (Scania), the Sound, and the Baltic. The Hansa towns to the west or to the east of Denmark were excellently placed to gather this great harvest. The second and complementary reason was that the nations of the North—Denmark, Norway, Sweden, and the Wendish and Slavonic peoples of the Baltic—were anarchical and ignorant. Therefore the German traders, headed by the two leading cities, Bremen and Lübeck, were able to gather in the produce of the fisheries. If they did not fish themselves, they alone could buy the fish collected by the natives of those countries. The power which enabled them to monopolize the fish also gave them exclusive access to the tallow, flax, timber, hides, and furs of Scandinavia and Russia. Their policy was simple, and was widely imitated in after times. When Pieter Bott, the first Governor-General of the Dutch East India Company, sailed to take up his command, he stated what he considered as the policy he was appointed to carry out. It was to take care that no other people should trade with the Spice Islands. The Hansa was resolved that its members only should trade to the North. Even a German city which would not join the League was to be crushed, if not by mere physical force, at least by boycotts. A town which would not obey the general rules in all points was " dishansed " (turned out and boycotted). We hear much to-day of the tyrannies of Trusts, and hear of them as a new development, yet it is certain that the most overbearing Trust of our days has nothing to teach the Hanseatic League, and that none of them approaches its power even remotely.

Open rivals or valued friends were treated alike when they trespassed on the preserve of the Hansa. It had, as a matter of course, need of friends, for it made its profits by selling its fish salted and dried, its tallow, wax, pitch, timber, hides, and furs to Western and Southern Europe. Therefore it negotiated treaties, and sought leave to establish factories far and wide. It had one at Venice, the Fondaco dei Tedeschi (the Store of the Germans), on the Grand Canal. But at Venice the League had to deal with another like unto itself. The Venetians kept their guests in excellent order, and the Germans were not even allowed to occupy their Fondaco for the whole of any one year, lest they should obtain too strong a footing. In Russia the Hansa treated the natives as the Dutch did the people of Java. In Norway it dictated and monopolized. In the Netherlands, which were then affiliated to it, it had its headquarters at Bruges, and was very strong. In England, which in medieval times was chiefly an agricultural and pastoral country, it had, in addition to minor stations, the London "Steelyard." This establishment stood in and about where Cannon Street Station stands now, and took its name from the balance in which goods were weighed. The Steelyard was just such a place as the East India Company's Factory at Surat, and was no doubt one of its models. The Hansa obtained privileges from English Kings, just as the Company secured a "phirmaun" from the Great Mogul. In that factory it governed its own staff, who were supposed to be strictly celibate, and were in any case forbidden to marry the women of the country. Our Kings had granted it the right to pay lower export dues than native traders. This, of course, gave it a privileged position, which it abused. The Steelyard was not only a warehouse and market, but a tavern. Englishmen frequented it in search of regales of herrings and German wine, known generally as Rhenish, or particularly by such corruptions of the original names as Backrag—*i.e.*, Bacharach.

Until evil days began to come upon them at the close of the fifteenth century, the merchants and seamen of the Hansa brought the produce of the North to the West and South. They had establishments in France, Spain, and Portugal, but their great "staples" were in the Netherlands and in England. In the Netherlands they met the traders of Italy, and foremost among them the Venetians.

The trade of Venice was highly organized by the State. Eight trading fleets, or convoys, called "mudue," left Venice every year for markets stretching from the Black Sea to Flanders. At first the trade of Venice reached Flanders overland. After the beginning of the Hundred Years' War between France and England it was driven to use the sea route. The "mudue" were commanded by officers appointed by the Republic, and were manned by a system of conscription. Every five families were called upon to supply a man. The stability of the Government of Venice and the internal peace of the city were largely due to the absence of so great a proportion of the people in the "mudue." In England the merchants of the Steelyard were the chief importing and exporting body. This does not imply that Englishmen did not import or export, but that they traded through the factory of the Hansa. One of the accusations brought against it in its last stages was that it allowed Englishmen to benefit by its privileges—for a consideration, of course—and to the detriment of the King's revenue.

Much as the Hansa owed to England, it was resolute to keep English seamen from approaching its preserves. When complaints failed to remove their grievances, the Hansa traders had recourse to plain murder. In the reign of Henry IV. of England they drowned a hundred Englishmen whom they found at Bergen. The Norwegian port was a main station of the League, and not even the risk of incurring trouble for their factory in London could restrain them from killing English intruders out of hand. Nor were the English less ready than the "Easterlings" to butcher and plunder, while the seafaring men of all nations kept them in countenance. Spaniards and Englishmen retorted the charge of piracy on one another. The traders of both peoples fought on their own account, and carried on wars while their Sovereigns were at peace. When King Edward III. of England attacked the Spanish fleet off Winchelsea, he was on the best of terms with the King of Castile and Leon. His quarrel was with the "Marisma," the League of Spanish ports on the Bay of Biscay. It had plundered English ships in retaliation for plunderings by

English ships, and had intervened in the war between England and France. It would be an easy piece of compilation to collect hundreds of illustrations from the history of trade in all the seas of Europe. A few leading examples of a universal condition of insecurity will serve our purpose, and for the North we shall find little which is more instructive than the story of the Vitalians.

The history of the Vitalians is not the only, nor yet by many the last, example of the natural tendency of maritime war to breed piracy. But the Vitalians ran the whole course, from privateer to pirate, swiftly and with artistic completeness. As the fourteenth century drew to its close, the Scandinavian and Baltic countries were torn by the great conflict between Margaret of Calmar and her enemies. She was Regent of Denmark and Norway, and she strove victoriously to achieve a union of the three Scandinavian kingdoms—a very masterful woman, who well deserved the complimentary name of Semiramis of the North. On February 24th, 1389, she defeated her enemy, King Albert of Sweden, at the Battle of Falkoping, took him and imprisoned him at Lindholm.

Albert was a member of the family of the Dukes of Mecklenburg, and they fought for him. The young Duke John of Mecklenburg-Stargard, his nephew, held Stockholm for Albert when the rest of Sweden had yielded to Margaret. The old Duke John would have helped the young Duke if he could, but as his power was not great he had to cast about for resources. The towns of Rostock and Wismar, both members of the Hansa, in Mecklenburg, were true to their "natural lords," and not without ambition to forward their own interests as they saw them. In 1391 a conference was held at Rostock, and a general invitation was issued to all such as were disposed to live by plunder. All who were ready to adventure at their own risk and charges against Denmark and Norway, there to rob and burn, and likewise to carry victuals to the starving garrison of Stockholm, were assured that if they would come to Rostock they would not fail to receive letters of marque (described with not unpleasing candour as "Stehlbriefen"—*i.e.*, warrants to steal), and should likewise enjoy free harbour and free market for their booty. The Duke further invited volunteers on these terms to his Island of Poel, east of Neustadt Bay, and his town of Ribnitz up towards Zingst.

The invitation was not likely to fail of eager acceptance in the fourteenth century. Men ready to adventure, to rob, and to burn, mustered rapidly, led by the ancestors of the illustrious Moltke, and Field-Marshal Manteuffel, among others. They called themselves " Vitalienbrüder—that is to say, Victualler-Brothers—and also the " Likedeeler '—the Fair Dividers. They were recruited from among the broken men of many races, and were the maritime equivalents of the Free Companies, the " Ecorcheurs," or Flayers, who infested France in the Hundred Years' War. They asserted, mendaciously, that they were the friends of God, and added truthfully that they were the enemies of all mankind, except the cities which gave them free harbour and market. Of course, they took to plundering all they met, and the Hansa traders as well as others, though Rostock and Wismar were members of the League. They found so much profit in being receivers of stolen goods that they stood out against the sister cities. The Hansa which had first favoured Albert ended by coming to terms with Margaret, and helping her to obtain possession of Stockholm; but the Vitalians cared for none of these things. They had plundered Bergen, seized Wisby in Gothland, and they haunted Heligoland. A life of alternate plunder and sloth was happiness to them. They continued to find protectors among the persons of the robber-baron order. The most valuable of their patrons was Keno then Broke, Lord of Aurich, between Ems and Lahde. He was connected by marriage with Klaus Stortebeker, the most famous of the Vitalian chiefs. The name is not heroic, for Stortebeker is simply Old German for " Stürzebecker " (a tosspot). Nick Tosspot became a popular hero. Ballads were written on his achievements, both as a fighter and an unconquered absorber of strong drink. The Hansa cities were subject to fierce internal feuds between the capitalists and the wage-earners. The poor made a Robin Hood and his Merry Men out of Nick Tosspot and his fellow-Vitalians, Gödeke Michels and Wigbold, who had been a Professor at Rostock, till he " exchanged his chair for the quarterdeck." As the legendary Robin Hood was credited with the Earldom of Huntingdom, so Stortebeker was supposed by the ballad-mongers to have been a noble in disguise.

The alliance with Keno then Broke, gave the Vitalians the free use of the East Friesland havens and islands. From this basis they harried the North Sea. They plundered ships belonging to Lynn, and murdered the crews. The day when the British Navy would have made short work of such a common pest was not yet come. The duty of suppressing the Vitalians fell to the Hansa, led by the City of Hamburg. The Netherlands still belonged to Germany, and their cities were affiliated to the League. Simon of Utrecht, the Admiral of the League, was a Netherlander, and to him belongs the honour of having destroyed the Victualler-Brothers. His flagship, which bore the, to modern ears, odd name of *The Piebald Cow* (" Die Bunte Kuh "), also became famous in song. "*The Piebald Cow* from Flanders tore through the North Sea with her strong horns " and gored the Vitalians off it. After a series of actions round Heligoland and among the islands of East Friesland, the Vitalians were beaten down. Klaus Stortebeker and eighty of his companions, who allowed themselves to be taken alive, were beheaded at Hamburg on one day by the city executioner, Master Rosenfeld, with his double-handed sword in the correct old German way. His shoes were soaked in the blood flowing all over the scaffold. When an alderman condoled with him on the severity of the day's work, the indefatigable man replied that he was still fresh enough to slice off the heads of the whole Town Council! The end of the Victualler-Brothers came in 1402. Their life was, we see, a short one, but there are indications that it was, while it lasted, merry.

The incidents differ as to the details, but there is small difference in the essentials of the story if we turn from North to South, from the German Hansa to the Flanders Galleys of Venice. By galley in this case we are not to understand the long light craft of the Mediterranean used for war, but a substantial vessel, which could be, and was, rowed at need, but was masted, was built to carry cargo, and to bear rough usage by the sea. It may have been from the Venetians, who frequented our ports till the sixteenth century, that we took the name " galley," which continued to be used for undoubted sailing ships far into the eighteenth century.*

The Flanders Galleys appear first in official records under the date 1317. But long before they are heard of the Venetians had exported the spices and silks of the East, the currants of Greece, and their own manufactures to Northern Europe, and had brought back wool and other raw produce. In the earliest times all, and to the end part, of this commerce was conducted overland by caravan. Private adventures by sea preceded the galleys, which were a State enterprise, bearing some resemblance to the "regulated companies"—that is to say, corporations of traders endowed with powers to control trade, and established because the Governments of the day were unable either to govern or to protect their subjects at a distance Yet the Flanders Galleys were the property of the "Serene Republic," which hired them to traders, and appointed its own commanders, who took their sailing instructions from the Senate. Their number was not great—sometimes they were as few as two, and never more than five. None the less, their place in the history of sea-borne commerce is considerable, and they were a standard example of the methods of their age. It is to be observed that they did not wholly supersede other ways of trade. A Venetian might import wool overland while the cruise of the galleys lasted, but if so he paid a 30 per cent. import duty. A private adventurer might bring a cargo to Venice in competition with the galleys, but if he did he forfeited three-fourths of his freight to them. These penalties, if strictly enforced, which, given the gravity, consistency, and vigilance of the Government, was no doubt the case, would regulate the trade effectually.

The work of preparing the "mudua," or convoy of galleys, began in January. Ships were put up to auction by the Senate, and hired for such sums as sixty-seven or eighty-one

* See "Calendar of State Papers and Manuscripts relating to English Affairs existing in the Archives and Collections of Venice, and in other Libraries of Northern Italy," vol. i., 1202—1509. Edited by Rawdon Brown. London, 1864.

"lire." The comparative, and still more the effective, value of money in the Middle Ages is a subject of maddening obscurity. But we know that the "lira," for which the galleys were hired by the traders, was the "lira grossa," the great pound of twelve golden "ducats," or "sequins." Till we know what the value of a ducat was, this leaves us not much wiser than before. From the fact that £100,000 is stated to have been the equivalent of 400,500 ducats, this coin would be worth five shillings. But in England the exchange value was thirty-eight pence. Even if we take the higher estimate, the "Serene Republic" must have lent the use of the galleys of St. Mark at a very cheap rate. Eighty "lire grosse" of twelve ducats of five shillings is £240. But, of course, there is the question of the effective value of money in the Middle Ages, and for most of us madness lies that way.

The Senate named the Captain and Vice-Captain of the galleys, but the traders paid their moderate salaries, which for the chief never rose above 600 golden ducats for the whole voyage. He was paid in honour and importance. In Venice, where men "wed the sea with rings," sea service was part of the "course of honours" for any man who was qualified by noble birth to hold the great offices of the State. The Captain of the Galleys of Flanders was always a noble, and was expected to live in a style becoming his birth and office. A Venetian gentleman must have taken the post not for his pay so much as for the chance of distinction. He was sometimes allowed tonnage in lieu of part salary. Thus, in 1408 the Captain of the galleys was paid only eighty ducats for the voyage, but he was allowed to carry four butts of wine freight-free on the outward-bound voyage to London or Bruges, and 3,000 (? pounds') weight on the homeward-bound for any port he liked. The Captain was sometimes expected to do diplomatic work, as, for instance, to wait on the King of England with messages from the Senate, and "state the case." He carried young gentlemen with him to the number of four for each galley to be trained for the sea service, as Mr. Darcy, of the time of King Charles II., was sent with a "King's Letter" to Sir R. Stayner, and orders that he was to be trained and treated as a gentleman, and that the pay and rations of a midshipman were to be allowed for his support; so the Senate sent four young gentlemen to each galley to be rated "arbalasters" (crossbowmen), at a salary of seventy ducats, "that the noble youth of Venice may see the world, be inured betimes to toil and peril, and learn to expose their lives for their native land." The actual "shipmen" were the masters, mates, boatswains, sailors, and rowers of all medieval ships. Of rowers, there were 180 to each galley. They were generally recruited among the Schiavoni of the eastern shore of the Adriatic. In the north aisle of North Stoneham Church, near Southampton, there is a pathetic trace of their visits to English ports, in the shape of an inscription on a flagstone, which states that : " Here is the burial place of the corps [" schola "] of Schiavoni, 1491."

The route of the "mudua" was by Capo d'Istria, Corfu, Otranto, Syracuse, Messina, Naples, Majorca, the coast of Spain, and Morocco, Lisbon, to Rye. Here the galleys for England separated from those bound to Flanders. The first went to Sandwich, Southampton, London; the second to Sluys, Middleburg, or Antwerp. They were expected to be in the Channel by June. Strict orders were given as to the time they might spend in discharging and reloading. Fifty days was the favourite minimum allowed, but necessities of trade and various troubles might delay them for much more. They rendezvoused at Sandwich for the return voyage, and went home by the same route. They had need to be expeditious if they were to start in time to avoid the late autumn and winter storms. Sometimes they did not start in time, and we hear of galleys embayed and in danger in the Bay of Biscay. The delay was attributed to the fact that the galleys which went to London were not so prompt and punctual in clearing as those which went to the Flemish ports. These latter were often compelled to wait long at the rendezvous. In later times the favourite port of the galleys in England was Southampton.

The Flanders Galleys brought with them the spices and silks of the East, collected at Trebizond, Constantinople, Damascus, Aleppo, Alexandria, Cairo; the currants of Greece, cotton, and their own glass and earthenware. The author of the " Libel of English Policy " would have it that the Venetians brought only flimsy trash, and took away our honest money, to the great impoverishment of the realm. But the Venetians were also good customers for our wool and woollen cloths. From their own point of view they did us great service by introducing currants, for which our ancestors had, it seems, an unruly passion. Englishmen, according to one Venetian witness, when deprived of their expected supply of currants, had been known to hang themselves. This is an interesting early testimony to *le spleen britannique*, which, as every Frenchman knew, caused Englishmen to hang themselves by the thousand at every November fog. Our reputation for hanging ourselves on small provocation is ancient. The author of the " Libel of English Policy " was as wise as the persons who in later times scolded the East India Company for corrupting the nation with flimsy muslins.

Troubles would not fail the Flanders Galleys from land thieves and water thieves. They suffered from such modern pests as the tempting and, when occasion served, crimping tavern keeper. On February 3rd, 1408, the Senate made an order touching the galleys then fitting out for the Channel. The Senators had before them certain complaints the nature of which is sufficiently indicated in the terms of the order they gave to provide a remedy. " As the oarsmen of the galleys when in London and Bruges pledge themselves in the taverns beyond the amount of pay received by them in these ports, so that the masters are compelled to go round the taverns and redeem the men at very great trouble and expense, it is ordered that all who shall be pledged in taverns to the amount of four ducats each above the pay received by them shall be redeemed by the masters, and the money paid on their behalf to be placed to their debit. If any men shall pledge themselves beyond the sum of four ducats, the money is to be paid on their behalf, and placed to their debit ; and in addition a fine of 50 per cent. levied on each man, on the sum exceeding four ducats, the penalty to be shared like the penalty imposed on bankrupts. The masters may not rate these loans higher than they do the pay given by them to the crews."

The crews were paid at the rate of thirty-nine pence to the ducat. Oarsmen, sailors, and arbalastmen were entitled to an advance of one month's pay at trial rate while abroad ; pilots to six weeks. If they asked for more, they received only thirty-six pence or less for the ducat ; they had, in fact, to give heavy interest. It would be strange if we heard nothing of plain downright robbery. One example serves to illustrate the ways of trade at the time, and also shows what excellent justice was kept by Henry VII. In February, 1499, letters came to Venice from Jacomo Capello, Captain of the galleys, informing the Senate, among other pieces of news, that " a few days previously some of the galley crews were travelling over the country (near Southampton) selling their wares. When at a distance of twenty miles from Hampton some highwaymen attacked three of them, and killed two ; so the Captain sent to London to notify this to the King, who, although three months ought to have elapsed before doing justice, caused two of these thieves to be taken, and sent them to Hampton, where he had them hanged. His Majesty does everything in favour of Venetian subjects, and shows them great good will." Henry VII. was not a King who would allow his laws to be broken before his face, nor yet behind his back.

The King of England and the Republic were, as a rule, on terms of friendship. In 1465, when Edward IV. was King, the Knights of St. John appealed to him to use his good offices on their behalf with Venice. The King wrote, and the Senate answered, in a long despatch, giving an account of the quarrel between themselves and the Order. It was a very good example of a kind of dispute which was common for centuries, and touches the history of the sea trader very closely. In 1465 the Knights of St. John were still established at Rhodes. They and the Republic were at war with the Sultan Mahomet II. But Egypt was an independent Sultanate, ruled by Abousaid Khosch Kadam. The Venetians traded to Alexandria, and certain of their vessels came back from that port bringing Moorish merchants with rich ventures bound for Venice. They put into Rhodes on their way home, and were attacked by the order of the Grand Master on the pretext that they were carrying Moors.

Several Venetians were killed or wounded and their vessels were seized. The Moorish merchants and their goods were impounded by the Grand Master, Pedro Raimondo Zacosta. Of course, Abousaid Khosch Kadam behaved exactly as the Great Mogul was to do in later times, when he made the East India Company pay for the piracies of Avery, Kidd, and the like, in the Red Sea and on the coast of Malabar. The Egyptian Sultan confiscated Venetian goods at Alexandria, and threw merchants into prison. His hostility was a serious addition to the troubles of Venice. He had to be pacified by diplomacy, and he naturally insisted on the surrender of his subjects and their goods which had been assailed under the protection of the Venetian flag. It was a fair demand. Venice sent a fleet to Rhodes to expostulate with the Grand Master. When he proved recalcitrant, " the Captain-General of our fleet resorted to other measures." The Moors and their property were released and sent home. But, said the Senate, " according to the Barbary fashion we shall need a considerable sum to exempt our subjects. Your Majesty will judge, how very grievous these things are." They were the more grievous because the Grand Master, while posing as the enemy of all unbelievers when Moorish merchants were to be robbed, was known to be striving to make his peace with Mahomet II. A halo of romance hangs over the Knights of St. John, and no doubt they fought nobly in defence of Rhodes and Malta, and at Lepanto. Nevertheless, they were, till the end of the seventeenth century, among the worst pirates and enemies of peaceful trade in the Eastern Mediterranean.

Venice had certain difficulties, inevitable in those ages, with the King of England as with other Sovereigns. All States, Venice herself included, were then in the habit of laying an embargo on whatever foreign ships happened to be in their ports in war time, and making use of them as fighting ships or transports. The chronic quarrel between England and France gave rise to many incidents of this nature. The sufferers were not the Flanders Galleys, which belonged to the State, but private traders and " coggos "—sailing ships. They were frequently arrested, forced to serve, and detained for months, and Venice could do nothing to protect her subjects against this violence. But as might be expected, the Venetians suffered most from the common pirate and sea thief. Some effort is required to realize a state of things in which piracy was obviously looked upon as a resource for shipowners and mariners on the outlook for a job, and a ship with a competent piratical crew could be hired in broad daylight. That it was so is made manifest by the strange, eventful history of the alum ship in the year 1486. The Lord of Piombino of that date was on bad terms with the Pope, Innocent VIII., and was excommunicated. He loaded a cargo of alum in a Spanish vessel. The Pope held that the alum was confiscated to him. His agents in England were informed of the coming of the alum, and asked to capture it. Giovanni Ambrosio de Negroni and his partners, Florentine merchants in England, who acted for the Pope, hired English mariners to make prize of the Spaniard. They may have been encouraged by knowing that the shipper of the alum was excommunicated, but a less excuse would no doubt have served the turn. Be that as it may, " the mariners thus engaged attacked the Spaniard not far from England, both parties fighting for a long while, and many being killed and wounded. At length the English mariners, who upheld the interest of Christ's Vicar, were victorious, and took the captured ship into port in England." Another Florentine then turned up to claim the alum as having been consigned to him. After much dispute, presentation of Bulls of excommunication, and what not, the alum was handed over to him by the King's Council. Signor Giovanni Ambrosio was in a state of despair which " defied exaggeration," and he had some cause to be disturbed, for the Council was thinking seriously of bringing him to trial for suborning British mariners to attack subjects of the King of Spain, who was in amity with England. But Papal agents intervened, and he got off with the fright, and, of course, the loss of what he may have paid the mariners. Nobody seems to have thought of bringing them to book for being suborned.

If they were at all times ready to be hired to plunder. they were no less well disposed to protect for a consideration. As much as this may be gathered from a Decree of the

SALE, PURCHASE, AND PLUNDER

Senate, dated November 11, 1497. It instructs the Venetian agents in England to hire one or more vessels well provided at Southampton to give convoy to the *Pasqualiga* as far as Sicily. They might also enlist men enough in England to bring the crew of the *Pasqualiga* up to 120. We cannot believe that Venetian ships and men were lying idle to be hired as convoy at Southampton. The protection was to be given by an English force hired for the purpose.

This indifference to the lawlessness of the sea is even more conspicuous in the story told in letters out of England, delivered to the Doge and the Ambassadors while they were attending the sermon at St. Mark's on Christmas Day, 1488. From them it appeared that while Pietro Malipiero, Captain of the galleys, was on his way home from Flanders, and was near the Isle of Wight, he was attacked by three English vessels, and called upon to strike sail. The context shows that there cannot have been a mere question of the salute, which the Venetians would render as a matter of course, just as they expected a corresponding mark of respect in their own sea, the Adriatic. Nor is it certain that the English ships belonged to the King. Malipiero bore towards them, seeing they were English, " and saying they were friends. Then the English endeavoured to take the galleys, but the Master blew his whistle and beat to quarters, and the crew killed eighteen of the English, the ships pursuing the galleys into Hampton Harbour. The Captain wrote about the injury done him to the King, who sent the Bishop of Winchester to say he was not to fear, as those who had been killed must bear their own loss, and that a pot of wine would settle the matter." A good deal remains to be cleared up in this story, but it is obvious enough that the King took the fighting and the killing of his subjects lightly. Malipiero died on the cruise, but it is not said that his death was due to a wound in the action.

The discovery of the route by the Cape turned the course of trade with the East, and disorganized the commerce of Venice. The Flanders Galleys made their last appearance in 1532, after a career of more than two centuries. Before we leave them we must look at one incident in their later adventures, which gives far too good a picture of the sea life of the fifteenth century to be passed over. This is the famous attack on the four galleys commanded by Bartolomeo Minio, on August 22nd, 1485. It was made by seven ships flying the French flag, commanded by one "Colombo," *alias* Nicolo Griego. As Columbus is said to have been in the action, and as the Commander bore the same name, the affair has been diligently investigated. We are not concerned with the obscure early years of Columbus, and the story is nowise dependent on his presence. There is no sufficient reason to suppose that "Colombo" was so much as a fellow-countryman of his. He seems, in fact, to have been a Gascon of the name of Coullon, which is Old French for "Colombe," and is still a provincial word. One Guillaume de Cazeneuve, called "Coullon" or "Coulon," had done much service at sea, some of it of no very honourable character, for Lewis XI. The leader of the piratical affair of 1485 was this man's son, and Nicolo Griego was a nickname. In 1485 Lewis XI. had been dead for two years. France was governed during the minority of Charles VIII. by his sister, the Dame de Beaujeu, who, in 1485, was busy putting down a revolt of the nobles, headed by the future Lewis XII., and very appropriately known as "The Silly War." France was at peace with Venice, and the attack on the galleys was simply an incident in the attempt of the feudal anarchy to raise its head again, and an example of the lawlessness of the sea.

The story begins with the issue of the commission, and instructions given by the Doge Giovanni Mocenigo to Bartolomeo Minio, Captain of the Flanders Galleys, which in that year were four in number. It is an illuminated manuscript of 163 pages, and covers four large pages of small print when summarized by Mr. Rawdon Brown. The date is April 12th, 1485. The Doge gave minute instructions how Minio was to carry out a voyage on the lines named above. His own pay was to be 600 gold ducats for the whole cruise—perhaps £150. Thirty arbalasters, of whom four were to be "noble youths," were to be carried in each galley at a wage of nineteen lire of four light soldi a month, a sum which I do not undertake to translate. The Masters of the galleys were to receive a bounty of 3,500 ducats at the end of the voyage, the funds to be taken from " the unappropriated moneys of the Jews." The Captain was to buy four pieces of artillery for each galley in the West, and to deliver them to the arsenal on his return.

So the four Flanders Galleys sailed in due course. On September 18th there came to Venice Antonio Jodeschin, clerk of Antonio Loredan, Master of one of the galleys. He brought a story of disaster. On the night of August 20th the galleys had been joined off Cape St. Vincent by seven vessels flying the flag of Charles, King of France. They were commanded by Young Colombo, *alias* Nicolo (or Giovanni) Griego. Colombo lay by them all night, and attacked at daylight. The action lasted from the first to the twentieth hour. Two of the Venetian Masters, Michiel and Dolfin, were slain, together with other noblemen, and a due proportion, we presume, of non-noble persons. Colombo carried his prizes into Lisbon, where he transferred their cargoes to his own ships, and landed the Captain, the Masters, and merchants with " scarcely clothes on their backs." Be it observed that Portugal was on friendly terms with Venice, yet it does not seem to have occurred to the Portuguese King, John II., that he was called upon to act when pirates brought the ships of his allies into his harbour, and rifled them under the windows of his palace. As he had received personal civilities from Venice, he did provide the plundered Captain, Masters, and merchants with suits of clothes, and aid to reach home. Having stowed his booty in the holds of his seven ships, Colombo made off to Honfleur, where he was sure of a friendly reception.

The total loss to Venice was great, directly and indirectly. The town relied on the return of the Flanders Galleys for the wool required for its local weaving industry, and the outward-bound cargoes were valued at 200,000 ducats. The Senate took measures to make good the deficiency, or at least to allow it to be made. As has been said already, the Flanders Galleys had the exclusive privilege to bring wool from England during the term of their cruise. Of course, when the whole outward-bound convoy went at a blow, there arose a state of things very competently described by the Senate.

"At this present, however, by reason of the adverse and unexpected catastrophe of the interception of our galleys bound on the aforesaid Flanders voyage, we cannot hope to have wools this year from the island aforesaid, and as those brought by the last galleys are few and not sufficient for the need of this city; and on this account little work can be put in hand by the drapers who have come into the presence of the Signory, earnestly requesting that proper provision may be made, and setting forth the great detriment incurred both from the lack of purchasers exporting Venetian cloths for the whole of Italy, and even for foreign parts; as also because a great part of the poor of this city was maintained by the manufacture of woollens, which manufacture failing, their supply of food fails, and they perish by hunger, to the offence of God, and to the disparagement and detriment of our Signory, whose chief end has been to provide that all the poor may live and maintain themselves."

Therefore the Senate removed the restriction on the import of wool, and allowed all men to bring it in when and as they could. Whether the most serene Senate reflected that the loss of Minio's convoy proved the danger of confining an important branch of trade to one route and one set of ships, does not appear. We may be sure they did not consider that if the free-trader could step in to make good the failure of the privileged trader after a catastrophe, he could equally supply the city in normal times. It is hard, indeed, to persuade governing persons that commerce will look after itself very well, if only they will moderate their well-meant efforts to regulate it, and what they are pleased to call their protection.

The Senate could throw open the trade easily. To recover the stolen goods was not so easy. It was necessary to secure the aid of the French Government, and the Senate must have known (for it knew all the affairs of its neighbours wondrous well) that even if the Regent, the Dame de Beaujeu, was willing to help, her power was limited. For that very reason, no doubt, the Senators saw the great advantage of possessing a material guarantee. Orders were given to Melchor Trevisiano, Vice Captain-General on the sea, to sail for Alexandria, and there seize a great galleass belonging to the King of France, which was supposed to be in that harbour. He was told to use no more violence than was necessary to effect his purpose, to hurt nobody except such as should be injured in making resistance to capture, and to treat his prisoners well. As no use was made of a material guarantee, it would appear that the galleass was not taken. The Venetians had to do what they could by diplomacy. Heronimo Zonzi, Ambassador at Milan, was sent to France to expostulate and ask for redress. He did his best, and he received plenty of good words. The Regent spoke severely to young Colombo, and refused him a safe-conduct he asked for, in order that he might come to Court and propose a compromise. It is quite clear, however, that it was not in the power of the Dame de Beaujeu to bring Colombo to trial, and hang him high and short. She was a resolute, capable woman, and the royal authority had been greatly increased by Lewis XI., yet the townsmen of Honfleur, who were the receivers of the stolen goods, and had provided the crews of Colombo's ships, defied the law. They murdered a messenger of the Venetian Embassy, and when Zonzi himself came to the town he was attacked. High officials were concerned in the piracy, and favoured the pirates. In the end we hear of the recovery of 200 bales of spices, 150 bales of Malmsey, 30 bags of cotton, and 40 casks of currants. They were carried to England in English ships, for to have loaded them in French vessels would have been to entrust them to the very men who had carried out the robbery. Much of the plunder of the Flanders Galleys had been carried into Biscay and Brittany, and was never recovered.

It sometimes begins to be difficult to understand how trade oversea contrived to exist at all when it was subject to such outrages as this, which was far, indeed, from being a rare example, when pirates swarmed on every coast, and when the trader was fleeced by "Kings who wished to live at the expense of their neighbours," to quote a tart judgment of the Venetian Senators. But while we hear of the piracy and violence, the intervening years of successful trade pass unnoticed and fruitful. The commerce carried on was conducted for the benefit of poor and scattered populations, and could not have been great in bulk. The Flanders Galleys, we see, were never more than five, and in many cases were fewer. Even with peace and security, the markets were not of sufficient importance to support a much greater volume of trade. Such as it was, its profits were large. If they had not been very considerable, the Flanders Galleys could not have borne the expense of crews containing 180 Schiavoni oarsmen, thirty crossbowmen, sailors, and officers. A small trade rendering high profits on a small capital would be a fair description of this branch of Venetian commerce, and of most others of the Middle Ages. If the galleys came no more after 1532, the reason was not that they were driven away by pirates and oppressive Kings, but that the opening of the ocean route to India by Vasco da Gama in 1497 turned the course of the trade of the East, and that Venice, after making a futile effort to support the Mohammedan power of Egypt against the Portuguese intruders on the coast of Malabar, saw her great trade slip swiftly out of her hands, and sank from her leading place among trading powers.

CHAPTER V

THE OPENING OF THE OCEAN ROUTES

THE fifteenth century, an age of brutal wars, was also a time of quiet preparation for a nobler day. Prince Henry of Portugal, surnamed the " Navigator," was in the front rank of the men who prepared for the vast expansion of knowledge which was to come with the sixteenth century. He spent his life and fortune in endeavouring to open the ocean route to the East. It was highly appropriate that a work of universal human interest should be begun by a gentleman who belonged by descent to the royal caste which occupied the thrones of all Europe, but was not of any single people by race.*

As a Portuguese, Prince Henry was admirably placed at the extreme western limit of Europe, the natural starting-point for an explorer of the ocean. That he did not himself sail on any of the voyages he promoted between his settlement at Sagres, near Cape St. Vincent, in 1414, and his death in 1460 ; that they were but timid coasting ventures when compared to the world-wide flights of Vasco da Gama,

* Extreme futility, making believe to be patriotism, will have it that Henry was half an Englishman, because his mother was a daughter of John of Gaunt. But if a man is half of the race of his mother, John of Gaunt was only half an Englishman, for he was the son of Philippa of Hainault. His second wife, Constance of Castile, the grandmother of Henry, was the daughter of Peter the Cruel and Maria de Padilla. A half-English man and a wholly Spanish woman could not be the parents of a daughter who was English in any other sense than by training and allegiance. By virtue of them Henry was a Portuguese. If we must follow up his pedigree in all its ramifications, and allow something for each element, we must fix the percentage contributed by Celtic Kings of the Scots, Scandinavian ancestors of Rollo, Franks, Basques, Grand Dukes of Moscow, and Emperors at Constantinople of the house of Basil the Macedonian—and of how many more ?

Columbus, and Magellan; that he did not live to see the full fruits of his thought and sacrifice, are facts which do not at all detract from the honour due to him. We are not to despise the day of small things. The slow advance of Henry's Captains brought the knowledge and confidence which enabled Bartholomew Diaz to round the Cape of Good Hope in 1486, when the Prince had been dead for twenty-six years. When that had been done, the essential was achieved. Somebody would one day have followed Diaz. The pressure of the south-easterly trade-wind, and the inset of the currents on the coast of Brazil, which carried the Portuguese Pedro Alvarez Cabral within sight of Monte Pascoal in 1500, would equally have led to the discovery of the mainland of America. Columbus was great, but he was not indispensable.

Nothing came to the Portuguese Prince by accidents or in his sleep. The geographical knowledge of his time justified his scientific hypothesis that Africa could be circumnavigated by the South. He strove intelligently to reach an attainable end, moreover, he was consciously doing a work for the world. The establishment of the ruffianly Turkish Power was already throttling the trade of Europe with the East. The old caravan routes and the voyages from the Red Sea and Persian Gulf were menaced. The Italian cities, with Venice at their head, were becoming convinced of the necessity for finding another way of access to India. They helped Henry with capital, seamen, and shipbuilders, for they had not realized that the turning of the trade with the East on to the Cape route would depose them from their supremacy. They and he were alike stimulated by the ambition to extend trade, and with it the Christian faith. To bring the heathen into the fold of the Church was the aim of all men at that time—the chief aim with the nobler of them, and an aim with all, if only for their trade's sake.

Diaz had pointed out the way to India by the East in 1486, but Portugal hesitated. Then, in 1492, Columbus sailed from Palos in the service of Spain, and reached, as he believed, and died believing, the Indian Islands described by Marco Polo. His example stimulated Portugal and England.

In 1497 Vasco da Gama sailed from Lisbon to the coast of Malabar, and John Cabot from Bristol to the mainland of America. But nearly a generation was to pass before the Old World had discovered that another continent lay between it and Asia to the West. " Islands " continued to be discovered, and in due course were found to be parts of the New World. In 1513 Vasco Nuñez de Balboa crossed the isthmus of Darien, and saw the South Sea. Between 1519 and 1522 Magellan and Sebastian de Elcano, or Del Cano, the Captain who brought home the *Victoria*, the only surviving ship of his squadron, after the great explorer's death, revealed the Pacific. Meanwhile the Portuguese had reached Malacca in 1511, and Nankin in 1520. The whole world had doubled in size.

But the whole world was not to be doubled for all men without a long fight. Monopoly was the very soul of medieval sea-borne commerce, and every people did as far as in it lay what the Hansa had done in the North Sea and Baltic. It was not in human nature that the two leading nations of the age of discovery should have been prepared to share what they had found with others. Portugal and Spain were alike determined to act on the rule that he who finds keeps, and were so resolved before they fully knew what their find was. They had to settle between themselves what belonged to each, and to warn off all trespassing third parties. As the Spanish " Indies " lying out to the West were more accessible than the Portuguese, the first challenge was given to Spain. The serious attack on the Portuguese began with the foundation of the English and Dutch East India Companies about 1600.*

* Years after the voyages of Columbus and Alvarez Cabral, the French advanced a claim to have visited the coast of Brazil before the Portuguese. It has, unfortunately, happened that these bold adventurers of the Norman port had, in the words of the historian La Popelinière, quoted by M. la Roncière in his " History of the French Navy," "ny l'esprit ny discretion de laisser un seul escrit public pour asseurance de leurs desseins." Many large claims to priority of discovery in this epoch have been advanced by the French. They are all much like the pedigree of the poet Béranger's father, which was complete in all respects except probability and documentary evidence. French pirates and privateers did undoubtedly harass the trade of Spain and Portugal with their Indies from an early date, but that is a very different thing from a deliberate attempt to open a trade in the Portuguese and Spanish preserves.

The organization of Spanish and Portuguese trade with the Indies, West and East, deserves to be looked at with more than mere curiosity. It set the model which the English, Dutch, and French were to follow, to some extent, in the West Indies (using the term in the Spanish sense, as meaning all America), and very closely indeed in the East. That model was one of monopoly, general and particular. Each State confined the trade of whatever territory it could control to its own subjects, and within its limits it placed commerce in the hands of a privileged body. Portugal acted on this principle in the East Indies with the kind of folly which is called " carrying things to their logical extreme." The Spanish moralist, who wrote under the name of Baltasar Gracian, has been credited with the profound maxim, " Do not die the death of a fool, which is to die of too much logic." And that is what the Portuguese Government did. It endeavoured to limit the profits of the trade to the Crown. The King was to be the Royal Lion, and to take the lion's share. The traders were to be his officers and jackals, and to take what he was pleased to leave them. The lion of the fable was on the spot, and could take for himself. But the King of Portugal was at Lisbon, and far away from the coast of Malabar and the Straits of Malacca. His jackals could cheat him, and they did it so effectually that his profits ended by leaking away. The King, after a time, began to discover that the folly was a folly, and to cast about for improved methods. He grew wise too late, and the Portuguese trade in the East was rotted by corruption before ever the English and Dutch East India Companies rushed upon it.

We need not look for a double dose of original sin in the Portuguese. Our own Company and the Dutch went as far as they could on the same road as the Portuguese Crown. But they were subjects of strong States, and were retained from indulging in their natural disposition to die the death of the fool. Even so " the private trade of the Company's servants," which meant in many cases the defrauding of the Company by its underpaid agents, came near to the pilfering of the Portuguese officers.

Spain did not go so far as Portugal in its logic. The King

did not endeavour to concentrate all the trade in his own hands. He was content to take his dues and his share of the bullion of the New World, which to him was by far the most valuable part of its produce. In order to render the collection safe and easy, he restricted the trade to a privileged body of merchants and to the City of Seville. Seville lies too far up the Guadalquivir to be a convenient port, and the bar at the mouth, on which there is only 12 feet of water at the low spring tides, has always been an obstruction. "Seville" ended by being a species of term of art which included San Lucar de Barrameda at the mouth of the river, Cadiz, and the towns on the bay. It continued to be the seat of the Government of the whole trade till the eighteenth century. There the "Casa de la Contratacion" and the "Consejo de las Indias," the House of Trade and Council of the Indies, had its seat. This truly wonderful body was a combination of an Exchange, a Colonial Office, a Board of Trade, an Admiralty, and Trinity House, in so far as the course to the Indies ("carrera de las Indias") was concerned, a judicial committee of the Privy Council for hearing colonial appeals, and, to top all, a missionary, sacred image, and Prayer-Book (not Bible) society for the conversion of the natives. It inspected, surveyed, certified, and minutely regulated everything and everybody. We, too, confined the East India trade to a Chartered Company and to London; but we did not go to the same length as the Spaniards, being by the beneficence of Providence a less logical people.

These Portuguese and Spanish regulators set the course of trade, as far as the nature of things and the irrepressible tendency of mere human officials to feather their own nests allowed. Times of sailing and routes were naturally dictated by winds and currents. The seamen of Portugal and Spain soon mastered the general course of the trade-winds, monsoons, and ocean currents. The Portuguese learnt that the trade-winds in the Atlantic, and the monsoons in the Indian Ocean, follow the sun. The north-easterly trade blows far down when the sun is over the Southern Hemisphere, and the south-easterly trade reaches well beyond the line when he is over the Northern. They had not made many voyages before learning that the southerly monsoons blow in the Indian Ocean from May to December, and the northerly between December and May, with an interval of storms and unsettled winds at the time of the changes. They timed their going out and returning in obedience to the winds and currents as they grew to know them. They found that the best time to leave Lisbon was at the beginning of March, before the 10th. But the voyage could be begun in September. A different route was chosen when the ships sailed at the later date. If the start was made in March, the course taken was through the Mozambique Channel, because the ships would reach the northern end before the prevailing winds would be against them. If they sailed in April, they would be compelled to stop at Mozambique or Melinde till the wind changed; or if they did persist in going on, it would be a miracle if they reached Goa without damage to ship and loss of men. When they sailed in September, then their course was by the east of Madagascar. Vessels bound to Malacca sailed in October by preference, but they could go in February and March. When homeward bound, and from whatever port they started, they left late in December or early in January to obtain the benefit of the north-east monsoon. All followed the same outward course as far as Mozambique —by the Canaries, the Cape de Verd Islands, Ascension, Trinidad, Tristan da Cunha, giving a wide berth to the dangerous Cape of Good Hope, till they were 150 leagues to the East, and then turning north for Mozambique. On the return voyage the route was by St. Helena and the Cape de Verd. From Goa or Cochin to the Cape the course first taken was through, or to the east of, the Maladives, and then, in later times, by the Mozambique Channel. The wide sweep to the west on the outward-bound voyage was dictated by the south-easterly trades and southern connecting current of the South Atlantic, which runs down the coast of Brazil, then turns east to the Cape. Yet the Portuguese navigators soon learnt the danger of the inset of the current on the coast of South America. Therefore they strove to keep 100 or 150 miles off the land, as a modern sailing ship does, lest she should be brought up against the formidable Abrolhos half-way between Bahia and Rio de Janeiro. And wherever they were, the Portuguese and their successors had need to bear in mind the warning included in the Pilot Major Aleixo da Motta, in his sailing directions for the Indian Ocean. "Remember," said he, speaking with the authority of thirty-five years' experience—"remember that the latitudes of the islands and shallows are not always correctly marked on the charts; that there are many which are not marked at all; therefore, keep a man at the topgallant mast by day, and watch the course of your ship. Look for changes in the colour of the water, station a man on the bowsprit, reduce sail, and keep the lead in hand by night. Trust only in God and the good lookout you must keep." The maxim has a familiar ring to men of the race and speech of Cromwell, and it holds good for all time.

The vessels engaged in this trade are well known in history and romance as the Portuguese "carracks." The Portuguese calculated that a few great ships meant fewer risks of wreck than a large number of small, more power to repel attack, and a lesser number of officers.

They built carracks of a vast size (for the time) to carry the Indian trade. We have the good-fortune to possess an account of the carrack *Madre de Dios*, taken by the Elizabethan Earl of Cumberland, and a swarm of other vessels belonging to adventurers or to the Queen in 1592. The carrack and her cargo did much to stimulate the merchants of London to open a trade with the East. She was carefully measured by "one Mr. Robert Adams, a man in his faculty of excellent skill," and "after an exquisite survey of the whole frame, he found the length from the beak head to the stern (whereon was erected a lantern) to contain 165 foot. The breadth in the second closed deck (whereof she had three), this being the place where there was most extension of breadth, was 46 foot 10 inches. She drew in water 31 foot at her departure from Cochin in India, but not above 26 at her arrival in Dartmouth, being lightened in her voyage by divers means some 5 foot. She carried in height seven several stories, one main orlop, three close decks [decks going the whole length fore and aft] one forecastle and a spar deck of two floors apiece. [Not seven decks one above the other anywhere but four decks, including the orlop, or over-top which is the platform on the beams of the hold, forecastle, poop, and topgallant poop]. The length of the keel was 100 foot, of the mainmast 121, and the circuit about at the partners 10 foot 7; the mainyard was 106 foot long."

If we estimate the size of the *Madre de Dios* by the common system of measurement used in the eighteenth and early ninetenth centuries—if, that is to say, we multiply the keel by the extreme breadth, and multiply the product by half the beam, and then divide by ninety-four—it appears that she was a vessel of about 1,200 tons. But this was a fallacious standard, since the real capacity of a ship will depend on the depth of the hold, which would appear to have been great in the case of the *Madre de Dios*. She was ill-proportioned, and was obviously a mere adaptation of the medieval one, two, three formula, slightly modified. As her length over all was 165 feet, and her keel was 100, she must have had a great rake fore and aft, which would tend to hitching and scending, or burrowing her head down, and dipping her stern deep. This, of course, would strain her just where the wooden ships of the Old World were weakest, longitudinally. It is easy enough to make a ship strong from side to side, for the beams hold the ribs together. To make her strong fore and aft, where she is held together only by the keel and the decks, is not so easy. At the end of the eighteenth century vessels, certainly better constructed than the *Madre de Dios*, were commonly hogged, or bent up in the middle, after two years' cruising. With her poop and topgallant poop she was too much built up at the stern, and must have offered a great surface to the wind. Therefore she must have been very "ardent," must have had a tendency to come head to wind, and have been very difficult to steer on the wind. Mr. Robert Adams' report on her rigging, as far as Hakluyt gives it, shows that she must have been subject to a leverage she was ill-qualified to resist. The length of her mainmast was excessive. The word "mast," like many sea terms, sins by ambiguity. Sometimes it means the whole structure from the foot stepped on the

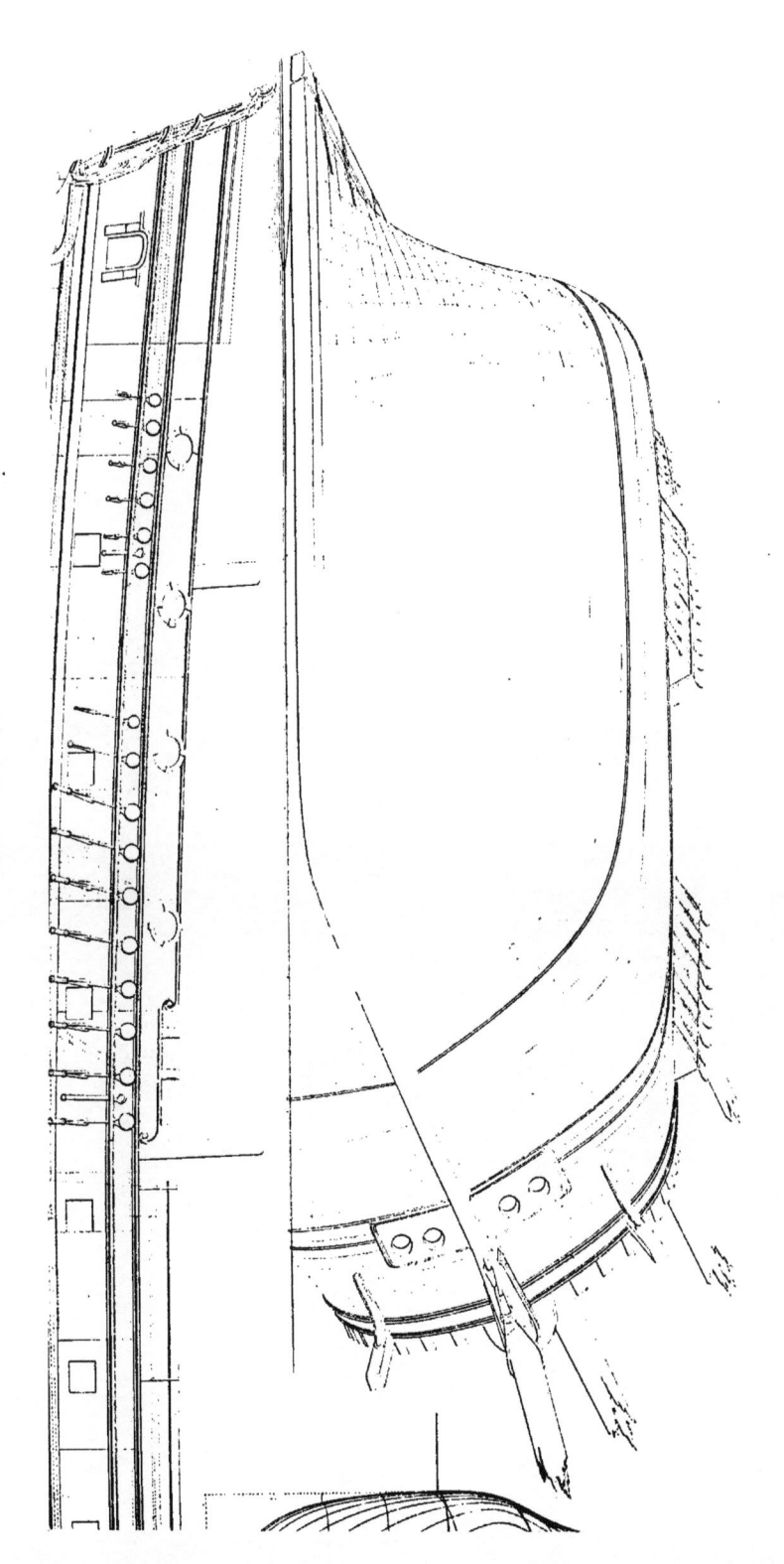

MERCHANT SHIP.
From Chapman's "Architectura Navalis Mercatoria."

THE OPENING OF THE OCEAN ROUTES 97

keel to the truck crowning the topgallant mast. But when used strictly, as it was by Mr. Adams, " mainmast " means the lowest of the divisions of the complete mast—namely, as much as lay between the keel and the maintop. Now, an English seventy-four of 1800 or thereabouts, a vessel of 1,900 tons or so, had a mainmast of 111 feet, as against the 121 feet of the smaller *Madre de Dios*. The mainmast of the carrack carried too large a mainsail. Her yard was 106 feet. The English seventy-four of 1800 had a mainyard of 99 feet. The strain of such a sail on such a vessel must have been prodigious, and the mast was heavy. Ten feet seven inches in circumference at the partners (the place where the mast passes through the middle deck of a threedecked ship and the upper deck of all others) is a measure which shows that the diameter of her mainmast must have been considerably in excess of the one-quarter inch to the foot of length allowed in after-times. After considering the weaknesses of the *Madre de Dios*, we are not surprised that the naval history of Portugal in its great day is rich in tragic shipwrecks. The Elizabethan seamen could make nothing of the carrack, and left her to rot in Dartmouth Harbour.

The defects of the carrack come, however, very short of supplying a sufficient explanation of the disasters of the Portuguese navigators. The style in which they were handled accounts for more. When Defoe's hero said that the Portuguese sailors with whom he lived for a time taught him all they knew, which was vice and bad seamanship, he may possibly have been influenced by British prejudice. Portugal has produced, and still produces, very fair seamen. But her commerce with the East was conducted in a way which gave their virtues little chance of displaying themselves, and made it inevitable that their faults should produce the maximum of evil. Let us look at a carrack through the eyes of an excellent witness—the Dutchman, Jan Huyghen van Linschoten, who went to the East Indies, and returned in the latter years of the sixteenth century:

"The partition of the ship [*i.e.*, the *Santa Maria*, in which Linschoten came home] is in this manner: the Pilot hath his Cabbin above in the hinder part of the shippe, on the right side, where he hath two or three rooms and never commeth [under hatches, nor] downe [into the foreship], but standeth only and commaundeth the Master of the ship to hoise or let fall the sailes, and to look unto his course, how they shall steer to take the height of the sunne, and every day to write and marke what passeth, and how they saile, with what tokens, winde, and weather they have everie day: the Master hath his Cabin in the same place, behind the Pilotes cabins, on the left hand, with as many places and roomes as the Pylot hath, where he standeth and commandeth with a silver whistle, and looketh onlie to the mayne maste and her Sayles, and so backwards: yet he hath the care of all the Shippe, and whatsoever belongeth to it, and commandeth all thinges, as to mend and make the sayls, which he cutteth out, and the saylers sow them: he looketh also if there be any fault in the shippe, and causeth it to be mended, and as need requireth, to draw their Cannon in, and again to put it out. If hee wanteth anything, as cloth for sailes, nailes, ropes, or any such like things, as are needful, he must ask them of the factor and purser of the ship, which presently are delivered unto him with a note of his hand in the booke to be accountable for it. The chiefe Boteson hath his cabin in the forecastle, and hath commandment and governement over the Fouke Mast [*i.e.*, the bowsprit (*cf.* the French "foc")] and the fore sails, hee hath also a silver whistle like the master, and taketh care for all things belonging to the Fouke maste and for the fast binding of the ankers. The Guardian or quartermaster hath his cabbin close by the great mast outwards on the left hand, for on the right hand standeth the scullerie and kitchen [where they dresse their meat]: he weareth a silver whistle, and hath charge to see the swabers pump to make the ship cleane, to looke to the ropes and cause them to be mended, and to the boate which he commonly ruleth. The Gunner hath his cabin inward from the maste hard by the Ruther under the first orlop, and must alwaies sit by the maine mast looking uppon the master both night and day, that as the master whistleth to will the gunners to draw in their pieces or to thrust them out he may bee readie so to doe, he likewise taketh care for the pieces and the thinges belonging to them; when they have cause to use them, the under Pilot doth nothing but helpe the chiefe Pilot, and watch his quarter; they have likewise two or three of the best saylers, that do nothing els but command in the Pilots roome when he sleepeth. The saylers have most of their Cabbins in the forecastle, and there abouts and the gunners behinde by the master gunner, under the upper decke, and doe nothing els but with their instruments put the great pieces forth, or draw them in as they are commanded. The swabers must doe all whatsoever they are bidden to doe by the officers but never touch the

Ruther; for the saylers doe only steere and rule the ship when need requireth, but not the pumpe, neither do they hoise up the maine sayle, for the souldiers and slaves use to do that, the swabers pumpe and the carpenter doth such worke as is to be done, the Cooper in like sort and the Calker, so that if the shippe were sinking not any of them will doe more than belongeth to his charge, and what further is to be done they will stande and looke upon it; the Captaine hath the gallerie and the Cabbin behind, he commandeth onely over the souldiers, and such as watch by night. The Pilot Master, and the Boteson are served in very good sorte with their silver lamps [lavers], beakers, cups, and bowles, every man by himselfe, [and are waited on] by their slaves and servants, and have enough of every thing, but the other saylers and swabers have not such store, but indure more hardnes, for every man must provide for himselfe, as we told you before."*

The wit of man might be taxed in vain to invent a system more certain to lead to division and indiscipline than this. There was no common authority in the carrack, but a partition of work and command which must have bred disputes. Men were encouraged to refuse to go beyond their limited function. It was the very opposite of Drake's wholesome rule that " the gentlemen should pull with the seamen," that all should work at what was the interest of all. The Italian traveller Pietro delle Valle, who belonged to the seventeenth century, adds a detail which condemns the Portuguese. Out of the excess of their fear that their rivals should become acquainted with the navigation of the Eastern Seas (as if Englishmen and Dutchmen could not learn as they themselves had done), they would not allow any of their own officers to learn navigation, or to become familiar with the soundings of the waters they visited. If, therefore, the navigators were removed by death in action, or by disease, there was nobody to take their places, and many ships were lost for that very reason. He praises the liberality and good sense of the English, who did all they could to extend knowledge, on the sane calculation that the better the sea was known the easier would it be to find competent navigators.

Linschoten was of opinion that the dangers of the Mala-

* " Voyage of Linschoten to the East Indies." Edition of Hakluyt Society, vol. ii., pp. 231-233.

dives had less to do with the many shipwrecks of the Portuguese than " the unreasonable lading, and charging of the ships, the unskilful seamen, and the slacke visiting or searching of the ships to see if they bee fit to sayle, and have all things that they want." His own voyage home provided a case in point. The carracks did not sail together, but hurried on each as it could get away for the rendezvous at St. Helena, meet there, and come to Lisbon in a convoy. The *Santa Maria* fell in with the *Saint Thomas* four days after passing the line on January 30th. The *Saint Thomas* recognized her by her new white coir cordage, and hurried away to be first at St. Helena, " of which they do use to brag." " By this and such like signs of pride the Portingales do often cast themselves away," says Linschoten, and so did the *Saint Thomas*. For, persisting in endeavouring to pass the Cape against a violent westerly gale, she " by the great force and strength of the seas, together with the overlading, was stricken in pieces, and swallowed in the sea, both men and all that was within her, as wee might well perceive, comming into the Cape, by the swimming of whole chests, fats, bailes, peeces of mastes and dead men tied unto bords, and such like fearful tokens."

The *Santa Maria*, an old weak ship, was like to have met the same fate. She was driven back repeatedly; her yards were damaged, her rudder broken, and she was compelled to jettison her deck cargo. The crew were in despair, and were thinking of running for Mozambique. But they saw the " 'corposanct' [the St. Elmo's lights]—lights on the main yard and many other places, which shewed like a candle that burneth dimly and skippeth from one place to another, never lying still." They saw five, which the " Portingals call Coroa de nossa Senhora, this is Oure Dear Ladies Crowne." When they were aware of the electric flame which the ancient seamen called Castor and Pollux, or Helle and Phryxus, and we the " Compasant," the master or chief boatswain whistled and commanded every man to salute it with " Salve corpo Santo " and a " misericordia," and with a very great cry. " And therewithall our men being all in great feare, and heaviness and almost out of hopes began again to revive and to be glad, as if thereby they had been fully assured of better comfort." So they fought on, repairing damage as best they could, and, returning towards the Cape every time a shift of the wind brought it behind them. They had good cause to struggle on, for if they were driven to run to Mozambique to refit, they would have lost their voyage for that year, and that would have been cruel for the seamen, since every man would have been left to subsist " at his own charges " while in harbour.

We share all the emotions of Linschoten as he reads how, time after time the *Santa Maria* reached the latitude of the Cape, only to " fall into the wind," and to be driven back, running with a single foresail in mortal terror of being brought side on to the following sea.

" And allthough we sailed before the winde, yet we had danger enough for that the sea came behinde and over our shippe, and filled all the Hatches, whereby we were compelled to bind our mastes, Cables, and all the shippe round about with Ropes, that with ye great force of the Sea it might not stirre and flye in peeces. [It would seem that, like the sailors who carried St. Paul, they undergirded or frapped the *Santa Maria*.] And forced we were to Pumpe night and day having at each end of the Fouke yard [fore yard] a rope that reached to the Pilot, and at each rope there stoode fifteene or sixteene men, the Pilot sitting in his seate, and the under Pilot behinde upon the sterne of the shippe to marke the course of the Sea, and so to advertise the other Pilot. At the ruther there stoode ten or twelve men [the *Santa Maria* had a helm, not a wheel] and the other Saylers upon the hatches to rule the sayles, and as the waves came and covered the shippe the under Pilot called, and then the chiefe Pilot spake to them at the Rudder to hold stiffe and commaunded the ropes that were at the Fouke yarde to be pulled stiffe, the Saylers likewise, and the chiefe Boatswaine standing on the Hatches to Keepe the ship right in the waves, for if the waves had once gotten us about, that they had entered on the side of the shippe, it had certainly been said of us ' Requiescant in pace.' "

Three months and three days after she sailed from Cochin, the *Santa Maria* did at last get into green water and floating reeds. The crew found they were round the Cape—" out of hell into Paradise." They had wondered why God suffered them, being " so good Christians and Catholiques," to pass with so great torments when he allowed the Englishman Cavendish, a " hereticke and blasphemer," to get round " easilie." A swallow which flew aboard was welcomed as a favourable sign sent them by the Blessed Virgin. They had become mutinous, and were so later on, when they cursed the officers for having failed to provide the ship properly. The officers, for their part, recriminated on one another, the Master asserting that he had been careful to provide stores, but that the Captain had corruptly sold them at Cochin, and had pocketed the price. It is but just to add that Linschoten qualifies his assertion that the different classes of the Portuguese crews would not help one another by telling how, at one crisis, all hands—an Admiral and the officers included—but their hands to the pumps. How the *Santa Maria* did at last reach the Azores; how she suffered further dreadful miseries, heard of the failure of the Armada, of the expedition of Drake and Norris to Lisbon, of the disasters of the " flota " from America, and the last fight of the *Revenge*, it does not fall to us to speak here. The moral of the story is sufficiently given by Linschoten. He says that, wretched as it was, this voyage of the *Santa Maria* was fortunate in comparison with many others. Such ships, such seamen, such workmanship, could subsist only by the help of an absolute monopoly. From the day they had to face the competition of Englishmen and Dutchmen, the Portuguese were doomed to ruin.

The Spaniards were called upon to deal with more complicated, and yet withal easier, conditions than the Portuguese. In the earliest days of their conquests in America they had only to conduct their trade with the West Indian Islands. But after the conquest of Mexico by Cortes (1519-1522), and of Peru by the Pizarro brothers between 1524 and 1539, and their first permanent settlement in the Philippines under Miguel Lopez de Legaspi (1564-65), their commerce with their possessions was settled on three lines, all meeting in Central America and Mexico, like the legs on the shield of the Isle of Man. These were the direct trade from old Spain to America; the trade between the west coast of South America and Panama, and the trade between the Philippines and Mexico, carried by the Acapulco ships. After their experience of the many miseries of the voyage of Garcia Jofre de Loaysa in 1525-26, the Spaniards shrank from facing the dangers of the Straits of Magellan, which would have given them the equivalent, or more than the equivalent, of the stormy passage round the Cape of Good Hope. They tamely left the Dutch officers, Le Maire and Schouten, to explore the route by the Horn in 1616-17.

Of these three by far the most important was the first, which they called " la carrera de Indias "—the course to the Indies. It also was dictated largely by the nature of things—the winds and currents. The Spanish seamen soon discovered that the West Indies were swept by the steady easternly trade-wind, which they named the " brisa," and we after them the " true breeze "; that it sets up a surface current to the west in the Caribbean Sea; that winds and currents are turned by the mainland; that the offshore winds, named by them " Vendavales," helped the navigator along the coast; and as early as 1513 Ponce de Leon and Antonio de Alaminos had observed that the Gulf Stream sweeps round the western end of Cuba, pours through the Straits of Florida, and then turns to the eastward. The line of least resistance for a sailing ship, and especially for one very ill fitted to sail on the wind, when trading to the Indies, was to go out to the south-west, reach the " brisa," enter the Caribbean Sea through the Lesser Antilles, and come home by the Straits of Florida and the northerly route. And this loop or oval was the " Carrera de Indias." The trade of the western side of America was brought to Panama, and carried over land to Nombre de Dios, and in later times to Portobello.

The Spanish Kings did not endeavour to keep the trade to themselves as the Portuguese Sovereigns did; they were content to take their dues and their share of the silver of Mexican and Peruvian mines — one-fifth. In order to collect their revenue with greater ease and security they limited the trade to Seville. The name must, however, be understood to include more than the place itself. The Guadalquivir, on which Seville stands, is a tidal river, and will carry ships drawing as much as 20 feet of water up to the city; but the Guadalquivir is obstructed by a formidable bar at its entrance. At the low spring tides the depth of water on the bar is only some 11 feet; at the high tide it is about 22 feet. During the neap tides the depth ranges from 14 feet at low to 17 feet at high tide. Large ships could enter and leave the river only on the high spring tides, and then only when the wind was in their favour. June, July, and August are bad months for leaving the river, because the wind is then commonly settled in the south-west and south, and so blows right in the teeth of a ship endeavouring to cross the bar outward bound. Under the pressure of these necessities the Government was compelled to relax its rules, and to allow the name " Seville " to cover San Lucar de Barrameda in the mouth of the river, Cadiz, and the towns round its bay.

If it had appeared a possible thing to the paternal rulers of the sixteenth century to allow the persons interested to conduct their business in the way they found most profitable, there can be no doubt that Cadiz would have become the headquarters of the Indian trade at an early date; but it was for generations allowed to be only a rendezvous for the home-coming convoys, and for outward-bound ships as they were loaded and slipped over the bar of San Lucar, one or two at a time. Generations of loss and trouble were required to beat the Spanish people and Government out of a pig-headed adherence to routine. Meanwhile the " carrera de Indias " was ruled by the already named " Casa de Contratacion " and " Consejo de las Indias " (House of Trade and Council of the Indies). They regulated everything and everybody. The swarm of officials they employed battened on the trade, and were more fatal to the sea-borne commerce of Spain than all the armed enemies who attacked it, and all the storms of the ocean. The " Casa " and the " Consejo " were separate parts of the same organization. It went through various changes in the course of its history, and in the end became a nuisance to the Government which established it, as strongly framed and long-enduring bureaucracies have become in many other countries. It was finally broken down in the eighteenth century.

The Spanish trade to the Indies sailed on the course already named under the meticulous control of the Consejo and Casa de Contratacion. Certain changes were allowed as time went on. In early days the outward-bound fleets were ordered to touch at the Canaries; in later, they went direct to Dominica. When the attacks of pirates from Barbary and France forced the Spaniards to sail in convoy in 1502, they first went in one body. After that the rule was that the " flota " or trading fleet sailed to Dominica by the Canaries, touching in early days at Gomera, but later at Gran Canaria. At Dominica the ships bound to Mexico and the Great Antilles separated from those going to La Tierra Firme, the Spanish Main. The Spanish Main was not, as romance has hastily supposed, the main sea, but the mainland from Darien to the mouth of the Orinoco.

By 1574 this arrangement had become inconvenient, and a Royal Order (Cédula), dated October 18th of that year, laid it down that two " flotas " were to sail every year—one for Mexico, as soon as might be after the first spring tides in May, and another for Cartagena and the Main, in, or as soon as might be, after August. It might even go in October. There was a General in command of each, with his flag in the "capitana," and an Admiral in the " almiranta " as second in command. The General was a political and military officer. The Admiral was the naval authority. This absurd division of command was usual with the Spaniards as with the Portuguese. The " capitana " and the " almiranta " carried a third less cargo than other vessels in order to allow room for an escort of soldiers, and to permit them to keep their guns always mounted. By this time the Spaniards had given up touching at the Canaries. After 1521 the " capitana " and " almiranta " were found to be insufficient protection, and the Government established the " Armada Real de la Guardia de la Carrera de Indias " (the Royal Squadron of Guards for the Course to the Indies). It consisted of warships, and was paid for by a tax of 5 per cent. on the whole trade. It sailed with, or just after, the second " flota " in autumn, and its duty was to round up the trade from the Main to Mexico. The general rendezvous was at the west end of Cuba. On the way out the " flotas," loaded with European goods, which made but poor prize, were little molested.

They were assailed on the way back when they were bringing the colonial produce and the bullion.

The trade from Peru and Chili was ordered to be at Panama by March in the dry, healthy season, for convenient transport over the isthmus to Nombre de Dios and Portobello. Fifteen days were required to bring the bullion from Potosi to Arica, eight days by sea to Callao, and twenty days from Callao to Panama, stopping at Paita and Trujillo to pick up the silver. The cold wind from the South Pole blows along the west coast of South America; therefore a sailing ship could make her voyage from south to north in a third of the time required to sail from north to south. From Panama to Chili might be a six months' voyage, but from Chili to Panama it lasted for two, and the going and returning had been done in less. The " flotas " from the mouth of the Guadalquivir took from twenty-five to thirty days to reach Dominica. Their stay in the danger belt between the Azores and Cadiz would be from fifteen to thirty days according to weather. The Acapulco ships from Mexico to Manilla took two and a half months to go by the equatorial winds and current, and four months to come back by the longer northern route out of the current and in favourable winds. Of course this trade had to carry the burden of a swarm of officials—Generals, Admirals, guardians of the bullion, surveyors and accountants, " Veedores " and " Contadores." It is obvious, too, that all these elaborate rules made to provide safety had a counteraction. English and Dutch traders who frequented the Spanish ports became as familiar with the course of the trade as the Spaniards. They knew, and their countrymen knew from them, that when they wished to assail the Spanish trade all they had to do was to prowl round the Azores, and it would run in their way.

The Spanish trading ships were of smaller size than the Portuguese carracks; they ranged, in fact, from 200 to 500 tons as a rule. The warships of the Armada de Galeones might be vessels of 1,200 tons, but the size generally preferred was 500. In quality they were as poor as the carracks, but the Spaniards were more open-minded than the Portuguese. After the disasters of the Armada and following years they strove to improve the proportions and construction of their vessels. The Elizabethan seamen noted a marked increase in the seaworthiness of their ships.

It cannot be said that there was any improvement in their seamanship. The Spaniards are not naturally drawn to the sea. The discoveries of Columbus did promote a sudden outburst of maritime adventure; but the purpose of the adventurers was to reach the Indies and stay there. It was in vain that the Spanish Government strove to encourage seamen. Those engaged in the " carrera de Indias " were exempted from direct taxation; soldiers could not be billeted on their houses; they were allowed to form a " marisma " (a corporation of seamen which had its hospital and privileges). But these encouragements failed to encourage. Jealous as the Spaniards were of allowing foreigners to enter the Indies, they were driven, by lack of native seamen, to employ Levantines. A Spanish law officer, Don Eugenio de Salazar, who made a voyage to San Domingo in 1573,* has left an account of his experiences. He notes the presence of the Levantines, and quotes one of their chanties. The reader will see at once that it is a jargon of Spanish and Italian. Don Engenio confesses that he could not understand it all. The " mayoral," gang leader, or petty officer, sang the lines, and the men chanted " O ! O !" at the end of each as they pulled :

> " Bu izà
> O dio—ayuta noy
> O que somo—servi soy
> O voleamo—ben servir
> O la fede—mantenir
> O la fede—de cristiano
> O Malmeta—lo pagano
> Sconfondi—y sarrahin
> Torchi y mori—gran mastin
> O fillioli—dabrahim—
> O non credono—que ben sia
> O non credono—la fe santa," etc.

I am as much puzzled as Don Engenio, and would not wish to be called upon to give a literal translation; but in a general way the chanty is an invocation to God, a profession

---

* See the volume called " La Mar Descrita por los Mareados " (" The Sea described by the Seasick ") in the " Disquisiciones Nauticas," of Don Cesareo Duro.

of faith, and a denunciation of Mahomet, the Saracens, and the sons of Abraham, who do not believe in the holy faith of Rome.

The numbers of the crews seem high, judging by a modern standard, but were not appreciably greater than in English vessels engaged in the oversea trade in the seventeenth century. Don Juan de Escalante, who wrote sailing directions for the West Indies* in the reign of Philip II., gives the rule for the due manning of ships as follows : " For a vessel of a hundred tons twelve able seamen, eight ordinary seamen [" grumetes," Anglicé "grommets "], and three boys; for one of two hundred add eight able seamen, four ordinary, and one boy ; for each successive hundred tons add able and ordinary seamen, on the same sliding scale, and one boy till you reach the ship of five hundred tons, which carries thirty-four able and eighteen ordinary seamen and seven boys. The galleon of a thousand tons carries one hundred and fifty able and twenty-nine ordinary seamen, and twelve boys, without including officers. The small vessels do not carry Captain and master, but only a master."

It is no wonder if between badly-built ships, lack of natural aptitude, poor pay, excessive regulation, which crushed all independence of character, to say nothing of official corruption, the seamanship of " la carrera de Indias " was bad and disasters were numerous. The sea became hateful to the Spaniards.

Yet with all their defeats and their final failure, the fact remains to their credit that the Peninsular seamen first explored the ocean routes. They revealed to all the world the passage by the Cape, to the West Indies, to China, and round the world, the course of the currents, the peculiar blowing of trade-winds and monsoons. Their pupils bettered their instruction and laid hands on their inheritance ; but these pupils started with the knowledge the masters gave. Therefore at the head of all the seamen of the ocean stand the names of Bartolomeu Diaz, Vasco da Gama, Columbus, Magellan, and Sebastian del Cano.

* " A la Mar Madera," p. 471, Don Cesareo Duro.

CHAPTER VI

THE INTRUDERS ON THE EAST

IN the year 1604 peace had just been made with Spain, and the Ministers of James I. were called upon to provide for the security of trade. On the advice of the most influential of them, Robert Cecil, Lord Salisbury, it was decided that the wisest course was to confine the right to conduct commerce to a company. The reasons given by him were that the burden of affording protection ought to fall on the merchants, and that some organization must be formed to raise the funds required to pay the Consuls appointed to Spanish ports. He assumed that the State could not be expected to discharge these duties out of its own resources.

At a time when £30,000 a year was all the Crown could spare for the maintenance of the navy in peace, and when the permanent armed force maintained was limited to the winter and summer guards in the Channel—small handfuls of little ships—it would have been folly to suppose that squadrons could be stationed in distant seas. And if the King could not protect, neither could he control. Englishmen who committed offences against one another in remote seas, or who made trouble with other nations, and thereby provoked reprisals by which the whole trade suffered, could escape punishment. No doubt they had offended within the jurisdiction of the Lord High Admiral, which included the high seas. But how was his jurisdiction to be enforced on men who had misbehaved among the Cyclades, or on the coast of Sumatra? Years might pass before the offence was known in England, and then the offender had to be found and the witnesses collected. The case of England was that of other States, even of the Dutch Republic, which was compelled by its constant hostilities with Spain to keep a powerful naval force always in commission. This inability of all Governments to protect and control supplies one of the most material reasons for the establishment of the chartered companies, which play so great a part in the history of maritime commerce and of colonization. No doubt there were other reasons, such as habits, ways of thinking, and customs of trade inherited from the Middle Ages. But the chartered companies would not have been the important bodies they were if the Governments of Europe had not been compelled by the narrowness of their resources to allow traders engaged in foreign commerce to form organizations for their own protection, and then to endow them with jurisdiction and the right to maintain armed forces, so that they could discharge those functions of control and protection which in modern times are everywhere taken over by the State. To these companies was left the task of opening new lines of trade, and in some cases they were expected to provide warships for the service of the State.

The number of companies formed was great. Every maritime nation created at least one, and some produced several. Only a few of them attained to considerable prosperity.*

Only three of them immediately concern us whose business is with the sea trader—the Dutch, the English, and the French East India Companies. Even the Levant Company, founded in 1581 to promote trade in the Mediterranean, cannot demand a special notice.† The first chiefs of the East India Company had belonged to the Levant Company, which supplied the model and much knowledge.

I place them in this order—first Dutch, then English, then French—not because it is their chronological order, but because the Dutch was the first to be fully organized and

* The policy of employing chartered companies was revived in the nineteenth century and in Africa, but for the purpose of inland settlement, and not for maritime commerce. "Les Grandes Compagnies de Commerce" of M. Pierre Bonnassieux is a useful summary of the whole subject, and gives copious references to authorities.

† The South Sea Company of later days was of the first importance, but it comes properly under the head of the Spanish Main.

developed. " The Governor and Company of the Merchants of London trading into the East " dates from 1600, and the Oostindische Vereenigde Maatschapij from 1602. But the London Company was a loose association of merchants, with a permanent Governor and Council, who united to open a trade with the East. It was not even an English, but only a London association. It began by forming out of its own members successive "separate voyage" companies, and did not establish a joint stock till 1612. The Dutch Company burst on the seas armed at all points.

Until the year 1580 the Dutch had been content to carry on a lucrative coasting trade, which was the prolongation of the commerce of the Hansa, with which their cities had been allied. They were the intermediaries between the north of Europe and Lisbon, then the centre of the Indian trade. Dutch merchants were settled in Lisbon, and made voyages to the East, as we have seen that Linschoten did. But in 1580 Philip II. of Spain enforced his claim to the Crown of Portugal. As he was also by inheritance Sovereign of the Netherlands, and the Netherlanders were in rebellion, he excluded them from Lisbon. His purpose was to punish and weaken them. What he actually did was to drive them to invade the Portuguese Indies in self-defence. They, as we had already done, endeavoured to open a way by the north of Asia, and found it blocked by ice. Then they determined to make a front attack, since they could not turn the flank. The way was known to them, and they were aware that the English merchant, James Lancaster, had made a profitable voyage between 1591 and 1594. So in 1595 a Dutch expedition of three vessels sailed under command of Cornelius Houtman, who had been settled in Lisbon (as Lancaster had been), and had sailed east in Portuguese ships. Houtman's expedition suffered much—lost one ship and three-fifths of its men—but it reached the Spice Islands, and brought back rich cargoes. The stimulus was sufficient. Jacob van Neck sailed from the Texel in 1598 with eight ships, and three others left at the same time. Van Neck made a most profitable voyage, and a swarm of eager sea traders followed the lead given by him and by Houtman. As they went every man for himself, they competed with one another, and, of course, they sent up the price of spice in the islands, and brought it down at home. Moreover, they quarrelled with one another. The States-General saw necessity for regulation. So they called together the merchants concerned in the trade, and proposed that they should form a United East India Company. The merchants agreed, and in 1602 the company was formed. It was a very great thing. All the Seven United Provinces joined to make up the capital of six million and odd florins, some £550,000. The exact figure is disputed. The company was endowed with a monopoly for twenty-one years. It received wide rights of jurisdiction, was authorized to coin money, maintain warships and troops, build forts, and make peace or war in the name of the Statholder, since the natives could not be supposed to know what was meant by the States-General. It had a governing body at home in which the State of Holland took the lead, since it had contributed half of the capital. The headquarters were at Amsterdam, with boards in Zeeland, Delft, Rotterdam, Hoorn, and Enkhuizen. Armed as it was, the Dutch company laid a heavy hand at once on the islands of the Indian Ocean. Its first Governor-General, Pieter Both, sailed in 1609. In 1619 it fixed its capital at Batavia, in Java, on the ruins of the native city of Jacatra, under the rule of the third Governor, Jan Pieterz Koen. Its mere weight was enough to depress the Portuguese power, which was already honeycombed by vice, and had, moreover, suffered heavily by the fall of the friendly Hindu kingdom of Vizyanagar, after the Battle of Talikoot in 1565, and the consequent establishment of hostile Mohammedan States in the Deccan. The seventeenth century was the flourishing period of the Dutch Company. It drove the Portuguese from Ceylon between 1638 and 1658, and it seized Malacca in 1641. At the height of its prosperity in the latter half of the century it possessed 150 ships engaged in the home trade, and thirty ships of war. The shareholders received a dividend of 40 per cent.

The London Company was preserved for great destinies, but it looked small and weak in its early days beside its highly organized rival, the Dutch Maatschapij. I say

London Company deliberately, not only because it was officially as well as accurately described as being composed of merchants of London, but because there is a very real reason for distinguishing the parent body and the great " John Company " of the eighteenth century. The London Company was essentially a private enterprise of a small body of capitalists recognized by the King. As it owed much to his favour, so it suffered from two corresponding evils. In the first place it was liable to be fleeced by him, and was dependent on him for protection. James I. and Charles I. did fleece it, and they were also tempted to allow interlopers to intrude into its monopoly. They were weak, and could give the company no protection. In the second place the company excited the jealousy of traders in the outports because it was confined to Londoners, and the dislike of Parliament because it was a " royal " body, and had never received Parliamentary confirmation. Therefore, after the Revolution of 1688, it was opposed by a new company favoured by Parliament. The two fought like cat and dog, till the common sense which generally comes to the rescue of the most violent body of Englishmen taught them to combine. They invited Earl Godolphin, the Lord High Treasurer of Queen Anne, to arbitrate between them in 1708, and out of his arbitration there came the " United Company of the Merchants of England trading into the East Indies," the " John Company," which conquered India, and which was also " a combine," if ever there was one.

Different as the Dutch and the English companies were in their origin and destiny, they had one point in common. The States-General or the Statholder might levy heavy fees when the company's charter came up for renewal at intervals of twenty-one years. King or Parliament might squeeze the Honourable East India Company when it asked for the renewal of its privileges. Both did extort fees for renewal, and heavy fees too. But the companies were allowed to conduct their affairs themselves, and they were composed of capitalists who supplied the funds and directed the use of them with sagacity. We come to quite another body when we reach the French Company, the third of the trio which long ruled the commerce of the Eastern Seas.

King Henry II. of France is credited with the remark that his subjects would do no good in the trade with " the Indies " (by which he meant America at least as much as the East), because they would not persevere. We ought, in fairness to add that it was difficult for them to persevere. The wars of religion delayed French enterprise. The troubles of the reign of Louis XIII. and the minority of Louis XIV. had very much to do with the evil fortune of the French Company established in 1604. It dragged on miserably, and subsisted at the end by selling the right to make East India voyages to private adventurers. The important French Company, which made a bid for the dominion of India, dated from 1664, and the favour of Louis XIV. It started on disastrous conditions. The King, as has been justly said, did not aim at helping the shareholders to good dividends, but wished to engage the purses of his subjects in support of a general policy. Commercial ventures cannot flourish on these principles, and the French Company did not flourish. There was too much Court, and there were too many courtiers about its headquarters. Gentlemen, who well remembered that they had fees to receive, and only forgot they had duties to perform, infested the management. The history of the company was deplorable—one long story of financial enbarrassment, Government interference, combinations with other companies, and separations from them. That it did attain to a considerable position in India during the eighteenth century was due to the capacity and energy of three able Frenchmen—who in succession governed the factory at Pondicherry—to Martin, Damas, and Dupleix.

However it had been managed, the French Company of 1664 would have started at a disadvantage, for it came late, and when the best stations were occupied by the Dutch and the English. The Dutch had placed their headquarters in Java, had dominated the Spice Islands, and had seized a long line of posts extending by Sumatra, the Straits of Malacca and Ceylon, to the Cape of Good Hope. The English, after endeavouring to divide the Spice Islands with the Dutch, had turned to the mainland of India, and had struck their roots deep on both its coasts. Monopoly, it is almost superfluous to say, was the very breath of their nostrils. The English were more liberal towards the natives than the Dutch. From the first they had the sense and fairness of mind to see that the Indians would be best disposed to trade with them if they were allowed to make a profit. The guiding rule of the Dutch was expressed in the words of their first Governor, Pieter Both, quoted above. It was that where they were masters nobody was to make a profit except themselves. But as against their own countrymen and foreign rivals, Dutch, English, and French were equally monopolists. No Englishman was allowed to come to work for himself " within the Charter of the East India Company "—that is to say, from the Cape of Good Hope to the Horn, going eastward—unless he came with a licence. All were equally ready to drive away a foreign competitor. Hence there arose a state of things not new, for we have seen a very full-blown example of it in the case of Hansa, but nearer to us, more interesting, more intelligible, because more in the daylight, than the greed and ferocity of the dim North during the later Middle Ages. It was a state of competition in trade, carried on by aid of the long gun, the musket, and the cutlass.

We must not be misled by the renown of the English East India Company's ships of later days. The famous Indiamen of the end of the eighteenth century were vessels of 1,200 and 1,400 nominal tons. Their real measurement was greater, and some of them were as large as Nelson's *Victory*. But they began to be built as late as 1781, when the company decided to cause five ships of from 1,100 to 1,200 tons to be constructed for the China trade. In earlier days the Indiamen were of smaller proportions, ranging from 300 to 750 or 800 tons. A few ships of 1,000 tons were employed in early days. One large Indiaman was built by the company, and launched in the presence of King James I., his Queen, and his eldest son, Prince Henry, on December 30, 1609. She was baptized the *Trade's Increase*. She sailed under the command of the company's " General," Sir Henry Middleton, on April 1st, 1610. But she came not back. She proved to be clumsy and leaky, and was burnt on the beach at Bantam, where she had been placed for repairs.

Her salvage was sold for the sum of 1,050 rials. Even if we suppose these to have been silver rials of the value of sixpence, the company had a very bad bargain in the *Trade's Increase*. As a rule, the Directors abstained from attempts to imitate the Portuguese carracks. As late as 1794 the company decided that ships of about 1,400 tons were proper for the China trade. For regular ships, carrying rich cargoes to India, a tonnage of 820 was judged sufficient, and vessels of from 480 to 520 were considered large enough to bring home " gruff goods." This name of odd suggestion meant " Indian return cargoes of raw materials—cotton, rice, pepper, sugar, hemp, salt- petre, etc." The large vessels carried silks, muslins, tea, and fine goods generally. They also carried the passengers, who, after the full establishment of the company's dominion in India, became a source of profit. The British dominion in India, and the trade of the East, were such great matters, and figured so largely in our policy, that we are inclined to-day to take it for granted that the number of vessels and men employed in its trade was large. But in 1793 the company decided that it must have thirty-six vessels of the 1,200-ton class, and forty of the 800 class to meet all needs. As it held the monopoly of the trade, this represented the whole of the British shipping trading with the East. The nominal tonnage, stated in round figures, and without pretence to minute accuracy, was 90,000. The number of men employed, allowing four white sailors per hundred, would be about 3,500. Compared with the figures of modern trade, the flowering time of " John Company " was a day of little things, but, then, it was also the day of the laying of the foundations.*

A good deal of business and of human nature are con- nected with the supply of ships to the company. It began by buying at second hand. The vessel variously called by the barely intelligible name of the *Mare Scourge*, and also the *Malice Scourge*, was bought from the adventurous Earl of Cumberland. She was measured for 600 tons, and she cost £3,700, a little over £6 a ton. The *Susan*, of 240 tons,

* *Cf.* Peter Auber, " Analysis of the Constitution of the East India Company," 1826, pp. 648-688.

was bought from Alderman Bannyng for £1,600, on condition that he was to buy her back for half that sum at the end of her voyage. In other words, the company freighted her for an indefinite period at the very moderate figure of £3 7s. a ton. In 1607, when the first voyage had brought great profits, and the future looked promising, the company leased a yard at Deptford, and began to build its own ships at the rate of about £10 a ton. The *Trade's Increase* and the *Peppercorn* were the first launched. The reason which dictated the establishment of the yard was the difficulty of finding vessels strong enough for the long Indian voyage at a time when voyages were generally short and ships lightly built. The Earl of Cumberland's ship had been built for war, and so probably was the *Susan*. When, after 1607, the company wished to hire additional ships, it was asked the outrageous figure of £45 a ton. This was no market price, but an attempt at extortion. After maintaining its own yard for twenty years, the company decided to adopt the practice of hiring its vessels. About 1627 the quarrel with the Dutch was raging, and the company had suffered heavy losses. It found that too much of its capital was tied up in the yard, and in vessels which, in the conditions of the time, were worn out in four voyages.

A reader moderately familiar with the nature of business and of business men will make a safe guess as to what ensued. Directors, shrewd men, with a quick eye for profits, took to building ships and hiring them to their own company. It was an arrangement more advantageous to the director than to the shareholder. After the amalgamation of the old and the new companies in 1708, Parliament began to turn its attention to this business of the supply of shipping. The company was no longer "unfettered by legislation." Directors were forbidden to supply ships, which in future were to be hired by open tender from the Commander and two owners. But saying is one thing, and doing is another. The mere fact that a special class of strong vessel was required for the Indian trade tended to throw the supply into the hands of a ring. And a ring there was. It was named the Marine Interest, and sought to obtain as much as possible for its ships. A pull-builder pull-company fight went on throughout the eighteenth century. The company appears on the whole to have been fleeced.*

The ships were not owned by the company in the sense that the Cunard or the Royal Mail owns its ships. They were hired for so many voyages at so much a ton, the company binding itself to freight a stipulated number of tons, which were generally less than the official measurement. Thus a ship measuring 850 might be freighted at 799. By the higgling of the market the price per ton tended to fix itself at £32, but in war time, when war insurance was to be paid, the Marine Interest insisted on £10 more. The whole question of "war extraordinaries" figured largely in the company's contracts. When an Indiaman was worn out, another was hired to replace her, and was said to be "built upon the bottom" of the first. The member of the Marine Interest who had built the one claimed a right to build the other. Hence arose what was called the "hereditary bottoms." Towards the close of the eighteenth century the shareholders rebelled under the leadership of the more public-spirited directors against the monopoly of the Marine Interest, and destroyed it in 1796.

Some light is thrown on that very obscure subject, the progress of the art of shipbuilding, by the records of the company. Until 1790 a vessel was looked upon as worn out by four voyages. The voyage in normal conditions would be eighteen months, but it might be greatly prolonged. In 1790 the company decided that as a ship could make three voyages without being under the necessity of stripping off her sheathing, if the fourth were made the repairing voyage, she would last for six. In 1810 the figure was increased to eight by leave of Parliament. A ship of 1790 was no doubt better put together than one of, say, 1730, and, moreover, the introduction of copper sheathing about 1780 had lengthened the life of all vessels. But the decision to make eight and not six voyages the official life of a ship was due to economy. The price of timber was already rising. Within a generation from 1810 it had increased to the point at which the use of iron was becoming compulsory except to

* The story will be found at length in Mr. Auber's "Analysis."

peoples who, like the Americans and Scandinavians, possessed large forests within easy reach of their ports.

As with the ships, so with the men—or, at least, the officers. They were not "covenanted servants," as the clerks and factors in India were. But they were taken for four, six, or eight voyages according to date, and had a moral right to re-engagement. When the company in 1796 decided to make an end of " hereditary bottoms," it compensated the commanders at the rate of £4,000 each. The sum it had to pay between 1796 and 1808, in order to free itself of " hereditary " claims, was £348,000.

The constitution of the company's crews is a subject well worth looking at, not only for its own interest, but because it throws a vivid light on the whole history of the merchant service, British and foreign, till quite recent days. One thing the reader must be asked to do, and that is to clear his mind for once and for all of the belief that the British merchant ship was ever wholly manned by British seamen. He will often hear that in some golden age it was so manned, and he will no doubt continue to hear the statement repeated with that audacity of assertion and brazen indifference to evidence proper to popular delusions. When it is thought necessary to produce proof, the Navigation Acts are quoted, as if they did impose the obligation to man British ships with British seamen only, or agreed with one another, or were rigidly obeyed. In the long series of Navigation Acts, which began with the Commonwealth, and ended in the early part of the reign of Queen Victoria, there are many differences. Their general tendency was to make it obligatory to carry " the King's natural-born subjects " to the extent of three-fourths of the crew. But a native of Minorca was a natural-born subject of the King so long as the island belonged to the Crown—that is to say, from 1714 to 1783. So were British negroes in the West Indies. An exception was always made for ships sailing within the charter of the East India Company, which might be manned entirely by Lascars, Seedy Boys, and Chinamen, so long as they did not come west of the Cape of Good Hope, or east of Cape Horn.

The Navigation Acts did, indeed, endeavour to limit

the employment of Lascars to the seas within the charter, and of negroes to voyages among the West Indian Islands, or between them and the mainland of America. But the legislators who passed these laws could not ignore certain patent facts. One of them was that, as Sir Charles Napier the Admiral said in 1817, the population of Great Britain and Ireland was never equal to manning the Navy and the Merchant Service at once. In war-time, when the fighting began, the Navy swept all the seamen it could lay hands on into the men-of-war. A great gap was created in the Merchant Service. It was filled up by foreigners. The manning clauses were suspended, and foreigners were tempted to come in by the promise that they should be allowed to take out letters of naturalization at the end of two years, and enjoy all the rights of a natural-born subject, including that of commanding a British merchant ship. The second fact was that a crew not only might be, but very commonly was, reduced by death or "accident"—*i.e.*, desertion in a foreign or Indian port—so low, that it was not sufficient to work the ship. In that case foreigners or Lascars could be shipped in the necessary numbers. The question what was a necessary number in the case of the Lascars was long in dispute. The company pointed out that as the Lascars were not equal to white sailors in physical strength, it would be most unfair and dangerous to enforce a rule that they must be shipped one for one to supply deficiencies. Very late in the history of the company a kind of counsel of perfection was hit upon by Parliament, and it was laid down that if an Indiaman carried four white sailors per hundred tons register, she was to be counted properly manned, whatever might be the the number of her Lascars. But this was no more than a counsel of perfection. If the ship was short-handed at Amoy or Canton, and white sailors were not to be found, what was to be done? Parliament could prevent the company from reshipping the Lascars it brought to London as seamen for the outward-bound voyage, and compel it to take them back as passengers. It did, with the result that the company was forced to keep them idle in lodging-houses near the docks. They became a scandal, which culminated when one of the Lascars was flogged to death by a serang (a foreman) in 1814. But they were always employed on the homeward-bound voyage, and that from an early date. In 1711 Charles Lockyer, an experienced servant of the company, published "An Account of the Trade in India." Among other observations, he noted the danger that the native traders and shipowners of Surat, then a port belonging to the Great Mogul, might learn to use the Cape route to Europe for themselves. He gave his opinion that it would be desirable to avoid engaging Lascars on the homeward voyages, lest they should learn too much. "But," he added, "on the foot things at present are they must needs be employed, for they [*i.e.*, the homecoming ships] have sometimes scarce hands enough on board to carry them thither, much less to beat about the Cape homeward bound, when they are diminished, and enfeebled by sickness and other accidents." And on that foot things have remained to this day, when complaints may be heard that the employment of lascars is a novelty and a danger.

Lockyer, writing more than a century after the trade to India had been diligently followed by the Cape route, speaks of the diminution of crews and the enfeebling of the survivors by sickness as common occurrences. He would not have thought it necessary to write his useless warning against the employment of Lascars on the homeward voyage if they had been shipped only on rare occasions. But he knew that his warning was useless because sickness was so rife, and death so busy, that ships were habitually undermanned before the time came to turn homewards. So it had been from the first, and so it was to be for long. Nothing is better proved, or more shocking, than the enormous expenditure of human life in sea trade within the tropics until quite recent times. To-day, if cholera breaks out in a steamer carrying passengers to South America, and ten of those on board her die, it is a startling event which spreads panic along the coast, and fills the newspapers with clamour. Yet she may carry from 1,200 to 1,500 crew and passengers. Turn to the letters written to the London Company by its servants at sea in 1608,* and hear one of them reporting

* *Cf.* "Letters received by the East India Company." F. C. Danvers, 1896.

the fortunes of the *Hector*. " In this my conclusion," he says, in brief, official style, " I will not omit to certify your worships of what men have died this voyage, and have been lost aboard our ship." There were ten in all, of whom two were drowned. Observe, too, that the writer dates from Socotra before the ship had reached India, and that these losses occurred between August 4th, 1607, and June 19th of the following year. He makes no comment, obviously because he saw nothing exceptional in this loss. When a writer has to record only three or four deaths in a period of similar length, he piously gives thanks to God, who has visibly extended His protection to His unworthy servants. And beyond all doubt to God were the thanks due, and not to the care of man.

The merchants and Captains of the time could not plead ignorance. Sir Richard Hawkins had noted during his voyage to the South Seas in 1593-94 how it was quite possible to keep a crew in fair health by taking reasonable care. It is true that his " observations " were not published till 1622, but his remarks cannot have been unknown. And even if the teaching of Hawkins was forgotten, the company's men must have known that Sir James Lancaster, the pioneer of all their ventures, had kept scurvy and fever at arm's length in his own ship during his voyage of 1600-1604. Not ignorance, but recklessness, supplies the true explanation of the long reign of scurvy on the ocean. We are not to blame the Commanders. They suffered with the others. Late in the eighteenth century Nelson when cruising in the North Atlantic, was prostrated by scurvy. It would not even be quite just to blame the employers, whether they were a company of merchants or the State. The London Company in its early days treated its servants meanly in the matter of pay, even when it was making profits of from 90 to 240 per cent. on its investments; but it took care of their morals with Puritanical piety, and it provided for their intellectual benefit by sending books to its ships and factories. Bibles and books of theology and divinity made up the bulk of these lit'le libraries, but they included Hakluyt, so that the company's servants might " refresh their minds with varieties of history." And here it may be remarked, by the way, that the sailors and "merchants" who went to the ends of the earth for the company and suffered infinite distresses were not without grace of art. In the midst of all the troubles of Sir Henry Middleton's ships at Mocha and Cambaya, treacherous capture by Turks, escapes, blockades, reprisals, we hear repeated mention of Mr. Bowles, his cornet and treble viol, and his books of music. When Captain Saris sailed on the first English voyage to Japan he had in his cabin a picture of Venus and her son "somewhat wantonly displayed in a frame." We have it under his own hand in a letter to his worshipful masters of the company, and he tells them further that certain Japanese women who visited his ship mistook it for a picture of the Virgin and Child. They went down on their knees and said their prayers, for, as they confessed to Saris in a whisper, they were secretly Christians.*

If the men of the sixteenth and seventeenth centuries were free from the vulgar and Philistine belief of the eighteenth century that it was unmanly to play on a musical instrument, or to enjoy pictures, they were indifferent to pain and needless risk of death for others and for themselves. They were not necessarily brutal to individual sufferers, but they took it for granted that disease and death were incidental to adventure, and they acted as if they thought precaution useless. They had, indeed, so much to contend with that they had some excuse for being without hope of avoiding the miseries of the sea. Their ships were but small, and as they knew they might be called upon to fight, they carried large crews. The first fleet sent out by the company consisted of three vessels, measuring among them 1,400 tons. They carried 240 men. All were not sailors. Before trade was settled and there were agents to be found in every port, it was necessary to send merchants, factors, supercargoes, to conduct the trade. Some of them were sent out to found factories; but long after factories had been established, merchants, supercargoes, and clerks were carried in the ships. At the risk of being reproached

* "Memorials of the Empire of Japan." Thomas Rundall, Hakluyt Society, No. 8, 1850.

with repetition, I must point out again that as the ill-balanced sails of these vessels—the nearly useless spritsail, and the excessive mizzen—rendered them ardent and unable to tack, they were forced to wear—that is to say, to turn on their heel—and so lose, perhaps, two or three miles by drift whenever they were beating against the wind. This, of course, increased the length of the voyage. With overcrowded ships, slow progress, and no rational precautions of diet—no vegetables, no fruit, no lemon nor lime-juice, only salted beef and pork (the " salt-horse " of the sea slang), dried peas and beans, and ship's biscuit, more or less mouldy and full of weevils, what could come but scurvy?

Let us take two typical voyages, and begin with the ships which left England in April, 1607, under the command of Captain Keeling as " General." The Commander of a squadron of war or merchant ships was then the " General " and his ship was the " Admiral." Keeling was a good officer and a cultivated man. He had probably passed from the service of the Levant Company, as many others did, and had in the Mediterranean acquired that " Arabic tongue " which was to be useful to him in the East. It was, of course, not the classical and literary Arabic, but the language as it was, and is, spoken in seaports. The troubles of the voyage came by no fault of his. His ships, the *Dragon*, the *Hector*, and the pinnace *Consent*, lost sight of England on April 17th, 1607. Teneriffe was seen on the 30th, and Mayo, in the Cape Verd Islands, on May 7th. On June 6th they saw " Fernando Forania," which, properly named, is Fernam de Noronha, the fantastic island of peaks, shaped like gigantic heads of monks with their cowls drawn over their faces, which lies south of the Equator, north-east of Cape San Roque in Brazil, and is to-day a telegraph and penal station. They were now two months out. As English seamen of that time had not yet mastered the currents of the South Atlantic, Captain Keeling had miscalculated. He came too near Fernam de Noronha, and so met the full force of the south-westerly current, which sets in to the coast of Brazil, while he had to contend with the south-east trade-wind which was then blowing strong and far up. Till July 30th the ships remained beating about against the wind, which forced them back, and in the current, which dragged them to the shore. They ought to have kept at least 120 miles to the east of Fernam de Noronha, as a modern sailing ship will take care to do, unless she is bound for Pernambuco. It is a proof of the little care then taken to collect observations and render them accessible that, though Lancaster had commanded a raid on this very coast in 1594, so good an officer as Keeling knew no better than to allow himself to be carried wide of his course. By July 30th the ships had reached São Agostinho in Pernambuco. The scurvy was raging among the crews. An expedition on its way to the East Indies could not venture to go into the Portuguese port of Recife for provisions. Yet go somewhere they must—or die. It shows how strong the medieval tradition still was that a council of officers and merchants was held in the " Admiral." One man proposed one place and another another, " all by our General disliked. Then he himself to us nominated ' Serro Leone,' upon the coast of Guinea. His notes for the navigation of it, and his reasons good, it was of all concluded to put for the same."

They recrossed the Equator and reached Sierra Leone on August 6th. There they found " a king and people niggers, simple and harmless," and were refreshed. They crossed the Equator for the third time, and were on the latitude of Fernam de Noronha by August 25th, well to the east, and they sighted the Table Mountain on December 17th. The scurvy had broken out again since they left Sierra Leone, so at the importunity of all, " and for pity taken of our weak and sick men," the " General " put into Saldanha Bay, by which they meant Table Bay—not the place so-called now —on December 18th. Fresh meat was purchased at a trifling price from the natives, and they sailed again on January 1st, 1608. The Cape was rounded on the 3rd, and St. Lawrence —*i.e.*, Madagascar—came in sight on February 17th. A stop was made at Augustine Bay on the 19th until the 28th. On March 14th they were in latitude 14° 30', and headed for Zanzibar, but fell to leeward of that port, and so made that way to Socotra. At Socotra they found native ships from Surat, and the General's Arab tongue helped him to the weighty information that, if he did not hasten, the westerly winds would make it impossible for him to reach Aden for four months. They had reached the island on March 26th, and they left on the 29th, only to be driven back by a storm, and to be imprisoned till August. This, at least, was the fate of the *Hector*. The *Dragon*, which was bound for Bantam, in Java, was able to go on her way in June. We see, therefore, that these ships, carefully appointed and commanded by a capable man, spent just a few days less than a year in reaching Socotra, which was only a stopping-place on the way to their destination. The story of the voyage enables us to understand why the company's agent, who reported their fortunes, did not see anything out of the way in the loss of eight of those on board her by disease. They had made, on the whole, a not unprosperous voyage.

In this case ships and men were fresh from home. On the backward voyage, when both were tried by much cruising in the East, the case was like to be notably worse. The journal kept by Captain Nicholas Downton of his fortunes during his return from Bantam to Waterford in 1613 in the *Peppercorn* is our witness for a voyage made in bad conditions. The *Peppercorn* had sailed in 1610 with Sir Henry Middleton. She was a small vessel, built in the company's yard at Deptford. Middleton had met with adverse fortune, and did not live to see England again. In the beginning of 1613 he decided, " after divers conferences and good considerations moving thereto," to send the *Peppercorn* back with her loading in advance of the other ships.

Downton began by a false start, and did not actually get away till the 7th.* By the time they were clear of Java, " before we doubted thereof, we had on our lower orlop among our casks 20 inches deep of water." The leak was due to " no less then two trenail holes . . . in the stern, by the negligent carpenters which built . . . hath been so left open, the least of which without God's merciful preventing might have drowned us all."† On the same day

---

* " East India Company's Records," pp. 241-251, Danvers.
† The trenails, or tree-nails—pronounced " trennels "—in a wooden ship were " long, cylindrical oak or other hard-wood pins, driven through the planks and timbers of a vessel to connect her

began a series of entries to be frequently repeated. Captain Downton recorded the death of " Alex. Wickstead our minister," the first of twenty who died before, or just after, the *Peppercorn* came to an anchor at Waterford. These entries punctuate the journal at short intervals. Mr. Wickstead had died on February 13th; Edward Pope died on the 22nd. " On the 4th day at 2 in the morning died Abraham Bouns, cooper, and Robert Blunt, about break of day in the morning following." And so it goes on. The crew, in fact, was sickly with flux—*i.e.*, dysentery—when the voyage began, and the ship indifferently fitted. Downton had already noted that before they were done " making a pridie ship "—*i.e.*, a trim ship—they had infinite trouble to provide " a tight room " to keep their bread in, " in regard of the innumerable sort of cacara, a most devouring worm with which this ship doth abound to our great disturbance." The cask " being 26 tons, decayed and weak, rotten and leaky one with another," was to hold their water, " and the cooper we had to mend them," says Downton callously, " three parts dead already and the fourth part he soon finished "—as we have seen. In such conditions did the *Peppercorn* wallow along. " On the 7th day (of March) a storm in hand, our ropes break, our sails rent. God sustain us." " On the 25th day I pray God to withhold all deserved plagues from us. At noon our ship came afire by the cook his negligence o'er guzzled with drink, digged a hole through the brick back of the furnace and gave the fire passage to the ship's side, which led to much trouble besides spoil to the ship." The name of that " negligent o'er guzzled " cook was Richard Hancock, and his death is recorded on May 1st. Of the splitting of the main bonnet and the main course, of how, " for want of fit sail to carry," they were forced to " lie a hull," to drift without sail till damage could be made good ; of how by " the labouring of the ship and beating her bows in a head

---

various parts." It looks ill for the way in which work was done and surveyed in the company's yard at Deptford that the *Peppercorn* should have suffered from this weakness. The shipwrights must have fitted her with " devils "—that is to say, they stopped the outer and inner ends of the trenail holes with small bits of wood to make a show, and, of course, stole the trenail itself.

sea " they took in water, 20 or 24 inches of it, and spoiled all their powder, with the doubtful exception of two barrels, does the journal discourse in grim brief phrases. On May 7th, four months after leaving Bantam, Downton found his ship had well overshot the " Cape Bona Speransa," though his untrustworthy instruments had told him he was thirty five leagues short of it. He put into Table Bay on May 10th, where he met the *Hector* and *Thomas* outward bound, and was relieved; but in spite of their help he sailed on the 15th in evil case. Now they sped away with a swift current to the north-west in hopes to find water and green food at St. Helena. On June 3rd they made ready their " rotten boat," in hope she might serve their turn ; but, alas ! when on the 8th they came about the north-east point and opened the roadstead in sick longing for land, for many of the men were touched with " the disease of the sea."—*i.e.*, scurvy— they saw two carracks " against the chapel." St. Helena still belonged to the Portuguese, who would have treated all poachers on Indian waters as pirates. In the unbridled world of romance the poor little *Peppercorn*, leaky, rotten, eaten up by " devouring worms," manned by a diminished, sickly crew, would have demonstrated the invincible valour of Englishmen. In the sober world of history, Captain Downton could only regret that the solitary *Peppercorn* was too weak to enforce respect, and bear up for England unfreshed.

Overworked, hag-ridden, tormented by vermin and scurvy, some of the ship's company began to see visions. On July 2nd Mr. " Abraham Lawes conceives he is poisoned, for that his stomach falls away, and he hath often inclination to vomit, for he saith he was so at Venise when he was formerly poisoned." Poison and witchcraft were the nightmares of the sixteenth and seventeenth century. The sufferings of Mr. Lawes were the reward of drunken habits. On the 14th he again declared his conceit of being poisoned, " and by none of the worst in the ship," but named nobody. On the 27th he died, and the surgeon " took good note of his inward parts.' They had crossed the line on July 18th, and on August 11th they descried Fayal and Pico—the Peak of Teneriffe. A sail came in sight next day, and they struck their topsail in hope to speak with her ; but every stranger was a possible pirate in those days, and, no doubt in fear, she bore away. On the 21st Downton notes that " men daily fall down into great weakness." As they approached home they began to see more sails, but nobody would come near them. On September 7th is the entry, " a great storm, our case weak, God be our help, comfort, and defence." Downton tried to reach Milford, but was forced to make for Waterford. First, for more security and safety of ship and goods from practice of lewd people, by riding within two forts ; secondly, for hope of supply there of what we wanted ; and lastly, for speediest conveyence of letters to the company to London. The Channel and Irish Sea were, in fact, then swarming with pirates, and the *Peppercorn* was in as much peril at home from her own countrymen as ever she could have been from Malay praus or Portuguese carracks.

Two days after reaching Waterford he wrote :

" RIGHT WORSHIPFUL,
" If the Indian Company at present had view of my decrepit and wretched person, I could expect no better censure from the generality for the use of my hands, legs, and feet than at first I found of the graver sort by the seeming defect of my tongue, which then was no other than the lame instrument of a passionate mind which remedeliless infirmity hath often of wise and worthy men been favourably forborne."

Yet he was resolute to stand to his ship, and asks for stores and ten honest sailors to bring him round to London, for he dared not trust all of the twenty-six survivors of his crew of forty-six " in case of pirates attempts."

He had good cause not to trust all his men. Early in the voyage one of them, Francis Pindar by name, had raised a mutiny to compel him to name a favourite of theirs as cook, the " o'er guzzled with drink " R. Hancock, who so nearly set the *Peppercorn* on fire. All through the voyage Pindar had given trouble, and he had the support of others like to himself. Downton believed that Pindar and his mates were capable of seizing the ship and disposing of her loading for their own advantage. As will be shown in another place, they would have had no difficulty in finding a purchaser on the West of Ireland. He caused one of his rascals, whom he does not name, to be laid by the heels in the fort at Waterford on a charge of piratical intentions. The man revenged himself by bringing a charge of piracy against his Captain. Downton was arrested on a warrant from the Earl of Ormond. One imagines that on this occasion the seeming defect of his tongue, that "lame instrument of a passionate mind," was not concealed. If Captain Downton swore and cursed, he had some excuse. But he was soon released, and after toils greater than had been overcome by Ulysses, the much-enduring man brought the battered *Peppercorn* to Blackwall.

Such was the sea life of the early seventeenth century in these long voyages, and it changed for the better by slow steps and during long years. All in it was not heroic, and of the men who lived it not a few were but sinister ruffians. Captain Richard Cock, the company's factor in Japan, has much to say about the evil behaviour of English and Dutch seamen. He was of opinion that parents and guardians at home, who were pestered by unruly young men, were accustomed to ship them off on these voyages to the Far East in the reasonable hope that they would never come back. Scurvy and the "flux" disposed of many of them. Others, like John Roan of Bristol, mariner, whose story is told by Cock, "found the end of the world in the middle of a ladder." Roan had murdered John Peterson, a Dutchman, at Firando by stabbing "him into the left breast and so to the heart [with a knife] that he never spoke a word but fell down dead." Roan was tried by a jury chosen from the crews of the *Elizabeth*, the *Palsgrave*, the *Moon*, and the *Bull*, English ships, then at Firando. His country found him guilty, and he was hanged at the yardarm of the *Elizabeth*. He, like nearly all the pirates, murderers, and mutineers we read of in those times, made a penitent end. When the game was up, when the defeated sinner was sober and sorry for it, when he saw the gallows waiting, and behind it the, to him, most indubitable vision of the " flames of hell and the horns of the devil," he never failed to endeavour to put himself right for his exit from this world and passage into the next. Roan made a becoming last speech. " He confessed before his death that he killed the said man, being in drink, and not knowing what he did, wishing all the ship's company to take example by him, to beware [of course] of women [the woman whom Thou gavest me, as our Father Adam said, and as his sons repeat], and wine, which had brought him to that untimely death. He died very resolutely, and received the sacrament by Mr. Arthur Hutch (Preacher) before he went to execution. Captain Robert Adams was forced to put the rope about his neck with his own hands, for none of the ship's company would do it, if he should hang them, and so told him to his face."

The Dutch were not lacking in reciprocity of good offices, for they brought to justice one " John Johnson von Homberg for killing M. Avery (purser's mate of the *Elizabeth*), five or six Englishmen standing by at the doing thereof (they having first made the man so drunk that he could scarce stand upon his legs), and cut his head off within their own house "—a shameful scene beside the orderly execution of Roan. The brutality of these pioneers of European trade with Japan had its share, no doubt, in bringing about the expulsion of all of them. They did not confine their outrages to one another, but broke out against their hosts. The Japanese had very substantial reasons for closing their ports, and confining European trade to the Dutch at one point and under severe restrictions. They saw what the intrusion of the European meant in the Philippines and elsewhere. They saw, too, during the twenty years or so of the existence of the English and Dutch factories that the European brought lawless violence with him. As they had not yet come to the point at which it was possible for them to master the arts of Europe, and so secure the right to rule the strangers who came among them, they did well to slam their door in the face of Roman Catholic missionaries, Dutch and English factors, and the likes of John Roan and John Johnson von Homberg.

Meanwhile, it is to be noted that such persons as these

were more or less controlled. In the end it was Captain Downton, and not the mutinous Francis Pindar, who won. Among the Dutch there was manifestly enough better order than in the English ships of the earlier eastern voyages. The Dutch Company was fully organized, and had at its command from the first a strong armed force to support authority. The fact, which was undeniable, that their ships suffered less from bad health than ours was partly due to better regulation ; but it must be mainly accounted for by the greater recklessness of the English sailor. It was not wholly by the neglect of his superiors that the English sailor died of scurvy and the " country fevers " in such enormous numbers. Such men as Pindar and Hancock (and their name was legion) would have rebelled against being compelled to drink a glassful of lemon-juice every morning on an empty stomach. In the unhealthy ports of the Indian Ocean Englishmen, whether sailors or " merchants," rushed to indulge in liquor in a fashion which seemed insane to the Dutch, who yet were not sober men. Therefore they suffered far more from dysentery. Along with the foresight, the honest dealing, the heroism of the better sort, there is to be found the blind longing of the mere human brute for an intense sensation of animal joy. For that they risked their lives, and they were prepared to obtain it by swilling raw arrack, and were at all times contemptuous of prudence. Therefore, they served as mere raw material, to be used up in making a breach, or as manure for the field, which wiser men have tilled to their profit ; but therefore, also, they were intrepid in the face of peril, and as contemptuous of danger as of caution.

ENGLISH SAILORS.

were more or less controlled. In the end it was Captain Downton, and not the mutinous Francis Pindar, who won. Among the Dutch there was manifestly enough better order than in the English ships of the earlier eastern voyages. The Dutch Company was fully organized, and had at its command from the first a strong armed force to support authority. The fact, which was undeniable, that their ships suffered less from bad health than ours was partly due to better regulation; but it must be mainly accounted for by the greater recklessness of the English sailor. It was not wholly by the neglect of his superiors that the English sailor died of scurvy and the "country fevers" in such enormous numbers. Such men as Pindar and Hancock (and their name was legion) would have rebelled against being compelled to drink a glassful of lemon-juice every morning on an empty stomach. In the unhealthy ports of the Indian Ocean Englishmen, whether sailors or "merchants," rushed to indulge in liquor in a fashion which seemed insane to the Dutch, who yet were not sober men. Therefore they suffered far more from dysentery. Along with the foresight, the honest dealing, the heroism of the better sort, there is to be found the blind longing of the mere human brute for an intense sensation of animal joy. For that they risked their lives, and they were prepared to obtain it by swilling raw arrack, and were at all times contemptuous of prudence. Therefore, they served as mere raw material, to be used up in making a breach, or as manure for the field, which wiser men have tilled to their profit; but therefore, also, they were intrepid in the face of peril, and as contemptuous of danger as of caution.

ENGLISH SAILORS.

CHAPTER VII

IN THE EASTERN SEAS

THE world beyond the Cape of Good Hope was everywhere full of violence. It always had been before the Portuguese came as the forerunners of direct European commerce. They made no change, neither did their successors and rivals from England, Holland, and France. When the European intruders came to a balance and an understanding, the old native disorder went on. It arose as from the soil, the sea, and the very bones of the peoples. If the repressing hand of civilization were lifted even for a single year, perhaps only for one month, it would come up again as inevitably as exhalations rise out of stagnant water.

From antiquity the sea trader had been subject to pillage at the hands of all who dwelt on the shores of the great trade routes. From the Gulf of Persia and the Red Sea, by the seashore of Mekran, and the Bay of Cambaya, along the coast of Malabar, round the Bay of Bengal, through the Straits of Malacca, across the Indian Archipelago, and on to the seas of China and Japan, it was always the same story. There was trade, and there were merchants, and there were those who robbed. We call it " piracy" for lack of a better name. If, as a strict use of terms demands, we apply the name pirate to the mere broken man and robber who lives outside of the law, then perhaps it was not piracy. It was at first a form of that desire to take advantage of a good thing which led lords of the land to seize on the goods of strangers who died within their limits and on wrecks, and to levy tolls, which were but " baksheesh " and blackmail, at fords and in mountain passes. It was on a par with the morality of the worthy people who protested against the building of a lighthouse on the south coast of England, because they had hitherto profited much by the wrecks which the goodness of God sent them every winter. They foresaw with a sincere sense of wrong that a valuable part of their means of subsistence was about to be lost. In the early days of the South Sea Company one of its agents in Madrid begged for leave to come away. His health was bad, and he knew that if he died in Spain the Inquisition would annex his goods as belonging to a stranger and a heretic, to the ruin of his poor family. The King of France would have done as much, simply because he was a stranger. The many peoples between the Bab-el-Mandeb and the Sea of Japan, who assailed every passer-by when they were strong enough, or who traded with friends by special arrangement, and robbed all others, acted on just the same principle. Whoever was not one of themselves, or an assured friend known to be capable of making unpleasant reprisals, was fair game. So it had been in the West, and so it was in the East, but more universally and more persistently, because it was long before great controlling Powers arose to keep order.

Here is a small example from the year 1716, chosen because it is so normal, so usual.* In that year the company, or, rather, its President and Council at Bombay, had to turn from other pressing occupations, to bring to his bearings a potentate, whom our historian calls the "Rodger" of Carwar. We should now say the Raja of Karwar, a port of less importance than it once was, lying to the south of Goa, in latitude 14° 49′ north and longitude 74° 8′ east. The seamen of the early eighteenth century, who as yet had no Harrison's chronometer, and were generally out in their longitudes, put it a full degree too much to the

* See "A Compendious History of the Indian Wars," by Clement Downing, 1737, pp. 15-20. I quote a minute part of a copious title-page, which promises accounts of the "Rise, Progress, and Strength of Angria the Pyrate," of the proceedings of "Commodore Matthews" in the Eastern Seas, and of pirates other than Angria, and also gives the leading notes in the author's life as officer in the East India Company's Marine Service, and engineer to the Great Mogul. Downing gives a curious picture of a phase of British history in the East. His little book is very rare, and deserves to be reprinted. Learned societies have spent their funds on books less worth preserving than Downing's.

west. Karwar, therefore, was on the route of the southern coast trade of Western India. It lay on the " starboard side," says Downing, of the River Kalinda, which falls into a bay with islands. The possession of such a place was a temptation to " piracy." There was a factory first established by the interloping association of Sir William Courten, and then taken over by the company. It carried on trade in fine muslins, and, of course, paid its footing to the Raja. But, though sufficiently enlightened to tolerate legitimate trade up to a point to be fixed by himself, the Raja was not proof against sudden temptations to revert to pillage. In 1716 he was subjected to one which was too much for him.

Mr. Bennet, a merchant of Surat, had come down the coast on a voyage to the Bay of Bengal somewhat late in the year, and too near the setting in of the south-west monsoon. His ship was driven ashore to the north of Karwar. Mr. Bennet had with him £15,000 for purposes of trade enclosed in iron boxes. Knowing the effect which the sight of this loot would infallibly have on a small Raja of the Malabar coast, he applied to the head of the Karwar factory for a guard. Except within the dominions of the Great Mogul, and while his greatness lasted, all factories were more or less forts, and had their armed men. A sergeant and fifteen men were sent to carry the treasure to the factory, and part of it was safely stored before the Raja found out what was going on under his very nose. When he did learn, he descended on the salvage party with a troop of horse, seized between £6,000 and £7,000, and, to make sure that the ship should give no further trouble, caused a large hole to be made in her. If this sort of thing had been done by an official of the Mogul in his great days, there would have been an authority to hear complaints and give redress. But there was nothing to be done with the little Rajas of the Malabar coast, except to take them by the throat and make them disgorge. The President at Bombay sent ships and soldiers to bring Karwar to reason. Both were officered by white men, and there were English sailors; but the bulk of the crews and troops were Lascars and Topassies— *i.e.*, Hat Men, half-bred Portuguese, and natives. We are so much accustomed to the immense military superiority of

Europeans and European-led natives in India, that we forget that it was not always so complete as it became in years after 1716. In the present case we cannot say that it was as manifest as it ought to have been.

To begin with, a detachment was sent to land through the surf. The boats, light galleys called " gallivats," were overturned, and the soldiers struggled ashore, with their powder wet and useless. The Raja's cavalry charged them. The English officers were wounded and taken, and so were forty of the Topassies. The Raja kept the white men, whom he tried to force or wheedle into his own service, and he cut off the noses of the Topassies. In the meantime the Raja had cut the factory off from the sea by throwing a boom across the mouth of the river. The first feeble effort having failed, more men were sent, to the number of 2,000, under command of Captain Gordon, " a gallant gentleman." They were landed in a more rational style, formed in a hollow square, with doctors and stores in the centre, and marched forward, led by Gordon. The Raja's cavalry threatened and his musketeers fired; but 2,000 more or less drilled men, commanded by white officers, even if they were only clerks who did military work at intervals, were amply sufficient to dispose of the Raja, if decently led. Unhappily, Gordon was disabled, and the command fell to one who was not " a gallant gentleman." He faced about at once, and made for the boats. To complete the scandal, some of the Raja's men got between the retreating force and the boats. The hollow square, which was not allowed to go forward fighting, had to sweep them away, and did so. After this shameful failure, the authorities at Bombay decided to end where, considering the quality of their land officers, they would have done better to begin. They established a blockade of Karwar. The Raja speculated in trade, and was interested in two ships which were coming from Muscat with Arabian horses, 100 in each. They were seized by the blockading ships, and he was brought to see reason, give up the treasure, release his prisoners, and pay for the damage done to Mr. Bennet's ship. It is to be observed that during these transactions, which lasted for months, he had failed to take the factory.

I certainly do not tell this story because it is a glorious one for the civilizing power, nor yet because it is particularly interesting, but because it is characteristic. The outbreak of the Raja was a typical example of the kind of childish and greedy explosion of violence which all Europeans trading to the East had to be prepared to meet at any moment. There were exceptions. While the Mogul Empire continued to be a reality, it could keep a reasonable measure of order, and would give protection to the foreign trader, when once he had received his permit to trade. But the Empire was confined to Northern India, and, as a rule, the Oriental Sovereign was just such another as the foolish Raja of Karwar, who could not resist a chance to seize a treasure-chest, though, if he had been capable of reflection, he would have foreseen that the English could do what in the end they did. But he could not think, neither he nor his like. Therefore in the end the European was driven to conquer, since it was only by being master that he could be sure of his safety.

Yet honesty imposes the obligation to confess that the Europeans did not become an influence on the side of order till they had fought out their quarrels among themselves. And that was not for two centuries and a half, or more. During that long period their activity tended to intensify whatever old and deeply rooted belief that men of other races were enemies who would plunder if they could and who were therefore to be plundered whenever possible, there was in the vast Eastern Seas. In so far as they acted on native morals at all, they did it by weakening them, and therefore diminishing such controlling power as there was. The Portuguese came to the East with the belief that they alone of all European peoples had a right to be there; with a deep contempt for the heathen, who, in their opinion, could possess no legitimate authority, and was by rights born to be the slave of the Christian, and with a fierce hatred of the Moslem and the Jew. Wherever there is trade there are Jews, and they were on the Malabar coast. To the Moslem it was always a just and pious act to conquer the Christian, and to the Christian it was never wrong to subdue and destroy the Moslem. In the faith that " paiens ont tort et Chretiens ont bon droit," the simple creed of the author of the "Chanson de Roland," the Portuguese had fallen on the trade of Western India and the Red Sea. For the heathen, who had never conquered them at home, they had more toleration than for the Moslem, who had once been their master. They would join with the Malabar "pirate" chief Timoja to seize Goa. For the "Rumis"— that is to say, for the traders who came from the Turkish, which had once been the Roman, Empire—they had no toleration. To have to learn, as they did, that the Venetians were helping their Moslem enemy only served to exasperate their rage. Venice, after lending her capital and skill to create the naval power of Portugal, found that it was turning aside the trade of the East to her detriment; therefore she helped the Turk. The rabid fury of Christian rivals was added to the disorders of the East. Holding, as they did, that the Christian had every right, and the unbeliever none, the Portuguese recognized no moral obligation towards those whom they looked upon as fair spoil. What they could take by open force they took. When it was necessary to piece out the hide of the lion by the skin of the fox, they lied and deceived. They helped the son to poison the father on condition that he gave them an establishment. When they had it, they enslaved him. This they did at Ormuz, in the Persian Gulf, that they might control the trade of Persia. All lies, said Mahomet, shall be counted for sin to a man on the day of judgment, save three: the lies he tells to reconcile friends who have quarrelled, the lies the Captain tells to deceive the enemy in war, and the lies husbands tell when they make promises to their wives. The unbeliever was always the enemy, and had no claim to the truth.

For a century the Portuguese set before the Oriental the example of a morality like his own, applied by a stronger power than his. They ruined the trade of the Rumis from the Red Sea to Malabar, and wherever they went they disturbed and they degraded. If they did not drive all ships save their own off the Eastern Seas, the reasons were, first, that they were not numerous, and then that they soon extended the limits of the just use of fraud and violence, and became unspeakably corrupt. A native shipping existed beside them for the port-to-port trade, and it im-

INDIAN PRINCE.

the "Chanson de Roland," the Portuguese had fallen on the trade of Western India and the Red Sea. For the heathen, who had never conquered them at home, they had more toleration than for the Moslem, who had once been their master. They would join with the Malabar "pirate" chief Timoja to seize Goa. For the "Rumis"— that is to say, for the traders who came from the Turkish, which had once been the Roman, Empire—they had no toleration. To have to learn, as they did, that the Venetians were helping their Moslem enemy only served to exasperate their rage. Venice, after lending her capital and skill to create the naval power of Portugal, found that it was turning aside the trade of the East to her detriment; therefore she helped the Turk. The rabid fury of Christian rivals was added to the disorders of the East. Holding, as they did, that the Christian had every right, and the unbeliever none, the Portuguese recognized no moral obligation towards those whom they looked upon as fair spoil. What they could take by open force they took. When it was necessary to piece out the hide of the lion by the skin of the fox, they lied and deceived. They helped the son to poison the father on condition that he gave them an establishment. When they had it, they enslaved him. This they did at Ormuz, in the Persian Gulf, that they might control the trade of Persia. All lies, said Mahomet, shall be counted for sin to a man on the day of judgment, save three: the lies he tells to reconcile friends who have quarrelled, the lies the Captain tells to deceive the enemy in war, and the lies husbands tell when they make promises to their wives. The unbeliever was always the enemy, and had no claim to the truth.

For a century the Portuguese set before the Oriental the example of a morality like his own, applied by a stronger power than his. They ruined the trade of the Rumis from the Red Sea to Malabar, and wherever they went they disturbed and they degraded. If they did not drive all ships save their own off the Eastern Seas, the reasons were, first, that they were not numerous, and then that they soon extended the limits of the just use of fraud and violence, and became unspeakably corrupt. A native shipping existed beside them for the port-to-port trade, and it im-

MURDER OF INDIAN PRINCE.
FROM F. VALENTIJN'S OUD EN NIEUW OOST—INDIEN.

proved. The native merchants of Western India, and of Surat in particular, who built ships of teak, adopted European models. Their own people supplied them with Lascar sailors and Seedy Boys, the men who served the Mogul Admiral, the Sidi, or Cid (the Lord). And this shipping grew better. At the close of the seventeenth century the Surat shipbuilders had adopted English models. Fine teak ships were built for the company and for the Crown in the eighteenth century at Bombay. Moorish ships, as the Europeans called them, were to be found all over the Eastern Seas, from China to Madagascar.

Why did they never go beyond them? It was not because their men feared to make the voyage. From the very beginning, Portuguese, English, and Dutch employed the Lascar sailors. They came and they went back with the knowledge that the " sea of darkness " could be passed in safety. There never was a time in the seventeenth century when Moorish ships could not have traded to Europe. France, which had so far no trade to the East of its own, would have welcomed them and their cargoes. England and Holland could not have said them nay. Shah Jehan, or Aurungzebe, could have compelled reciprocity by threatening their factories with extinction, for in his dominion they were helpless. Charles Lockyer, as we have seen, thought it quite possible that the merchants of Surat might one day take the Cape route themselves. There is but one answer to the question—bounds have been placed on the capacity of the East to learn.* The Indian shipbuilders, merchants, and seamen could make the vessel. When Captain Downton, in the sixth " separate voyage," chased a Moorish ship in the Red Sea, she fairly outsailed him. Some of these craft were of 1,000 tons, equal to the largest Europeans in bulk. But the Oriental could not acquire the knowledge of navigation, nor develop the confidence of command. He shrank from making the great voyage alone. His genius was rebuked before the European, and he commonly gave the command of his ships to an Englishman, Dutchman, or Frenchman. And though he could fight at

* Japan may seem to have proved the contrary. But is the Japanese exception fully established? And is Japan quite " the East " ?

sea, he could not fight well enough to compel respect. Great Mogul ships, which carried the pilgrims to Jeddah, and much wealth in merchandise, were taken easily by European pirates, who would never have dared to attack an English or Dutch Indiaman of the same size and equal armament. The greatest Indian Power could not protect its own ships. It could only force the European merchants to do the work by threatening to put them in prison, and ruin their trade if they refused or failed.

When the English and Dutch broke into the Eastern Seas, they began by adding to what the Portuguese were doing. They never did it quite as much, for there was an utterness of corruption in Portuguese India, and a puerile unreason to which the men of the North never attained. But, nevertheless, they proved to the Oriental that the Europeans could plunder one another as heartily as Malay or Malabarese could pillage all strangers. When the people of the Indian Archipelago saw Sir James Lancaster provide himself with a cargo by transferring one from a Portuguese carrack, we may be sure they did not trouble themselves with high political considerations, or reflect that this was a legitimate operation of war. They simply saw one European rob another, as they themselves would rob another Asiatic when they had the chance. And it was long before they saw anything else—they or any other Eastern people from the Mozambique Channel to the Sea of Japan. The trade of Europe with the East was built up by men who came holding money, or a sample of goods, in one hand, and pistol or cutlass in the other. " Sell to me, or I will plunder you, and perhaps kill you too," said Europe to Asia. " Keep away from my preserve, or I will do you a damage," said one European to another, and the answer was apt to be : " I do not allow that it is your preserve," or, " You claim more than you have a right to, and if you try to bar my road, I will put my mark on you." And that dialogue went on among men of the same race, for the chartered companies, the monopolists, would keep their warren to themselves, and the interloper was resolute to intrude. The struggle was at its hottest in the seventeenth and eighteenth centuries.

It was the heroic age of the merchant skipper. He was not merely the seaman who took the ship out and brought her back, he was the merchant, too, and in conditions which compelled him to be fighter and diplomatist. It was the case with all, but more—far more—with the English skipper than with any other. The Portuguese at once established a Government in the East in a bad way. The Dutch did the same in a far better way; but the English were content with a miminum of government, and left the men free to explore, to act, to negotiate. The Dutch skipper was a skipper and nothing else. The English skipper was half an ambassador, and he was not seldom at the end a ruling man in a factory which was on the way to become a State, or to help to make a State. Lancaster, a merchant and skipper, Sharpegh, Downton, the Middletons, Best, Saris, who were the same, and, in later generations, Sir John Gayer, Macrea, and many others, who became Presidents at Bombay or Madras, were sea captains. They had little enough support from home; commonly, indeed, they had rebuke and obstruction. But just because they were not mere parts of a great machine, such as was the Dutch Company, they were free to prove what men who have the root of the matter in them can do with an unsettled world to fight in, and the determination to achieve something solid. " Ainsi sera quiconcque en groyne "— the defiant motto of the Duchess of Brittany, "So shall it be maugre the beards of eastern sinners and timid directors," was the tacit rule of them all.

The life of Sir Henry Middleton affords two good examples of the fortunes of the sea trader in insecure times. In 1604 he sailed for the East with the *Red Dragon*, *Hector*, *Ascension*, and *Susan*. The squadron " broke ground " from Greenwich on Sunday, March 25th. It was fortunate to begin a voyage on a Sunday, and, as all the world knows, of ill omen to begin on a Friday. All the world does not know that there is no harm in sailing from an intermediate port and in the course of a voyage on a Friday. A careful Commander could put himself right with fortune by " breaking ground " on a Sunday. A short run out and back would do it, or even the shifting of the ship's place from one part of the harbour to another. It was only necessary to count either of them as the beginning of the voyage. The actual start might then be made on a Friday with safety. In this case the actual start was made on Sunday from Greenwich, but a delay was made in the Downs to muster the crews. A first examination seemed to show that they were incomplete, but when the squadron was finally on its way, so large a number of stowaways came out of hiding that the ships were found to be overmanned; a shift of the wind made it impossible for Middleton to land the excess, and so the intruders were necessarily carried on the voyage. Some of them had cause to regret that the wind did " souther " on Middleton when he was off Plymouth. By the time the squadron was off the Cape, which was not till the end of July, the scurvy was raging. " The wind at south-west, a gentle gale," says the historian of the voyage, " the general commanded the tacks aboard, intending to go about the Cape, but our sick men cried out so lamentably, for at present there were sick of the scurvy at least eighty men in our ship, not one able to help the other, who made a petition to the general, most humbly entreating him for God's sake to save their lives, and to put in for Saldania [Table Bay], otherways they were but dead men. The general perusing their pitiful complaint, and looking out of his cabin door, where did attend a swarm of lame and weak diseased cripples, who beholding this lamentable sight extended his compassion towards them, and granted their requests."*

Neither inhumanity nor zeal had moved Middleton to go about the Cape without stopping. He was especially instructed by the company not to touch at the " Saldania in anywise for the inconveniences of that island noted unto us by men of good experience." He was also stringently instructed that when it was necessary to land for refreshments he was " to give order to the preacher to prepare himself to preach to the people, being come together out of the several ships, making his choice of such fit arguments and places of Scripture as may be most agreeable to the

* " The Last East Indian Voyage," in publications of the Hakluyt Society, No. 19, edited by Mr. Bolton Corney, 1854.

time and occasion, whereby the whole company may be exhorted and taught the better to carry themselves in the general business; and that the preacher may have the more comfort in his ministry, we pray you be careful that all due respects be given him, not only for yourself, but by the whole company, that his doctrine and exhortations by contempt or neglect of his ministry, return not without profit." We may take it that men of good experience had told the pious company of occasions on which the preacher had been subjected to the interruptions such as those of the son of Belial, who cut short the sermon of Brother Felix Faber in the galley of Venice. It may well have taxed all the authority of Middleton to maintain quiet in the congregation if the weak and diseased cripples were compelled to listen with the smell of the land in their nostrils to a Puritanical preacher improving the occasion; but we do not hear that the preacher was called upon for his services, when, after seventeen days of effort, the ships did at last make Table Bay. They did obtain fresh meat—perhaps by the use of the tongue employed by Sir James Lancaster, when he came into the Bay on his first voyage for the merchants of London. "Then he spoke to them in the cattle's language which was never changed at the confusion of Babell, which was 'moath' for oxen and kine, and 'baa' for sheepe, which language the people understood very well without any interpreter." Having abated the scurvy by help of meat obtained not without some difficulties from the natives, the squadron went on and reached Bantam in December—ten months after leaving home.

They had now come to what the company's instructions call the "merchandising port" of the voyage. Middleton's orders were to pick up what cargo the company's agent at Bantam, William Starkey, had collected, send them back in some of his vessels, and go on with the others to the Moluccas to open a trade. The merchants of London, who were, in fact, laying the first stones of the foundations of the British Empire in India, had no prophetic knowledge of what they were about. Their most ardent wish was to reach the Spice Islands, and tap that valuable trade; but if they did not foresee the conquest of Hindustan and the Deccan, neither did they realize what a wasp's-nest they were sending their General into. The Moluccas had long been the scene of a sanguinary scuffle, in which the actors were native Kings of Tidoré and Ternate, the Spaniards, and the Portuguese. It was, said Southey, the most wicked history he had met in the course of his extensive reading, and a fifth was now added to the combatants. The Dutch had struck in. The English had made peace with the King of Spain and Portugal in 1603, and hoped to enjoy good trade in the Moluccas; but the Dutch had not made peace, and were not to make it for many a long year. They did not even make their twelve years' truce till 1609. Peace or no peace, truce or no truce, it was their fixed determination to keep the Spice Islands to themselves; so when Middleton left Bantam on January 16th, 1605, he had an enemy to deal with on whom neither he nor his directors had counted.

He carried a foe with him who was terribly familiar to all in those seas, but more especially known to the English. Hardly have the *Red Dragon* and the *Ascension* left Bantam before the history of their voyage begins to abound in such entries as these: "This day our purser, William Griffen, and Master Foster died, both of the flux." "The seventeenth day died of the flux William Lewed, John Jenkens, and Samuel Porter." "This day died Henry Stiles our master carpenter, and James Varnam and John Iberson, all of the flux." "At night one of our men leaped overboard, having the calenture, and three more died of the flux—their names were William Bellidine, William Pooter, Gideon Marten, and James Vennes." It was the well-grounded belief of Dr. Johnson that of those who die in war "a very small part ever felt the stroke of an enemy; the rest languished in tents and ships amid damps and putrefactions; pale, torpid, spiritless, helpless, groping and groaning, unpitied among men, made obdurate by long continuance of hopeless misery, and were at last whelmed in pits, or heaved into the ocean, without notice and without remembrance. By incommodious encampments and unwholesome stations, where courage is useless and enterprise impracticable, fleets were

A KORA-KORA.

From F. Valentijn: "Oud en nieuw cost-Indien."

silently dispeopled, and armies sluggishly melted away."*
Early trade was a kind of war, and subject to its laws. Of
the " thousands and tens of thousands " who died to prepare
the expansion of modern commerce, only a comparatively
small part " felt the stroke of an enemy " or perished in
shipwreck.

When Middleton did reach Amboina and begin to open
a trade with the Portuguese garrison, the Dutch turned up.
Gaspar de Melo, the Portuguese Captain, had been on the
whole friendly, and was loud in professions of his determination to defy the Dutch ; but when they came he made a
tame surrender, for which he afterwards lost his head.
When the natives saw that the Dutch were masters, they
declined to trade with us. It was the same story at Tidoré
and Ternate. In vain did the *Red Dragon* rescue the King
of Ternate and certain Dutch friends of his when they were
fiercely pursued by the men of Tidoré, who were in alliance
with the Portuguese. The King of Ternate was trembling
when he scrambled out of his " caracara " (Kōra, Kōra)
on to the deck of the *Red Dragon*, and Middleton, thinking
he was cold, lent him " a black damask gown, laid with
gold lace, and lined with unshorn velvet, which the King
put upon his back, but never had the manners to surrender
it again, but kept it as his own." The monarch of Ternate
and his Dutch friends were profuse in advice to Middleton
to avoid the people of Tidoré and the deceitful Portuguese.
He thought he could manage the Portuguese, and went to
Tidoré. Whether his confidence was justified cannot be
known, for while he was negotiating, and the Portuguese
appeared to be friendly, up came the Dutch, blew up the
Portuguese fort, and spoiled our trade. They spirited
away even native canoes coming to deliver goods already
paid for. In short, the Hollanders wiped their boots on
the servants of the Worshipful Company. The fury of the
insulted English glows on the pages of the narrative of
the fourth voyage. " He [the King of Ternate, to wit]
said the Hollanders did threaten him to forsake his country,
and to establish a factory in Tidoré if he did let the English

* " Thoughts on the Late Transactions respecting Falkland's
Islands."

tarry in the country and establish a factory. They [the Hollanders] saying we were thieves and robbers, and so, if he did trust us, he should find us; saying that Holland was able to set out twenty ships for England's one, and that the King of Holland was stronger by sea than all Christendom besides; with many untruths of their own people and country's commendations, and disparagement of our people and country and of all other Christian princes. If this frothy nation [the rage of our injured countrymen disturbed his judgment in words. The Dutch may be many things, but ' frothy ' they never were] may have the trade of the Indies to themselves, which is the thing they hope for, their pride and insolence will be intolerable."

The *Red Dragon* and *Ascension* had other adventures, but this much of their cruise is all we need look at to learn how European was treated by European in the East. There was worse to come when the Dutch fairly attacked our ships at sea and took them by force. The *Red Dragon* herself was destined to be one day taken by them after a stout fight. Worse than all was the horrible story of torture and hypocrisy enacted at Amboina in 1620 by the Dutch factor, Van Speult, on the unhappy English merchants. Take the Amboina story by itself, and it is difficult to believe that our ancestors, who left it unavenged for years, and then accepted a compensation in money, had any measure of honour and spirit. Van Speult, an excitable coward, eager to please his masters of the Dutch Company, trumped up a charge of conspiracy against the English merchants in Amboina, and extorted confessions from them, not only by the use but by the illegal misuse of torture; for the application of torture was regulated by law, and Van Speult disregarded the law by which he professed to act. I fear that when the news of the outrage at Amboina reached the ears of the merchants of London, they were less affected by the cruelty shown to Towerson and his companions than by the loss of the trade.* The time was not

---

* Let us take Dr. Johnson's advice, and clear our minds of cant. If Van Speult had had any rational reason for believing that Towerson and the others were engaged in a conspiracy to seize the island, he would have done nothing contrary to the then usual practice of England by making use of torture to an extreme degree. Torture

very far off when the servants of the London Company in their Island of St. Helena were to show that they could trump up charges, inflict the death penalty, and flog men and women brutally, with as little regard for evidence and as little humanity as ever was shown by Van Speult. And these persons were countrymen living under the company's rule, with their wives and their daughters. The Captains and factors who served the London merchants were not guilty of the monopolizing greed of the Portuguese and Dutch; their reasonable claim was to be allowed to trade freely where no other people had an established monopoly. Nobody can, I think, read the letters sent home by them, or examine accounts of what they did, without coming to the conclusion that the English in the East in early days showed much moderation and self-restraint. If "advocati diaboli" from Portugal and from Holland were to reply that this virtue was imposed on them by the King's orders, that they were not to assail the Portuguese subjects of his friend King Philip III., and, as regards the Hollanders, by the fact that the Dutch Company was a much better armed concern than their own, I am afraid that it would be necessary to leave those foreigners in the undisputed possession of their opinion. The company's servants were certainly not incapable of displaying what Dr. Johnson called "the morality of a sailor,' and forcing trade on reluctant customers.

Though the company clung to the hope of sharing the

---

was constantly used at that time—not, as Lord Burghley put it, with fine discrimination, in order to obtain evidence, but for "discovery." In common criminal cases it was not used, because nobody was much concerned to know what had been the past, and who were the friends of a common homicide, horse-thief, or shop-lifter, because the prisoner was carefully deprived of all means of defence, and because it was never necessary to prove the prisoner guilty, but only to find a jury which could be packed or coerced to say that he or she was guilty. But where, as in cases of witchcraft or treason, it was thought desirable to know by whom the prisoner was instigated or helped—to obtain "discovery"—then torture was used. It had been employed in 1614 just before the Amboina affair, for the purpose of compelling a Puritan divine of the name of Peacham to confess that he was guilty of treason. The case against Van Speult was not that he applied the torture, but that he cannot possibly have believed in the existence of the conspiracy which he set about to discover. But did the councillors of King James believe in the guilt of Peacham?

Spice Islands with the Dutch till it was forced to desist, it applied itself early to the discovery of alternatives. In 1610 it sent out a squadron of three ships—the *Trade's Increase*, a ship of a 1,000 tons, the *Peppercorn*, both built in the company's yard at Deptford, and the *Darling*. The launch of the *Trade's Increase* was a great event. She was the largest merchant ship so far built in England. The King, Queen, and the Prince of Wales, Henry, were present. The voyage was popular, and many distinguished persons took shares. Sir Henry Middleton went in command, and he took with him a staff of " merchants " and clerks who were to conduct the trade under his direction. His orders were to make for Surat and the Red Sea, establish factories if possible, send his chief merchant, Mr. Femmel, on a mission to the Mogul, and end up in the Indian Archipelago. There was an element of exploration in his voyage. He was to make notes of currents, tides, anchorages, and all such knowledge as was of value to trade. The company would not have been what it was, and the Governor, Sir Thomas Smith, would have been greatly wanting to himself, if Sir Henry had not been weightily exhorted to see that prayers were said, piety practised, and all such conduct as was calculated to deprive the venture of a blessing—drunkenness and gambling being prominently named—rigidly suppressed.

A whole chapter, as large as this or larger, would be required to do justice to the Sixth Voyage. We will confine ourselves to one episode of a long story, because it shows us the sea trader contending with the brutality of Asiatic potentates. The reader will take it for granted that the voyage began on April 4th, 1610, and met the usual fortunes on its way to the Red Sea, and that it was close to its hoped-for " merchandise ports " by the close of the year. Middleton had now to deal, not with monopolizing Dutchmen and small Malay " Kings," but with the Pashas and Agas of the Sultan whose garrisons dominated the coast of Arabia, and who one and all proved themselves to be " unspeakable Turks." There was, to begin with, the Governor of Aden— a ruffian. He, and, indeed, all the rest, went on a common rule. They would allow goods to be landed, but they would permit no trade or payment till they had the leave of the Pasha in Sena'a, who was their chief. A Spenlow and Jorkins see-saw was kept up by all of them, and they took care to be on the right side for their own interests by impounding not only whatever portable property the English might send ashore, but also such sailors or merchants as came within their reach. Then they hectored and demanded ransom. The General, his Captains and merchants, seem to have been fairly well aware of the character of the official Turk, perhaps because some of them had gained experience in the service of the Turkey Company. Yet they allowed themselves to be deceived—it may be because the Turkish Pasha and Agas, being so far away from home and in so wild a world as the Eastern Seas, were even more mendacious and violent than they were in the Levant. They were inordinate in grasping at baksheesh, and were encouraged by the docility of the traders who came from India, and the Pilgrims who landed at Jeddah on the way to Mecca.

The Governor of Aden gave the English a preliminary taste of the quality of Turkish officialdom by his unreason, insolence, and grasping. Middleton, in the hopes of doing better, and in any case in order to put his fortune to the test, went on to Mocha with the *Trades Increase* and *Darling*, leaving Captain Nicholas Downton with the *Peppercorn* to treat with the Governor of Aden. At Mocha he found another Turk of the same character, but of a more deceptive, crafty, and deadly quality. There were negotiations, formalities, questions of Custom dues, and so forth, to be cleared up, and of course Jorkins at Mocha could do nothing without the consent of Spenlow at Sena'a. The Mocha partner was Regib Aga, and his senior at Sena'a was Jaffier Pasha. Regib was what the sailor would call very, let us say, excessively politeful. He invited Middleton to land, to put goods on shore, to bring his carpenters and men to put together the pinnace which had been brought out in parts from England. Middleton was plainly enough suspicious, but the Aga was plausible, the squadron was in need of provisions, and it was desirable to get the pinnace put together. So he landed, taking with him some sixty of his crew and merchants and the parts of the pinnace. Then came an episode which gives the impression that Regib Aga, besides being a liar and extortioner of the first water, had a vein of undergraduate practical joker. He assured Middleton that such a distinguished guest as he was must be duly honoured in public ceremony by being clothed in the " Grand Senior's Vest." The General had, perhaps, an uneasy British feeling that he would look like a fool; but he reflected that he must stay for months at Mocha, and must needs be on good terms with the Aga. So he consented to be received by the whole official world in full dress, clothed in a vest of cloth of gold, mounted on a horse which the Aga held for him, and went through a burlesque of the ceremony observed when an Ambassador was formally received by the Grand Vizier. Then he found out the quality of his host.

One evening, while the English were off their guard, they were attacked by a mob of the Aga's men. Eight were butchered and the others made prisoners, fourteen among them being wounded. At the same time three boats put off to seize the *Darling*, which was lying somewhat near the shore. The *Darling's* crew, relying, it would seem, on the fallacious civility of Regib Aga, were not keeping watch; but when their deck was invaded by his ruffians they rallied at once. The forecastle and poop of the vessel of the time were commonly screened off from the waist by barriers called " cobridge heads," which were loop-holed for musketry fire. There are many instances of ships being boarded at the waist and afterwards cleared of boarders by the crew which had rallied behind the " cobridges "; and this is probably what happened in the case of the *Darling*, for the Turkish soldiers would naturally attempt to scramble aboard where the side was lowest. Three of the *Darling's* men were killed, but they despatched twenty-six of the Turks and sent the others off quicker than they came, and with payment of an instalment of their deserts.

The outrage took place on November 28th. Until December 22nd Middleton and the fifty wounded and un- wounded merchants and sailors with him were imprisoned at Mocha " in irons both feet and hands." The *Trades*

Increase and *Darling* lay off the port in need of stores, not knowing what to do, and the *Peppercorn* was at Aden contending with another Turk of the stamp of Regib Aga. On December 22nd Middleton and part of the prisoners were sent up to Sena'a to be put at the disposal of the Pasha, Jaffier. If the Aga did not send them all, the reason was that he kept back the carpenters, who were forced to work at the pinnace in irons. The Turk meant to keep her for himself when finished. The prisoners were marched up country under a strong guard by night, and mounted on "asnecoes." On the way Mr. Pemberton, one of the merchants, contrived to make his escape by pushing into the bush and getting off undetected; but hear his own account of the adventure, as given to Middleton in a letter written in the following March :

" To satisfy your worship of my arrival and safety after I gave you the slip, was thus ; having taken a conceit of captivity under these heathen tyrants [*i.e.*, believing they were being carried off to slavery], and there seemed to my judgment to prove no loss [*sic ?* less] by the Aga's working, I watched my time, and slipped aside and travelled down to the seaside about seven or eight miles to the southwards of the ships, where, going by the seaside, I found a canoe, but never an oar, but God so provided for me that, wading along with her to windward, found two gengathoes and with them an oar with a pole, which pole I put out like a bowsprit and with my garter made it fast, and thereon hung my shirt, and with the oar, though with much ado, and great pain, steered her, but could not guide her so well as I would, but came December 23rd on the offside of the *Increase*, and so far that had it not been for one poor fellow, under God, I might have been in danger of perishing, this being about nine of the clock in the morning, but blessed be God, I arrived all spent with labour and want of drink, having drunk all my own water that nature could afford me, for which blessing with many other, God make me thankful."

While Pemberton was enjoying the reward of his bold push for freedom, his commander and shipmates were enduring the miseries of a fourteen days' march to Sena'a, and the brutal reception given them by Jaffier Pasha when they did reach the town, "where," so Middleton records in his letter of advice unto all English ships to shun the Red Sea, "for a welcome we were anew imprisoned and the most part clapped in weighty irons, where at last, coming to have sentence of the Pasha, he adjudged all our goods on shore, with our pinnace, confiscate to the Grand Turk's use, and praising his own mild nature in not making us captives or putting us to the sword, accounting it a great good turn to let our persons depart."

After abundant bullying in the true old Turkish fashion, Jaffier Pasha allowed the English prisoners to return to Mocha on condition that thirty of the best of them were to remain as hostages in the hands of Regib Aga. He retained them as a security that the English ships would not retaliate by intercepting the native trading vessels from India which were due by the end of May. The Pasha declared that he acted by orders from Constantinople to punish the unbelievers for coming so close to Mecca, the Holy Place of Islam. He added that Regib Aga had acted by his orders. These were palpable lies, and, in fact, the Pasha and his subordinates were beginning to be afraid that they had gone too far. So long as the English ships were free to act they could blockade Mocha, and even stop the pilgrim traffic to Jeddah. Then they would cut off the supply of baksheesh, and not improbably bring the wrath of the Sultan down on his officers. The Turkish plan was to paralyze the ships by retaining the hostages, till the trade from India was safely delivered, and then it would be in the discretion of the Pasha to keep or to break his promises.

This was exactly how the situation appeared to the man to whom the command of the ships had passed when Middleton was captured—Captain Nicholas Downton of the *Peppercorn*, who had been left behind at Aden. Downton had sailed for the brilliant privateering Earl of Cumberland in the Elizabethan times. It is as certain as a thing not directly proved can be, that he was the Nicholas Downton who distinguished himself in command of one of the Earl's ships in the destruction of the Portuguese

carrack *Cinco Chagas* (the *Five Wounds* of Christ). It is
probable that he had sailed for the Turkey Company, for
he knew the nature of the Turk well. He was a man who
reminds the reader of his letters* and reports, of Shakespeare's Fluellen, the rather pedantic officer in whom
there was none the less much care and valour. He wrote
laboured English, manifestly copied from the antithetical
euphuistic style popular in his youth; but he wrote sense,
and it was not seldom the case that the force of his meaning pierced direct and penetrating through the buckram
cover of his words. Downton came up from Aden after
the capture of Middleton. He did not transfer himself to
the *Trades Increase*, as he was entitled to do, but remained
in the *Peppercorn* to keep a vigilant watch on certain bad
elements in her crew. Some of the English prisoners were
released by the Pasha's orders, and some of the *Peppercorn*'s
men who had been seized at Aden contrived to escape
and rejoined him at Mocha. To Downton it was perfectly
clear that Regib and Jaffier were not to be trusted, and that
the best way of compelling them to release their prisoners
was to blockade Mocha, but the native ships were not
due for some time, and he had to consider the position of
the captives. When Middleton was allowed to return to
Mocha an exchange of letters took place between him and
his officers who were still free. Pemberton, who had a
pretty talent for planning escapes, suggested that the
General should disguise himself with dirt and make a run
for the boats. The Turks, who were playing with the
English till it was safe to be brutal, allowed them to correspond freely. Pemberton's plan seems to have hurt
Middleton's sense of dignity. His prudence and his very
pardonable anxiety as to the safety of himself and his fellow-
captives caused him to be considerably disturbed by the
fierceness of Downton. The "Lieutenant-General," to give
him his official title, sent what he confessed was "a bragging
letter" to be delivered to the Aga. It threatened furious
reprisals. Middleton did not send on the letter, which had
given the captives a fright. Some of them were, in Down-

* My account of the events in the Red Sea is based on "Letters
received by the East India Company," vol. i., edited by Mr. F. C.
Danvers.

ton's opinion, "fear-blasted fellows." The General implored his second in command to hold his hand, to remember that the trade was not yet due, and to look for water and fresh provisions on the west of Abyssinia. Downton did find refreshment among the "Abescins" and obeyed Middleton for the present, but told him plainly that he could not consent to take orders from an imprisoned commander. It is highly probable that if Middleton had been still a prisoner at the end of May, Downton would have kept his threat to make the " scale " of Mocha—*i.e.*, the " scala " or " échelle " as trading ports were called in the Levant—unapproachable.

Before that time Middleton had escaped with fifteen of the prisoners, and by a device not much more dignified than Mr. Pemberton's. He learnt that Regib was going in state to a villa to hold a feast. Having warned the boats of his ships to be ready to take him, he made his guards drunk with arrack, and caused himself to be carried down to the landing-place in a barrel. The details of the escape cannot be made out clearly. There was plainly a rush at the end, and an alarm in the town. While Middleton and fifteen others reached the boats, all were not so fortunate. We hear of the " unwieldly fat " of Mr. Femmell as having been his ruin, but how does not quite appear; a letter signed by him and another merchant, Mr. John Williams, throws a limited light, somewhat after the fashion of Mr. Pickwick's dark lantern, on a scene of agitation. The " we " and the " I " alternate till it is not possible to say what happened to which. " Our ill fortune in not escaping proceeded of two causes: the first, Thomas Eves, the armourer, going down to the bridge to put something into the boat, and returned a swift pace till he passed the Aga's house, then he took off his shoes and ran through the streets with all the force he could, whereupon all the town rose after him. The second cause was the foolish dealing of that idiot and white-livered fellow the coxswain, who, seeing us hardly pursued, and we waving to have the boat sheer in, we being in the water up to the armpits, fell to leeward of us, it was no small grief to us to hear your worship reprehending, asking what he had done, nay, if he had stayed the boat where they sheered in, we had gotten her. My pistol, I thank God, was a means to save my life, for two soldiers at once assailing me, I placed two bullets in one of them, who lieth by it, I hear, the second purposing to have cloven my head. I warded it with my pistol. The blow was so violent that his sword fell out of his hand into the sea. By this time there came a Turk who knew me, and protected me from further harm. We hope that in due time we shall be delivered, and must have patience during the limited [*i.e.*, the appointed] time, till which we beseech your worship's forbearance."

Whether the obese Mr. Femmel or Mr. Williams made this effective use of his pistol, I cannot say. Poor Mr. Femmel was not destined to see deliverance. Before the end of the limited time came, he was dead. The Aga asked him to dinner, and Mr. Femmel was so rash as to threaten to bring him into trouble at Stambul. Regib smiled affably, but Mr. Femmel died after that dinner, and an examination of the body convinced the surgeon that he had been poisoned.

When he was again on his own quarterdeck, the General acted as Downton had advised. Their little tiff made no difference in their friendship. Middleton was by nature a moderate man, and he did no more than was necessary to secure the release of his crew, the return of the pinnace, and some compensation for confiscated goods. He was also a just man, and it pained him to see that the compensation would come, not from the pockets of Jaffier and Regib, but from the Indian traders, who would be forced by the Turks to pay the cost of raising the blockade. Finally, he had, as agent of the company, to consider that, if heavy loss were inflicted on these traders, their sovereign, the Mogul, would probably make English merchants, who wished to establish themselves in his dominions, pay, and so to some extent it turned out.

After months of trouble and loss in the Red Sea, the English left for the coasts of India in the hope of finding some compensation for their losses by trade. But they found the Portuguese in possession of the anchorage at Surat, and were unable to force an entry for themselves. Other months of loss followed, and Middleton did not even succeed in making effective reprisals on the Portuguese. The company's Captains were, in fact, hampered doubly. They knew that King James was desirous to maintain peace with Spain, which then included Portugal, and was peremptory in forbidding attacks on the Portuguese, though he allowed that his subjects might defend themselves if attacked. The company was entirely dependent on the King, and could not afford to offend him. Neither could its Captains quarrel too violently with native princes, to whom they had to look for favour. Therefore, they had to keep their reprisals within bounds. When on this voyage the English did seize a Portuguese ship at Dabul, Downton, who made the capture, took strong measures to prevent his crew from plundering her, and forced them to give up booty they had taken. The element of sheer freebooters who, in after times sailed with Kidd, Avery, Seager, Taylor, and others in those seas, was present in the company's ships, but was kept in check.

After months of little or no success on the western coast of India, Middleton and his council of merchants and captains had to decide whether it would not be better to go on to Bantam, and cut their losses in the Red Sea. But to have done this would have been to leave the Turk insufficiently punished. The natives, too, had shown no good will at Surat, and less scruple was felt as to injuring them. The Portuguese, who had shown themselves the most hateful of all (nothing could exceed the insolence of their officer at Surat), were also to be chastised if possible. Finally, it was known that another expedition had left England for the Red Sea, and there was good hope of meeting the ships there, when the united force would be able to bring Turks, Indians, and Portuguese alike to their bearings.

So they went back to the Red Sea, and there met Captain Saris—he who, first of all Englishmen, sailed to Japan—and Captain Towerson. The new-comers did not get on very well with Middleton. There was, in fact, a great deal of wrangling among the commanders, to which Downton attributed the comparative insuccess of their operations. Saris, who appears on the whole to have been a rather brutal man given to looking at an immediate advantage and not beyond, was all for extorting compensation from the native ships, since they were to be taken easily. Middleton would have preferred to find some more direct way of chastising the Pasha and the Agas. Saris, too, was rather extortionate in his demands of a share of whatever was obtained for his own expedition. The " Generals " came to something like an open quarrel, and their subordinates, among whom Downton was active, had considerable difficulty in settling a *modus vivendi*. In the end they did combine, of course at the cost of the native ships from India. When the Kings rage, the Argives are beaten, as we know. The operations have been described as of a semi-piratical character, and perhaps they were. In a general element of lawlessness, in which the Sultan's officers were the worst offenders, the English had to choose between anvil or hammer, and they were not disposed to be anvil. Compensation was obtained at the immediate cost of the Indian traders. Later on their grievances were produced against the company at Surat, and it did not prove easy to make a settlement. Saris parted rudely from Middleton without firing the salute which the sea manners of the age required him to give to his colleague.

It would be pleasant to follow the fortunes of all the Captains who took part in this campaign in the Red Sea. Middleton died at Bantam; Saris went far East to begin a great work; Downton, after making the voyage home described in the last chapter, returned in command of a " voyage " of four ships. He it was who inflicted the final defeat on the Portuguese at Surat, and established the English factory on a secure basis, or made it possible for the factors to establish themselves. After losing his only son during the fight near Surat, he, too, died, at Bantam, and was buried by the side of his old commander. But these tales have been told in other and more formal histories,* which record embassies, treaties, and wars. We are concerned with the life of the men. Middleton's troubles, sufferings, and retaliation are interesting because they are as complete examples as could well be found of what were the ex-

* They are fully told, with ample references to authorities, in Sir W. Hunter's unfinished " History of British India."

periences of all who came to trade in the East for generations. Such misfortunes as his might very well have befallen a trader in China down to the very middle of the nineteenth century, in the Persian Gulf or Red Sea, or among the islands of the Indian Archipelago, till quite as late or later. It is, in fact, only a few years since the crew of a steamer under the British flag were prisoners in Acheen, much after the manner of the merchants and sailors of the *Trade's Increase* and the *Peppercorn*.

Their experience must very soon have disposed of the illusions with which they came to the Eastern Seas. The Portuguese, indeed, came with the belief that they would find a variation of what they were already familiar with in Morocco. But to some extent the Dutch, and to a far greater extent the English, were prepared to meet with states such as they knew in Europe. They talked of the great and potent King or Prince of this or that, as they might have spoken of a King of France. Before a generation was passed, they may be found referring to the Mogul himself, who, indeed, was a potent sovereign in the Asiatic world, as the " toy-loving master " of the Governor of Surat. They were actually prepared to promote friendly relations with native rulers by supplying them with English wives. The request of a Malay Prince, that he might be provided with one, was seriously entertained, and only rejected by the company on the ground that, if she became a favourite, the native wives would poison her. A shareholder of the company was ready to supply his daughter—a virtuous gentlewoman well trained for a housewife, and of admired skill with her needle. That the proposal was only saved from being monstrous by being ridiculous did not occur to anybody. But that was in very early days. A few years of actual intercourse taught us that the " potent " chiefs of Asia were indeed but children of a larger growth, and too often of the stamp of the ill-conditioned little brat who thinks it amusing to inflict pain by cutting off the wings of small birds, or setting the cat's tail on fire. They soon learned to act on Middleton's counsel, as given in his " Letter of Advice," and to " trust not any, but stand upon your guard." They might have to submit to these children with the strength of men, but they knew them for what they were. The stupid unreason of such persons as the Pasha and his Agas in Arabia was too palpable not to be understood. It was, from the first, obvious that the English ships could blockade the ports, and cut off the trade. But the prospect of securing a little immediate booty blinded their puerile senses to the ultimate consequences of their acts.

We have seen the European traders in rivalry with one another, and in conflict with more or less dangerous native powers. Even the " Rodger of Carwar " was somebody, and the Pasha of the Grand Senior was a serious bully. But the sea trader had to deal with potentates who were below the humble level of the small Raja's of the Malabar coast—with mere chiefs of less than semi-barbarians. The process was always pretty much the same, and multiplicity of examples affords little novelty. It was the just observation of Thoreau that nobody need waste time in reading numerous accounts of common murders. He has only to satisfy himself by the study of one good example what the nature of common murder is, and then he may be sure that one specimen differs from another only in accidents both separable and unimportant. A trade bargain with a savage stands on the same footing, and when we have seen one, we have seen all. Mr. Robert Drury, who had certainly resided in Madagascar*—whether, as he affirms, in innocent captivity to native masters, or as some have plausibly suspected, in association with pirates—will show how the thing was. He had been redeemed by one Captain Mackett, who turned up on the coast to trade, and made himself useful by acting as interpreter. The fact that the goods which Captain Mackett, and other captains came to buy were just human beings, to be bought to labour as slaves in British plantations, or to be smuggled into slavery in Spanish colonies, makes but a trifling difference. The process would have been the same if they had been in search of pepper. Having premised that Drury, who was, as Captain Mackett was prepared to certify, " an honest, industrious man," spent a few days in accustoming his body to the

* " Madagascar ; or, Robert Drury's Journal during Fifteen Years' Captivity on that Island," second edition, 1731, pp. 430, 432, and 437.

long disused luxury of clothes, and his tongue to the pronunciation of English, and was then ready for service, we can let him speak:

"I accompany'd the two Captains [*i.e.*, Mackett and Bloom] to Ter Trimmonongarevo, to whom they went in order to settle some circumstances relating to the trade; this being the general custom all over the island. The King of each place makes terms, and settles one universal price, to which all the people are obliged to conform, and this renders trading very easy, and free from quarrels and disturbances. They presented the King with a fine gun, gilded on the barrel, and japan'd. ... A few days after came messengers from Ter Mourne desiring the Captains to come up the River Mernee, he having a great many slaves to sell, and being lame could not take a long journey, but would come down on the banks of that River to a town near enough for the trade. They agreed that the *Sarah* should go, so ordering a longboat out to sound before them, I went on board, and we sailed with an easy gale, but could find no convenient harbour or road in the mouth of Mernee; but three leagues on this side a convenient place for anchoring in a salt-water river was found, from whence the two Captains and myself went up the river a great way till a canoe took us in and carried us to the town where Ter Mourne was with his wives and people. ... There we remained four or five days, bought all the slaves they had, and agreed to send the long boat once a week while they stayed. ... We returned that evening to the ship, and the next day built a house for to carry on the trade in. The natives seeing our resolution to stay, they built several others near it to serve us with rice, milk, fruits, and other necessaries. [Query, the native strong drink, *toak*.] I went often to the town to hear news, but it was a month before the people came back from the wars. They came down the river in canoes, having had good success. At length the King arrived with the corpse of his brother, who was killed in the fight. He put off his burial for a fortnight, till he had settled affairs with us, and also given audience to his brother's embassadors, who were waiting for him. Capt. Mackett, hearing of his return, came up to town again well attended, with his trumpeter sounding before him ... and then all we white men, as well Captain Burgess, and the rest, as those who came with us, marched in order two abreast, the trumpeter sounding before the Captain, with a crowd of black mob after us, the shells blowing and drums beating in the King's pallisade to complement him. Deaan Toke Offu, who knew how to treat white men, had ordered two stools for the Captain and surgeon to sit on. After the usual complements of *Salamonger umbay*

CIVILIZING THE NATIVES.
From F. Valentijn: "Oud en nieuw oost-Indien."

reciprocally had passed, I being interpreter, we settled the matter of trade, and then the Captain made presents of a gun or two, etc., and the King presented him with a slave, etc. He also gave me a girl of twelve years old, which I sold immediately to John Pro."

They remained to make the King's Court look grand at a reception of ambassadors from another potentate, and then the slaves were delivered. If the scene had been the Island of Sumatra, the goods bought had been gums and spices, and the great man whose permission to trade was to be obtained by respectful address and acceptable present, all would have been done in just the same way down to the trumpeter. Till the eighteenth century had begun, the ships of the East India Company carried trumpeters who were the best paid of the petty officers. It was their function to add dignity to the approach of the Captain as he came, well-attended, and well-armed, with his weather eye lifting to detect signs of possible treachery, to open negotiations with Ter Trimmonongarevo and his like.

CHAPTER VIII

THE INTRUDERS ON THE WEST

In the thirteenth chapter of the nineteenth book of his " General and Natural History of the Indies: the Isles and Mainland of the Ocean Sea," Gonzalo Fernandez de Oviedo records this event:

"In the year one thousand five hundred and twenty-seven, an English Sea Rover, on the pretence that he was going about to discover, came with a great ship on his way back from Brazil on to the coast of the Mainland, and from there crossed over to this Island of Española, and came close to the harbour mouth of this city of San Domingo, and sent his boat manned by his people, and asked leave to come in here, saying that he came with wares, and to trade, and upon the instant Francisco de Tapia, the Alcaide [*i.e.*, commander of the fort] gave order to fire a discharge of powder from the castle at the ship, which was standing right into the port. And when the English saw that, they stood out again, and those in the boat took themselves off, and followed the ship. And indeed the Alcaide erred in what he did, for if that warship had come in, she could not have gone out again save with the leave of this city and its castle. So that seeing the welcome which was given them, they went back again to the island of San Juan [now Porto Rico] and having entered into the Bay of San German, had talk with those of that town, and begged food of them, complaining of those of this city [San Domingo to wit], saying that they had not come as enemies, but to trade with their money and wares if they were suffered, and some food was given them, and the ship paid for it with tin for making pots and other things, and went its way to return to Europe, where it is thought she never came, for never was that ship heard of more."

Who this Sea Rover may have been is not, and never will be, known. A mistake as to the date in Eden's translation of "Oviedo" led Hakluyt to think that the great ship which came from Brazil was the vessel in which Sebastian Cabot, and an Englishman named Pert, made, or are supposed to have made, for there is a doubt, an unsuccessful voyage to the West in 1516. Cabot in 1527 was in the service of Spain. The "English" Rover remains a nameless man, who, in the old pirate phrase, "hailed from the Sea," and was perhaps one of the forgotten Bristol adventurers, the forerunners of Hawkins and Drake. He plays his part in history as a species of herald come to assert England's claim to share with the Spaniards in the trade and wealth of the New World. The order he received to depart was Spain's refusal to accept the demand. When Francisco de Tapia gave his ill-considered order to warn the Rover off by a mere blast of powder, he was, in fact, uttering a defiance to all comers. That handful of powder was the beginning of a war, which in one form or another lasted for two centuries and a half. The cause of the war was the pretension of Spain to keep the New World to herself. The combatants were on the one side the Spaniards, on the other, and successively, the Adventurers of the sixteenth century, the Buccaneers of the seventeenth, and the Smugglers of the eighteenth.

This Spanish claim was based on the Bull of Alexander VI., which has long stood as the type of arrogant pretension. The Pope divided—so the common expression has it—the New World between Spain and Portugal, giving away what was not his to give. Francis I., the French King, and Elizabeth, agreed in refusing to allow any validity to the grant, and the refusal was very natural. Natural, too, as long as the fight lasted, was the ridicule which the assailants of Spain cast on the judgment of what they considered an incompetent court. Now that the fight is over we can afford to be fair even to Alexander VI. The just thing to say of his action in 1493 is that, being appealed to as arbitrator by the only claimants then in the field, he divided the "Indies" into the respective "spheres of influence" of Spain and Portugal. There should be nothing in the action to shock a generation which has seen the division of Africa among claimants whose rights were, in kind at least, identical with those of the Peninsular kingdoms at the close of the fifteenth century. At that time, too, the Pope was still, as he had been throughout the Middle Ages, the recognized arbitrator between Christian Kings. To say that he gave away the New World is to commit the not uncommon mistake of judging an act, not by what was known before or at the time, but by what was discovered later. In 1493 the existence of America was not suspected even by those who had seen it. Spain and Portugal, it was believed, had reached Asia by different sea routes. Now arose a dispute between the parties as to their respective " spheres of influence." Portugal claimed that the voyages of exploration sent out by Prince Henry had given her a prior right to the trade with the Indies; this right, too, had been recognized by Pope Nicholas V. in 1454. To this, however, the Spaniards replied that the Portuguese navigators from João Zarco and Tristram Vaz down to Bartolomeu Diaz had only established their country's right, which was not disputed, to keep the exclusive control of the road to Asia round Africa. They had acquired no right to stop the way for others across the ocean. Nicholas V. had had the African route only in his mind in 1454, and the Portuguese had then claimed no more. The Pope's grant must be applied in the light of greater knowledge. The argument was one day to be turned against the Spaniards themselves, but for the present it was convenient. A dispute had arisen which might lead to " the effusion of Christian blood." Neither the Catholic sovereigns, nor the King of Portugal, had anything to gain by fighting. They referred the dispute to the Pope, begging him to decide between them, and interpret the grant of his predecessor. Alexander VI. made what was, looking only to the circumstances before him, a reasonable compromise. He confirmed the exclusive right of Portugal to the sea route round Africa, and of Castile to the road across the ocean—to each the road which it had first found, and what it could reach by that road. Put in this way the arrangement was one which has nothing intrinsically absurd in principle, even to the nineteenth century. If it was absurd in fact, that was because of the existence of a multitude of material conditions, which were not, and could not be, known in 1493 to Pope or Kings, and because, also, of other intellectual or spiritual conditions of which some were not yet in existence.

It would no doubt be grossly inaccurate to say that the arbitration of Alexander VI. did not differ in any respect from that of, for instance, Marshal MacMahon in the Delagoa Bay dispute. The Pope of the Middle Ages—at the very close of which the world stood in 1493—was a very different personage from a President of the French Republic. He had a sanctity which Western Europe was still unanimous in recognizing. He had, too, claims to authority founded on the belief of the Middle Ages, or on use and custom, or even on simple forgery. His character gave a peculiar force and extension to his act. Whatever we may think of those claims, the Kings of the Middle Ages had been ready enough to profit by them, and Alexander VI. cannot be blamed for not giving up what his predecessors had been believed to possess. Among these powers of the medieval Pope, which were effective as long as the world believed in them, and a sword could be found to make them good, was the right to give away sovereignty over excommunicated or heathen states, and the islands of the sea. William of Normandy had thought the warrant good, and so had Henry II. Moreover, they had made it good. Ferdinand and Isabella for Castile, and João II. for Portugal, turned, in 1493, to the Papal authority as the Kings of the eleventh and twelfth centuries had done. Alexander VI. gave as his predecessors had given.

The details of the division between Spain and Portugal were not settled at once, nor finally by the Pope. Alexander VI., in 1493, on May 4th, decided that the spheres of the competitors should be divided by a line drawn from Pole to Pole 100 leagues to the west of the Azores or the Cape de Verd Islands. The terms prove the geographical knowledge of both arbitrator and claimants to have been limited. It was obviously taken for granted that all the islands of both these groups are upon the same meridian, which is far from being the case. The place of the line would vary materially according to whether it was measured from the most easterly or the most westerly island of either group. It was the interest of Portugal to put the line of demarcation as much as possible to the West, and of Spain to bring it as far as might be to the East. Moreover, the Portuguese soon persuaded themselves that in either case the Pope's award would confine them too closely to the coast of Africa. The Court of Lisbon, therefore, began at once to complain that the Pope had not fairly considered its interests, and had been too exclusively influenced by the Spanish Ambassadors. The quarrel did not lead to a rupture. A friendly conference was held at Tordesillas on the Duero in the Province of Valladolid, a town famous in Spanish history. The envoys came to a reasonable compromise. It was decided that the line of demarcation should be carried 260 leagues farther to the West, making 360 in all. The interval was to be measured from the Azores, which are themselves somewhat farther to the West than the Cape de Verd Islands. The diplomatists did their work with commendable thoroughness. It was settled that a delimitation commission of Spanish and Portuguese officers should sail to observe and fix the meridian. Care was also taken to put it down in black and white that the King of Spain's ships were not, when sailing to the line, to be considered as trespassing on the Portuguese preserve. The proviso is a pleasing illustration of the good diplomatists' love of having everything in writing. That the King of Spain would be practically shut out of his acknowledged territory, if he was not allowed to sail to it, is so self-evident a proposition that it seems hardly to require statement. The Treaty of Tordesillas was duly signed and sealed by the envoys of Spain and Portugal. It was then confirmed by the Pope, and became the basis of the colonial relations of the Spaniards and Portuguese. The date of the treaty is June, 1494, just one year later than the Pope's Bull. When Spanish and Portuguese explorers, sailing respectively West and East, had met in the Indian Ocean, the dispute was renewed in another form, and led to other conflicts and diplomatic disputes. But in this case the question at issue was the place of the line when it had been carried through the Poles and across the Eastern Seas. It was settled by a money transaction between Charles V. and the then King of Portugal, had comparatively little importance, and lasted but for a short time. The historic line, beyond which there was no peace, was the line of demarcation drawn 360 leagues to the west of the Azores from Pole to Pole.

Characteristically enough, its exact position was never settled in any formal way. No delimitation commission was ever sent out by Spain or Portugal. Both Powers had enough to do in taking possession of the vast estates which had fallen to them. They were content with a boundary which was marked accurately enough for all practical purposes. The line may be taken to be the fiftieth degree of longitude west of Greenwich, which strikes the continent of South America at about the mouth of the Amazon and leaves it at the southern end of the mountains of Santa Caterina. It thus cuts off a great cantle of the southern continent for the benefit of Portugal. Of this possession the Portuguese took seisin, when Pedro Alvarez Cabral, being then on his way to India to continue the work begun by Vasco da Gama in the previous year, was driven to the West by storms, and sighted the coast of Brazil at Monte Pascoal in the Aymores, in March, 1500.

But it was inevitable that the claim of the Spaniards should be disputed. The other maritime nations of Western Europe could not submit to exclusion from the New World. They would not have submitted to it permanently, even if there had been no great religious convulsion in the sixteenth century to shake the moral authority of the Pope's award. So soon as they had the power and the will, other States were sure to break through the imaginary barrier somewhere. The exact manner of the breaking was due to the condition of the Western Powers in the sixteenth century, and their relations to one another or to Spain.

The apparently undeniable proposition that a door must be either open or shut is not true of the diplomatic relations of nations. They often stand to one another on a footing which is neither one of open war nor of assured peace.

We have in our own time seen the agents of an English trading company come into collision with the Portuguese in a disputed territory at a time when the two Governments were at peace. The adventure of the South African Company in Mashonaland is a picture in little of a fight which went on in the New World in one form or another, and with a greater or less degree of ferocity, down to the signing of the Peace of Ryswick in 1697.

What happened (to sketch in large lines) was this. The Spaniard said: " I alone have the right to go beyond the line. Whoever else comes there is a pirate, and as that I will treat him whenever he is caught, unless he comes in war-time with a commission. Then he is a servant of my enemy, and entitled to be treated according to the custom of the wars. In peace he is a pirate." To this the other Powers replied: " We do not allow your claim, but it is not convenient for us to compel you to give it up by arms. So we note our protest, warn you that we do not hold our subjects forbidden to sail west, to trade with all who will deal with them, and to establish themselves wherever you are not in actual occupation. If you touch them, you do it at your peril." To their subjects the Governments said: " Go west if you please, but remember that it is for your masters to decide whether you are to be protected or avenged." The Spaniard and the adventurers accepted the duel on these terms. He thought it better to run the risk of all the harm adventurers could do him, than to concede the principle by acknowledging that foreign Governments might exercise jurisdiction within his bounds. Thus there arose a state of things singularly favourable to the adventurers. They knew that their Government would not punish them on their return for merely crossing the line. If they came back with profit, it would be for the Spanish Ambassador to prove that they earned it by piracy. This it would not be easy to do before an unfriendly court. If they were taken, the adventurers knew that they paid with their lives, but this risk they were prepared to run, and as they learnt the real weakness of Spain in the New World, they grew ever bolder, till they became the buccaneers of the seventeenth century.

The West Indies lay on the very road to Mexico, and were

the outposts of the Spanish possessions on the main. Therefore it was not until the Spaniard had been cowed by a long series of disasters that he was reduced so low as to be compelled to recognize the legality of foreign settlements. The struggle fills a series of chapters in the history of sea-borne commerce, which abound in picturesque incident, and in characters ranging from the height of heroism to the lowest depths of villainy and greed.

Although individual English adventurers were the first to follow the Spaniard to the New World, the direct attack upon him by arms was not begun by us. French pirates and settlers had made their appearance among the islands, and on the mainland, long before Hawkins, the pioneer of the Elizabethans, made his famous voyage in 1563. The reasons for our delay are not far to seek. Their own internal affairs, and their troubles with Scotland, gave Englishmen abundant occupation during the reigns of Henry VIII., Edward VI., and Mary. It was the prevailing policy of the crown to maintain the " Burgundian Alliance," to keep on friendly terms with the ruler of Spain and the Low Countries, with which we had great trade. Moreover, he was a natural ally against France. Whatever part of their strength Englishmen could spare from domestic troubles was directed for years towards efforts to obtain possession of a route of their own to the East. Portugal had the route by the Cape of Good Hope, and Spain the route by the West. Before claiming to share in either of them, Englishmen made an effort to secure a road for themselves to the North-East. They failed, but their merchant adventurers succeeded in establishing an English factory at Archangel, and opening the trade with Muscovy.

Until Elizabeth had been some four years on the throne the Englishmen who found their way to the New World as traders either took care to avoid the districts actually occupied by the Spaniards and Portuguese, or sailed from Seville with a licence. The only known examples of the first class of ventures are the " two sundry voyages made by the worshipful Mr. William Hawkins of Plymouth, father to Sir John Hawkins, Knight." Old Mr. William Hawkins, the founder, or, at least, the earliest known member of a family of active seafaring men, made his first voyage in 1530. It was mainly noteworthy as having set an example which his famous son was destined to better. In a tall ship of his own, the *Paul of Plymouth*, he sailed to the coast of Guinea, and there " he traffiqued with the negroes and took of them elephants' teeth, and other commodities which that place yieldeth." The other commodities did not include that peculiar African article of export in which his son was destined to do a large business. It was not yet known that negro slaves found a good market in the Spanish Indies. Mr. William Hawkins did not aim at selling to the Spaniards, but at acquiring goods to sell in England. From Guinea he sailed over to the coast of Brazil, " and behaved himself so wisely with those savage people that he grew into great familiarity with them." A native King agreed to aecompany him back to England, and Hawkins left one Martin Cockeram as a hostage for the chief's return. When the *Paul* reached home, " the Savage King " was taken up to be stared at by the Court, which " did not a little marvel and not without cause, for in his cheeks were holes made, according to their savage manner, and therein small bones were planted, standing an inch out from the said holes, which in his own country was reputed for a great bravery [*i.e.*, finery]. He also had another hole in his nether lip, wherein was set a precious stone about the bigness of a pease; all his apparel, behaviour and gesture were very strange to the beholders." The climate, probably not unaided by strong drink, killed the savage King. He died at sea, on board the *Paul*, as she was on her way back to Brazil in 1532. William Hawkins was in fear lest the natives should refuse to return the hostage Cockeram, but " the savages, being fully persuaded of the honest dealing of our men with their prince, restored again the said pledge, without any harm to him, or any man of the company." Martin Cockeram lived for many years in Plymouth, and, indeed, lives now in the pages of " Westward Ho !"

It was one of the consequences of the long struggle between Francis I. and Charles V., that French adventurers were the first to make a serious attack on the West Indies. These men did not sail with the King's commission, but for the Admiral Coligny and his party. They were therefore Huguenots. All of them were not "of the Reform," but the leaders were, and it was they who inspired the spirit in which these voyages were made. That spirit was one of bloodthirsty ferocity. It was the misfortune of the Huguenots, to use the most charitable word, that what Voltaire called the tiger element in the French character was peculiarly conspicuous in very many of their partisans. Among their seamen it wholly prevailed. No quarter was given by the French pirates except where there was a certainty of securing a large ransom. It was their uniform practice to cut the throats of the Spanish crews which they were able to capture, and that fact must in justice be accepted as some palliation of the ruthless severity shown by Don Pedro Melendez in Florida. The history of sporadic expeditions of pirates is inevitably obscure. Constant complaints from the Spanish colonists of ships taken, and crews massacred, is almost all the record of them which remains. One story stands out with peculiar distinctness in Spanish records, and may be taken as the type of much else. In 1535 a certain Jacques de Sorie captured Havannah, sacked and burned the town, and then butchered the Spanish prisoners who had surrendered on promise of quarter. Out of mere devilry, as it would appear, he hung up the negroes whom he found in the place, and shot them to death. Protestant writers who have made much of the slaughter of Jean Ribault and his companions have preserved a judicious silence about Jacques de Sorie. We may be very sure that when Pedro Melendez came to Florida in 1564, the memory of the Havannah massacre in 1555 was very fresh in the minds of the Spaniards. The English were led to the same field by John Hawkins. In October, 1562, he sailed from Plymouth with three small vessels, steered first to the Canaries, and thence to the coast of Guinea, where he had collected a cargo of negroes. With this "prey" he crossed the Atlantic, and during the summer months of 1563 he disposed of his slaves in Hispaniola, to the great satisfaction of the planters, and by the connivance of the King's officers, standing on his guard the while. Hawkins was well qualified by birth and training to begin the work.

He was the second son of old Mr. William Hawkins, of the *Paul of Plymouth*. He had been bred to the sea in his father's ships, and had heard from him and his old sailors of the voyages to Brazil, which had been made about the time of his own birth. The trade of Plymouth was largely for wine to the Canaries. In the islands he would learn a great deal more, which was useful to him. In particular he learnt " that negroes were very good merchandise in Hispaniola; and that store of them might easily be had upon the coast of Guinea." Unquestionably, too, he would be told more than this. He would find Spaniards to tell him that the creole population already formed in the islands, and on the main, was by no means unwilling to obtain goods which had not paid the King's dues, that the settlements were far apart, unfortified, often without garrison, generally destitute of firearms, that the King of Spain maintained no armed ships permanently in the Indies. There would be no want of informants to tell him that the severe limitations imposed on the licensed trade from Seville made it almost impossible for the legitimate trader to supply the wants of the planters. The common instincts of human nature made it certain that they would have no great scruple as to supplying themselves by the help of the smuggler. The adventure, in fact, presented many chances of profit counterbalanced by little or no appreciable risk. The opportunity was good, and Hawkins was the man to take advantage of it.

In 1562 he laid his plan before " worshipful friends " in London—his father-in-law Gonson, Sir Lionel Ducket, Sir Thomas Lodge, Sir William Winter. The Hawkins family could perhaps have found the capital themselves, but as there was a risk of trouble with the Council, it was advisable to have persons of position engaged who could give support at Court. The worshipful friends thought the risk worth running for the general advantage of the kingdom, and the particular good of their own pockets. With his own capital and the help of the other adventurers, Hawkins fitted out three little ships—the *Solomon*, of 120 tons; the *Swallow*, of 100; and the *Jonah*, of 40, and sailed from Plymouth Sound in October, 1562, for the Canaries.

First he sailed to Teneriffe. His visit to this port may have been partly due to the necessities of trade, but it is probable that he had another motive. From a passage in Sparke's long account of the voyage which followed this one, it appears that Hawkins had then on board a Spanish merchant, whom he found a prisoner among the Tangomangos. The man was of no recorded use to Hawkins, but, if he was a smuggling agent of the planters, he would naturally take care to be found by the " English corsair " in captivity among some convenient " Tangomangos." It would be an excellent excuse. From the ease with which Hawkins conducted his trade on the first voyage, there is every probability that his coming was known, the places he was to visit had been fixed upon, and that he was supplied with charts and a pilot. There is, then, a considerable likelihood that his visit to Teneriffe was mainly to settle the necessary arrangements, and that " worshipful friends " in London were not the only adventurers. From the islands Hawkins went on to the coast of Guinea, where he " got into his possession, partly by the sword and partly by other means, to the number of three hundred negroes at least, besides other merchandise which that country yieldeth." With his cargo he stretched across to the coast of Hispaniola, and there, at Isabella, Puerto de Plata and Monte Christo, " had reasonable utterance " of his goods, human and other, receiving in exchange pearls, hides, ginger, sugar, and " other like commodities." He was a cautious man, and stood well upon his guard, but he had no difficulty in conducting his trade, and was back in England in September after a very prosperous voyage. It raises a further presumption that Hawkins was acting with some Spanish partner that he loaded two vessels with hides and the " like commodities," which he sent to Spain. He cannot possibly have been so ignorant of the Spanish laws as to suppose that he would be allowed to sell these cargoes in Spain without question. If he was, his mistake cost the adventurers the value of the two cargoes which were confiscated, and would have cost an English agent sent with them a long imprisonment, if the man had not had the sense to escape in time. If we knew the truth, we should probably find that there were Spanish smugglers in the plot who thought they could do a stroke of business at home, and who failed.

Hawkins raised a loud cry of thieves over his cargoes, and talked of a loss of £20,000. He alleged to no purpose his stock excuse—namely, that bad weather had forced him on the coast of Hispaniola, and that he had only sold a part of his cargo by leave of the authorities to pay for necessary provisions and repairs. As a matter of fact, the voyage had been extremely profitable, and had gained him great reputation—not with the Queen, perhaps, as yet, and certainly not with Cecil, who seems never to have liked him, but with the courtiers of the anti-Spanish party. Elizabeth, who shared the tastes of her time to the full, and would indulge her favourite courtier, Leicester, to the utmost limit of safety, was induced to favour the adventurers so far as to permit them to hire a ship of the Royal Navy—an old German-built vessel called the *Jesus of Lübeck*. No doubt this was a purely commercial transaction. The practice of hiring out the King's ships when they were not wanted for service was common, and had obvious attractions to a poor and thrifty Sovereign. We may be sure that Elizabeth took care to be well secured against loss. We may be equally sure that she knew for what purpose the ship was wanted, and was disposed to favour it as long as showing favour suited her convenience.

Between the sea rover, the merchants, the courtiers, and the Queen, an adventure of the same nature as the last, but on a larger scale, was prepared for 1564. When Hawkins said, as he afterwards did, that, because he sailed in a ship hired from the Queen, he was on her service, he was saying what was technically untrue. But it was by no means the most audacious falsehood he told in his life. He was on the Queen's service after a fashion not uncommon at the time. He was, in the French phrase, " un agent désavouable et désavoué." His scheme might prove profitable, so, if he could get security, he should have the ship, and nothing was to be done to hinder his sailing. If he succeeded, the Queen would take her share of the profit—not openly, not allowing the thing to be made a matter of account, but not the less effectually. If it failed, the adventurers must pay the freight of the *Jesus of Lübeck*, and her value in case of total loss. If they made trouble with Spain they must expect to be disavowed. They would be at her mercy, which would be, more or less, according to her liking for them personally, the influence of Leicester, and the necessities of her political position. The bargain looks one-sided, and would assuredly not have tempted men who wished to enjoy the pleasures of security, but these men were adventurers in an adventurous time. They played for great prizes, and with the knowledge that they might some day be called upon to stake their lives. They took the risk, relying on luck, on their own courage, on the influence of Leicester, and on that element of manly pride in the Queen's nature which was very likely to nerve her to turn fiercely on any man, native or foreign, subject or sovereign, who pressed her too closely to do a base thing.

The expedition sailed on October 18th. It consisted of four vessels—the *Jesus of Lübeck*, of 700 tons, a " capital ship," according to the expression of that time, and about as large as most of the Spanish galleons. Her consorts were the *Solomon*, of 140, the *Tiger*, of 90, and the *Swallow*, of 30 tons. Some thirty miles or so out at sea Hawkins fell in with another small squadron bound, like his own, to Guinea. It also included a vessel belonging to the Queen, called the *Minion*, under the command of one David Carlet. The two bodies of adventurers agreed to keep company together. Bad weather scattered them, and Hawkins ran into Ferrol, where he spent five days repairing damages, and drawing up a code of signals and sailing instructions which passed for a model of good order. The small ships were always to keep ahead and to windward of the *Jesus*, and to speak with her twice a day. The signals were scanty and rude. They did not go beyond a few signs, flags by day, or a light and a discharge of powder by night, to show that the Admiral was going about or wished to speak with the others, but they included a signal of distress, and a private signal by which the ships could, if they happened to be scattered, know one another when they met again. They were to give three yaws and strike the mizzen thrice. The general instructions as to conduct were all contained in one admirable formula : " Serve God daily, love one another, preserve your victuals, beware of fire, and keep good company."

While they were at Ferrol, the *Minion*, which had lost company in the bad weather, came in with dismal tidings—one of her consorts had been blown up by the carelessness of the gunner, and the Minions, though they had saved most of the crew, were too depressed to appreciate the friendly salute with which Hawkins greeted them after the manner of the sea. Their disaster doubtless served to enforce his advice to his own ships to beware of fire. From the Galician port they all went on to the Canaries. At Teneriffe there took place a little passage of negotiation with the local authorities which was characteristic of much that was to follow. As Hawkins was coming to an anchor, he hoisted out his pinnace to row ashore, intending to send a letter to " one of the governors " of the island, his friend Peter de Ponte, which was in the original, no doubt, Pedro del Puente. As he neared the shore, he was aware of " men levelling of bases [small boat guns] and harquebusses to them, with divers others to the number of fourscore, with halberts, pikes, swords, and targets." The sight did amaze Hawkins all the more because he was within range, and did not well see how he was to get out safe. He was not the man to lose his head, and so hailed the shore to say " that he was an especial friend to Peter de Ponte, and had sundry things for him which he greatly desired," telling his men in the meantime to row out of danger, which they did. Then, from among the divers persons there came forth one Nicholas de Ponte, son of Peter, and entered into talk with the English. The result was that Hawkins had leave to anchor, and that after a space Peter de Ponte came over from Santa Cruz, " and gave him as gentle entertainment as if he had been his own brother." The interpretation of an apparently purposeless show of hostility is probably this —that Pedro del Puente had orders from home to forbid all intercourse between the islanders and Hawkins, and that he made just so much show of obeying as might, with the help of some judicious despatch-writing, make it appear that he had done his duty, under the cover of which demonstration he conducted a little private trade with the English smuggler.

From Teneriffe Hawkins went on to the Cape de Verd Islands, where he found that the natives had grown civil by much intercourse with the French. Perhaps because he thought that their " civility " would be a material addition to their value for purposes of domestic service, he laid a plot to kidnap a good few of them for export to the Spanish Main. Some of the sailors of the *Minion* were so base as to reveal this project to the natives, who fled beyond reach. Hawkins separated from a countryman who spoiled his market, and went on with his four ships to the coast of Senegambia, where he fell upon a people called the Sapis, who lived in islands in subordination to a fierce cannibal race from the continent called the Camboses. The narrator of the voyage, a person of an observing eye and an irrepressible unctuous piety, made curious observations on native manners and customs, as to filing the teeth, tatooing " as workmanlike as a jerkin maker with us maketh a jerkin," their burial customs, military tactics, polity and morals. Hawkins kidnapped some of them, and carried off much of their fruit. His loss was one man, who, being " more licorous than circumspect," went ashore for " Pompions," alone, and was surprised by the natives, who very properly cut his throat, " thus," as Southey says, " taking no undue vengeance " on the only invader they could reach. Thence Hawkins dropped down the coast, and entered the River " Callowsa," where the Portuguese rode. Their anchorage was some way up the river. Hawkins " came thither the five and twentieth, and dispatched his business, and so returned with two caravels loaded with negroes." The Portuguese afterwards complained that ships of theirs had been plundered by Hawkins on this coast, and it may be that the business he despatched was the conveyance of negroes already taken by them to the hold of his own vessels.

On this same river was a native town, of which the Portuguese told him that it not only contained much gold, but that there were not above forty men in it, and a hundred women and children. There were at least a hundred slaves to be got—to wit, the women and children after the men had been massacred. Hawkins undertook this not very arduous adventure gladly, " because the Portugals should not think him of so base a courage, but that he durst give them that and greater attempts." But the result was to show that " Portugals are not to be trusted," as the narrator severely observes, for when Hawkins sent forty men in boats to land below the town, and they had scattered in search of the gold, women, and children, they were suddenly and fiercely attacked by no less than 200 grown male negroes, who drove them to the boats, and were like to have made an end of them in the ooze, but for the strenuous exertions of the commander himself. He brought off ten negroes, with the loss of Captain Field of the *Solomon*, and six others killed and twenty-seven wounded. Hawkins, " in a singular wise manner carried himself with a countenance very cheerful outwardly as though he did little weigh the death of his men, nor yet the great hurt of the rest, though his heart inwardly was broken to pieces for it." For some time he continued on the coast, filling up with negroes as he could catch them. His farthest point south was Sierra Leone. Here war was raging between native Kings, and a battle was imminent. The English from the decks of their ships saw over the tops of the trees the glare of the fires kindled by the black warriors. They would have waited to hang about the coming struggle and chaffer with the conqueror for captives, but the contagion of the coast was among them; they were fairly well stored; and it was the part of a prudent man to temper enterprise with caution. On January 26th, 1565, Hawkins left his black fellow-slave-hunters behind, and steered for the West.

The voyage across the Atlantic was delayed by calms so persistent that there was a serious risk of heavy loss of negroes, but " Almighty God, who never suffereth his elect to perish," sent a favourable breeze. The slavers dropped anchor at Dominica, an island then inhabited only by the Caribs, where they watered at a brackish pool. After ten days' stay the squadron went on. Hawkins was now at the gate of his market, which this year was the Main, and not Hispaniola. He had, as has been noted above, a Spanish merchant on board, whom he had found among the Tangomangos on the coast of Senegambia, probably by arrangement. In any case he would not fail to obtain useful hints from his passenger. He turned south, and passing close by the rocky little Testigos, steered for Margarita, an island off the coast of what is now Venezuela, shaped like a dumbbell, two lofty masses of rock connected by a long narrow isthmus.

Here Hawkins's men made their first acquaintance with potatoes, which "are the most delicate roots that may be eaten, and do far exceed our parsnips and carrots," and with the pines "more delicious than any sweet apple sugared." As usual, he was soon on excellent terms with the planters. The "alcalde" of the nearest Spanish settlement, an elected officer, gave him hospitable welcome, but the King's Governor was less tractable. He retired to the mountain, taking not only the Spanish inhabitants of the chief town, but the very Indians with them. The Indians in the neighbourhood of the anchorage, who had at first been friendly, were mustered in a body with their bows and arrows by three Spaniards on horseback, and marched off to the hills. A pilot who had been hired was forbidden to go, and Hawkins learnt that a caravel had been despatched to San Domingo with news of his presence on the coast. Finding that there was nothing to be done in the way of trade, and that he could not hit on a watering-place, Hawkins, after a delay of some days, stood over to Cumaná on the mainland. Here he found only a few soldiers who were too poor to buy his negroes, and, leaving them, sailed along the coast westward, after buying flour and vegetables. It was still lying desolate, inhabited only by Caribs, who endeavoured to tempt the English on shore by showing gold. The bait was declined, for the wind was fair, and Hawkins eager to reach a market. If the English had landed, they would, so the Spaniards afterwards told them, have assuredly been led into an ambush by the Carib cannibals, who only showed gold, knowing it to be a temptation the white men rarely resisted. Passing between the Island of Tortuga—not the famous buccaneer stronghold, but another of several of the name in the West Indies— he at last came to a place of trade. This was Borburata, "a snug little inlet about three cables deep, and nearly two cables wide, with depths of 9 to 6 fathoms almost alongside the beach at its head." The other sides are skirted by a coral ledge to a short distance, leaving a channel in the middle about a cable wide. It lies just beyond Puerto Cabello, and its lagoon surrounded by pestilential swamps. Puerto Cabello was not yet occupied by the Spaniards, who had their settlement at Borburata. Hawkins appeared off the port on April 3rd—about five months after his departure from Plymouth.

Anchoring his ships outside, he went in himself in his pinnace to speak with the Spaniards. He represented himself with more truth than he commonly expended afterwards, as an Englishman who had come to trade, and begged for a licence. The Spaniards answered that they were forbidden to deal with foreigners, and must, as became good subjects, obey, wherefore they asked him to go elsewhere. Hawkins replied to an invitation, which was probably not very sincerely meant, in a fashion which closely resembled the manner of the Norman pilgrims as described by M. Michelet. These pious travellers carried goods to traffic for their subsistence on the way to shrines. When they were asked for toll, they hitched the handles of their swords round, and pleaded the piety of their purpose. It was generally held that they had made good their right to exemption. In the same spirit, though with different formulas, Hawkins answered that going farther was out of the question. He had an armament of the Queen's with him, and many men whom he must support. Without trade, this could not be done, and, their princes being at amity, he saw no reason why the subjects should not deal amicably to their mutual gain, " and with much other talk persuaded them not to fear any dishonest part of his behalf towards them, for neither would he commit any such thing to the dishonour of his prince, nor yet for his honest reputation and estimation, unless he were too rigorously dealt withal, which he hoped not to find at their hands." The hint was as clear as friendly language permitted, and had satisfactory effects. The inhabitants of Borburata, whose whole conduct proves that they only wanted a decent show of compulsion to quote as an excuse for illicit trade, gave him leave to come in, adding that they would send to the Governor of the province for a licence, which might be expected to arrive in ten days.

So Hawkins brought his four ships in between the ledges of coral, and anchored in the deep water at the bottom of the Bay. Water and fresh provisions were obtained from the shore; then, being comfortably berthed, he reflected "that to remain there for ten days idle, spending victuals and men's wages, and perhaps in the end receive no good answer from the governor, it were mere folly." So he took the next step. He applied for leave to sell thirty lean and sickly negroes, who were likely to die upon his hands, but would recover well enough on shore. The officers and "town-dwellers" assembled in council thought this fair, all the more because Hawkins, always a marvel of reasonableness, pointed out that he could not pay for his provisions unless he was allowed to sell those negroes. The leave was given, but for some days no buyer appeared. This delay seemed suspicious to Hawkins, and he went ashore to inquire into the reason of it. He was told that leave had only been given to the poor to buy negroes of little price, and that they had sent their money to the hills when his ships were seen off the port, and could not readily get it back. There was, in fact, much higgling of the market under strange conditions. The "town-dwellers" hung back in hope that fear of missing his licence would force the Englishman to sell his negroes cheap. He, again, was resolute not to part with them at an unremunerative figure. At last, seeing that the Borburatans were as eager to buy as he to sell, he threatened to go if they did not come to terms. This threat had the effect he calculated. The "town-dwellers" crowded round him, imploring him to have patience, and finally assuring him that, licence or no licence, they would buy his goods. Pacified by this assurance, he remained, and some negroes were sold.

The budding traffic was again checked by the Receiver of Customs, who, when the buyers paid the King's dues, refused to receive them, and told them to hand the money over to the poor. This frightened the buyers, who thought it not at all unlikely that they might be called upon to pay again; so they abstained from making further purchases.

Hawkins was too good a man of business to frighten his customers, and decided to wait till the Governor came. In a few days he arrived, and then the slaver repeated his story, with a larger admixture of fiction and a greater explicitness of menace. The Captain "made petition" to the Governor, "declaring that he came thither in a ship of the Queen's Majesty's of England, being bound to Guinea, and thither driven by wind and weather, he had need of sundry necessities for the reparation of the said navy, and also great need of money for the payment of his soldiers, unto whom he had promised payment, and therefore, although he would, yet would not they depart without it."

The Governor, who had no force of his own, and knew that the colonists would give him no support, who, besides, was, as the result showed, not unwilling to do trade on his own account, made a virtue of necessity. Leave was granted, but before business could fairly begin there was another hitch: the King's dues were put at thirty ducats per negro, which was a prohibitive duty. If it was to be paid, the price of the negroes must be raised; but the Borburatans refused to go any higher. It was clear that somebody must give way, and Hawkins decided that it must be the Custom House. His patience being now exhausted, he landed "a hundred Englishmen well armed with bows and arrows, harquebusses and pikes, and marched to the townwards." This spectacle brought the Governor down to treat. Hawkins pointed out how unreasonable an import duty of thirty ducats was, and how mainfestly seven and a half was enough, which sum, if the Custom House would not take, "he would displease them." On this basis the market was established, and a brisk trade was done. After some further chaffering, higgling by the Spaniards, and threats to go from Hawkins, the local demand was satisfied, and the English sailed; they had been a month at Borburata. While they were there a French ship called the *Green Dragon* came in from the coast of Guinea. From her Captain, Bontemps, Hawkins learned that the *Minion* had been brought to grief in Africa by the Portuguese. The mention of the *Green Dragon*, which remained at Borburata when Hawkins sailed, is one more proof that we were not the only adventurers on the Spanish Main. Captain Bontemps was, no doubt, engaged in the same smuggling business as his English friend.

From Borburata Hawkins sailed along the coast to Curaçao, which he found uninhabited, but swarming with wild cattle, the descendants of animals turned loose by the Spaniards. In after-times the number of these animals in the West Indian Islands, particularly in San Domingo and Cuba, became a curse to the people who had introduced them, for they afforded an ample supply of fresh provisions to the Buccaneers. Passing by the Island of Oruba and the pearl fishery at La Rancheria, the English adventurers reached Rio de la Hacha, on the coast of what is now the Republic of Colombia, a little town at the mouth of a river, on May 19th.

At Rio de la Hacha there was a repetition of the transactions which had already taken place at Borburata. Again Hawkins told his story of storms and necessity; again the Spanish officials made a show of resistance, and the colonists haggled over the price; again Hawkins landed men, and the show of opposition melted at once. Towards the end of his stay some soldiers arrived, bringing firearms and four " falchions " or cannon. There had been none in the town before, which explains the trifling resistance offered by the King's officers, even if they had been zealous. Four armed ships, with 150 men, made a commanding force among the small, widely-scattered and ill-provided little settlements on the coast. The appearance of these cannon made a change in Hawkins's tone. When at the end of the trading he asked for a certificate of good behaviour, he was told that he should not have it till he was under way. He accepted the condition, stood out with his ships, and returned in his pinnace for the certificate, which was given, with much exchange of courtesies from both sides. It was, indeed, not Hawkins's cue to fight, but to trade. The use of arms was with him a means; commerce was the end.

On the last day of May the four ships sailed from Rio de la Hacha, bound for San Domingo. Our adventurers were as yet insufficiently acquainted with the force of the westerly current of the Caribbean Sea. They did not allow for it, and were carried to leeward, which, in the West Indies, always means to westward, of their destination. Their landfall was made in Jamaica. Nor did their disappointments end there. Heavy mists were hanging over the island when they first caught sight of it. The Spanish merchant, misled by the haze, mistook Jamaica for his native San Domingo. In his delight at the prospect of again reaching home, he threw away his old clothes and put on his new (it is, by the way, strange that his wardrobe should have afforded so many resources if he had been long a captive among African savages), and then confidently went on to point out this or the other man's land as they ranged along the coast to the west. The end of it was that the squadron was allowed to fall to leeward of Jamaica. Hawkins cursed the Spaniard for a plague to himself and to everybody else. The mistake was especially annoying because it had carried the ships to leeward of Santa Cruz in Cuba, where there was hope of securing good store of hides. Time was now wearing on towards the hurricane months, and the ships were becoming foul. It was decided that enough had been done, and Hawkins made his way home by the normal route round the west end of Cuba and through the Florida Strait. Touching at the Island of Pines, where they met their first storm, they rounded Cape Antonio and stretched up to the Dry Tortugas—which, again, are not the home of the Buccaneers, but a cluster of sandy islets lying almost due west of the Florida Cays. A last attempt was made to trade with the Spaniards, and Hawkins came over to the north coast of Cuba with the intention of putting into Havannah, which was not yet the great port it afterwards became, but was already a favourite anchorage of the Spaniards on their way to and from the Gulf of Mexico; but he was destined to be unlucky with his foreigners on this voyage. A Frenchman whom he had on board, an old Huguenot pirate of course, misled him. The ships overshot Havannah, and Hawkins, finding that he was getting too close to the Great Bahama Bank, turned his face homewards. He ran through the Florida Strait. On his way he relieved Laudonnière's Colony at St. Augustine, and would willingly have done more if the French Huguenot had not thought it wise to trust his fellow Protestant no farther than he could see him. From Florida the English ships went home, not without difficulty. Their provisions ran short, and they were " in despair of ever coming home, had not God in His goodness better provided for us than our deserving." On the banks of Newfoundland they took some cod, and met two French vessels, from which they bought more. And so " with a good large wind, the twentieth of September we came to Padstow in Cornwall, God be thanked, in safety, with the loss of twenty persons in all the voyage, and with great profit to the venturers of the said voyage, as also to the whole realm, in bringing home both gold, silver, pearls, and other jewels great store. His name therefore be praised for evermore. Amen."

The success of his second voyage had more than fulfilled all the promises made by Hawkins to his friends at Court. Sixty per cent. was the profit of the adventurers, and if the Queen received less in payment for the use of the *Jesus*, it was the only occasion in her life on which she was content to forego attainable money. The following October would have seen Hawkins on the sea again, but by this time Philip was thoroughly angered. The delicacy of her relations with the Queen of Scots, and the Queen's partisans in England, made it too dangerous to offend the King of Spain, so Elizabeth forbade all such adventures in 1566. Hawkins could afford to wait. He was now formally made a gentleman by the grant of a coat of arms, in which a very significant Demi-Moor, proper, chained, figured as crest over a rather commonplace display of bezants and a lion, or, on a field sable. Silva, the Spanish Ambassador, invited him to dinner, and reported his assurances that his conduct in the West Indies had been a model of friendly propriety. If his ships sailed in 1566, he did not go with them, and it is not probable that he risked the Queen's anger by sending them again to the West Indies. The ordinary business of the firm would give employment to those men of his crews of whom he did not wish to lose sight.

In 1567 there came a change. Philip was threatened by an open rebellion in the Low Countries, and the Queen of Scots was going to ruin. Hawkins, on the advice, in all probability, of friends at Court, applied successfully for leave to sail again. He argued that if his men were sent adrift they would turn pirates, and promised emphatically to be of good behaviour in the West Indies. The facts that he made no concealment of his intention to repeat his former voyages, and was allowed to go, prove that the Queen was as ready as any of her subjects to break down the Spanish prohibition of trade with the New World.

The new squadron was made ready at Plymouth during the summer of 1567. It consisted of two Queen's ships, the *Jesus* and the *Minion*; and of four vessels belonging to the Hawkins family, the *Angel*, the *Swallow*, the *William and Mary*, and the *Judith*, in which Francis Drake went as Captain. The object of the armament was perfectly obvious to everybody, and extorted protests from Silva; but the Queen knew that Philip's hands were full with the Low Country troubles, and this year she refused to repeat the order to stop, which she had given when in danger.

While he was lying in the Catwater a Spanish packet on her way from Flanders to Spain came into the Sound with her flag flying. Hawkins immediately fired upon her, and continued to fire until the flag was hauled down. The master of the packet, a Fleming, declared that such a thing had never happened to him in any English port in the seventeen or eighteen years of his service. It was an act partly of mere uproarious horseplay, but partly of calculation. The Spaniard was compelled to anchor out in the sound, where he was attacked at night by some of the more or less Protestant privateers, who were always cruising in the Channel for the promotion of pure religion and the collection of plunder. Several prisoners whom he had on board for transport to Spain were rescued. It requires a large dose of credulity to believe that the whole transaction was not arranged betwween Hawkins and the privateers. The Spaniards protested, and Elizabeth made an ironical pretence of inquiry into this outrage against the security of her harbours. Hawkins replied, as he was expected to reply, with a lying but plausible excuse, to the effect that he had only prevented the Spaniard from entering the overcrowded Catwater, and was ignorant of the subsequent attack. The

Queen would do nothing beyond listen to Silva's severely-worded protest with an air of much compunction. Much innocent merriment was doubtless excited by this story about Court, and in the Plymouth beer-shops—very justly, too, for the farce was played with contagious zest, both by the Queen and the " bold sea rover."

On October 2nd Hawkins sailed. A storm, which lasted from the 7th to the 11th, scattered the ships, and the *Jesus* was so roughly battered that the adventure seemed likely to be cut short at its beginning. The Admiral had been turned back, and was running for port before the south-wester, when the wind changed and blew fair. At once the voyage was resumed, and the *Jesus* was steered for Gomera, which had been appointed as the rendezvous. On November 4th Hawkins, having provided himself with water and fresh provisions, left the island for the Cape de Verd. On the way an incident occurred which proved that the English had come out this time prepared to deal very freely with all they met upon the sea. Four Portuguese vessels, which were conducting a French corsair of Rochelle they had taken, fell in with Hawkins. He at once attacked the Portuguese and overpowered them, releasing the corsair, which joined him, and followed his fortunes to the disaster at San Juan de Ulloa. At the Cape de Verd he made an attempt to kidnap some of the " civil " negroes who had eluded him on his former voyage. It was unsuccessful. The " civil " negroes defended themselves with poisoned arrows, and very few of them were taken. Their poison was apparently a kind of curari, for several of the English wounded died in the course of a few days " in a strange sort with their mouths shut." Hawkins was himself hit badly, but recovered by applying garlic to his wound, on the advice of a negro, if Job Hortop remembered rightly.

This unfortunate experience left the English adventurer only the more disposed to steal his brooms ready-made. He confined himself during the rest of his stay on the coast of Africa to, with one exception, plundering the Portuguese slavers. The English dropped into this river of Senegambia, or into that, pillaging the Portuguese of their pillage, and conveying it to their own holds. The last incident of their stay on the coast was a fight with seven Portuguese at Rio Grande. They were driven on shore, but the crews escaped into the bush with their captives, who, let us hope, found means to cut their throats. We were at peace with Portugal, of course, but it claimed to keep Africa to itself as Spain did America, and, being a weak little Power, was even more severely punished for its pretensions.

What was needed to make up the cargoes taken from our competitors was obtained by a means which Hawkins shall be allowed to describe for himself. After telling how we searched " with all diligence the rivers from Rio Grande to Sierra Leone " (the nature of the searching has been described above, from authorities who had not the same reason to keep to general terms), till the country sickness appeared in his ships, he goes on :

" But even at that present instant, there came to us a Negro, sent from a king oppressed by other kings his neighbours, desiring our aid, with promise that as many negroes as by these wars might be obtained, as well of his part as of ours, should be at our pleasure; whereupon we concluded to give aid, and sent 120 of our men, which the 15th of January assaulted a town of the negroes of our allies adversaries which had in it 3,000 inhabitants, being very strongly impaled and fenced after their manner, but it was so well defended that our men prevailed not, but lost six men, and forty hurt, so that our men sent forthwith to me for more help, whereupon considering that the good success of this enterprise might highly further the commodity of our voyage I went myself, and with the help of the king of our side, assaulted the town both by land and sea, and very hardly with fire (their houses being covered with dry Palm leaves) obtained the town, and put the inhabitants to flight, where we took 250 persons, men, women, and children, and by our friend the king of our side there were taken 600 prisoners, whereof we had hoped to have had our choice ; but the negro (in which nation is seldom or never found truth) meant nothing less ; for that night he removed his camp and prisoners, so that we were fain to content us with those few which we had gotten ourselves."

It would need little change of phrase to fit this narrative

to the pen of Tippoo Tib. Job Hortop, who speaks highly of Hawkins's courage and conduct in the fight, adds that 7,000 negroes were driven into the mud of the river, and there smothered. The figure is large, but if the town contained 8,000 inhabitants, and only 850 prisoners were taken, a considerable margin must be allowed for massacre. Five Portuguese were found in the captured town, whose lives Hawkins magnanimously spared. When the actors in these scenes talk of themselves as " God's elect,' one understands better the rising of the gorge which helped Ben Jonson to draw " Tribulation Wholesome " and " Zeal o' the Land Busy." In our time we may remember that this man was received at Court, promoted high in her service by Elizabeth, and borne with as confidential agent by Cecil and Walsingham—and then, be it said again, we had better abstain from moral rebuke of the Spaniard.

Hawkins now left the coast and made his way to Dominica. The voyage, which extended from February 3rd to March 27th, 1568, was painful. From Dominica Hawkins, whose squadron had been increased by the addition of the French corsair, and perhaps by one or two of the Portuguese caravels manned by prize crews, repeated his voyage of 1565. He sailed along the Main. At Borburata, which had shortly before been pillaged by French pirates, he put in to refit. It would be tiresome to repeat incidents which did not differ materially from those of the former voyage. The slavers remained upon the coast from the end of March till the end of July, trading as before with the Creoles, after more or less genuine opposition from the King's officers. Whether because he was more certain of support at home, or because he had grown bolder with his experience of the real weakness of the Spaniards, Hawkins was on this occasion less scrupulous than before in drawing the line between smuggling and piracy. Some of his vessels, which had been sent ou in advance to Rio de la Hacha to reconnoitre under Drake, drove a Spanish packet ashore. When Hawkins himself arrived he landed 200 men, who easily overpowered the resistance of about half that number of Spaniards who could be collected to oppose him, and he then occupied the little settlement. Once in possession, he did a good trade with the Creoles, and even with the King's officers who visited his slave pens by night. At Cartagena, to which point his voyage extended, he could do nothing. It was too well guarded, and the Governor did his duty. After four months spent on the coast of the Main, Hawkins had still a balance of negroes undisposed of; but he could not afford to linger about an exhausted market, and therefore sailed north to the Antilles.

According to his own narrative, it was now his intention to make his way home by the Florida Strait, and he would have done so if the "furicano," which assailed him on August 12th when at the west end of Cuba, and a second, which shattered the *Jesus* some days later when the ships had reached the north side of the island, had not made it absolutely necessary for him to seek a harbour in the Gulf of Mexico. This story need not be accepted as quite literally true. It is unlikely that Hawkins would have left the West Indies without an attempt to sell his remaining negroes. Probably he hoped to succeed in Cuba, but was driven to leeward by the storms. It was now the height of the hurricane months. The storm would give him a pretext for putting into a port, and his unsold slaves gave him a motive to make the most of his pretext. He decided to steer for San Juan de Ulloa, the port of Mexico. On his way there he fell in with three small Spanish vessels bound to San Domingo with passengers. Hawkins made prize of the ships, and seized the passengers as hostages. Guided by the snow-capped peaks of Orizaba and the Cofre de Perote, which are visible over the flat Tierra Caliente of Mexico for 150 miles at sea, he came outside the port on September 16th. There was a certain risk in visiting Vera Cruz, which was near the very heart of the Spanish Power in the New World; but Hawkins, emboldened by impunity, and aware that the town itself was small and unfortified, might well calculate that the eight or ten ships of which his squadron now consisted would be an overwhelming force. With it he could extort leave to enter, and provisions when in. Moreover, it was not unreasonable in him to suppose that the Creoles of Mexico would be as willing as settlers elsewhere to take his negroes off his hands.

On September 16th, a Thursday, he appeared off the port. The officials were in daily expectation of a convoy from Spain, and they took Hawkins's ships for the vessels they were looking for. A boat put off with the harbour officers. It was not until they were alongside that they learnt that they were in the hands of the English corsair. Hawkins, as usual, was profuse in plausible excuses and peaceful professions. He told his stock story of bad weather, and asked leave to come in, merely to refit, making it quite clear that with leave, or without it, come in he would. The officials were helpless. Permission was given Hawkins to come in, and a promise was made that a messenger should go at once to the City of Mexico to obtain the Viceroy's licence for trade. Before night the English ships, their prizes, and their French ally, were in what was destined to prove a fatal trap to all but two of them.

The harbour of Vera Cruz is bad, but it is the only one upon that coast. It is formed by the little rocky island of San Juan de Ulloa or Lua, which lies at a distance of from 400 to 600 yards from the shore. Between the island and the mainland there is about three-quarters of a mile of fairly good anchorage stretching from north-west to south-east. San Juan de Ulloa was in after-times covered by a castle, which is still in existence. In Hawkins's time it was a mere bare rock, standing about 3 feet above the level of the sea, with water enough on the inside of it for much larger vessels than his to moor themselves to it as to a natural quay. The town of Vera Cruz was a small, unhealthy place, little used except for warehouses and offices at the coming and sailing of the yearly convoys. It was estimated to contain about 140 men capable of bearing arms, and was unfortified. If he had not been disturbed from without, Hawkins might easily have played his own game here, as he did at Borburata, and have sailed, after disposing profitably of his negroes, with the satisfaction of having defied the King of Spain's laws under the very nose of his Viceroy of Mexico; but on the day after he had entered the port the expected convoy turned up from Spain, and the slaver found himself for the first time during his cruises in a position of very serious difficulty indeed.

The Spanish convoy consisted of thirteen vessels, one of them, the "capitana" of Don Francisco Lujan, the naval officer in command, being in fighting trim, and the other twelve heavily laden merchant galleons. These last were, no doubt armed, as all vessels except mere coasters were at that time, but they certainly were not so heavily gunned as several of Hawkins's own, and they were crowded with cargo, as well as severely tried by the voyage. On board one of them came the new Viceroy of Mexico, Don Martin Enriquez.

The truth about the week of fraud and violence which followed can only be approximately known. If a report summarized by Don Cesario Duro is to be trusted, Enriquez and Lujan refused to parley with Hawkins at all. They shipped the fighting men of Vera Cruz, sailed into the harbour, and sunk, burnt, and drove out all the English, after a determined fight, and with serious loss to themselves. This was the absolutely correct course, and if there were nothing against it but the word of Hawkins, who on his own showing never hesitated to lie, we might accept it as substantially true. It is, however, contradicted, not only by him and his followers, Hortop and Philips, but by Herrera, the official Spanish historian, who was almost a contemporary, and was well informed. Their account, too, is nowise inconsistent with general probability. Putting all four together, we may describe the course of events as something like this, with pardonable confidence: When Hawkins saw the convoy outside the port, he realized that he had before him only a choice of perils. To let the Spaniards in without conditions would have been to put the rope round his own neck. He knew not only that they denied his right to be in Vera Cruz at all, but that he had, by capturing Spanish vessels on his way there, committed acts of downright piracy. A demand for a sight of his commission, and upon his failure to produce what he did not possess, a short shrift and a long drop would be the immediate consequences of putting himself at the mercy of Don Francisco Lujan. Looking only at the circumstances immediately before him, the obvious course was to keep the Spaniards out.' He asserts that he could have done it, and probably with truth. He had either found guns on San Juan de Ulloa, or mounted ship-guns of his own there. With a battery on the island and the fire of his ships, he might safely calculate on holding the mouth of the harbour against one man-of-war, which was probably no larger than the *Jesus*, and a dozen deeply-laden galleons covered with barnacles.

But this simple course would have brought Hawkins's neck into more remote but equally serious peril. He had solemnly promised the Queen to cause no trouble in the West Indies, and although he had felt it safe to interpret his engagement with some laxity, it was possible to go too far. By excluding the Spaniards from the anchorage of Vera Cruz he would have put them at the mercy of the first "norther." These formidable storms are common in September, and if one blew while the Spaniards were outside San Juan de Ulloa they would be driven on shore. The convoy was estimated to be worth £1,800,000. If all that property and the lives of hundreds of men were lost through his act, Hawkins knew that he would have to answer for it to the Queen. Such an outrage would be more than Philip could possibly endure. He would demand satisfaction under threat of war, and it was as near as might be certain that Elizabeth would sacrifice Hawkins.

Placed as he was between the devil and the deep sea, the English rover took a course which offered many dangers, but a chance of safety. He decided to let the Spaniards enter their own harbour on conditions. Delgadillo, the Captain of the port, whom Hawkins held as a hostage, was sent on board the Spanish flagship with a message. It was to the effect that the Viceroy should be allowed to enter his master's harbour, if he would confirm the arrangement already made with the local authorities, give Hawkins leave to refit and depart in safety, and leave the Island of San Juan de Ulloa in possession of the English. This last was an indispensable condition, for, if the island were in the hands of the Spaniards, they had only to wait for the first "norther" and cut the cables of the English ships, which would then have driven helplessly on shore.

We can understand, and, if we are moderately fair-minded, have some sympathy with, the speechless rage which filled Enriquez and Lujan on the receipt of this astounding message. They were in the position of men who find themselves met at their own garden-gate by a footpad with a blunderbuss, who not only insists on food and lodgings, but on being treated as a gentleman. To throw the fellow off his guard by pretended submission, and then cut him down, was a course which would hardly cause the most honourable of men excessive scruple, even now. In the sixteenth century it was the obvious resource. Enriquez gave his word, with no intention of keeping it further than he saw occasion. The man, said Lujan, is a pirate, and we are not bound to keep our promises to him. It is possible, too, that by the code of honour of the time they considered that, by insisting on retaining his hold on San Juan, Hawkins left them free. He did not trust their word, and was therefore not entitled to more compliance with the promises made him than he could extort.

Three days had been spent in messages and disputes. On Friday the Spaniards appeared off the port. On the Monday they entered. Tuesday and Wednesday were days of sleepless watching on the part of the English and of quiet preparation on the part of the Spaniards. Hawkins, though he raised a loud outcry over the treachery with which he was treated, knew well that the promises made him must be understood to be as honest, and no more than as honest, as his excuses for being in Vera Cruz. He fastened his ships by the head to San Juan de Ulloa, and carried anchors out into the harbour to hold them by the stern. His squadron was collected at one end, with the Spaniards at the other, of the island. Nearest to the enemy was the *Jesus*; behind her the *Minion* and the small ships; his own four, the French corsair, and the prizes taken from the Portuguese, were behind the *Minion*. The Spaniards counted them as ten sail. On the island were his battery, with its guns trained on the Spaniards, and his men with their matches burning. For forty-eight hours there was a show of peace. The Viceroy landed and left for the City of Mexico. Then among the Spaniards there began to be a great display of activity—more, it seemed to the English, than was justified by the necessity of preparing for the discharge of the ships. Boats full of men came off from the shore—to the number of 1,000, said the English. They were, say the Spaniards, the 140 fighting men of Vera Cruz. There were suspicious movements among the galleons, and portholes which had been closed when they entered were seen to be open and provided with guns. Lujan was, in fact, quietly filling two fireships and getting his guns in order. As the Spanish convoys were seldom molested on their voyage out to America, they had doubtless put some of their guns in the hold to leave more room between decks, and these were now got up. Hawkins complained, and insisted on this being changed, and on that. Lujan listened, complied, assured him that there was no cause for uneasiness, adding one more to the score each time. At last, on Thursday morning, the measure was full. The wind was blowing fair for an attack down the harbour, from the Spaniards to the English. Lujan decided that the time had come. Some movement among the Spaniards, or on board them, caught Hawkins's eye. He sent his sailing-master, Barret, with another protest. This time the answer was the arrest of the messenger and a trumpet call from the flagship. Then the fight blazed up.

The attack did not find Hawkins without a plan. At no period of his life did he appear to better advantage than now, when the peril was come upon him. The huckster disappeared, and the Devonshire seaman fought for his life and his booty with hand and with headpiece. His scheme was good enough. It was to cover the smaller ships with the *Minion* and the *Jesus* till, with the help of the battery on the island, he could effect his retreat, even if he could not overpower the Spaniards. But success in carrying out this plan depended on the steadiness of his men, and, unfortunately, the courage and seamanship of Hawkins's crews were far better than their military discipline. So soon as the Spaniards had opened fire, they landed the townsmen of Vera Cruz and others from their ships on the island. Under the command of Delgadillo, this detachment charged the battery so fiercely that, by Hawkins's own confession, his men were seized with a panic and fled to the ships. The crews on board were no steadier. At the first movement of the Spaniards they cast off their fastenings and began to haul off from the rock to the middle of the harbour. Some had even begun doing it before the Spaniards fired, and the sight may have had a share in causing the panic on the shore. This promptitude saved the ships from being boarded from the island, but it was at the sacrifice of all the men in the battery, who were put to the sword by Delgadillo, with the exception of three who took to the water and swam on board. The guns they had left behind were now turned on their vessels, crowded together in the middle of the harbour, and attacked by Lujan in his "capitana," supported by the admiral ship of the galleons and a great hulk crowded with men. Before the *Minion* and the *Jesus* could get well clear of their moorings, the Spanish ships were laid alongside them, and the Spaniards, with a well-justified confidence in their numbers and their skill in the art of the sword, endeavoured to settle it by boarding. The *Minion* was in great danger, but Hawkins brought part of his own crew to her assistance, and her deck was cleared. Then the *Minion* hauled herself out by her warps. Before the crew of the *Jesus* could do as much for her she was three times boarded, and the enemy was only kept out at a heavy loss of life to the English crew. Still, by a division of labour, by hard fighting on the part of some, and hard hauling on the part of others, all working with cold steel or handspike for their lives, she, too, was hauled out.

When he had shaken off the Spaniard and could look about him, Hawkins, who had borne himself most stoutly, could see little that was not dismal in itself and ominous of worse. Their masts above the water were all that showed of the *Angel* and the *Swallow*, sunk at their anchors by the fire of the battery the English had raised for their own protection. Of the smaller vessels, the *Judith* alone proved of any use. Drake wrung her clear, but the others were deserted in a panic by the crews, which crowded into their boats to escape to the larger vessels. The *Jesus*, the *Minion*, the *Judith*, and the Frenchman alone were in a state to show fight, and they were in a ring of fire from ships and shore. At the game of gunnery the English had the advantage, for their ordnance was heavier, their powder was stronger, and the practice of their men always greatly better than the Spaniards'. But in the narrow space in which they were now penned there was no room to manœuvre, the odds were long against them, and, most fatal of all, their own guns and their own powder were battering them from the island. Soon the four became two. The Frenchman got up anchor and endeavoured to turn to windward of the Spaniards. A chain shot cut his mainmast just above the deck, and it went over his side. The game was up for him. Captain "Blond," as Hortop calls him, could only provide that his ship should be of no use to the Spaniards. He fired her, and came aboard the *Jesus* in his pinnace. The *Minion* fell down the harbour out of range. Thus the *Jesus* was left to bear the brunt alone with the little *Judith*. Very soon it became clear that the *Jesus* also must be deserted. Her spars were cut to pieces. There were six shots through the mainmast, and the best of her crew were dead or dying. Night was coming on, for the fight had begun about midday. To keep up the fight with the *Jesus* till he could transfer his slaves, gold, and hostages to the *Minion*, then to fire his ship and escape in his boats, was all that it was now possible for Hawkins to do. The *Judith* was summoned alongside. Drake came at the summons, and took the first lading of stores—that is, of slaves—to the *Minion*.

While this work was going forward Hawkins was everywhere on the side where his gunners were answering the Spanish fire—and not without effect. On board the admiral galleon there had been an explosion, for which the English not unfairly took the credit, and she was blazing. With orders and with praise, with pious exhortation and with jest, Hawkins kept up the heart of his men. He called for a tankard of beer to drink the health of all good gunners. It was dashed out of his hand by a shot, and he claimed his escape as a good omen. But his tough valour was all in vain. Lujan sent the fire-ships down on him. The fire-ship was a terrible danger to wooden vessels with inflammable canvas hanging at their yards. So the Spaniards were to feel twenty years later in Calais road. So the broken remnant of the English adventurers felt now. The crew of the *Jesus* ran from their guns, the dreadful selfishness of men in flight seized on them, and each thought only of himself. Master of himself in flight as in battle, Hawkins jumped into a skiff with two men, and rowed strenuously after the *Minion*. Very hardly he was received on board her, and there were many who could not be taken at all. In boats, or swimming with appeals for rescue, men crowded round the *Minion* and *Judith* as they sailed out of the harbour. Numbers were hauled on board till the vessels were crowded like their own slave-holds, but more were necessarily left to the little mercy of the Spaniards.

So ended the famous treachery of the Spaniards at San Juan de Ulloa. There was indeed little enough scruple on the part of the Spaniards as to the telling of lies, as little as there was in Hawkins himself, either then or some years later, when, with the consent of Walsingham, he entered into a pretended scheme to betray a part of the Queen's fleet to Philip II., with the patriotic object of cheating the Spanish King out of his money, and of information as to his designs on England. On the evening of this day of fighting the rover seemed in no case ever to trouble the King again. He was a fugitive in one small, much-battered, and overcrowded vessel. Of all his squadron the little *Judith* alone was with him. The *Jesus*, crowded with dead and wounded men, was left behind to be taken possession of by the Spaniards, who found on her the hostages Hawkins had retained unhurt, many slaves, and much prize in gold or jewels, the produce of piracy and smuggling on the coasts of Africa and the Main.

CHAPTER IX

THE SPANISH MAIN

"To pardon a pirate may be injurious to mankind, but how much greater is the crime of opening a port in which all pirates shall be safe ? The contraband trader is not more worthy of protection. If with Narborough he trades by force, he is a pirate ; if he trades secretly, he is only a thief. Those who honestly refuse his traffic he hates as obstructors of his profit, and those with whom he deals he cheats, because he knows that they dare not complain. He lives with a heart full of that malignity which fear of detection always generates in those who are to defend unjust acquisitions against lawful authority, and when he comes home with riches thus acquired he brings a mind hardened in evil, too proud for reproof, and too stupid for reflection. He offends the high by his insolence, and corrupts the low by his example " ("Thoughts on the Late Transactions respecting Falkland's Islands," Dr. Johnson, 1771).

WHEN Dr. Johnson wrote these words he was, it may be, thinking as much of the hastily and dishonestly enriched Indian Nabobs, who were then a conspicuous and offensive element in London society, as of armed smugglers on the Spanish Main. Yet this passage of his " Reflections " was well in place. Everybody knew why the British Government had suddenly decided to enforce a dubious claim to the Falkland Islands. Their intrinsic value was trifling. Treeless, barren, swept by the icy winds which blow up from the South Pole, they were in themselves worthless for agriculture, and at that time their pastures, which are now of some merit, were no attraction. But they contain some good harbours, and they lie on a level with the eastern entrance to the Straits of Magellan. The decent reason for insisting on taking possession of them was that they would serve as a headquarters of a whaling industry. The real motive for endeavouring to make a settlement on them was that they were thought capable of supplying a depot and taking-off place for the contraband trade with South America. To secure access to this market was the wish alike of the most important Governments in Europe, and of those who ventured on their own account with what Dr. Johnson called the " morality of a sailor "—that is to say, with the determination to trade by force if they could not obtain permission. So late as the close of the American War of Independence the British Government would have restored Gibraltar to Spain in exchange for Trinidad, which lay at the gate of " the Main." Seventy years earlier it had taken advantage of the weakness of the Spanish monarchy to impose upon it the famous Asiento Treaty.

It is very necessary to appreciate the true character of this contraband trade. Many writers have denounced with force and justice the dog in the manger policy of the Spaniards, who, though not themselves a manufacturing people, persisted in endeavouring to shut their widely-spread American possessions to the direct trade of other peoples. But the sale of goods was not the only object of the contraband trade. They, too, could, and did, enter the Spanish colonies through the ports of the mother country. Because Spain had few manufactures, she was compelled to purchase the produce of other nations for re-export to her colonies. The trade might have been so conducted not only with profit, but without delay. A glance at a globe, which is not, as all maps of large areas are, misleading, will show that Spain lies on the road from Europe to Central and South America. The trade was so conducted, and that by foreign capital, from the early sixteenth century. Spanish ship-owners and merchants were to a great extent only the agents—the *prête-noms* of foreign capitalists. The reputation of the Spaniards for probity, which was so ill-justified by the conduct of their Government, was based on the acknowledged fact that they rarely took advantage of a technical legality or a state of war to defraud their foreign correspondents. But since the trade could have gone on openly or under a thin disguise, what need was there for contraband ?

There were several reasons why it should arise. The Spanish Government, with characteristic obstinacy, would persist in endeavouring to do the impossible—to exclude the goods of foreigners, which it knew by long experience to be indispensable. In its dire need for money it taxed and fleeced the trade of its ports to strangulation. It was enslaved to the theory that the wealth of a people consists in the precious metals and coined money. It would not free the trade in silver. By outrageous taxation and obstructions it drove the foreigner to the use of armed contraband in America. And then the import most desired in its colonies was " ebony," the " pieza de Indias."* The slave-trade could not be conducted through Spanish ports. What the foreigner mainly desired to obtain from Spanish America was the silver of Mexican and Peruvian mines, and the laws of Spain forbade the re-export of bullion or coined money. This silver was not valued only because it was the then most generally useful commercial metal, but because it was indispensable for the eastern trade. Europe has, ever since it began to trade with India before the Christian Era, exported to it incalculable quantities of the precious metals, and especially of silver, which have been engulfed and hoarded. The re-export of bullion was forbidden in the laws of all countries, but the prohibition was relaxed to meet the imperative necessity of the Indian market. The

* This little bit of Spanish has long been a curiosity, and few Spaniards could now say what was its original meaning. The literal meaning is "piece of the Indies," or "Indian piece," which, until itself interpreted, means nothing. The "pieza de Indias" was seven spans (quartos) of healthy negro flesh and blood. The " quarto " was the fourth part of the yard (vara) of Castile, which is divided into 3 feet of 12 inches, and four spans of 12 digits. The vara is to the English yard as 836 millimetres of the French metrical scale are to 911—that is to say, that it is about 3 inches shorter. When, now, a cargo of slaves was to be sold in a Spanish American market, it was shoaled or sorted into batches of men, women, and children able to work. Children-in-arms were thrown in. The trader did not wish to find himself left with children or undersized men and women on his hands, after the stoutest had been picked out by the purchaser. The members of the batch were then measured in spans, and the total divided by seven. It was then sold as so many "piezas de Indias " at such or such a price the "pieza." There might be more or fewer individuals than "piezas," according to the composition of the batch. In later times "piezas de Indias " came to mean simply the imported negro, or "negro bozal," as distinguished from the negro born on the plantation and bred in slavery.

Indiaman commonly sailed with some goods and a mass of silver coins. To avoid a too open disregard of its own laws a European State required that these coins should be, in great part at least, Spanish. Spanish coins were struck for the trade in England or Holland. But they were also imported from America. Spain was the chief, all but the only, producer of silver from the sixteenth century downwards, and her own mints were in Mexico or Peru. But for the demands of Eastern trade it is highly probable that the mines of Spanish America would have been closed by the end of the sixteenth century. As the silver must be obtained, and could be got only from the Spaniards, there was an unceasing effort to secure it in America or Spain by permitted trade if possible, and when not by contraband or violence. And the most certain, though not the only, way of coming at it by contraband was to smuggle negroes. The earliest adventurers within the sphere of Spain began the trade. We have seen it opened for England by John Hawkins, who did but sail in the wake of Frenchmen. He kidnapped negroes on the coast of Africa, and sold them by force or fraud in Spanish America. The example he set was followed by his countrymen, by the Dutch, and the French, while the slave-trade lasted, and Spain retained her possessions in the New World. The English island Jamaica, the Dutch island Curaçoa, the French island Martinique, were depots of slaves brought from Africa to be smuggled into the Spanish possessions. If we ardently desired to acquire Trinidad, our motive was the wish to use it for the same purpose.*

Much which is suggested by the words " Spanish Main "

* The history of this side of commerce has still to be written. We have done very little to elucidate our own share—perhaps because it is not quite pleasant for the country, which, when it had stocked its own colonies to overflowing, took the lead in abolishing the slave-trade, to confess that it had no more ardent wish for many generations than to be the greatest kidnapper and smuggler of blacks in the world. Much light has been thrown on it by the doctoral thesis of M. G. Scelle ("La Traite Negrière aux Indes de Castille," Paris, 2 vols., 1906), and by "Les Relations Commerciales et Maritimes entre la France et les Côtes de l'Océan Pacifique," of E. W. Dahlgren, translated from Swedish, Paris, 1909. Something may be learnt from the treatises of Don Dionisio de Alsedo, republished under the somewhat misleading title, " Piraterias y Agresiones de los Ingleses," etc., by Don Justo Zaragoza," Madrid, 1883.

either does not belong to our subject, or touches it only indirectly. The Buccaneers, for instance, had but little connection with the sea trader. What connection they had was mainly in the illustration they afforded of what could hardly fail to happen when a power claiming dominion could not shut out intruders entirely, and would not allow them to come freely. At the close of the sixteenth century Spain had effective possession of the Greater Antilles, Cuba, Hispaniola (Hayti), Porto Rico, and Jamaica. She had no real hold on the lesser islands of the West Indies. If she could have occupied them, or if she could have maintained a permanent naval force to exclude all foreigners, the Buccaneers could never have come into existence. But she had no population from which to supply colonists. The few Spaniards who at that time emigrated to America went to the mainland, and she had not the resources for maintaining a permanent force. If she could have frankly recognized her inability to exclude the whole world, and could have allowed foreigners to settle peacefully in the unoccupied islands, then there would have been no reason why there should have been any Buccaneers. But Spain could not fight hard, and would not fall soft. She would only make erratic efforts to expel the settlers, and then leave the islands from which they had been expelled ungarrisoned. In the early seventeenth century there were repeated occasions on which such expulsions were carried out. Of course, the squatters came back so soon as the invaders were gone, and they came back exasperated, impoverished, persuaded that there was no security to be looked for in the neighbourhood of the Spaniard, and also that he was too weak to control them effectually. In such condition a predatory population came inevitably into existence. The Buccaneers and "Brothers of the Coast" were the direct product of Spanish policy. As Spain sank into the decadence of the middle seventeenth century, they became aggressive, and the predatory adventurers of the Antilles overflowed into Central America and the South Seas.

The Buccaneer wars belong to the middle and later part of the seventeenth century—to the interval between the establishment of the English in Jamaica, and the French in Martinique and Guadéloupe, and the final heart-broken recognition by Spain of the fact that she could not preserve the New World to herself. The contraband trade began long before there were any " Brothers of the Coast," and went on while the Spanish dominion in America endured. It arose and it lasted by the very facts of the case. The Spaniard himself, with his well-known capacity for creating a sententious proverb, has found a formula in which to state the conclusion of the whole matter. "He who would bring back the wealth of the Indies must first take the wealth of the Indies out with him." In sober business language this means that capital is required to develop a colony. Now, the Spaniard had but little capital. Seamen, artisans, traders, are as needful as capital, and though Spain has produced all three types, she has never had many of them. Her best trading element she ruined, knowing well what she was about, and doing it for the love of God, when she laid hands upon her Jews, and expelled all of them whom she could not emasculate and cow into bad copies of the real Spaniard by a religious persecution unsurpassed for efficiency. The true Spaniard was, in the first place, a herdsman, and then in less degree he was a vine-dresser and a tiller of the soil. His first purpose in the Indies was to grow rich at a stroke by plunder. When that was impossible, then he wished to grow rich speedily by means of slave labour on plantations, in cattle stations, or in mines. What capital he could not obtain by pillage—and it was much the greater part of what he required—and whatever instruments or goods he had to use, he must needs bring from Europe. And Spain could supply neither from her own resources. The success with which the Iberian peoples (for Portugal must be taken in with Spain) established themselves as masters of the vast region stretching from Mexico to the Pampas of what is now Argentina, was a remarkable feat of colonization. The rapidity with which the New World was covered by countless herds of cattle and flocks of sheep, the descendants of animals imported from Europe, is proof of the Spaniard's natural capacity as a herdsman. It is not so easy to decide what we are to say of his equally rapid success in forming a population attached to him by consanguinity and loyal to him for many generations. It was not done with any regard to morals. The sexual morality of Spanish America (which, I repeat, includes Portuguese) is to this day the lowest of any people with a claim to civilization and Christianity. What it is, it is by inheritance. The Inquisition strove hard by precept, and by punishments of incredible severity, to eradicate the belief of the medieval Spaniard that concubinage is no sin except when the woman is a wife, and the element of adultery is introduced. It met with some success at home. In America it utterly failed. The leading type of the settler from either of the Iberian kingdoms was that Jaõ Ramalho, whose provable descendants are numerous in the Brazilian State of São Paulo to this day. Ramalho was left behind, either because he was marooned, or because he remained of his own free will, among the Tupi Indians of the Serra da Mar very early in the sixteenth century. Being an armourer and a handy man, he found favour with the " King " Tibiriça, who gave him a daughter in marriage. The tribe was not monogamous, and other daughters of other Tupis were given to Jão Ramalho, to win his favour, or the aid of his arts. When he died, at a great age, he was the patriarch of a tribe of three hundred and more children, grand-children, and great-grandchildren. They had their encampment on the hill now covered by the city of São Paulo. They were known as the " Mamalucos," and they were the guides of Portuguese conquest and exploration in the hinterland. We know his story, and we know that there were thousands like him whose biographies are lost. War left multitudes of native women to work for Spanish masters and bear them children. Their offspring formed the bulk of the Spanish population. Pure-blooded Spaniards were (and are) hardly to be found, except in towns and among new-comers. They were looked up to and they led, and the cross-breeds, proud of their Spanish blood, thought true whites had the right to be masters.

This population was scattered thinly over a continent and a half. It had needs which the mother country could not supply. The whole commercial history of Spain is one long, contumacious and inevitably unsuccessful fight to keep out the foreigner—that is to say, with the nature of things. Spanish rulers strove to keep the trade in Spanish hands. They would not allow their own native shipowners and merchants to sail at their own risk and to go where they pleased, lest they should be tempted by a base lucre of gain to carry for the foreigner. They regulated, they limited, they fixed certain ports as the only places of trade, and they enforced convoy. As the market extended in America, and while Spain, strangled as she was by insane fiscal regulations, grew poorer, and in all probability less populous, while she certainly grew more idle, largely because it was so difficult for any man to see any fruit of his labour, her rulers could think of nothing but of more and ever more regulation. They met every demonstration that Spain could not supply her colonies by mere dogged persistence in the old course. When their subjects at home and in America took, in sheer self-defence, to contraband, all the rulers could do was to threaten, lament, and make fresh regulations. Meanwhile the poverty, which was mainly their own work, prevented them from paying their servants, and the very agents they employed to exclude the foreigner were left to choose between taking his bribes and dying of starvation. If some power at once irresistible and mischievous had set itself deliberately to organize a state of things in which a contraband trade must arise, and in which contraband was justifiable, it could not have done better. If Spain could have succeeded in excluding all foreign trade from her possessions in America, she would have done it at the cost of ruining them completely.*

It naturally came to pass that the first field of the contraband trade which arose because Spain would have it so, was the " carrera de Indias " described in Chapter V. There was, however, a secondary route of less fame and later

* Dr. Johnson once startled his company by shouting that patriotism was the last refuge of a scoundrel. If he had been surveying this part of our subject, he might have said that it is the parrot cry of a fool. The Spaniards were very patriotic, and would have given a short shrift to any man amongst them who had spoken of surrendering their "rights." Meanwhile they profited individually by the contraband. But as patriotic Spaniards they would hear nothing of concessions, and so they persevered in maintaining their dignity till the knife was at their throats, and all was lost.

origin—that between Cadiz and the River Plate. It could not be included in the round of the " flotas " and " armadas de galeones," because of distance and position. When the Spaniard Solis first entered the miscalled river, which is in fact the estuary of the Paraná and the Uruguay, he hoped that he had found a stream leading to Peru, the country of the silver mines. Therefore he named the estuary the Rio de la Plata, the river which bears the silver, not the silver coloured. Its muddy waters, charged with the silt brought down by the heavily-laden Paraná and Uruguay could never have earned the compliment. On the south side the Spaniards, in time, founded the station which took its name from the chapel dedicated to Nuestra Señora de los Buenos Ayres (Our Lady of Fair Winds). The etymology which accounts for the name by the fine air or good climate of the place, is fantastic. Buenos Ayres is no port—only a spot on a line of shallow coast which the deposit of the rivers renders yearly more shallow.*

The first settlers might well seem to deserve the reproach of those " blind " early Greeks who planted themselves on the eastern shore of the Hellespont, and neglected the Golden Horn. On the other side of the Rio de la Plata lies the natural harbour of Monte Video. But Monte Video is open to the south and south-westerly winds—the Pamperos, the most dangerous of that coast. Moreover, the north side of the estuary was in dispute between Spain and Portugal. Monte Video was for a long time little more than a stopping-place, where vessels on their way to Buenos Ayres put in for a pilot.

The Spaniards made small use of Buenos Ayres as a shipping-place for treasure, though it was used for that purpose in war, when hostile fleets blockaded the ports of Central

* The modern harbour of Buenos Ayres is a work of engineering. The approach to the docks is made by two channels—the north and south—dredged, and kept open by incessant dredging. Vessels drawing 20 feet of water can just grovel over the mud, and when the wind blows off shore they not uncommonly ground right in, or on the way to, the docks. The day when the whole estuary will be a mud flat is perhaps too far off to be calculable. Yet it comes slowly nearer. A comparison between old and modern pilotage books shows that the depth of water in many parts of the estuary is now 2 and 3 feet less than it was when the Spaniards first came.

America. There were drawbacks to the value of Buenos Ayres as an outlet for the trade of Peru.* The upper stretches of the rivers were unmanageable. As the Spaniards, after crossing the isthmus of Panama, spread down by Peru to Chili, and then turned across the Andes, they reached the rich lands of Salta and Tucuman, now the most northerly provinces of the Argentine Republic. Then they found their road to the south barred by a great belt of waterless salt desert. Trade arose and was carried on by caravans of carts with enormous wheels, drawn by droves of spirited little Creole horses. A caravan left in one year and returned in the next, and sometimes it never came back, for the desert was raided by savage Indians, and swept by duststorms. By that route came the produce of the lands east of the Andes. The manufactures which Spain allowed her colonists to receive, or which they obtained by contraband, went back by the same way. It would, seemingly, have been easier to let the trade of the Pacific coast and of Salta and Tucuman come in and out by the Pacific ports. But the Straits of Magellan are too dangerous for regular use by sailing ships. Their natural route was round the Horn. The way was shown in 1616-17 by the Dutch merchant Lemaire and his colleague, the skipper William Schouten. They came, not to smuggle nor to pillage on the Spanish coast, but to turn the Charter of the Dutch East India Company, and reach the Spice Islands by a route not expressly forbidden. They did reach the islands, and were promptly impounded by the company as interlopers. Yet they had shown the way, and it was used for military expeditions and privateering not seldom, and during one curious episode for trade.

Lemaire and Schouten are not men to be dismissed with a bare reference. They are too much at home in our immediate subject for one thing, and then for another their feat had certain consequences. Be it repeated, to begin with, that they came interloping. The Dutch Company, though less assailed than the English, had enemies. There were

* The reader may note that the old Viceroyalty of Peru, until it was divided in the eighteenth century, meant the possession of Spain in South America.

merchants in the Netherlands who thought it hard that they could not trade to the Spice Islands for their own account. One of them was Jacob Lemaire. Reflecting on the matter, he came to the conclusion that the company's charter only gave it a monopoly of the trade to the East by the routes known in 1602—by the Cape and the Straits of Magellan. If, now, another route could be found, could it not be lawfully followed by the free-trader? What a court of appeal would have said to this reasoning we can confidently guess, but to the enterprising trader, and the bold Dutch seaman whom he joined in fellowship with him, it looked sound. They formed the plausible scientific hypothesis that there must be a passage into the Pacific south of the Straits of Magellan. So they sailed to find it, and proved they were right by passing between Staaten Island and the Tierra del Fuego, and then rounding the Horn. From that point they struck diagonally across the Pacific, as Magellan had done before them, and reached the Moluccas. Their feat brought no good to them. The company would not listen to Lemaire's ingenious reading of its charter. The explorers' ships were seized, their men taken into the company's service, and they were imprisoned as interlopers. Lemaire died on the way home, and Schouten, though he was honoured as an explorer, could never recover damages from the company. But they had shown others a better way into the South Seas than the formidable Straits of Magellan. " South Seas " was the, for long, generally used misnomer for the Pacific. Vasco Nuñez de Balboa, who first looked at its waters from the peak of Darien, saw it to the south of him, and called it the " Mar del Sur." As the name America, which was first given to what was supposed to be an island newly discovered by Amerigo Vespucci, spread by use and wont over the two Americas, so the " Mar del Sur "—South Sea—grew to be the whole North and South Pacific in current language. By a process not to be defended on rational grounds, but sufficiently intelligible, the Atlantic was frequently called the North Sea simply because it was not the same body of water as the Pacific, improperly called the South Sea.

The route to the islands of the Indian Ocean, and then

by a diagonal course across the South Pacific, was used, but not much. The Spaniards discovered that the best route was by the equatorial current and the easterly trade-wind. If the navigator were coming from Europe to the Philippines by the Straits of Magellan, the longest way round was the shortest road home for him. The best thing he could do was to come up the coast of South America by the southerly wind from the Pole (which alone renders much of it habitable) and strike west by the equatorial current. But if it was easy to go from east to west by this route, to come back from west to east against wind and current was all but impossible for the ships of the time. Yet the skilful navigator can always find wind and waves to obey him. Andres de Urdaneta, who sailed to the Philippines in 1564 with the first Spanish settler, Miguel de Legaspi, formed his scientific hypothesis. He calculated that by going north to the fortieth parallel he would find a wind from the west corresponding to the westerly winds of the North Atlantic. He put it to the test, and proved that he was right. His return voyage was the last great service rendered by Spanish seamen to seamanship and navigation. As the chart of the Pacific was when Urdaneta completed his return voyage, so, not wholly, but in the main, it remained till the voyages of Captain Cook.

The Spaniards made as good as no use of the route to South America, either by the Straits of Magellan or by the Horn. They were bound to the "carrera de Indias," and to the transport of goods across the isthmus of Panama and down by the sea to Peru. All goods brought by this broken and laborious way came burdened by cost of carriage and the long series of custom dues levied by the Spanish Government. Therefore Peru was particularly ill-supplied among Spanish colonies. Yet it was rich in silver, and there was a class of wealthy people ready to buy, and, as experience was to prove, very ready to profit by a contraband trade. Its market would have been known, even if it had not been revealed by the raids of the Buccaneers. The wish to reach it was lively in Europe. In 1669 the Government of Charles II. sent out Captain John Narbrough to see what could be done to open trade.

He came back to report that there was no trading to be done except by force—the opinion which provoked the reprobation of Johnson. England and Holland were busy elsewhere. The opportunities for contraband presented by the Pacific coast of South America were neglected till France stepped in.

French goods—fine cloths, lace, paper, and playing-cards—had found their way to South America in considerable quantities already by Cadiz and the Fair of Porto Bello. But in time the French began to realize that they had everything to gain by going direct to the Peruvian market, and bringing back the silver coin, for themselves. The trade was an absolutely perfect one according to mercantile theory of the time, for France would get rid of her manufactures, and would bring in " real wealth "—to wit, the precious metals. The relations of the French Government to the contraband trade which did arise were curious. They varied from direct encouragement to indirect encouragement, given in the form of permission to make " voyages of discovery," which all the world knew well were to be voyages of contraband to Peru, and from that again to strict prohibition when King Lewis XIV. wished to please the Spanish Government.*

The story was further complicated by the formation of great companies. The French Government had as great " a rage for regulation " as any other. It endeavoured to control the trade with distant regions through companies for China and the South Seas. They were all ill-managed, full of dissensions, lawsuits, and rivalries, and all became bankrupt long before the wrecks of them were swept into the great abyss of Law's Mississippi Company in 1720.

Wisdom cries aloud in the streets, and no man marks her. When Law's universal company was being formed certain merchants of Marseilles petitioned against it. " Our experience," said they, " has shown us that not one of the

* The story would go far beyond my limits. The reader will be rewarded if he consults " La France et les Côtes de l'Océan Pacifique " of Mr. E. W. Dahlgren, and an article by him in vol. lxxxviii. of *La Revue Historique*, pp. 225-263—" Le Comte Jérôme de Pontchartrain et les Armateurs de Saint-Malo." Also the second volume of " La Traite Négrière " of M. Scelle.

general companies has ever succeeded in France, and that all have become bankrupt. It is certain that what is called a company in which the State interferes will never have the confidence of traders or of foreigners." And that was the conclusion of the whole matter, and for the reason the petitioners gave—namely, that when men were allowed to work for themselves " cupidity supported industry," and all exerted themselves; but when they were " regulated," then they fell into a dull routine. That is the history of the China Company, the two South Sea Companies, and the French East India Company itself.* They did practically nothing. If the French did work up a considerable trade in the South Seas, the credit belongs to the interlopers, and among them mostly to the crafty and enterprising seamen and merchants of the Corsair town, St. Malo. The flourishing time of their trade began in 1700, with the establishment of the Bourbon dynasty on the throne of Spain. It has been said that the French Government obtained leave from King Philip V. for its traders in the South Seas. But this was not the case. The French Government did obtain an " asiento," a contract for the supply of slaves, but its " asiento " company took no part in the South Sea trade. The Spanish Government never ceased to protest against the visits of French traders to Peru, and Lewis XIV. was disposed to satisfy it. He checked the trade quite as much as he encouraged it, and as for the interlopers, the chief difficulty they had to contend with all along was the hostility of their own Government, which they were constantly called upon to defy or to bamboozle. The conduct of the Spanish Government was characteristic. The utter disorganization of its administration, the rotten-

* It ought, perhaps, to be added that the French Government not only insisted on regulating, but did its work of regulation with incoherence (see E. W. Dahlgren, *op. cit., passim*). The comparative success of the Dutch and English Companies is no argument in favour of the company policy of Colbert and Lewis XIV. They were corporations of privileged men of business who were called upon to pay for their privileges, but were allowed to manage their own affairs. The French Government's policy, for which that meddlesome and pedantically dictatorial person, the " great " Colbert was largely responsible, was essentially similar to the policy of the Consejo de las Indias, and Casa de la Contratacion, which regulated Spanish commerce out of existence.

ness of its galleons, the disappearance of its seamen, and the hostile fleets of England and Holland throughout the whole War of Succession, continued to make it impossible to send the regular convoys to the West Indies. Spain could neither supply her colonies nor bring in her own silver. Yet she endeavoured to prevent her French allies from doing the work, or accepted their help grudgingly and from time to time.

It speaks well for the enterprise of French shipowners in St. Malo, Nantes, Rochelle, and Marseilles, that within the space of some sixteen years, beginning in 1695, they contrived to send as many as 200 vessels (according to the Spaniards) to Peru, to flood the colony with French manufactures and other produce, and to bring back bullion coined and in bars to the value of many millions of "livres."* In 1709 a number of these adventurers, who were brought back, little to their liking, under escort of a King's ship, confessed to having with them 31,000,000 livres, which the King, in his royal way, condescended to "borrow" in whole or in part. In his royal way the King never repaid the loan, and the Malouins, who were the chief losers, were fain to console themselves by inventing the legend that they, loyally and patriotically, of their own free will and mere motion, lent their 31,000,000 livres for the relief of His Majesty's treasury in that the worst year of the Succession War. This was clever of them, but it was cleverer to conceal large parts of their bullion as they did. In addition to the long list of South Sea voyages which are recorded, there were others which were concealed from the authorities. Ships slipped off without a permit from the Minister of Marine, and came back without telling him where

* It is necessary to be on one's guard in estimating the value of the "livre." The French themselves have been much in the habit of using the word as if it were the equivalent of franc. But the "livre," which was "a money of account," has varied in value from a pound sterling, divided into twenty "sous" of twelve "deniers," down to less than a franc. During part of the reign of Lewis XIV. it was worth two francs and a half, but it sank (see the Vicomte G. D'Avenel's "Histoire Économique de la Propriété," etc., 1894, vol. i.). The treasure brought from Spanish America was frequently calculated in "piastres." The "piastre" (which is still generally quoted as a standard of value in rural Normandy) was slightly more valuable than the "écu" of four livres.

they had been. The bullion they brought was of immense value to France. What amount of good it did to the men who actually brought it is another question.

To give a list of these South Sea voyages would be an easy mechanical task. To show the men and their way of life is not so easy. The narratives, as far as I know them, are not so rich in humanity and colour as our own Elizabethan and Jacobean voyages, or even as Dampier or Woodes Rogers. The " Relation du Voyage de la Mer du Sud aux Côtes du Chily et du Pérou," of M. Frezier, is, indeed, excellent in its kind. But it is excellent because it gives a valuable account of the condition of the Spanish possessions on the Pacific coast of South America in 1711, 1713, and 1714. Frezier, " Ingénieur ordinaire du Roy," was not only not a seaman, but he frankly confesses that he detested the sea, and was perfectly uncomfortable in his ship, the *Joseph*. His function was to make scientific observations, and report on the position and state of the Spanish harbours, and he discharged it well. As a rule the scientific work was well done on these voyages. The observations were carefully taken, and the charts based on them beautifully executed. But the men ? and how did they live ? Well, it has to be confessed that the self-assertions, vain jactitations, malicious mutual accusations, official pedantry, and, in a general way, the Jack-in-office spirit which have been so ruinous to French colonial enterprise, were too prominent among the officers. The men we see less of, and what we do see leaves the impression that, if it was always possible to recruit crews for these South Sea voyages, the reason was not that the men gained much, but that if they had remained at home they would probably have been pressed into the navy, where they would have been even worse off. We hear too much of " poor sailors " left unpaid or cheated out of the fair profits of their little ventures.

When we turn to a particular voyage, we find without surprise that it bears a close likeness to the visits of Hawkins to the Main. The conditions were the same, and the events could not differ widely. Let us take, for instance, the voyage of Beauchesne, executed in 1698-1701. It was to have been a great affair undertaken by the South Sea Company

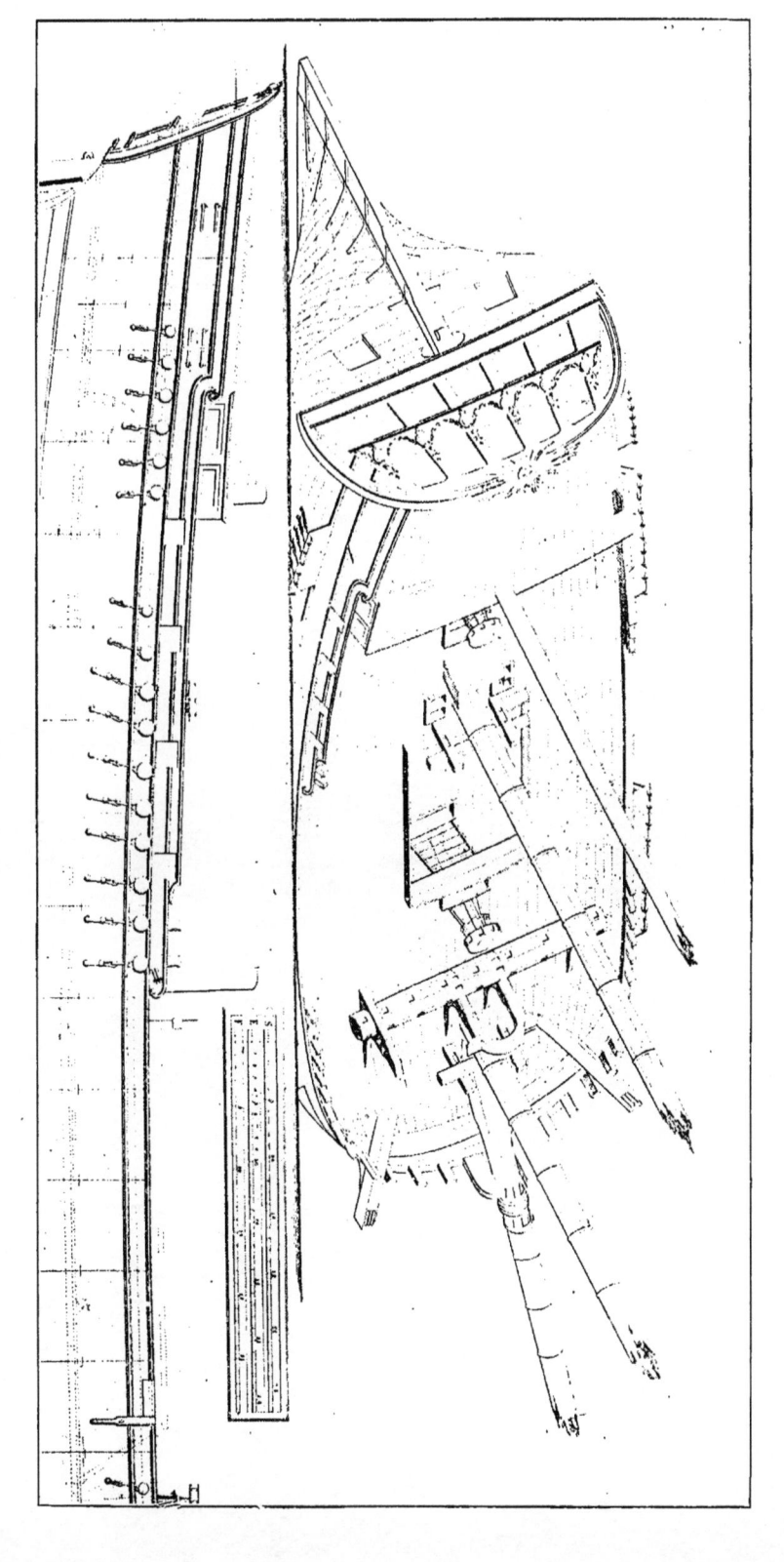

MERCHANT SHIP.
From Chapman's "Architectura Navalis Mercatoria."

To face page 214.

with views of colonization. Soldiers, workmen, and a corps of cadets were to have been carried. That nothing might be lacking, the services of an old "Phlibustier"—*i.e.*, Buccaneer—of the resounding name of Jouhan de la Gilbaudière, were secured. Gilbaudière had been in the South Seas with the Buccaneers, had gone through many adventures, had been, among other troubles, wrecked in the Straits of Magellan, where he and his messmates had built themselves a small vessel out of the ruins of the larger one, and had in her found their way home. Obviously, he was a man capable of being useful, if he could be kept in order. But the grand plan was frittered down to a contraband voyage. There were difficulties in getting the capital together, and the merchant adventurers fell out. The cadets were allowed to haunt the taverns of La Rochelle, where they spent their money and incurred debts. Greatly indignant at the way in which they were treated, they grew outrageous, and threatened to burn the company's agent, M. de Roddes, alive in his lodgings. M. de Gennes, who was to have commanded, threw up his commission in disgust. His second, Beauchesne, also resigned, but was persuaded to resume service, and finally sailed with four vessels—the *Phelypeaux, Maurepas, Bonne Nouvelle*, and *Nécessaire* (which followed the others)—on December 17th, 1698.*

M. de Beauchesne was plainly enough the very man for the work. He took his ships through the Straits of Magellan, where his crews suffered severely, and where he erected a pillar to mark his taking possession of the island, which he named after Lewis the Great. It is now the Isla Carlos III. Then he went on to Valdivia, sending his second, M. de Terville, ahead. At Valdivia Terville was at first fired at, and found it necessary to anchor out of range of the fort. Communications were, however, opened. As the Spaniards were notoriously respectful to the clergy, the French chaplain was sent as envoy. At first all seemed to go well. The Spanish officer apologized for firing at the white flag of France, on the ground that it had been shown by the only foreigners they ever saw in those waters—the pirates.

* The voyage of Beauchesne made a stir in its day, and left traces. For the copious bibliography, see Dahlgren, *op. cit.*, p. 132.

Friendly professions were exchanged. The Spaniards produced a liquor which the French called " guildive," and described as stronger than brandy, injurious, and disagreeable to drink. They did drink the Governor's health in it once, and they thought once enough. To make things still more pleasant, the Spanish Governor invited the envoys to dinner, and told Terville that he might anchor close to the fort. The Frenchman brought his ship, the *Maurepas*, in, and was actually preparing his return dinner to the friendly Spanish officials, when the fort opened fire. It was the story of the treachery of the Spaniards at San Juan de Ulloa on a meaner and a smaller scale. Nor were the results equally disastrous to the victim. Three men were killed in the *Maurepas* and others wounded, and some damage done to the ship. But, as Terville piously observed, God visibly protected him by sending a nice breeze from the east-north-east. He cut his cables and got to sea just in time to meet Beauchesne, who was coming up the coast.

It was plain that no trade was to be done at Valdivia. Beauchesne, who, even if he had had the necessary force, would probably have been too much afraid of getting into trouble at home to attack the town, went north, looking for chance to trade. For a time the colonists obeyed the order of the Viceroy, and would have no communication with the Frenchmen. They may very well have doubted whether he was in truth only a smuggler, and not a Buccaneer. At last, when Beauchesne was on the point of giving up the venture as hopeless, and going away to India, the townsmen of Arica opened communications with him. Though his goods had suffered on the voyage, he was able to get rid of them at remunerative prices at Arica, at Ilo, to which the merchants invited him to go in order that he might be better concealed, and, in fact, at many points on the coast. The Viceroy thundered and threatened to send armed ships, which, however, never appeared. In the end Beauchesne sold his cargoes and returned by Cape Horn, with 400,000 livres of bullion " very well satisfied with the Spaniards, but not at all with the Viceroy."

What the Viceroy's share in the story was is not so very clear. The Count of Monclova, who then held the post, was a gentleman of the enviable name of Portocarrero Laso de la Vega. He had been Viceroy in Mexico from 1685-1688, had then in the ordinary course of promotion passed to Peru, where he held office for an unusually long period, and where he died. What is known of him says a great deal as to the contraband trade. He left a fortune, estimated at 14,000,000 piastres, in possession of his widow and son. They elected to remain in Peru, where the Count's colossal fortune—say £3,000,000—was stored in the great Franciscan convent at Lima. Fear of accident on the voyage had no doubt a share in helping them to come to the decision to remain. But they had another reason. They had no wish to carry the fortune to Spain, where it might have been subject to the indiscreet curiosity of the King's officers, and they were wise. At a later period the Government of King Philip V. cast its eye on the Count's hoard. The King said that Monclova was no doubt a very honourable man, and that, but for his lamented death, he would have been able to give a most satisfactory explanation of the origin of those millions of piastres; but as a matter of fact, no account had ever been given, and His Majesty thought that at least a million of the fourteen might reasonably be subtracted to meet the needs of the Crown. Whether the Countess and her son, who were firmly recalcitrant, were ever forced to disgorge, I cannot undertake to say. The lady was certainly resolute in refusing to leave the "oyster bed." And what have the fortune of the Viceroy and the obstinacy of his lady to do with the contraband trade? Well, when a Viceroy heaps together 14,000,000 of piastres in fifteen years or so, it is pretty obvious that he was not content with fair economies on his official salary. He took bribes, and took them, among other things, for permitting the unlawful trade, and that explains much. It is antecedently probable that the merchants who came on the quiet to trade with Beauchesne had first settled to an arrangement with His Excellency.

This is as much as need be said here concerning the French share in the contraband trade of the Viceroyalty of Peru. It went on till the Regency of the Duke of Orleans, and was then stopped by the French Government itself. The Duke sent out a squadron which drove the French ships away. His reasons were that he wished to please the King of Spain, his cousin, a little, and that he wished very much to please the British Government, because he desired to obtain its support.

At the first blush it is not quite obvious why the British Government should have desired to see the contraband trade of the French ships stopped. But the thing is simple enough. The British Government had, indeed, no wish to stop the contraband, but it did wish to confine the trade to British subjects. The point was very well put by Lord Lexington, British Envoy in Spain in 1712, in the course of a despatch to Lord Dartmouth, Secretary of State in the Ministry of Harley. " Therefore, I think we had better stick to our clandestine trade, which, by the Assiento, we have entirely to ourselves exclusively [sic] to all the world . . . and make it as difficult to others as we can." Lexington's despatch referred to the reasons he thought there were why Great Britain should not insist on a reduction of the dues charged on its goods exported to Spanish America through Cadiz. If we could secure a monopoly, it mattered little to us what dues were charged, since, in the end, they would be paid by the consumer in America—by the King of Spain's own subjects. And Great Britain had taken measures to secure the monopoly. To obtain a share in the trade of the Indies had been a great object with the Powers concerned in the War of Succession, and, as it drew to a close, various proposals were made, if not exactly for throwing it open, at least for making it more accessible. Spain would have been well advised to meet the reasonable wishes of European trading nations, but she behaved like herself. The Spaniards had to pay for the follies they inherited, and still persisted in taking for wisdom. Moreover, Spanish commerce could have held its own against competition in America only, if it had been free from the obligation to pay fees and export duties at home, and had enjoyed preferential rights in the New World. But the treasury of Philip V. could not dispense with the export duties. Therefore it was bound to endeavour to maintain the old system, by which the Indies were to be kept as a preserve for Spanish trade, and Spanish trade was to pay for this boon by being outrageously fleeced in the mother country. In order that it might have its way, the Spanish Government was prepared to pay for support. No support looked so well worth having as that of Great Britain, now beyond all question the leading naval Power. It was helped, and even pushed, to take this course by King Lewis XIV., who insisted on speaking for the Spanish Government during the peace negotiations, and who, for his own part, was prepared to sacrifice the commercial interests of his subjects in America in order to obtain peace. He knew what he was doing, for the British Government had made no secret of its intention to exclude French trade from Spanish America.

The price paid to the British Government for consenting to the restoration of the old Spanish system of trade in the Indies was tempting. Spain ceded to the Crown of Great Britain the exclusive right to import slaves into Spanish America for thirty years, beginning in April, 1713, and ending in May, 1743. In the full blaze of her glory, England took as the just reward of Marlborough's victories, and her own eminent merits as the defender of the freedom of Europe, the privilege of being the only lawful kidnapper and Tippoo Tib of the decadent monarchy of Spain. Four thousand eight hundred " piezas de Indias " might be imported in one year, and $33\frac{1}{3}$ " pesos "—*i.e.*, pieces of eight or dollars—were to be paid per " pieza " up to the number of 4,000. And that was not all. The Spanish Government undertook to allow one British vessel of 500 tons to accompany the " flota " to the fair at Portobelo, and there sell her cargo duty free. The Crown ceded the rights given to it by Spain to the South Sea Company. More negotiation went on. Details were modified or adjusted. The size of the " permitted ship "— " navio " or " nave de permiso "—was increased to 650 tons. It was settled that the company might establish factories at necessary points—Cartagena and Panama, and Buenos Ayres ; that its factors might acquire houses and land, and travel up country in the way of their business. Small vessels might be employed to carry stores to the factories. When the British diplomatists endeavoured to obtain leave for these small vessels to approach the coast of Spanish possessions on their way to and fro, the Government at Madrid plucked up spirit to say no. The right would have been abused to promote clandestine trade. The diplomatists did not insist, perhaps because they considered Spain far too weak to control the company.

It is surely not necessary to labour to prove that this famous arrangement, known as the " Asiento," or Contract Treaty, while making a pitiful appearance of saving the rights of Spain in her Indies, did, in fact, hand her trade over to the tender mercies of the British South Sea Company. The exclusive right to import slaves authorized the company to insist on keeping all competitors out. The machinery provided for the slave-trade could be used to promote contraband, and the opening afforded by the "nave de permiso" needed no demonstration.*

Here is a typical voyage ordered to be made for the South Sea Company by Captain Nathaniel Smith " to Angola and Buenos Ayres,"† in the *Essex* in 1724. Captain Smith was provided with " a certificate in Spanish under the company's seal, attesting that your ship is freighted by them on account of the Asiento, which certificate you are to produce in the Spanish West Indies as occasion serves to prevent any seizure and molestation, and deliver back the same to us at your return." " Spanish West Indies " meant to the company what " Las Indias " meant to the Spaniards—namely, the whole of their possessions in the New World. Captain Smith was also provided with " a copy of the Assiento Contract, which you are to observe, and not give any scandal to those of the Roman Catholic Religion." Goods to the value of £3,599 1s. 2d., together with " negro provisions amounting to £284 9s. 4d.," were shipped in the *Essex*, and Captain Smith was told what he was to do with them. He having signed his bills of lading, " we," the Court of Directors, " direct that, according to Charterparty, you take the first opportunity of wind and

---

* Of course, there was a vast deal more in the history of the South Sea Company than is stated here, or belongs to my subject—its financial relations to the British Government and the " Bubble " of 1720.

† " Instructions to Captains," in South Sea Company papers, MS., British Museum, 25,567.

weather, and sail from Gravesend, making the best of your way to Angola in Africa ; where being arrived you are to use your utmost endeavours to dispose of the cargo to the greatest advantage of the company, and therewith purchase four hundred negroes, or as many as can be procured, at as reasonable rates as possible, and with such provisions for them as shall be necessary to be purchased there, the negroes to be between the ages of ten and thirty years, and to be as near as may be half males and half females. And if after purchasing the said four hundred negroes and provisions there shall remain any surplus of the said goods and merchandize, you are to invest the same in gold and elephants' teeth to be delivered to the company's order at the Port of London, or bring the said surplus goods home, *unless our factory at Buenos Ayres shall require you to leave all or any part of the said surplus goods as necessaries for themselves or negroes. In which case you are to leave the same with them taking receipt.*"

The italics are mine, and the words are instructive. They show how easily the vessels authorized to carry the slaves under the Asiento Contract could be used for a contraband trade. The company could put any fancy price they liked on the goods they sent out to be bartered for negroes at Angola, and could ship what they pleased. The £3,599 1s. 2d. of the instructions might simply stand for a greater value, and represent goods not suitable to sell in Angola, and to buy 400 negroes at reasonable prices. The company contemplated the probability that there might be a surplus. If the Captain could purchase " elephants' teeth and gold " on good terms he might, but he is not told that he must. The possibility that he would still have a surplus when he reached Buenos Ayres was allowed for. If he had, he was to deliver them to the factory, should the factors apply for them. What could be easier than to take care to see that there should be a surplus ? It would be the business of the factors to provide for landing the goods and merchandise, and selling them to the Creoles.

The instructions go on to say : " Having taken in your negroes at Angola, you are to proceed direct to Buenos Ayres in the River Plate, in the Spanish West Indies, stopping at

Mount Video in the said river, and sending your boat up the north side for a Pilot." At Buenos Ayres the negroes were to be landed within fifteen days. The company was intelligently careful to provide for the delivery of the cargo in good condition. The decks of the *Essex* were to be regularly washed with vinegar as an antiseptic, and the negroes to be diverted by music and play. Exact musters of the blacks were to be taken at short intervals. No bodies were to be thrown overboard without a due certificate of death from the surgeon, witnessed by officers. Failure to take these musters correctly, and to make record of the number, and causes of deaths in the human cargo, would entail loss of head-money by the Captain and surgeon. When the blacks were landed, the Captain might stay for sixty days to ship hides, taking care to put his water-casks and provisions between decks, so as to leave the hold free for cargo. It is to be observed that the Court of Directors in this part of their instructions leave no room for the possible surplus of goods and merchandise Captain Smith might have on hand when he reached Buenos Ayres. When the hides were shipped, Captain Smith was to make his way home, and not to put into any Portuguese port on the way, lest he should be fleeced by official exactions. When the voyage was from Angola to the Antilles, there were, of course, differences in detail. But this was the round of the ships engaged in carrying out the "Asiento"—to Africa to buy blacks, to "the Spanish West Indies" to sell them, and in a quiet way to dispose of surpluses of "goods and merchandize" by contraband.

As for the South Sea ship, the trick played with it is a commonplace. It was regularly fed by tenders, and was used as a floating storehouse for British manufactures.

Everything would appear to have been in favour of the company, and yet on the whole the hopes based on the Asiento Treaty were disappointed. For one cause of its failure, or comparative failure, we could not blame the Spaniards. There was no lack of Englishmen who could not see why the company should have all the contraband to itself. Interlopers competed with it from England in large ships, and from Jamaica in small vessels. These latter were the direct representatives of the Buccaneer element in the population of the island. Spain had herself to thank for their existence. If her colonies were carcasses infested by vermin, the fault was primarily her own. But because vermin are naturally produced, they are not the less loathsome. British naval officers who spoke of the Jamaica smugglers with the feelings of gentlemen, judged them to be swaggering rogues and sanguinary scoundrels. The company suffered from their competition. The doings of these men are inevitably obscure. They loved the darkness for obvious reasons.

With the company we are fairly in the open air. It tried to defraud, and it did defraud, the King of Spain's revenue, and it succeeded by bribing his officers. Of course, it did meet with officials who were not to be bribed. Whenever these men could detect misuse of treaty rights, they imprisoned and confiscated. This was the fortune of war, and could be borne with philosophy. It was more painful to have to endure measures of rigour when applied by officials whom the company had bribed, and that also happened. The corrupt official who had pocketed his dishonest gains might then wish to earn praise for zeal in the King's service. In that case he descended on the " contrabandista," well knowing that his old friend dare not complain.

The South Sea Company made handsome profits in a legitimate way from time to time. For instance, its factors could easily discover what goods would sell best when the fair at Porto Bello was officially opened. When a " flota " was coming from Spain, and the fair must be declared open at a known time, the company's agents would take care to have their ship on the spot early. They could afford to undersell the Spanish traders, who, being ruinously taxed at home, must sell dear to cover charges. On one occasion, not long before the outbreak of the war of 1739, the company did in this way make a clean sweep of all the money brought to purchase goods at Porto Bello just before the convoy from Spain turned up. The Spanish traders suffered a dead loss. They really deserved no better for not forcing their Government to drop a proved absurdity, but we can understand that they were very angry. So was the King, and so were his Ministers, and as we can hardly expect them to recognize cheerfully that they were blockheads for mulishly adhering to a stupid routine, we can understand why they were upset by the loss of the revenue they would have received if the " flota " had come back with a good load. Of course, these exalted persons came to no such humble conclusion. What they did was to try to get round the Asiento Treaty by sending out a convoy of small ships, and denying that they constituted a real "flota." When the company claimed the right to send a permitted ship, it was refused, and told that it ought to distinguish better. Quarrels of this kind bore their fruit in the war of 1739.

Meanwhile there were other and heating causes of dispute. They all really come to this—that the company was for ever trying to get more than it had a right to, while the Spanish authorities strove to keep it to the letter of the bond. High-handed and peremptory things were undoubtedly done by Spanish officers. Early in its history the company had to complain that Don Blas de Lezo, the officer who afterwards helped to defend Cartagena against Vernon, had threatened to hang one of its Captains at Buenos Ayres. I do not find what answer, if any, Don Blas made to this complaint. My patriotism is not of a sufficiently refined quality to cause me to assume that the company's skipper was wholly meek and innocent. Years of pretty close intercourse with the British skipper has led me to the conclusion that his conscience is large in the matter of contraband. Whatever may have happened at Buenos Ayres on that particular occasion, it is easy to understand that any Don Blas employed to prevent contraband would be excusable for being worked to fury by the spectacle presented by the " nave de permiso " at the Porto Bello Fair. She was allowed to be of 650 tons. When a Spanish officer who was not to be bribed insisted on measuring her, she would turn out to be of 950 tons. And she was not alone. When the fair opened, thirty to forty small vessels laden with goods would turn up from Jamaica under pretence of bringing her provisions. By bribery or by mere push and swagger, the goods brought by, or supplied to, the "nave de permiso" would be rushed in duty free. Of course, the legitimate trade was ruined.

Again, Spanish officials who meant to do their duty were quite naturally enraged when they discovered that year after year a regular convoy of trading vessels, armed, or with an armed convoy, came from Jamaica to the mouth of the River Coclé, which is formed by the union of the Penonome and the Rata, and falls into the Caribbean Sea on the east coast of the province of Panama. They worked in harmony with native "contrabandistas." At the beginning of the war called "Jenkins's Ear," in 1739, there were three notorious companies of these smugglers—the Real Jurisdiccion (Royal Jurisdiction), the Apostolado de Penonome (Apostolate of Penonome), and the Sacra Familia (the Holy Family). They acted together, had built a fort at the mouth of the Coclé, had storehouses on the mountains along the paths to the South Sea. In the South Sea they had vessels, which carried the goods smuggled by them across the mountains down to Peru. The existence of this organization explains the determination of the Spanish Government to enforce the right of search. British vessels found prowling along the coasts of Spanish colonies were always presumably on their way to some such place as the smugglers' fort at the mouth of the Coclé.

The British traders were by no means successful in confining the clandestine trade entirely to themselves. The Dutch and French took a share. The Dutch island of Oruba was a notorious centre of smuggling of negroes to begin with, and when British competition had reduced that trade, then of other articles of commerce. The method was simple, and so easy of application by everybody, that it may be quoted from a contemporary account as an example of the whole thing.

"Occasionally vessels from Holland would bear away directly for a Spanish port, and, as they enter it, make signals of distress, pretending that they have sprung a leak, are in imminent danger of sinking, and obliged to seek for shelter in the port of a Crown allied to the Republic. As soon as they come to an anchor they inform the Governor of their distress, and, as a full proof thereof, make him a very considerable present. Leave is obtained to unload the ship. The King's officers register the packages as they enter the warehouse, the doors of which are sealed when the goods are all in. The business is then done in the night by the back-door. The European goods are taken out, and the bullion, indigo, cochineal, etc., are very exactly packed in the cases, and placed as they stood before. To enable those who have bought the goods to sell them publicly, the Governor is petitioned to allow the foreigners to dispose of as much of their cargo as may pay the expenses of the repairs. Thus the whole process is transacted with the forms of justice."*

The Spaniards, be it repeated, brought it all upon themselves. Their colonists had quite as much to do with it as the foreign smugglers. At the same time, it must be allowed that, so long as the Asiento Treaty lasted, Spain could not alter the old system of trade. If she suppressed the "flotas" and "galeones," and allowed her subjects to go to the Indies as they pleased, she thereby deprived the company of the "nave de permiso," which could go only with the Spanish convoys. Great Britain would have insisted on her bond. Spain was at last beginning to be aware that some change must be made. We can therefore understand that the Spanish Government should make no secret of his intention to refuse to renew the Asiento when it ran out in 1743. Great Britain was by no means pleased with the prospect of losing its privileged position. In the meantime the power of Spain had somewhat revived since 1713, and she was able to patrol the Indian Seas more effectually. A "blow up" would almost certainly have come in any case. The pretext was provided by " Jenkins's Ear."

" Jenkins's Ear " must be understood to be a symbol. As for the actual Robert Jenkins, Master of the *Rebecca*, of Glasgow, who gave his name to the war which broke out with Spain in 1739, we may safely affirm that there was such a person. It was also a fact visible to his contemporaries that he had lost one of his ears. A writer in the *Gentleman's Magazine* for 1731 asserts that he was received

* Quoted from Captain Thomas Southey, " Chronological History of the West Indies," vol. ii., p. 302.

in audience by King George II. In 1739 he was summoned to attend to give evidence before a Committee of the House of Commons, but there is no evidence that he did attend, and no record of what he said if he came. It is also matter of record that in 1731 a story that he had been ill treated by the Spaniards off the west of Cuba was current in Jamaica. Beyond these facts all is uncertain. His own story was that, while he was on his way home from the West Indies in 1731, his ship was overhauled off Havannah by a Spanish revenue boat ("guarda costa"), commanded by one Fandino. The Spaniards ransacked her for contraband, and as they could find none, revenged themselves by hanging him up, letting him down, cutting one of his ears off, and swearing in a most arrogant manner that, if the King of England had been there, they would have treated him in the same way. Finally, Fandino, who is habitually called "the infamous," allowed Jenkins to continue his voyage. He went on his way, carrying his ear with him, and made a deposition when he reached Glasgow. It was then that he was brought to London, was favoured with an interview by the King, told his tale, and showed his amputated ear.

And then a strange thing happened. Nothing more was heard of Jenkins for some seven years, when he suddenly became a popular hero in the midst of a growing press and parliamentary agitation in favour of a war with Spain. Kind members of Parliament gave him another chance to recount his wrongs, and sympathetically asked him to tell them what were his emotions at the awful moment when his ear was cropped by the infamous Fandino. He answered, with every appearance of that spontaneity which is born of intelligent coaching: "I commended my soul to God, and my cause to my country." And then another strange thing happened. No sooner had Captain Jenkins served his turn, and a war with Spain been obtained by the press and the opposition, than the man went back to the obscurity whence he came. When the excitement which produced the war had worn itself out, the fable of "Jenkins's Ear" became a byword. And nothing was more natural, for the story reeks of fraud. It is a most suspicious circumstance that the story of the outrage was reported to Rear-Admiral Charles

Stewart in Jamaica, immediately after the offence was committed. The thing did not happen in a market-place before a crowd, but in a solitary ship at sea, and on her way home. How came the news to reach Jamaica with such promptitude? If the whole tale was concocted beforehand by Jenkins and his friends in Jamaica, all engaged in the clandestine trade, and all eager to blow up a war with Spain, nothing is easier than to understand how it came to be current in Jamaica. And if Jenkins had a good case in 1731, why was not our Minister at Madrid, Sir Benjamin Keene, instructed to make strong representations to the Government of Spain? Walpole was anxious to maintain peace, but he showed repeatedly that he could take firm measures with Spain. Here was an admirable opportunity for checking the excesses of the " guarda costas "—a proved case of a gross outrage. George II. was not at all a meek man, and it is not to be believed that he would have passed over an insult to his flag and his person, if he did indeed hear Jenkins's story and believed him. As for the use made of the man in 1738 and 1739, it will be easily understood by those who recollect the process by which " outrages " were worked up in the London press when the war in South Africa was being brought about.

That Jenkins lost his ear somewhere and somehow must be believed. That he lost it in the pillory, as unfriendly commentators afterwards asserted, is improbable, for there would have been record of the sentence. We need not believe that he lost it in a drunken brawl. There is probability in the supposition that he was mutilated by some Fandino or another in one of the collisions which were of weekly occurrence in the seas of the West Indies, for they were swarming with armed smugglers and pirates manned by criminal adventurers of all nations. That may well have been the case. We have many notices of vessels overhauled and pillaged by ships which alternately showed the black pirate flag and the Spanish colours. The Spanish man-of-war flag of the time was not the red and yellow ensign now familiar, which was adopted in the reign of King Carlos III. (1759-1788), but a red St. Andrew's Cross on a white ground. It would be the obvious interest of a pirate to pretend to be a " guarda costa." Touching the infamous Fandino, it should be recorded that he was an historical person, a half-breed who sailed with a crew largely composed of blacks and Indians. He was taken during the war by Captain Frankland, after a fierce resistance, and was sent to England as a prisoner.

Jenkins, his ear, and his story, are mythical, with an irrecoverable basis of fact. But they are very characteristic of " the Indies," as they were in the middle of the eighteenth century. They were full of outrage, but let us listen to a witness who wrote, with ample knowledge, at the time, and not for the public or for effect—Rear-Admiral Charles Stewart.*

The Admiral does not deny that outrages were perpetrated by the Spaniards, but he goes on to say (the italics are mine):

" *The question will be whether we, by carrying on the clandestine trade, are not ourselves the authors of our complaints.* . . .

" It is undeniably true that that trade is carried on at our own risk, and therefore the vessels are good prizes if they are taken ; yet, as those vessels go armed, or as it has been customary to allow them convoy, and therefore is carried on in defiance to the law of the country, it don't appear strange that they do retaliate the injury by robbing those people they can get the better of.†

" It is without doubt irksome to every honest man to hear such cruelties are committed in these seas, but give me leave to say that you only hear one side of the question, and I can assure you the sloops that sail from this island [Jamaica] manned and armed on that illicit trade has [sic] more than once bragged to me of their having murdered 7 or 8 Spaniards on their own shore. *To prevent these cruelties has been one reason for allowing convoy to that trade.*

" It is, I think, a little unreasonable for us to do injuries and not know how to bear them. But villainy is inherent to this

* See *English Historical Review*, vol. iv., p. 741 *et seq.*

† It was not the business of Rear-Admiral Stewart to be a literary man and write neat sentences, but we must confess that the capacity of the average English man of action to express himself intelligibly had not improved since the beginning of the seventeenth century. I do not believe that Middleton, Lancaster, Saris, or Downton— though *he* was a starched stylist—would have written so confused a sentence as this. Yet the Admiral's meaning can be made clear. He obviously wished the Duke of Newcastle, to whom he was writing, to understand that, since we encouraged armed smugglers to carry on a clandestine trade, which the Spaniards were entitled to suppress by force, we must expect to learn that these same smugglers would be capable of revenging themselves by violence for the repressive measures of the Spanish authorities.

climate, and I should be partial if I were to judge whether the trading part of this island or those we complain of among the Spaniards are most exquisite in that trade. . . .

"I was a little surprised to hear of the usage Captain Jenkins met with off the Havana, as I know the Governor there has the character of being an honest man, and don't find anybody thinks he would connive [at] or countenance such villainies. But Porto Rico is the first place that it is necessary to reform.

"I can't help observing that I believe I am the first military person who has stood up in defence of peace and quietness, and for delivering up vessels, against a parcel of men who call themselves merchants; but except two or three of them that has signed the letter, they are no better than pedlars, and one of them formerly in jail for piracy."

Whoever will place the two sentences of Rear-Admiral Stewart's report to Newcastle, which I have printed in italics, beside the previously quoted passage from Lexington's despatch to Dartmouth, will have before him in a compendious form all the law and all the prophets touching "Jenkins's Ear." That ear remains as the historic symbol of the armed illicit trade and chronic mutual outrage of the West Indies and Spanish Main. The responsibility for causing the crimes of whole generations of fraud and brutality, rests first on the Spaniards. They grasped at far more than they could hold, and they persisted with a plentiful lack of political sagacity and administrative good sense, in clinging to a claim of exclusive possession which they could not enforce, and to a system of regulation of trade which, in its effect, was disastrous to honest commerce. But other nations must bear their share of the blame. The Powers which arranged the great settlement of the world at the Peace of Utrecht—Great Britain, France, and in a less degree Holland—were in a position to dictate the terms upon which Spain should retain possession of the Indies. Unfortunately, they had debarred themselves from the right to claim free access to the Spanish colonies. Every one of them enforced a rigid monopoly of the trade of its own plantations. Their policy differed from the Spanish not in principle, but only in being more intelligently applied, and by the fact that they could supply their colonists and the Spaniards could not. In the reign of Charles II., the Secretary of State, Lord Arlington, laid it down as a rule that, while the English should try to obtain access to the Spanish colonies, the Spaniards were to be plainly told that on no condition would they be allowed to trade with the dominions of His Majesty the King of Great Britain and Ireland. It is very unlikely that the Spaniards would have accepted reciprocity, but it was never offered.

Among the Powers which thus failed to settle the bitter old question of the trade to the "Spanish West Indies," Great Britain was not the least in fault. She used her superiority in naval power, which was as great at the end of the reign of Queen Anne as it was at the fall of Napoleon, to obtain exclusive privileges for herself. She took the Asiento — the contract for supplying Spanish America with negroes—through the experience of previous Asientistas. French, Genoese, and Portuguese, had proved that the slave-trade in itself was hazardous and rarely profitable, and she took it as a shoeing-horn for the clandestine trade. To make the Asiento more profitable, she obtained the "nave de permiso," and she secured that easement with the deliberate purpose of making it the pretext for a wholesale illicit commerce. She consented to the reimposition of the old Spanish law of trade to the Indies, because she obtained the power to defraud and abuse. She encouraged the illicit trade conducted by armed smugglers. The Spaniards, insulted, defrauded, hectored, were exasperated by provocation. They retaliated partly by endeavouring to enforce observance of the strict letter of the Asiento, partly by commissioning revenue boats, the "guarda costas," which were frequently mere privateers, with the privateer's universal tendency to become a pirate, who had to look for their reward to the contraband they might capture. They fell upon everything they found near their coast. The illicit traders retorted by murder and counter-piracy. At this game British ships were at a disadvantage, for there were fifty of them in the West Indies for one Spaniard. Under pretence of preventing "these cruelties," British authorities took to sending war-ships to protect men whom they knew to be armed smugglers, in the pursuit of their illicit trade. If ever there was an example of *le cant Britannique*, it was this. The Spaniards retaliated by attacking convoys they found near their coasts, even when they were under the protection of British men-of-war. Any such convoy might be engaged in smuggling.

Only the weakness of Spain and the fact that her King, Philip V., was occasionally insane, and, when he was in possession of his small senses, was intent on obtaining establishments in Italy for the sons born of his second marriage with Elizabeth Farnese of Parma, to the neglect of the real interests of his kingdom, explains the existence of such a state of things from 1713 to 1739. Spain did, to some extent, revive in those years, and as she grew less weak, she became more resentful of the Asiento Treaty and its consequences. War was the inevitable end.

War is not our business, but this one had a great deal of trade in it. We persisted in thinking that the Spanish-Americans wished to trade with us, and many did. Our first hope was to seize the Spanish colonies in South America, and so obtain possession of the silver mines. After the failure of the attack on Cartagena and of the plan for an attack on Panama across the isthmus, we fell back on sending a squadron to the coast of the Captain-Generalty of New Grenada ("hodie" Colombia and Venezuela) to cover the traders. The squadron was commanded by Sir Charles Knowles.* It attacked La Guayra and Puerto Cabello, and was beaten off with loss at both places. The trade was interrupted by the Spaniards on shore. Don Dionisio de Alsedo, the Captain-General, broke up the chief smuggling station in the "Coclé," burnt the fort, killed a number of the native smugglers, and cut off their heads and hands, which were jerked and exposed "in terrorem" in market-places.

The Spanish Government took a more effectual measure. Seeing that it could no longer carry on the trade by means of the "flotas" and "galeones," it suspended the laws of the Indian commerce, and authorized the "Register ships"

* There is no more curious figure in the list of British naval officers of the eighteenth century than Sir C. Knowles. His life is exceptionally well known, and may be read in Charnock's "Biographia Navalis" and the first volume of the *Naval Chronicle*. He was the natural son of that Sir Charles Knollys who claimed to be Earl of Banbury, and of whom it is recorded that he could not succeed in getting tried for killing his brother-in-law in a duel because the judges said he was a peer, and ought to be tried by his peers, and the House of Lords would not recognize him.

to come and go as they found opportunity. "Register ship" is a term the reader will meet often in the history of British naval wars in the eighteenth century. The name had been used from of old for vessels authorized to go to Buenos Ayres, apart from the "flota." The whole trade was now thrown open to them, and with, in the main, good results for the Spaniard. As their times of sailing were not announced, and they were free to go from any port, and to take the safest courses, it was far more difficult to intercept them than to stop the "flota." If the Spaniards had been wise they would have dropped the ancient methods wholly. But they did try to return to them, and it was not till 1778 that they threw the trade open to single ships sailing from thirteen authorized ports at home to twenty permitted ports in America. "Tarde llega el desengaño" (The truth is seen too late), says the melancholy Spanish proverb. To that we may add another no less gloomy: "Da Dios habas à quién no tiene quijadas" (God sends the beans when the grinders are gone). It was too late for Spain to do in 1778 what she ought to have done long before.

A volume the size of this would be required to tell the whole story of the trade with the Indies. I can only provide a sketch and indicate the character of the thing. But it would be a serious omission to ignore the end of the Asiento Treaty and the "nave de permiso." When the peace was made at Aix la Chapelle in 1748, Spain undertook to revive the South Sea Company's privileges for the four years which had to run when war broke out in 1739. By this time the company had begun to doubt whether these same privileges were worth having, while English traders in Spain were able to show that the patriotism of the Spaniards led them to boycott British goods in retaliation for the illicit trade. What we gained on one side of the ocean we lost on the other. The company accepted £100,000 in satisfaction of all claims, and the Spanish Government paid gladly to be rid of a thorn in the flesh. Few historians have omitted to note that nothing was settled at the Peace of Aix la Chapelle as to the right of search. But the British Government had no occasion to trouble itself about the right of search if it no longer meant to protect the clandestine trade.

CHAPTER X

THE PIRATE

" And because pirates frequently infest the coast of Africa, and the Rovers of Salley may trouble you, you are to be very circumspect, and not leave your ship, or speak with any other without absolute necessity, but always keep a good guard, and look out, both at Sea and in Port, to prevent surprise." (Instructions given by the Court of Directors of the South Sea Company to Captain Nathaniel Smith of the *Essex* for a voyage to Angola and Buenos Ayres. Given at South Sea House, 17th January, 1723, O.S.).

"The Court of Directors of the South Sea Company think themselves bound in a most humble and dutiful manner to represent to Your Majesty that by their late advices from their Factory at Jamaica, and others, they are informed there are in those seas and in the Gulf of Florida great numbers of pirates' sloops with 80, 100, and 150 men each, who by their frequent piracies render all the trade in those seas very dangerous, not only to the said company, but also to all others, not doubting but that Your Majesty will from princely wisdom, etc., etc.

"They [the ' pirates' sloops '] have lately taken the *Dragon* sloop with five and twenty thousand pieces of eight,* and the *Royal Africa*, with negroes belonging to this company, and the *Widah*, and a merchant ship of 24 guns, 70 men, richly laden, belonging to private traders with many other ships, sloops, and vessels. . . . That the said company are also informed of very great robberies committed by a pirate formerly inhabitant of Jamaica, known by the name of the Mulatto, who has got together 2 or 3,000 men, and fortified himself in the Island of Providence " (The South Sea Company to King George I., August, 1717).†

---

* The " piece of eight," familiar to our boyhood from Robinson Crusoe, was a piece of the value of eight silver reals of the value of sixpence ; therefore it was a dollar—" duro," " peso," " scudo," " écu "—not always exactly, but near enough for rough calculations.

† South Sea Company's papers in Manuscripts of the British Museum, volume of " Instructions to Captains, and Letters," 25,555.

THE PIRATE

THESE two short passages from the letter-books of the South Sea Company will do duty as shoeing-horn for what has to be said concerning the relations of the sea trader, and the pirate. No history of piracy can be given. A history implies a succession of events, a growth or decay of institutions, the existence of some state, tribe, or corporate body with some coherence and life of its own. But piracy was a condition. It existed, increased, flourished, declined, or disappeared according as the organism on which it preyed was healthy or diseased, strong or weak. Pirate, like other words, may be used in a figurative sense. The " Sea Tories " who fought for the Stuarts in the English Civil Wars were called pirates by their enemies. So were the Jacobites who sailed with the commission of King James II., after his expulsion from England. Barbarous invaders of settled states have been called pirates ; but to apply that name to the Norsemen is not more rational than it would be to call Alaric and Alboin brigands. I am not persuaded that the term as applied to the Mohammedan states of Barbary, which carried on perpetual war with the Christians, is not a misnomer. As for " hostis humani generis " (enemy of the human race), it is a term of " rhetorical invective," used to scold a heinous offence.

The pirate pure and undeniable was simply the sea-robber, and whether he was to be active and mischievous or no, did not depend upon himself. How came it, then, that a pest which all men, so one must suppose, would hurry to stamp out was allowed to reach the height it had manifestly attained when the South Sea Company petitioned the King in 1717—a time of high civilization and of well-established law and order ? Let us consult a pirate who spoke with the authority of long experience, and who handled his subject with a firm, not to say a philosophic, grip.

Among the minor personages of the reigns of James I. and Charles I. was one Sir Henry Manwaring, whose name was, as a matter of course, and for the greater pleasure of the trivial pedant, occasionally spelt with eccentricity and that lavish doubling of consonants popular at the time (it costs nothing to double a consonant and yet makes a show), as " Maynwaringe," and so forth. He comes in and out of the Calendars of State Papers, generally in the way of mere reference, or as about to do something which was never done. As the name was not uncommon, as there were more Henry Manwarings than one, all these references may not be to the same person. Our Henry Manwaring was the undoubted author of a discourse on the "Begginings, Practises, and Suppression of Pirates,' dedicated to King James I., and we may take it for granted that he was also the compiler of the "Seamen's Dictionary," a very useful little book, drawn up for the instruction of the Duke of Buckingham, who was favourite to James I. and Charles I.*

If we had only Manwaring's word for himself, we might hesitate to believe him, for the man was a manifest liar where his own conduct was concerned. But a Captain Manwaring is spoken of as a notorious pirate by Monson, in the passage in which he gives an account of his operations on the coast of Ireland in 1614. This was no doubt the gentleman (for gentleman he was by birth) who dedicated the "Discourse" to King James I. as a proof of gratitude. "To my most gratious Soveraigne that represents the King of Heaven, whose Mercy is above all his works."†

The ex-pirate, as we see, knew the style which would please King James. His Majesty's poor petitioners were safe in going to the very border of blasphemy. Manwaring had been a pirate, had been pardoned, and appointed to a place in Dover Castle. He had much to thank the King for. To be sure, he had been a very mild pirate—if he said sooth, which those may believe who can. He had, he all but says as much, carefully abstained from robbery while engaged in his late course of piracy, and had deserved well of the merchants, as their certificates in his favour proved. If it had been his task to speak for another gentleman of the same way of life, he would have had no hesitation in describing his errors as "Pulchrum scelus" (a beautiful crime). But for himself, bowed down with remorse (with

* The "Seamen's Dictionary," after remaining for some twenty years in manuscript, was printed during the first Civil War, and reprinted after the Restoration.

† I know of no printed copy of this piece of work. The manuscript showily, but neither exactly nor really well, penned, and adorned with poorly executed illuminated letters, is in the British Museum, Reg. 17, A. xlvii.

his tongue in his cheek), he would not venture to lay any such plea before " his most gratious Soveraigne that represents the King of Heaven."

Impudent rascal as he plainly was, Manwaring was no fool, and he knew what he was talking about. We can quite agree with him that the consistent enforcement of the law is a check on evil-doers, even if we cannot accept the case in point which he quotes to King James.

" So likewise in my commonwealth of most uncivil barbarous seamen (the common sort of seamen, I mean), that are of all men the most uncivil and barbarous. I could never have subsisted as I did if I had ever pardoned any notorious offence, though committed by my truest followers, by which constant severity I kept them all in a short time in so good obedience and conformity, that for five years I never had any outrageous offence, but had them all aboard my ships in as good civility and order, as it could not have been much better in a civil state, for questionless as the fear of punishment makes men fear to offend, so the hope of being pardoned makes them the apter to err." A milder mannered body of men never scuttled ship, nor cut a throat.

Nevertheless, when our authority drops romancing about himself, and sets forth his views on the suppression of piracy, he goes to the root of the matter. If you wish, he says, to clear the country of foxes you stop the holes. If you wish to make an end of piracy, take care that the pirate shall have no port in which to refit his ship, and sell his booty. It was the possibility that piracy might be made profitable, which in the long run accounts for its prolonged existence. Other causes there were. One of them is presented, under the species of eternity, by Kingsley :

" Oh, sweet it was in Aves to hear the landward breeze
Aswing with good tobacco in a net between the trees,
With a negro lass to fan you, and to listen to the roar
Of the breakers on the reef outside which never reached the shore."

Freedom from the dull routine of peaceful work, and joy, even when they were to be had only in the intervals of toil and distress—these attractions accounted for much. But there must be some refuge where a man could enjoy them, some market where booty could be spent to purchase pleasure. The fox must have his hole. Where none was to be found he could not subsist.

When James I. was on the throne, the Isle of Aves of the pirates was on the west coast of Ireland. It is full of good anchorages, where the sea rover could careen his ship and rest. They were, as Manwaring says, not " commanded." There were no forts, no garrisons, no forces of law and order at hand. Law and order were represented by lords and gentry, and what their standard of morality was in the west of Ireland long after the beginning of the seventeenth century, the reader may learn with more satisfaction than I can afford him, by turning to Mr. Froude's " English in Ireland," and reading his flawless narrative of the plunder of the wrecked Danish Indiaman by the Crossleys of Ballyhige. About the year 1620 the Crossleys would have been in league with some pirate to take the Indiaman at sea. Sir William Monson has left an admirable description of an Irish family of the Crossley stamp, of the name of Cormat, the genial father, his affable daughters of easy virtue, his hospitable hall, and his harper who provided music, and of the merry life they all led with their pirate guests, till Sir William caught them in a net, and his carpenter, working diligently all night, set up a gallows opposite the front door.

The pirate paid for supplies and safe mooring by gifts of wine and brandy plundered at sea. He was met by agents of traders from London itself, who bought his goods, and with the price he adorned his sweethearts. Manwaring describes with the downright candour of his age: " The nymphs recruited not only in Ireland but in England, and as far away as Denmark," who peopled this pirate's Cythera. The dangers rewarded by these pleasures were not very serious. There was the sea, to be sure, and its perils. Now and then there was a well-armed enemy to be fought or avoided. From time to time Governments were taken with spasms of activity, as when Monson was sent after robbers who had become no longer tolerable. But on the whole it was not very perilous to be a pirate. In the first place, the risk of capture was small when very few warships were kept regularly in commission, and several of them would be employed in carrying ambassadors and other formal duties. There was no regular police, and except in countries which maintained galleys, no penal system. Local authorities, even when they were zealous, had to act with local levies, which were often not available in time. If a pirate was taken, the choice was between hanging him and letting him go. To hang a whole crew was a harsh measure, when, as was generally the case, some were young, and many would plead that they were " perforced " men—had been compelled to join the pirates. Our instructive authority Manwaring says—and he was no doubt right—that this excuse was commonly fraudulent. Men offered to join if the pirate Captain would give them an excuse by threatening them. He says that he gave his " perforced " recruits a certificate, so that they might be the more willing. He adds that, as they thought their necks safe, they were the most violent of the crew. When a pirate was taken, the usual course was that followed by Monson himself. A few of the prisoners who had formerly tasted of the King's mercy, and had shown no amendment, but had returned to their evil courses, were hanged as an example. The others were pardoned, or pressed for the navy if their services were needed. They were bold fellows, and capable of being useful if properly directed. No wonder that the bulk of these pirates felt a comforting conviction that even if they fell into the hands of the King's officers, their Captain and leaders would be the only members of the company to taste of the King's justice. No wonder either that Monson was able to recruit a useful body of former pirates in the Shetland Islands. From poachers they turned gamekeepers, and were of real use. Add to these permanent conditions in favour of the pirate, the fact that Governments, when provoked to activity, were much in the habit of issuing promises of pardon to all who would come in by a certain day. The pirate who had " come in on a proclamation " was a known and even a familiar type.

Yet piracy was a heinous offence, and the pirate a heinous offender. So they were, and legislators did not spare denunciation and threats of punishment. The Act of the twenty-seventh year of Henry VIII. against " Pirates and

Robbers on the Sea " was eloquent on the subject, and propounded a remedy. " Whereas Pirates, Thieves, Robbers, and Murtherers upon the Sea, many times escape unpunished because the Trial of their offences hath heretofore been ordered before the Admiral or his Lieutenant or Commissary, after the course of the Civil Laws, the nature whereof is, that before any Judgment of Death can be given against the offenders, either they must plainly confess their offence (which they will never do without torture or pain) or else their offences be so plainly and directly proved by witnesses indifferent [*i.e.*, impartial] such as saw their offences committed, which cannot be gotten but by chance at few times, because such offenders commit their offences upon the sea, and at many times murther and kill such persons being in the ship or boat where they commit their offences, which should bear witness against them in that behalf, and also such as should bear witness be commonly mariners and ship men which for the most part cannot be gotten ne had always ready to testify to such offences, because of their often voyages and passages in the seas, without long tarrying or portraction of time, and great costs and charges, as well of the King's Highness, as of such as would pursue such offenders ; For the Reformation whereof ;——" effectual measures were to be taken. To put it shortly, " such offenders " were in future to be sent before a jury, and tried by the ordinary criminal procedure of England as if they had offended on land. The difference between the two procedures was profound. The nature of the Civil Law was that it aimed at obtaining certainty as to the guilt of the prisoner ; the nature of the English, or Common, Law was that it was content with the " oath of twelve good and lawful men " forming a jury, who were prepared to affirm that the prisoner was guilty.

The superiority of our native procedure was obvious. A resolute fellow who was not very sensitive to pain could beat the Civil Law by standing the torture. He had no such resource against the oath of the twelve good and lawful men. If he refused to plead he was pressed to death. If he did plead, put himself on his country, he was not allowed to employ counsel except on points of law and flaws in the indictment. He had to find the flaws for himself, and the only opportunity given him to find them was on the day of his trial, when the indictment was read to him in Latin—a language not very familiar to persons likely to commit offences within the jurisdiction of the Admiral. His witnesses were not allowed to be sworn, and therefore were not liable to be punished for perjury. The jury was always told that an unsworn witness was not so credible as a sworn one. The witnesses for the prosecution were sworn, and were therefore supposed to be more credible. To complete the efficiency of our procedure, the Judge could fine, imprison, or refuse to discharge a jury which would not find the verdict he wished it to give. The Civil Law was feebleness itself when compared to a system which could dispense with evidence, refused the prisoner all means of defending himself, and threw the responsibility of declaring him guilty, not on the Judge, but on a committee of twelve men, who divided the burden of the sin of sending an innocent man to death among them, and who, moreover, could soothe their consciences with the plea that they acted under compulsion applied by the Bench.

Such a procedure as this was far more effective than all the instruments of the torture-room, and yet it failed to check piracy. Its failure is intelligible enough, and for a simple reason. First it was necessary to catch your pirate. The free pirate, who was revelling in an Irish harbour on the proceeds of his last cruise, was not to be intimidated because another man was found guilty by a jury at Exeter, and hanged as an example. The Law of Henry VIII. was simply one of a shipload of enactments which endeavoured to supply the lack of an efficient police by threatening offenders with frightful penalties. The offender, who knew that he had an excellent chance of getting away uncaught, was not disturbed a jot by the thunder of the law. It was to equally little purpose that the lawgivers took to applying pressure to merchant Captains to make them defend their ships. The 22 and 23 Charles II. told the skipper that he must not depart from his ship after discovering a pirate on any pretence whatever. It also declared that if his vessel was of 200 tons, carrying sixteen guns, or if of less size and armament, then when his assailant was of less than twice his strength, he must defend his ship under penalty of being declared incapable of ever commanding a ship again. And William followed Charles, and George followed William. Merchant sailors were promised that they should be qualified for Greenwich Hospital if they were wounded while defending their ship against a pirate. But it skilled not. The merchant skipper assailed by a real pirate swarming with men was not to be nerved to heroism by the prospect of six months imprisonment if he took command of another ship after surrendering without fighting, and supposing he did get home.* After Henry, Charles, William, and George, had done their best, " The Mulatto," with his pirate sloops, was infesting the Gulf of Florida, and continued to do so till his fox's hole at Old Providence was stopped.

We always come back to this stopping of the holes. The entire history of the suppression of piracy comes to nothing else. The process began at home. As we have seen, there was a time when piracy was based on the ports of every maritime nation in Europe. That state of things had come pretty well to an end by the seventeenth century, except for outlying territories, of which the west coast of Ireland was the most frequented and the most notorious. It was admirably placed to serve the turn of " Pirates, Thieves, Robbers, and Murtherers on the Sea," whose field of operations extended from the banks of Newfoundland on the west to the Sound on the east, and from Iceland in the north to the coast of Morocco in the south. In King James's time, so Manwaring reports, the pirates did not go so far south as the Coast of Guinea. When the South Sea Company issued its instructions to Captain Nathaniel Smith, of the *Essex*, they were swarming on the Guinea Coast. The Cromwellian conquest, and the immense extension of the English navy which accompanied and followed the Civil War, had driven them out of the Irish " ports for mariners " to distant seas. Even before that rout they had been subject to certain restrictions. The ships of the King of Denmark checked them in the Sound ; the warships of England and

* And how could the penalty be enforced unless the Commander of a merchant ship was required to carry a Master's certificate which was not then the case ? He had only to change his name.

Holland were to be feared in the Channel; the "armada de galeones" of the King of Spain were to be met on the approaches to Cadiz and the way to the Isles. Yet they had an ample field on the Atlantic, and inside the Mediterranean they had another refuge.

The story of the piracy of the Mediterranean must be left aside for a space, while we follow its fortunes on the ocean. The very power which forced the pirates from Ireland supplied them with a new opening, and did it by means of the Navigation Laws. These laws worked in harmony with the monopoly of the East India Company. Their aim was to restrict the trade of the Colonies to the mother-country, so that, whatever they sent out, with few exceptions, should go to England for consumption or re-export, and that whatever came into them should come from or through England. Now, these restrictions, imposed with a single eye to the good of the mother-country, were grievous to the Colonies. They were peculiarly offensive, because they compelled the colonists to receive the products of the East through the London Company, and at a dearer rate than they could have obtained them at by direct trade. Hence arose a peculiar and very far-ranging form of piracy.

We have seen from the experience of the company's first Captain that an active trade went on between India, the Red Sea, and the Persian Gulf, in native ships sailing from the Bay of Cambaya and the Coast of Malabar. If the colonists in America were not free to trade directly with the East, there was one thing they could do: they could sail to the mouth of the Red Sea, plunder the country ships, and bring the produce of their cruise back to the ports of the Plantations. And that is what they did. By the end of the seventeenth century the great "pirate round" was to sail from New England to the Coast of Malabar, Bay of Cambaya, Red Sea, and Persian Gulf, plunder the country ships, and return home. Information on oath was given to the Secretary of State to the effect that "Thomas Too, William Maze, John Ireland, Thomas Wake, and others, who were all of them known as pirates, and had made several piratical voyages, from which they had returned with great wealth," were living in New England about 1698, and made no concealment of its origin. And why should they have felt any shame? They had, to begin with, the support of the very prevalent belief that there was no sin in plundering the unbeliever. Darby Mullins, one of Kidd's crew, declared that he had never been told it was wrong, and the pirates of the Eastern Seas avowed the profitable belief. "But," said one East India Company's officer, "some of the old hardened pirates said they looked on it as little or no sin to take what they could from such heathens as the Moors and Indians were." And then they had the general favour of New England, which resented the monopoly of the company and the barriers imposed on its industry. Lord Fairfax, Governor of Virginia in the early days of the Navigation Laws, declared that they weighed heavily on his Colony, which was Royalist and obedient, but were disregarded by the Puritan colonists, which were not loyal, and observed the laws only in so far as suited their convenience. Too, Maze, Ireland, Wake, and the others, were forerunners of the patriots who, within a century of 1698, gave the signal for the War of Independence by throwing the tea into Boston Harbour.

Here, again, it was the possession of a safe "fox's hole" which allowed the piracy to exist. Too, Maze, and the others, had stations on the way to the East. The West Indies afforded a large choice. The Greater Antilles were loosely held by the Spaniards. Jamaica was in English hands after 1655, but it was a headquarters of piracy itself. As for the Lesser Antilles, they were either occupied by half or wholly piratical settlers, or were empty. It was easy for the pirates to provide themselves with stations where they could receive ammunition and naval stores or recruits from New York or Boston, and keep a storehouse. On the other side of the Cape was the great Island of Madagascar, unoccupied by any Power capable of exercising control. The general lawlessness of the West Indies, due to the weakness and obstinacy of the Spaniards, who could not occupy them effectually themselves, and would not recognize the legitimacy of foreign settlements, was, of course, all in favour of the pirate. So was the condition of the East. Except where the Dutch Company ruled in

Java and the seas around it, there was no force to control them. The coast peoples of India had ships worth plundering, but they had no navies. The English Company had power over its own servants, but it had no Admiralty jurisdiction ; therefore it could not try and punish a pirate. When it applied to be empowered to hold Admiralty Courts, the Admiralty lawyers at home, moved, as we are forced to suspect, by the great consideration of fees, opposed the grant. They thought it would be enough to authorize the Company to arrest pirates, and send them to London for trial. The American Colonies were also without jurisdiction. So even if the will to punish piracy had been good in New England, the authorities had not the power. Offences committed on the coast and the high seas were committed within the jurisdiction of the Lord High Admiral, and must be tried by him, his Lieutenant, or Vice-Admiral, or Commissioner. Where there was none, the offender could not be tried. At home there were Vice-Admirals of the Counties, and Admiralty Courts empowered by Henry VIII.'s laws to try offenders in the English manner, but there were none in the " Plantations " of North America nor within the limits of the Charter of the East India Company.*

The company was often chastised for the sins of the pirates, but it would appear that there was no reason why they should not have continued to flourish for a long while if they had self-restraint enough to abstain from assailing British or Dutch trade directly or in an outrageous manner. But as Kingsley's Old Buccaneer put it, " Scripture says an end of all good things must be." The pirates were brought to their downfall by the undesigned co-operation of a set of persons who came together from the ends of the earth—namely, John or Henry Avery or Every, *alias* Bridgeman, Cogi Baba of Chulfa—*i.e.*, Shulfa, the Christian suburb of Ispahan—the Great Mogul, and the distressed Spanish Government.

At the close of the seventeenth century Spain was at the very depths of decay. It could not longer build nor even man ships for the defence of its colonies, but was forced to

* The Vice-Admiralship of a county is now a dignity, but the President of the Admiralty, Probate, and Divorce Division is a Vice-Admiral.

hire them abroad. As the English appeared to the Spaniards of that time rather less dangerous and hateful than the Dutch, they betook themselves to England in 1694 to charter vessels to protect the coast of the Main, and bring the bullion from the Peruvian mines to Spain. They hired two English vessels, the *Charles II.* and the *James*, and brought them to Corunna. But the same penury that reduced them to this makeshift rendered them unable to pay the stipulated freights and advances. These ships lay at Corunna waiting for money, and the crews were left idle. It was a position full of temptations. The men may well have begun to doubt whether the funds to pay their wages would ever be forthcoming. Meanwhile there were the two ships with their armament. What could be easier than to take possession of them, and join the New Englanders in the Eastern Seas?

It would have been strange if no one among the English sailors who manned the *James* and the *Charles II.* had made the proposal while the sailors were yarning on the forecastle or sitting in the wine-shops of Corunna. Avery was the man who did, and who had sufficient power of persuasion to carry a part of the crews with him. He had in all probability been on a cruise to the East. He could navigate, and was very fit to show the road. At his instigation part of the crews of each ship mutinied and seized the *Charles II.* Her Captain, Gibson, who was ill below when the mutineers made the capture, bitterly reproached Avery with disloyalty and ingratitude. The pirate, for so he was already by the mere fact of the seizure of the ship, bore his reproaches patiently. He said he was a man of fortune (by which he meant one who had to trust to fortune), and must follow his fortune. It is to his credit that he protected Captain Gibson and seventeen of the crew who remained loyal. They were provided with a boat to take them to the *James*, and were allowed to carry their clothes with them; then the *Charles II.* went on her way to the Red Sea.

The history of Avery's cruise has not been written in trustworthy detail, but we know that he joined other pirates at Perim, and that they took, among others, a large

Mogul vessel, which they called the *Gunsway*—*i.e.*, " Gunj Suwaie " (Exceeding Treasure). This historical episode was used in his characteristic style by Defoe, who first wrote what claimed to be a life of Avery, and then founded upon it the " Life, Adventures, and Piracies of Captain Singleton." In reality the capture of the Mogul ship was a disaster to all the pirates. Whether or no she carried a lady of the Imperial family as passenger, the Court was interested in her cargo. The pirates bullied the passengers, and they let the vessel go after rifling her of money and jewels. For the moment they thought they had done well. The money, divided at the capstan head, gave every able seaman a thousand pounds, and to Avery two thousand. He may have concealed jewels which he ought to have thrown into hotchpot. However that may be, they had " made their voyages," had gained enough to make it worth their while to return and enjoy their booty. As a matter of course, they sailed to New England. They made a purse among themselves—Avery subscribed £40—to bribe the authorities, and then they scattered.

While the crew of the *Charles II.* were making off, the Mogul was punishing the East India Company—as his predecessors had several times done—for the sins of the pirates. It was in vain for the company to plead that it was not to blame, and had no control over the offenders. The Emperor was not unnaturally exasperated by the insult, and would not distinguish between one European and another. A similar outrage on a Mogul ship perpetrated by the Portuguese nearly a century before had been revenged with good effect on their settlements. Aurungzebe, then the Emperor —the Great Mogul—made the obvious calculation that similar measures would produce similar results, and in the main he was right. The company had already found that piracy was becoming a serious danger to themselves, and now they made every effort to bring about its suppression by the British Government. It was under the stimulus applied by the company that effectual measures were at last taken.

The despatch of Captain Kidd in the *Adventure* galley to suppress piracy in the East was not one of those effectual measures. It is not necessary to go into his well-known story.* Here, as always, piracy was beaten by being deprived of its harbours of refuge. In 1698 the Government issued the usual proclamation offering pardon to all pirates who would come in before April 31st, 1699, and surrender to certain officers named. An exception was made for piracies committed east of the Cape of Good Hope, and Avery and Kidd were excluded by name. This pardon, limited as it was, had precisely the effect attributed by Manwaring to earlier proclamations. It enabled a certain number of rascals to come in, and wipe the slate clean preparatory to beginning again at the first good opportunity. But it was followed in 1701 by the passing of the Act for " the more effectual suppression of piracy."

The preamble of the Act contains a lamentable and shameful confession of the failure of the State to provide for the security of the seas. After the necessary reference to the Act of Henry VIII., it goes on : " And whereas that, since the making of the said Act, and especially of late years, it hath been found by experience that persons committing piracies, robberies, and felonies on the seas, in or near the East and West Indies, and in places very remote, cannot be brought to condign punishment without great trouble and charges in sending them into England to be tried within the realm, as the said statute directs, insomuch that many idle and profligate persons have been thereby encouraged to turn pirates, and betake themselves to that sort of wicked life, trusting that they shall not, or at least

* I leave it aside the more willingly because it is to me unintelligible. The mere material facts are sufficiently known. It is the meaning of them that escapes one. We are asked to believe that such men as Lord Chancellor Somers, the wise and virtuous, Lord Orford, Lord Romney, Sir F. Harrison, and Lord Bellomont, did the following amazing thing : They took an old West India privateer (*i.e.*, parcel pirate), and sent him out to the East with an *unpaid* crew, on the understanding that he and his men were to share one-fourth of whatever they could recover from the pirates. Three-fourths were to go to the syndicate. It was idiotic, if it was honest, and the bitterest Tory never asserted that Somers and his Whig associates were fools. The follies of the wise are not unknown, but contemporaries who thought highly of the intelligence of Somers were really to be excused if they did believe that some villainy lay at the back of a scheme which was so manifestly the work either of a rogue or of a fool And I repeat that it was impossible for them to think of Somers as a fool.

cannot easily be questioned for such their piracies and robberies, by reason of the great trouble and expence that will necessarily fall upon such as shall attempt to apprehend and prosecute them for the same : and whereas the numbers of them are of late very much increased and their insolencies so great, that unless some speedy remedy be provided to suppress them by a strict and more easy way of putting the ancient laws in that behalf in execution, the trade and navigation into remote parts will very much suffer thereby"—the following "strict and easy way" of putting the ancient laws into operation shall be adopted.

From henceforth a pirate might be tried " in any place at Sea, or upon the land, in any of His Majesty's Islands, Plantations, Colonies, Dominions, Forts, or Factories," by naval officers or other official persons appointed under the Great Seal of England or seal of the Admiralty of England. The court was to consist of seven qualified officers, or if the full number could not be collected, then by three, of whom the Governor, or Lieutenant-Governor, or Member of Council of a Colony, Chief or President of a Factory, and Captain of a man-of-war, is " always to be one." These three were empowered to select four others, who must be English merchants or planters, commissioned or warrant officers of a man-of-war, Masters or mates of merchant ships. The seven could appoint their own Registrar and Provost, and could inflict the death penalty. The decision was by a majority, and was taken in secret. It was the process of a naval court martial. The prisoner who would not plead was held to have confessed. His witnesses were to be sworn, and he could cross-examine through the President of the court. Any Master of a merchant ship who betrayed his trust, or any seaman who laid violent hands on his Commander in order to obtain possession of a ship, could be tried. It is obvious that Parliament foresaw difficulties with the plantations. The tenth clause says that " whereas several evil-disposed persons, in the Plantations and elsewhere, have contributed very much towards the increase and encouragement of Pirates, by setting them forth, and by aiding and abetting, receiving and concealing them and their goods, and there being some defects in the laws for bringing such evil-disposed persons to condign punishment," they shall be tried as provided by the Act of Henry VIII.—namely, by a court authorized to exercise Admiralty jurisdiction—and punished in the same way as principals. Distrust of the colonies is openly displayed in the fifteenth clause, which provides that the refusal of colonial authorities to yield obedience to the Act should be a forfeiture of the colony's charter.

In addition to threatening evil-disposed persons, the Act gave masters and seamen who had defended their ship a right to a reward of 2 per cent. of the freight of the ship and goods, to be levied on owners and shippers by authority.

This Act went far to stop the fox-holes. Cases might arise where it was impossible to form a court for each of duly qualified members. In those of the American colonies which were thinly populated and unsettled, notably in North Carolina, the pirates could still lurk in creeks and woods; but when excluded from New England, they lost their best market. The more prudent dropped the trade; the more reckless began to make themselves a pest at home, and then they were hunted down. In the East the company was able to deal with them, so soon as it was armed with jurisdiction. The pirates could still hang about the coast of Madagascar. A few of them, finding that the sea had become too dangerous, settled on shore in the island. These, the so-called Kings of Madagascar, were able, since they possessed firearms, to enslave natives whose labour supported them. They lived in bestial comfort, selling cattle and vegetables to passing ships in return for gunpowder and strong drink. But the old free days of cruising round the Bab-el-Mandeb, or Perim, plundering the country ships, and going off to a safe refuge in New England, were over.

Apart from fear of native reprisals, the company had other reasons for praying the Royal Government in aid. The appetite comes with eating, and the pirates had begun to assail its own ships, and then some of its sailors had begun to yield to the temptation to join the New England heroes, and go off to a way of life in which there would certainly be no discipline, there would almost certainly be plenty to drink, and there well might be a pocketful of coin to win. In 1686 the *Cæsar* was attacked on the coast of Gambia when on her outward-bound voyage by a whole squadron of piratical vessels. The result of the action showed how contemptible they were as enemies. The *Cæsar* was carrying a few European soldiers for the defence of the company's factories. Her Captain was not disposed to yield without a fight, and in an engagement of five hours he beat the pirates off. They had succeeded in killing only one of his men and in wounding eight. The *Cæsar* was, of course, more heavily armed than the average merchant ship would have been, and the presence of the soldiers gave her a considerable advantage. Yet the pirates were five to one. But real fighting was not their business. They were out " on the plundering account," as the phrase was, and had no wish to pay too dear for their plunder. Piratically disposed mutineers could run away with a company's ship, as the crew of the *Mocha* did, after murdering their Captain, Edgecombe, and sending twenty-seven loyal men adrift in a boat, and as the crew of the *Josiah* ketch did, without murder. The *Josiah* was retaken by two of the men who had been forced to join in the mutiny, and who ran away with her while the real pirates were ashore in the Laccadives. The *Mocha*, renamed the *Défence*, and then again renamed the *Resolution*, had a longer career. Her first " Captain," Stent, was got rid of—murdered or marooned—by his fellow-pirates, and then she fell to one Culliford, who had been the ringleader in the *Josiah*. After carrying on in her for some two years with the usual daring—that is to say, pillaging the weak and running away from the strong (the company's ship *Dorrill* beat him off in the Straits of Malacca)—he " came in on a proclamation,' and though he was tried and condemned at home, was never punished. The impunity of such a man as this could have no other effect than to encourage imitators.

The lurking-places were not all stopped at once. We have seen that twenty-four years after the Act of William III. was passed the Gulf of Florida was swarming with pirates. The West Indies and the coast of the Spanish Main continued for long to give them refuge. First comes the fact that they were for long ill-occupied, and in many places not occupied at all. Therefore it was always possible for prowling ruffians to find some creek far from a town, and out of sight of the police, where they could hide. But what was even of more importance was that these regions were divided between Spain, England, France, and Holland—Powers which were at war among themselves, with brief intervals of peace, from the middle of the seventeenth century till 1815. All employed privateers, and the privateer, as Nelson said, was always half a pirate. When peace came, and he was thrown back on honest industry, he frequently became a pirate altogether. It is safe to affirm that every naval war was followed by a recrudescence of piracy. When the great wars came to an end in 1815 the revolt of the Spanish colonies in America had exactly the same effect. The so-called Colombian Navy was nothing but an association of pirates of all nations. They sailed under the Colombian flag, but it was a mere cover for piracy. We need not blame the South American Republics too severely; they were only doing what European potentates had done for centuries—what, as we have seen in the case of the Vitalians, had been done by the German enemies of Denmark when they invited all who would rob and burn to come to their ports. We can obtain a very sufficient view of what it all meant nearer home than the West Indies and the Spanish Main.

The Eastern Mediterranean supplied somewhat similar conditions and manners, and for them we happen to possess an excellent English witness.*

If we can believe our author, A. Roberts—and his statement is credible enough—he was shipwrecked at the haven of Nio in His Majesty's hired ship, the *Arcana* galley, in 1692. While he was endeavouring to arrange for a passage

* "A Collection of Original Voyages," Captain Hack, 1699; "Mr. Roberts: his Voyage to the Levant, with an Account of his Sufferings amongst the Corsairs, their Villainous Way of Living, and his Description of the Archipelago Islands." This was "A. Roberts," who is not to be confounded with George Roberts, who had adventures with pirates in the Cape de Verd Islands, and whose "Four Voyages" were published in 1726. The book is one of the many attributed to Defoe, had obviously enough been at least dressed up by some literary man, and is of dubious authority, and withal long-winded.

BARBARY PIRATES PLUNDERING THE "ADMIRAL TROWBRIDGE."
From "Mariner's Marvel."

to Scio in a Greek ship a " crusal " or corsair came in, and he was kidnapped by her crew. He says that, knowing how miserably men lived in a corsair, he would not have served willingly, but he makes no pretence of disliking the piratical life in itself. All his countrymen were not so fastidious, for the leader of the gang who kidnapped him was one Dawes of Saltash. Another of the crew was a Dane. The corsair was not a pirate pure and simple, but only in fact and practice. If the western seamen held the easy creed of Darby Mullins, that it was little or no sin to rob such heathens as the Moors and Indians were, the Moslem of the Mediterranean saw no sin whatever in pillaging Christians, and the Christians retaliated in kind. Small States did not scruple, under pretence of fighting Islam, to give commissions to adventurers whose real object was plunder, and who took it where it was to be found. Roberts gives a list of the corsairs he met during his sixteen months' captivity: the *St. Helena*, which had two Captains, Joseph Pretiosi and Angelo Franciso, Corsicans, of 20 guns, 30 " patereroes "—small pieces firing stones—230 men, flying Livornese colours—*i.e.*, the flag of Tuscany; the *Annuntiation*, Captain John Peragola, Corsican, of 22 guns, 16 " patereroes," and 230 men, Tuscan colours; *Caravel*, John Vecchio, Corsican, 12 guns, 8 " patereroes," 109 men, Portuguese colours; *Madona of Monte Negroa*, Captain Franciscain, Corsican, 16 guns, 10 " patereroes," 160 men, Tuscan colours; *Santa Barbara*, Captain Anthony Sicar, Provençal, 24 guns, 12 " patereroes," 200 men, Venetian colours; and two vessels of 36 and 6 guns respectively, belonging to the Order of Malta, and commanded by Knights. When we are told that French naval officers, Tourville and Suffren among them, began by serving in the caravans of the Order, it is to be understood that they were engaged in the service described by Roberts, which we shall see was just sordid piracy.

These vessels were fitted out by speculators, who belonged as a rule to Genoa or Leghorn. The essential part of the crew was provided by Corsican refugees and Italian criminals. Corsica, being in a chronic state of family feud, brigandage, and rebellion against its Genoese Sovereigns (it did not pass to France till 1768), supplied endless desperate adventurers by land and sea to all who would hire them. Italy provided men who could not stay at home except at the imminent hazard of the galleys or the rope. The Corsicans and the criminals served as trustworthy guards to the Captain, and terrorized the other elements of the crew. The full complement was made up of vagabonds tempted by lying promises at Leghorn or Genoa, or by poor wretches pressed out of the vessels captured in the Levant. As for the life they led, Roberts asserts that he would rather serve for seven years in the galleys than go through another sixteen months of it. We can well believe him. The corsair, as he saw him, was a very different person to the corsair of Lord Byron. He was, he says, compelled to serve as gunner, and was promised all the " patereroes " taken out of such prizes of all nationalities as they might capture. But for thirty-five " patereroes " and seventy chambers, which ought to have fallen to his lot, he received just two dollars and seven reals, which was all the money he saw in sixteen months' service. In fact, the Captain and his volunteers kept all the booty. As for " the life of the poor sailor here, I am sure nothing can parallel it for the badness thereof." They were kept hard at work, and their rations were bread three times a day, except on Sundays and Thursdays, when they were allowed a kettle of horse-beans boiled and well salted, with sometimes one-quarter of a pint of oil thrown on them as they boiled. A pickthank who would report anybody's misdemeanours to the steward might hope for an occasional sardine. Meat they never saw, except when some of the Captain's had turned bad. The Captain and his volunteers, in short, treated the bulk of the crew as ill as ever galley-slaves were treated by the authorities of the galleys. Desert the poor wretches could not, for the cruising-ground of the corsairs was the Archipelago, which sailors called for short the " Arches," and the islanders were too much afraid of the corsairs to protect runaways. Resist they could not, for fear of the volunteers and lack of arms. It was only when the volunteers were by some accident absent or reduced in numbers that the " perforced " men could mutiny. Now and then they did succeed in getting possession of a corsair and carrying her off. As a rule they were terrorized, beaten, half-starved, and kept from all share of the booty.

The adventures of these lurking scoundrels were much what might have been expected. During the winter months they lay in harbour in one of the islands refitting their vessels, when necessary, by pulling a prize to pieces; in spring and summer they haunted the Archipelago and the coasts of Cyprus, Syria, or Egypt, taking small merchant ships or kidnapping prisoners on shore to be held to ransom. The mere report that a Turkish or Algerine ship of force was in their neighbourhood was enough to make them show a clean pair of heels.*

It must be confessed that when the pirate is looked at by the light of authentic records he cuts a miserable figure. The romantic corsair of Lord Byron, a hero of " one virtue and a thousand crimes," was an invention. The melodramatic pirate Captain of Marryat or Michael Scott was the offspring of what ill-conditioned persons have called " the lying spirit of romance." The real pirate was a sneaking thief and an arrant coward. I have met no instance in which he put up a good fight. He did not even accumulate a treasure to be hidden away and sought for, like Kidd's hoard in Poe's " Gold Brig." A couple of thousand pounds was Avery's share of the loot of the *Gunsway*, and he was exceptionally lucky. A sluttish idleness and freedom to drink were the real attractions of the life.

Captain Charles Johnson's " History of the Pyrates " may be accepted as a fairly authentic picture. Of the man himself we know nothing, and the name was probably assumed. But whoever the writer was, he had access to letters and reports, and it is pretty clear that he was acquainted with some who had come in on a proclamation. Perhaps he was one himself, or had been a " perforced " man at some period in his life. His narrative has certainly verisimilitude, and it is borne out by evidence given in trials and last dying speeches and confessions made

* M. P. Masson's " Commerce Français dans le Levant au XVIIme Siècle," 1896, has much to say of Mediterranean piracy.

to the Ordinary of Newgate.* The stories he has to tell are inexpressibly dreary and monotonous. Some are variations on the history of Avery—the seizure of a ship by mutineers, a cruise, a few captures, and at the end a return to some lurking-place. Some are just the wretched fortunes of men of the stamp of the—for the most deservedly—distressed British seamen who hang about the door of H.B.M. Consul's office in foreign ports, or loaf around the harbour as beachcombers, cadging on the charity of honest sailors, or pilfering from the ships of their countrymen. In times when the police of the sea was ill done they found some pirate to join, and they robbed weak merchant ships or unarmed villages. When boldly faced, they were always beaten. Listen to the confession of that famous English pirate, Captain James Kelly, who was hanged on Friday, July 12th, 1700. He had begun his career in the *Dolphin*, Captain Yankee, "Commander on the privateer account." This means that Captain Yankee, under pretence of privateering, was a pirate. He hung about in the West Indies, and sent his plunder into Jamaica to exchange for provisions. Somebody peached. Kelly's story shows that it must have been so, and these vermin were always betraying and robbing one another. One Captain Jacob was sent to suppress Yankee and another of the same kidney then cruising with him. As he had the pirate's signal, the way was clear for him. "Captain Jacob," so Kelly told the reporter to whom he recounted his adventures on the day before "justice took place" at Execution Dock, "he came out on the Sunday morning, which was a thing not usual, and when he came near the ship [Captain Yankee's] he showed us the sign, which he was ordered to do if all was well [the pudding-headed Kelly means the signal their friends were wont to make]. The sea-breeze then setting in, he could not fetch the ship, so he fetched a trip off, and our consort then riding to windward the other ship [*i.e.*, Jacob's] tackt, and when he came within small arms trial

* There are some fine specimens among the broadsides preserved in the British Museum. They can be looked up under the name of Paul Lorraine, the ordinary (*i.e.*, chaplain) who assisted Kidd and not a few other ruffians, land thieves, and water thieves, at Tyburn or Execution Dock.

[*sic* ? shot] of our consort he hoisted the King's Jack upon his insignet staff, and called his men upon deck, which were about ninety red coats,* and then laid our consort on board, their men [the consort's] for the most part being drunk, so our consort was taken." So much for the sea, and now for the land. "We went to a great Indian town, St. Mark, and took it, and one of our consorts meeting with the Beef Stantion [cattle "Estancia," or station, of course, but the illiterate blackguard, with the gloomy view of to-morrow's gallows before his eyes, and the no doubt equally ignorant reporter, make wild work of all names], left twenty men to secure the cattle, and while we were in the town we were disguised at Sankto Mark [disguised in drink, to wit], and rousing all they [the inhabitants] could they assaulted us, and fell upon the men that kept the beef stantion and slew all but three or four." And the rest of us who were not too thoroughly "disguised" to move, ran away. And so it is a little more or a little less in the story of all of them. Chaloner Ogle suppressed Bartholomew Roberts and his gang on the Guinea Coast in much the way that Captain Jacob snuffed out Yankee. All our men drunk, no look-out, and no fight, is the general tale.

Whenever and wherever the law was ill-enforced, piracy arose in just the same way. Manwaring describes the rise and progress of a pirate crew in terms which might almost have been copied from Belon's account of the progress of the Levantine corsairs.† "Three or four hardy fellows bred to the sea join in an adventure, whereof the first beginnings are poor, for they have but some small boat, or frigate or brigantine [little rowing and sailing craft] ill-appointed. But for the rest they have a mariner's compass, and have also some arms. For provisions they have a bag of flour and a little biscuit, a skin of oil, honey, some strings of garlic and onions, which are food enough for a month.

* Were these soldiers told off to serve as Marines, or did the King's sailors wear red jackets? The navy had a narrow escape of being uniformed in red. Commodore Trunnion wore a red jacket when he boarded the *Renummy*.

† Quoted by M. Victor Bérard in his "Les Phéniciens et l'Odysée," 1902, to illustrate the ancient sea-life of the Mediterranean—from "Plurimarum Singularum Rerum in Græcia, Asia, Egypto, etc., ab ipso conspectu Observationes," 1589.

With that they go a roaming. If the wind keeps them in port, they draw their boat up on the shore, where they cover it with branches which they cut out of the wood with their axes, and they will light a fire with their flint, and make a damper with their flour, which they will cook on a tile or sheet of copper or hammered iron laid on two stones with a fire below." From that starting-point they advance by plundering fishing-boats, till they have gathered a few more like themelvses, and can seize a coasting craft. The next step is to prowl on some frequented route till they can one day surprise a trading vessel. For the pirate ships in reality were not long, low, raking craft of superior speed and picturesque appearance. They were just stolen merchant vessels with the armament such vessels would carry. They sailed no better in the hands of the pirate than they did when in possession of honest men. If there was an exception, it was when the piratical craft was a stolen privateer. As for the pirate Captain, he was simply the ruffian who happened to be able to get himself accepted as the member of the gang who was to carry on in pursuit, action, or flight, when somebody must give the word. At other times he had no more authority than another. If his gang had suspected him of concealing a hoard for his own benefit, his throat would soon have been cut. What authority there was in a pirate, apart from the natural superiority a strong and determined man has over weaklings and cowards (and even the strongest man must sleep sometimes, and can be killed by the weakest in his sleep), belonged to the regular bred seamen, on whose skill all depended. They took a full share, and gave as much as they pleased to such landsmen and boys as there were among them. What discipline could exist in such a company? And what fight could be made by a crew, when most of its members would be sure to surrender promptly to a well-appointed opponent in the hope of saving their necks, and some were forced men eager to escape at the first opportunity? No real resistance was to be expected, and little enough was made.

The *Times* gave a most authentic picture of the pirate of reality when on October 18th, 1811, it reprinted a letter which had appeared in its columns a century before. The writer, Colonel Christie, was an eyewitness, and tells his tale well. He had taken a passage in the packet *Coffee Planter*. The packet carried a crew of nine men, of whom six were down with fever, and one was disabled by the bursting of a musket. Her skipper, Hercules Jenkins, two men, and the Colonel, who lent a hand, had to manage her. She was overhauled in the Mona passage by a big schooner full of men, who first showed English, and then French colours. The schooner was in no hurry to come to close quarters. When her crew were satisfied that there must be but few men in the packet (a small brig), they at last plucked up spirit to call on her to surrender. Resistance was impossible, and a boat from the schooner took possession of the packet after the pirate had fired several times at her in mere wantonness. The boat's crew were of all colours, and, of course, bristling with weapons. Their leader was " a young Frenchman, half naked, with two fresh sabre-wounds on his right arm, of good aspect, and modest deportment." Of course they set to work to plunder, and in a short time the packet was taken into smooth water on the south-west side of the island of Mona. Here she was methodically plundered. Her Captain, who was forced to spend the night in the pirate, found her a sink of filth and foul smells. He could not learn where she came from. Naturally he could not, for she had no regular commission. There were about a hundred men in her of 140 she had originally carried. But she had lost heavily in an action with a Spanish packet from Cadiz, which made a stout fight. The pirates had finally got possession by boarding, and had massacred thirty-five of her crew of forty. About thirty of them were white, and as many pure blacks. The balance were of mixed race, and Colonel Christie saw red men among them. Some of her hundred were wounded or sick, and lay below, adding to her prevailing stench and dirt.

The intention of the pirates was to complete the transfer of the packet's cargo, and then burn her. It is to be observed that they did not so far propose to butcher their prisoners. Captain Jenkins, who had spent the night on the deck of the schooner in the rain, for the foul smells below in the dirty, overcrowded schooner were intolerable, returned in the morning to say that the packet was about to be burnt, and that he had been allowed to return to take clean clothes. At that moment another vessel came in sight. Captain Jenkins and the three Englishmen who could help him cut the packet's cable, and stood for the stranger. She proved to be the *Carmarthen*, from San Domingo, with a cargo of mahogany for Liverpool. She carried twelve guns and as many men. The pirate was far too cautious to tackle the new-comer till he had taken careful survey. While he was feeling his way another mahogany trader from San Domingo came in sight—the *Minerva*, indifferently manned and armed, but of imposing appearance. Hereupon the pirate made off. She was named the *Marengo*, commanded by Jean Augereau of Nantes ; and in Colonel Christie's opinion she sailed from Hayti, since she " could not well keep those seas without being recruited with the necessary supplies in one or other of the many creeks or minor harbours of that kingdom."

The Colonel was no doubt right in his estimate, for the negro " kingdom " of Hayti had been a nest of piracy ever since the insurgent negro slaves had thrown off their French masters. His story shows of how little use an armament was to a merchant—at least, in war time, when the navy of every Power was certain to press every man not needed to work the ship on the most economical scale. And then the Colonel's story brings us back to the old matter of the fox-holes. He was surprised to see the French flag flying in the West Indies, when the French ports had been conquered, and their privateers deprived of a basis of operations. When they were cut off from regular privateering they took to piracy, and Hayti gave them refuge.

The adventure of the *Coffee Planter* shows how very difficult it was for a mere merchant ship to resist attack by a numerously manned pirate. She was a packet, and carried mails. These vessels were in a way fighting ships, and there were many instances in which they made a determined fight against privateers. But they could not carry arge crews, and they were liable to be undermanned, as we see the *Coffee Planter* was. A merchant ship pure and simple was less able to resist than a packet. In war it was pretty certain that the press would cut her crew down to the quick, and a large part of it would be boys. I say nothing of foreigners, for they might have just as little wish to be butchered, robbed, or pressed by a pirate as an English sailor. Nor will I suppose that any part of her crew was of the stamp of the Francis Pindar, who vexed the soul of Captain Downton when he brought home the *Peppercorn* from Bantam. Suppose they were all good men and true, what could twelve men do to fight twelve guns? If the ship was assailed by a single opponent, she would have to fight only six guns; and if the Captain took the wheel and left everybody free to fight, she had two men per piece. Now, it was calculated that one man must be allowed to each 500 pounds of metal, and that one a strong grown man. A 9-pounder of 26 hundredweight would require a crew of five men. After 1780 the carronade was introduced. It was a light piece of large bore, and could be handled by fewer men than a gun proper; but then it had a very short range, and would be of no use for the purpose of knocking away the pirate's spars. It would be easy for an assailant full of men to board and overpower the small crew of a merchant ship by numbers.

We can still consult an older and more experienced witness to what the pirate was in himself than Colonel Christie. In the years 1719-20 Richard Lasinby, mariner, spent seven months as the prisoner of certain pirates in the Indian Ocean. His account of what he saw and suffered, and of what his captors did, survives among the Records of the India Office in three forms—a letter to the directors of the Company, a summary of the letter, and an affidavit.* Lasinby sailed as second mate in the *Cassandra*, Indiaman, with Captain Macrae. The *Cassandra* was attacked while watering at Johanna, or Anuyan, one of the Comoro Islands at the north end of the Mozambique Channel, by two pirate ships. They were commanded by one Seager, who can be identified with the Captain England who figures in the "History of the Pirates" (Stevenson's John Silver sailed

* "India Office Records," Miscellaneous Letters 13, Nos. 97, 98, 99. But see also Colonel John Biddulph, "Pirates of Malabar."

with England) and Taylor. The subsequent fortunes of these persons do not belong to our story, but are of some value as illustrations of the life and character of the pirate. Seager-England was marooned, turned ashore to shift for himself by his fellow-pirates, to punish him for having shown too much weak humanity in this very business of the attack on the *Cassandra*. Taylor made his way to the West Indies, took advantage of a Spanish proclamation, and entered the service of Spain.

Captain Macrae made a stout fight, but the pirates were too many for him. After losing a large part of his crew in action, he beached his ship, and took refuge in the woods with the survivors. The *Cassandra* was a valuable prize, and the pirates were very pleased with themselves and their luck. After a few days Macrae opened negotiations with them, and they were persuaded to come to an understanding. Some of the pirates were for acting on the maxim that dead men tell no tales. But England was energetic in defending Macrae, and he is said to have been helped by a one-legged pirate of ferocious appearance but humane leanings. Captain Macrae and the faithful men who followed him were allowed to go free, and the pirates gave them one of their own ships, the *Fancy*, in which to go to India. She was rotten and leaky, and, of course, they kept the *Cassandra*. They behaved with all the generosity of the brigand of the Russian fabulist Kriloff. He robbed the poor man of his milch cow and milking-pail; then, moved by pity for the poor man's hard case, magnanimously gave him back the pail, which was of no use to himself. Macrae reached India, and showed himself active in persecution of the pirates, which proved unfortunate for Captain England. His captors were infuriated by his ingratitude, and swore to burn him alive if they caught him again, but took good care to keep out of his way. Before allowing him to go they pressed Richard Lasinby.

Their reason for impressing the *Cassandra*'s second mate is easily understood. After transferring their men to the *Cassandra*, which they renamed the *Victory*, they sailed, at the end of six weeks, to Malabar. Until they were clear of Johanna the pirates would not allow Lasinby on deck. They threatened to murder him if he did not keep below. He had to sleep on the floor of the cabin beside the pirate's surgeon, who was, in fact, his gaoler. It is only in romance that the pirate Captain has his cabin to himself, and is waited on by fair captives in " very light clothing and very little of it." The real pirate Captain pigged with the others, and could do nothing but by their leave. When the *Victory* and her consort had reached the coast of Malabar, the Captain—who one gathers was Seager-England—called upon Lasinby to tell them the private signals of the company's ships. He professed, probably with truth, that he knew of none. The Captain flourished a broadsword over his head, and uttered dire threats. But the menaces of the pirates were worse than their acts to Lasinby. He was constantly threatened with death, but the worst that was done to him was that he was beaten once towards the end of his stay with them, at the instigation of one scoundrel who accused him of not showing sufficient respect. On this occasion several of the crew intervened on his behalf, saying it was a shame to treat him so. On the Malabar coast they took two small native craft of little value, and put their crews to the torture by " squeezing their joints in trees," to make them give information as to the movements of the trading ships on the coasts. When their supply of water began to run low, they went to the Laccadive Islands. Here they behaved with extreme brutality to the women and children. The men had fled to cover. A gale blew the ships off while part of the crews were on shore. When the vessels had regained their anchorage and re-embarked their men, it was decided to sail for the Dutch factory at Cochin. It was known to all old pirates that the Dutch would be good friends to whomsoever brought goods to swop or money to pay for food and drink.

On the way to Cochin they captured a small vessel belonging to Mr. Adams, of the factory at Tellicherry, and commanded by an Englishman, Fawk, with a Lascar crew. Fawk, who was " half disguised in liquor " when brought aboard the *Victory*, began to babble, and let out the unwelcome information that Macrae was already fitting out vessels to pursue his generous captors. Their anger was extreme, and broke out in furious threats as to what they would do if they caught Macrae, and the revenge they would take on Lasinby. Their belief as to the complacency of the Dutch was well founded. They were allowed to deal for provisions with one who passed by the name of Trumpett. The provisions consisted largely of arrack and sugar, which were received with jubilation and salutes. The happy pirates threw handfuls of coin into Trumpett's boat as he left the side. They also marked their approval of the conduct of the Dutch Governor by sending him a handsome table clock they had taken from the *Cassandra*, together with a gold watch for his daughter. When provided with drink and fresh meat, they decided " to keep their Christmas," and did so by a three days' drunk, during which they wasted two-thirds of their provisions. After hanging about the coast for a time, chasing to no purpose and running away at the sight of what looked like a serious force, they decided to go to the Mascarenhas Islands—better known as Mauritius and Réunion—then both in the hands of the French, and no less hospitable to pirates than the Dutch factory at Cochin. The result of " keeping their Christmas " was that they were reduced to 2 pounds of beef and a little rice per day for a mess of ten. Their chief subsistence was on arrack and sugar. At the islands they had the good luck to find a Portuguese vessel which had put in in distress, and was therefore at once easily overpowered. It carried a Viceroy of Goa, who was going home with bags full of diamonds. This last stroke of luck restored the good humour of the pirates, and they let Lasinby go. He took a passage in a French ship homeward bound, and at St. Helena was able to transfer himself to one of the company's vessels.

Here we may finally part with the pirate. We have seen him from the inside. His din and disorder, foul life and foul tongue, his bestiality to the weak, his avoidance of the strong, his elementary joy in arrack and sugar, his highwayman generosity, his dependence on the receiver of stolen goods, his gorging and his starvation. Stripped of tinsel, he is a common blackguard, whose nearest approach to worth was that at his best he did not kill in mere wanton cruelty.

CHAPTER XI

IMPRESSMENT

THE medieval codes had been concerned to secure the sailor his rights. Later, legislators were busy with him, but as a rule in the way of deciding how much and how often he could be forced to serve at a cheap rate. Impressment, the fear of it, and the devices by which it might be avoided, played a large part in the lives of the merchant seamen of all countries. No better introduction to what it meant and how it worked could be wished for than the report of the trial of Alexander Broadfoot at Bristol, on August 30th, 1743, for murder.

In that year the War of the Austrian Succession was getting into full swing, and there was a hot press for seamen. Captain Hanway, of H.M. sloop *Mortar*, stationed in the Bristol Channel, held a press warrant. It expressly provided that the impressment must be carried out by a commissioned officer, whose name and rank were to be endorsed on the document. On April 25th, when the sloop was at anchor in the King's Road, Captain Hanway sent out a boat on press duty, with orders to take men out of any ship it might meet. But he did not comply with his legal obligation to entrust the service of the warrant to a commissioned officer. There was only one in the *Mortar*, her Lieutenant, and—whether because his services were called for elsewhere, or, what is more probable, because Captain Hanway's experience had not led him to think that minute attention to the letter of the law was necessary—this officer was not sent in command of the boat. The *Mortar's* boat stopped a homeward-bound ship, the *Bremen Factor*, some leagues from the King's Road. Part of her crew boarded the vessel. They were told by her master that several of the crew had gone below. The *Mortar's* pressmen went down to the hold in search of them, and there they found Alexander Broadfoot, together with others. They were hailed by him with the question, What were they coming for? " We are coming for you and your comrades," was the answer. " Stand back !" cried Broadfoot; " for I have a blunderbuss loaded with swan-shot." The pressgang hesitated, and then Broadfoot asked : " Where is your officer ?" " He is not far off,' was the reply. It was enough for the rebellious sailor, who would appear to have been something of a sea lawyer, for it showed him that there was no officer with the boat, and he was, we may be sure, well aware that the service of the warrant was illegal. Having now, as he judged, the law on his side, he fired at once, killing one Calhoun on the spot, and wounding others of the pressgang. Nor was Broadfoot wholly in the wrong in thinking that he was entitled to resist. When he came to be tried before the Recorder of Bristol, Mr. Sergeant Foster (afterwards Sir Michael Foster of the King's Bench), that distinguished legal authority instructed the jury to find a verdict of manslaughter on the ground that the service of the warrant was illegal, and must therefore be looked upon as " an attempt on the liberty of the subject without any legal warrant."*

If this had been all, the case would hardly have earned the honour of a report in the " State Trials." But it was not all. Mr. Sergeant Foster, speaking from conviction, as we are prepared to believe, but not, perhaps, without a thoughtful eye to promotion, took the opportunity to deliver a pronouncement on not only the legality, but the humanity and essential justice of the impressment of seamen. To be candid, the learned Recorder's harangue was not free from a certain unctuous and complacent tone which may often be heard from the Bench, the pulpit, and the Senate— as the eighteenth century would have called Parliament— when well-endowed persons are lecturing others who are not endowed at all on their obligation to serve their country. Mr. Sergeant Foster descanted on the obvious justice of

* See Howell's " State Trials," vol. xiii., cols. 1328-1362.

compelling men who had voluntarily adopted the sea as a profession to defend their country in the way of their trade and in time of need. The cant in Mr. Sergeant Foster's speech was competently handled by Benjamin Franklin, who pointed out that the obligation to defend our country does not justify the rest of the population in throwing a peculiar burden on the sailor. It should put its hand in its pocket and pay fairly. He also applied the *reductio ad absurdum* with some force, for, said he, the economical administration of justice is a great public interest. Therefore, on the Recorder's own principles, it would be fair to shut him up in the Law Courts all the year round, and compel him to hear cases for scant pay and rough rations. The parody was at least adequate to the cant, and neither has a high value.

When we ignore the Recorder's rhetoric, and turn to his defence of the legality of impressment, it is beyond dispute that he was perfectly right. He expressly put aside the question how far the Crown was entitled to impress men for general military service. He might have said, truly, that English Kings of the fourteenth and fifteenth centuries had impressed men to serve in their wars in France. Queen Elizabeth had done the same. So had King Charles I. and the Parliament in the Civil Wars. Indeed, the impressment of soldiers lingered on until the War of American Independence. It was more uniformly enforced, and lasted far longer for the sea service, because of two reasons. The first was that the law dictated the compulsory employment in the Royal Navy of all such rogues and vagabonds as the orderly part of the community desired to be well rid of.*

* Here is the sonorous list of them as given in the Act of Queen Anne, "for the increase of Seamen, the better encouragement of Navigation, and the Security of the Coal Trade" (anno 2° and 3° Annæ, cap. 6). "And forasmuch as divers dissolute and idle persons, Rogues, Vagabonds, and Sturdy Beggars, notwithstanding the many good and wholesome laws to the contrary, do continue to wander up and down, pilfering and begging through all Parts of this Kingdom, to the great disturbance of the peace and tranquillity of the Realm, for the more effectual suppressing such disorderly Persons, to the end that they may be made serviceable and beneficial to their Country, be it further enacted by the authority aforesaid, That all lewd and disorderly Manservants, and every such Person and Persons, both Men and Boys, that are deemed and adjudged Rogues, Vagabonds, and Sturdy Beggars (not being Felons) by an Act of Parliament, made the nine and thirtieth year of the Reign of the said late

We are not concerned with the lewd serving-men, the rogues, vagabonds, and sturdy beggars, who were sent into the navy by the thousand, to be flogged, and to desert at the first chance. But the second reason touches us closely. The sailors were always liable to impressment, not because they were classed with rogues and vagabonds, but, on the contrary, because they were the skilled artificers whose services were indispensable, and who very rarely—well-qualified observers asserted that they never—entered a warship of their own free will. It may be asserted without qualification that until very recent days no navy trained its own men in peace, and that no State was sufficiently wealthy to stand the strain. Wars were periods of waste and loss which made it absolutely necessary to use peace as a time of thrift and recuperation. Therefore navies were cut down to a handful when peace was signed, and when war began again the skilled men who could hand, reef, and steer, set up rigging, or repair it when damaged, and handle a boat, had to be sought where they could be found among the men " bred to the sea," " the prime seamen," " the real sailormen," brought up from boyhood in merchant ships and fishing boats.

It may—it probably does—occur to most readers that there were better ways of obtaining their services, even if compulsion was to be employed, than the brutal and wasteful system, or no system, of impressment as practised in Great Britain. Well, the French were early of that opinion. The Ministers of King Lewis XIV., with the illustrious Colbert at their head, sought out a better way, with results which are highly instructive.*

Let us first see what was the problem which Colbert and

Queen Elisabeth for punishing of Rogues, Vagabonds, and Sturdy Beggars, shall be and are hereby directed to be taken up, sent, conducted, and conveyed, into her Majesty's Service at Sea, or the Service at Sea of her Majesty's Heirs or Successors, by such ways, methods, and means, and in such Manner and Form, as is directed for Vagrants by the said before mentioned Act of Parliament, made in the said Eleventh and Twelfth years of the reign of the said late King William the Third, for the more effectual Punishment of Vagrants, and sending them whither by law they ought to be sent."

* I have, in the main, followed the " Mémoire sur l'Inscription Maritime " of M. Jules de Crisenoy, a retired naval officer, published in 1870, but with reference to other sources.

all the Ministers of maritime States had to solve. Put in a nutshell, it was this : They had to make the seafaring population perform two incompatible functions simultaneously—to man the fleet, and also to supply crews for merchant ships and fishing boats. In 1686, when the French Royal Navy was fully organized, the King's Ministers came to the conclusion that the trade and fisheries of France employed 47,919 men and boys who could be drawn on for the navy. There were also known to be 9,311 Masters, qualified pilots, and other special men, such as skippers of fishing boats and apprentices, who were exempted from the obligation to serve. Now, when King Lewis was sending fleets of eighty sail of the line into the Channel, and also maintaining forces in America and the Mediterranean, as he had to do after 1688, it was a matter of very simple calculation that the maritime population of France was not equal to manning the navy, and was palpably unequal to providing crews for warships, merchant ships, and fishing fleets, at one and the same time.

In the beginning of the King's reign his Government had recourse to the press, pure and simple, as practised in Great Britain. There was much rebellious resistance by the men, and loud outcries from the shipowners. Colbert, whose heart was set on developing the industry and commerce of France, elaborated a scheme which was to have made the obligation to serve the King orderly, and therefore less harsh than the erratic press, and also to have provided certain compensations to the seafaring men. This was the much vaunted system, known as " Les Classes " under the Monarchy, then taken on, recast, and renamed the " Inscription Maritime " by the Republic. It had its official defenders in France, and its ill-informed admirers abroad. But it never worked, and that for the reason which makes it impossible for the greatest administrative genius to obtain a gallon of liquid from a quart. The seamen of France were to be registered in three classes. In each district the whole body was to be " shoaled," to use the term employed in our dockyards. They were to be called out in rotation, and when not needed were to receive half-pay. Moreover, the men were promised certain **advan-**

tages, such as exemption from the arbitrary direct tax, called the " taille." " Les Classes " did well enough when they were asked to supply the crews of a small squadron fitted out against the Barbary tyrants. When the war with Holland came on 1672, and a great fleet was to be manned, they broke down completely. The Government is found trying to sweep the whole seafaring population into the navy by wholesale impressment, as in England. The men are found, as in England, doing their utmost to escape. The King's Ministers are found adopting measures of coercion such as would have raised a storm of fury in England.

In 1673 M. de la Vaissière, Governor of Havre, announced that the wives and families of refractory seamen who failed to report themselves in three days would be expelled from the town. The Minister Seigneley approved of his vigorous measure, but added that the Governor must take care to enforce it. The Governor had good reason to know that his energy would be praised. In the previous year the Minister had written to the port authorities, telling them that this was not the time to apply for instructions from Paris. They must use all means, and lay hands on all the men they could find for thirty miles round the ports, in order to provide crews for the King's ships. Nor were such measures as these by any means exceptional. During the whole existence of the Ancien Régime it was the regular custom of the authorities to enforce the service of the men by attacking their families. The usual course was to put " garnisaires " into their houses—or huts, to speak accurately. " Garnisaires " were simply soldiers, who were billeted on the families of sailors and fishermen, and were to be fed in part by them. They were allowed, if they were not encouraged, to commit every kind of outrage.

The British Government cared little enough for what might happen to the families of pressed men, but it never endeavoured to enforce service in the navy by turning women and children on to the country roads to become vagrants and to die of starvation, nor yet by billeting soldiers on them, with full leave to beat and to rape. I would hesitate to commit myself to the proposition that the difference was due to the higher level of British humanity.

FRENCH SAILOR.

By Joseph Vernet.

Engraved by Le Bas for "Tableaux des Ports de France"

tages, such as exemption from the arbitrary direct tax, called the "taille." "Les Classes" did well enough when they were asked to supply the crews of a small squadron fitted out against the Barbary tyrants. When the war with Holland came on 1672, and a great fleet was to be manned, they broke down completely. The Government is found trying to sweep the whole seafaring population into the navy by wholesale impressment, as in England. The men are found, as in England, doing their utmost to escape. The King's Ministers are found adopting measures of coercion such as would have raised a storm of fury in England.

In 1673 M. de la Vaissière, Governor of Havre, announced that the wives and families of refractory seamen who failed to report themselves in three days would be expelled from the town. The Minister Seigneley approved of his vigorous measure, but added that the Governor must take care to enforce it. The Governor had good reason to know that his energy would be praised. In the previous year the Minister had written to the port authorities, telling them that this was not the time to apply for instructions from Paris. They must use all means, and lay hands on all the men they could find for thirty miles round the ports, in order to provide crews for the King's ships. Nor were such measures as these by any means exceptional. During the whole existence of the Ancien Régime it was the regular custom of the authorities to enforce the service of the men by attacking their families. The usual course was to put "garnisaires" into their houses—or huts, to speak accurately. "Garnisaires" were simply soldiers, who were billeted on the families of sailors and fishermen, and were to be fed in part by them. They were allowed, if they were not encouraged, to commit every kind of outrage.

The British Government cared little enough for what might happen to the families of pressed men, but it never endeavoured to enforce service in the navy by turning women and children on to the country roads to become vagrants and to die of starvation, nor yet by billeting soldiers on them, with full leave to beat and to rape. I would hesitate to commit myself to the proposition that the difference was due to the higher level of British humanity.

FRENCH SAILOR.

By Joseph Vernet.

Engraved by Le Bas for "Tableaux des Ports de France"

It is sufficiently explained by the difference in the systems adopted by the two countries. In Great Britain the sailor was personally liable, and could be forced to serve whenever he could be caught, but he was not under a legal obligation to come forward. In France the law bound the whole body to serve, and the failure to report for service was an offence. When the individual offender could not be found, he was struck at through his family. The greater cruelty of the press in France was, in fact, the direct—perhaps it was the intended—consequence of Colbert's well-meant organization. The burden was aggravated by other causes. If all the promises made to the French sailors had been kept, " Les Classes " would have been less hateful to the maritime population than they were. But they were not kept. The financial embarrassments of the Government of King Lewis XIV., in the middle and later years of his reign, and those of his successors at all times made it impossible for the Government of France to keep its promises. The half-pays, the exemption from the " taille," the hospitals, were never given. Colbert, when reminded of them, answered with callous impudence that the King had never intended to keep his promises. Nor was that all. The men were not even paid when actually in the King's service. Of course it became hateful. Men not only fled from it, but they did their utmost to escape from the trade which rendered them liable to so much suffering.

We must not overlook the essential fact that liability to be summoned into the navy was quite another thing than the burden of conscription as it is enforced to-day. The conscript serves in his youth for a period limited by law. The men of " Les Classes " were never free so long as they could work. Then the conscripts represent a percentage of the general population. When " Les Classes " were called out in a body, the skilled men of a whole trade were swept away, and it was paralyzed. When peace returned, the recovery was slow, and it was long before regular work was to be found. Our national complacency prompts us to believe that the maritime activity of France was ruined by the British Navy. This is, however, little more than a delusion of patriotic vanity. The fact that

France does not produce a bulky outward freight corresponding to the coal of England, the ores, timber, wool, and raw material of other countries, would have hampered the development of her shipping in any case. But if her maritime population, which had been full of life and promise in the early seventeenth century, grew stagnant and began to diminish at the close, the explanation is to be sought in the fact that the merchantman was sacrificed to the warship. The maritime population lost its best men, for the most energetic of them who survived the navy were the most successful in escaping to other ways of life. Colbert's plausible-looking scheme, and its successor, the Inscription Maritime of the Republic and the Empire, which lasted down to the Crimean War, can be judged and condemned by their last appearance. In 1854 the Government of Napoleon III. called out the whole strength of the Inscription Maritime. The establishment of the Imperial Navy was raised to 65,000 with an apparent ease and rapidity which were the objects of much unthinking admiration in England. The thing was done, and the doing of it killed the old Inscription Maritime. The loss inflicted on the shipping and fishing industries, the burden thrown on public assistance and private charity by the destitution of thousands of families, combined to convince all Frenchmen that the call could never be made again. The Inscription Maritime has been modified by a succession of enactments which have assimilated it to an ordinary conscription, and France has been compelled to form a peace establishment of specially recruited men.*

* It is not my cue to launch into general history, but I am unwilling to leave this part of my subject without noting my inability to agree with those who say that the naval power of France was sacrificed wholly to the necessity for maintaining armies. The large sums wasted by Lewis XIV. on his superfluous palace at Versailles, and the yet larger sums which, according to Saint-Simon, he spent on a yet more superfluous palace at Marly, would have more than sufficed to support his fleet. The treasures lavished by him and his successor on bedizened guards, persons of both sexes who rendered purely personal services, and a whole apparatus of Court show worthy of a decadent Chinese dynasty, would have covered the expense of training a corps of skilled seamen for their navy in peace several times over. The part which the swinish self-indulgence, greed, corruption, and smirking frivolity of ruling persons have played in the history of the world is too commonly underrated.

But there were peoples who pressed the merchant seamen, and who yet maintained a great sea-borne commerce in their own ships. There were, and it is incumbent on me to show how the feat was achieved. Observe, to begin with, that it was very little done. The successful nations were just two—Great Britain, and Holland till the day of her decadence in the eighteenth century. Neither of them succeeded on its own strength only. Both drew on alien populations to man their merchant ships in war time, and especially upon the seafaring men of Scandinavia and the Baltic.

It is impossible to understand the story without some reference to matters of legislation and policy.* The Navigation Laws are now shadows of once formidable names, and, to judge by what may be heard said of them from time to time, moulder unread in the limbo of repealed statutes. There was a long string of them, beginning with the reign of Richard II. and ending with Queen Victoria. It is, happily, no part of our duty to linger over these laws in so far as they strove to regulate the import and export of goods. Our concern is with the seafaring man. But we may pause for a moment to point out that one and all, from first to last, they aimed at carrying into effect the maxim expressed in the Scotch proverb, " We maun keeps our ain fish guts for our ain sea maws." Richard II. said that English goods must be exported in English ships. Well, there were not enough of them, and the owners, finding that they had been endowed with a monopoly, promptly put up their freights—the clever fellows ! Whereupon there went up a loud outcry from the merchants, answered by bullying rebuke of the inordinate shipowners by the Council of His Grace the King, who insisted that only reasonable freights should be charged ; to which the owners

* The reader who can consult "A Collection of the Statutes relating to the Admiralty, Navy, Shipping, and Navigation down to the Fiftieth of George III. inclusive," issued by authority for the use of naval officers in 1810, and will add " A Short Review of the History of the Navigation Laws of England," by a Barrister (*i.e.*, Lord Iddesleigh), 1849, will find what is essential to the subject as far as Great Britain is concerned. He can with advantage add, " Select Charters and Other Documents illustrative of American History, 1606-1775," by William Macdonald, 1899.

replied that if the law was not to benefit them it was no good, and a reasonable freight was any freight they could charge. There were re-enactments, and amending Acts, and withdrawals, and reassertions. Foreign States retaliated by declaring that their goods should be exported only in their ships, and that English ships coming to their ports for a lading should not be allowed to obtain one. Ruling persons went on running their heads against the nature of things, with the imperturbable resolution of the blue-bottle which *will* fly through the pane of glass. At last came Queen Elizabeth and swept it all away, declaring that English merchants could make use of ships of any nationality, subject to the proviso that, if they employed an alien, they must pay such dues as he paid.

Then, in 1650, the Council of State sent us on the old round on a bigger scale. It was moved by the discovery that its Royalist enemies were swarming into the West Indies and America. It shut their ports to Dutch and all foreign ships by ordinance. But if they could be excluded because they carried Royalists, why not when they carried other goods? They could, and they were, by the Act of 1651. After running the round between the reigns of Richard II. and Queen Elizabeth, we ran it again between the Council of State, which had cut off the head of Charles I., and the reign of Victoria—two periods of nearly the same length. The guiding rule was that the trade of British Colonies must be confined wholly to British ships, and that all goods must be imported either in British ships, or in vessels belonging to the country from which they were exported. This did not necessarily mean the country in which they were produced. The goods of an inland country —Saxony, for instance, or Switzerland—might be carried in the vessels of Hamburg or Genoa, because these were the usual places of shipment.

Similar conditions produced similar manners. The Navigation Laws of the new cycle went through the history of the old. How the New England Colonies defied and evaded them we have seen in the history of piracy. Foreign nations retaliated, and often with effect. British shipowners, finding they had a colonial monopoly, turned to colonial trades, and put up their freights. The Dutch, driven from our Colonies, undersold us in, and beat us out of, the Baltic and Mediterranean. Nothing is more flagrantly contrary to the truth than the common assertion that the Navigation Laws ruined the carrying trade of the Dutch. They only altered its course. A century after they had begun, the Dutch shipping was still equal to the British.

The attempt to devote " our ain fish guts " exclusively, or as exclusively as might be, to " our ain sea maws " was, of course, not limited to the transport of goods. If the ships were to be British, so the crews were to be mainly national. I abstain deliberately from saying British, in order to avoid the reproach of falling into a common error. At no time was there a legal obligation to man ships entirely with British seamen. The Council of State provided in 1651 that the majority and the master must be " of the people of this Commonwealth." The Act of 1672—the first of three passed in the reign of Charles II.—defined the restriction. It required that the master and three-fourths of the crew must be drawn from England, Ireland, and the Plantations, from which it followed that Scotchmen were excluded. After the union of 1707 they, of course, came in. Then began the age of extension and conquest. It became necessary to enlarge the terms which had been wide enough for Charles II., for William and Mary, or Queen Anne. The policy adopted in the new circumstances is summed up in the Act of Queen Victoria's regin (1846)—the last of them all.

As it is idle to paraphrase what is already well worded, the Manning Clauses of this Act may be conveniently quoted as they stand. The italics, of course, are mine :

" SECTION XIII. And be it enacted, That no ship shall be admitted to be a British ship unless duly registered and navigated as such, and that every British registered ship (so long as the Register of such ships shall be in force, or the certificate of such registry retained for the use of such ship) shall be navigated during the whole of every voyage (whether with a cargo or in Ballast) in every part of the world by a Master who is a British subject and by a crew whereof three-fourths at least are British seamen, and if such ship be employed in a coasting voyage from one part of the United Kingdom to another, or in a voyage between the United Kingdom and the islands of Guernsey, Jersey, Alderney, or Sark, or Man, or from one of the said islands to another of them, or from one part of either to another of the same, or to be employed in fishing on the coast of the United Kingdom or any of the said islands, then the whole of the crew shall be British seamen.

"XVII. And be it enacted, That no person shall be qualified to be a Master of a British Ship, or to be a British Seaman within the meaning of this Act except the natural born subjects of Her Majesty, or *persons naturalized by an Act of Parliament, or made denizens by Letters of Denization, or except persons who have become British subjects by virtue of conquest or cession of some newly acquired country, and who shall have taken the oath of allegiance to Her Majesty, or the oath of fidelity required by the treaty or capitulation by which such newly acquired country came into Her Majesty's possession, or persons who shall have served on board any of Her Majesty's ships of war, for the space of three years:* Provided always that the natives of places within the limits of the East India Company's charter, although under British Dominion, shall not, upon the ground of being such natives, be deemed to be British seamen. *Provided always that every ship (except ships required to be wholly navigated by British seamen) which shall be navigated by one British seaman, or one seaman of the country of such ship if a foreign ship* [" foreign ship " in this connection was one belonging to a conquered territory of British allegiance] *for every twenty tons of the burden of such ship, shall be deemed to be duly navigated, although the number of other seamen shall exceed one-fourth of the whole crew. Provided also that nothing herein contained shall extend to, repeal, or alter the provisions of an Act passed in the fourth year of the reign of His late Majesty King George IV. for consolidating and amending the laws then in force with respect to trade from and to places within the limits of the East India Company's charter.*"

The Act of George IV., while declaring that Asiatics should not be deemed to be British seamen, allowed them to be carried in any numbers and proportion to the crew, so long as there were four British seamen per hundred tons. It also provided that if British seamen could not be found, Lascars might be taken in lieu of them in whatever number was judged sufficient, leave being first obtained from local authorities. Finally, it declared that vessels trading from port to port wholly within the limits of the charter of the Company, including the Cape of Good Hope, were not under the obligation to carry any British seamen. And now to return to Queen Victoria's Act :

" XVIII. *Provided always and be it enacted, That it shall be lawful for Her Majesty by her royal proclamation during war to declare that 'foreigners having served two years on board any of Her Majesty's ships of war in time of such war shall be British seamen within the meaning of this Act.*"

Section XIX. permits British ships trading between places in America to be manned by British negroes, and with superabundant caution reaffirms that ships trading within the limits of the East India Company's charter " may be navigated by Lascars or other natives of countries within those limits." At the end power is reserved to the Crown to alter the proportions of British to foreign or Asiatic seamen by proclamation.

This Act was a summary of its predecessors, and contains no novelty of importance.

Section XVIII., for instance, simply repeats an Act passed by the Government of George II. on the eve of the Seven Years' War.

One thing is manifest, and it is that the legislators who made these laws, from the revolutionary Council of State downwards, never contemplated the possibility that British ships engaged in oversea voyages should be manned entirely by British seamen. A majority satisfied the Council of State, three-fourths were enough for Charles II., and then British seamen was made to cover all whose allegiance was British. Therefore, at any time between 1714 and 1783, while the Island of Minorca was a British possession, a ship owned by a native of the island, with a Minorquin Captain, manned by three-fourths of Minorquins and one of Greeks, would have been a British ship duly navigated. A glance at the words in italics will show that they introduce a mass of exceptions to the three-fourths rule. And we might add to the list. It might, and it did, occur that a British ship in a foreign port was short-handed through death or desertion. What was to be done ? Was she to sail undermanned, or not sail at all ? The suppositions are absurd. She bowed to *force majeure*, and shipped foreigners, as she was entitled to do. But it is no less clear that the British

Government never contemplated the possibility of manning both its fleet and its merchant ships in war even with a clear majority of British seamen. It invited foreigners to volunteer into its fleet, and tried to tempt them by offering them naturalization at the end of two years—one-fourth of the period of residence demanded from others who sought naturalization. And it suspended the manning clauses whenever war broke out. Charles II. did so of his own mere motion in 1664, and afterwards the suspension was ordered by Parliament, or by the Crown with Parliamentary authority.

Let us consider what this means. From the first war of Charles II.'s reign—1664—down to the Peace of Paris in 1815, was a period of 151 years. Sixty-five of these were years of war, during which our merchant service was open to foreigners without restriction. Any one of them who served for two years was free to become a British subject, and many no doubt did. Those who find a new and menacing danger in the presence of one-fourth or even one-third of foreigners and Lascars among the crews of British ships cannot be aware that they are being frightened by what has been the rule for ages.

And it was in the nature of things that it should be the rule. That what always has been will be for ever is a hazardous proposition to the eye of strict logic. But none the less we have to go by the guidance of the maxim that all presumption of time future is memory of time past. Now memory of time past shows that while there have at all periods been many maritime peoples, there have been but very few great maritime polities at any one time. While the conditions which allowed them to arise endure, then to those who have is given. They draw more and more to themselves. When the conditions fail they wither, and the "thalassocracy" passes to others or to another. One set of causes blighted the maritime supremacy of Venice, another atrophied the Netherlands. If science teaches all the world the use of a substitute for coal, which is within the reach of all, or more within the reach of some people other than our own than it is for us, or if our coal becomes too difficult and costly to work with economic advantage, then the thalassocracy of Britain will follow that of Athens, of Venice, and of the Netherlands. No effort of ours will avail to avert fate, as no muscular exertion can fill the lungs of one who is in an exhausted receiver.

It has also been always true that the predominant maritime State has been compelled to make use of men brought from beyond her own borders. The work to be done was more than her own people could provide. Athens could never have manned her triremes from the city alone. Venice employed the Dalmatian and the Greek. Holland was always open to the Scandinavian and the peoples of the Baltic. Great Britain strove to multiply her seamen by securing them employment in her merchant ships in peace, by forcing every ship to take apprentices, by directing the Guardians of the Poor to send pauper boys to sea. But she had more work to be done even in peace than her sons could overtake, and in war—why, at the beginning of the war with France in 1778 the Admiralty could declare that the number of known seafaring men in the country was but 60,000, and that a greater number of men had been carried as sailors in the fleet alone during the Seven Years' War. The Admiralty estimate of the seafaring population must be taken with reserve. Our ancestors had for long an insuperable dislike of a census. They had learnt from their Bibles that it was a sin to "number the people," and it may be believed that they were frightened by the use made of registrations by Continental Governments. These things smacked of designs on the liberty of the subject. But the Admiralty was not without means of making a rough estimate of the number of seamen.

In 1696 the Government of William III. had imposed a charge of sixpence a month on the wages of all seamen, whether they were serving in the King's ships or in trading craft, for the benefit of Greenwich Hospital. A small department for the levy of the sixpences from merchant seamen was established in 1712, in the reign of Queen Anne. Merchant Captains were required to make the deduction from the wages of their men, and to pay the amount on reaching port. The payment was made to Custom-house officials at the outports, and to the office of the Commissioners in London. Now, supposing that there had been neither fraud nor carelessness in the collection, that the levy was universal, and that the office had kept a separate account for each man, it would of course have been possible to estimate the total number employed with accuracy. Even so the Sixpenny Office could not have made a distinction between foreigners and the King's natural-born subjects, since all alike paid, and to the collectors the seamen were just so many tax-paying entities. But there was fraud in the collection, as was shown by the Naval Inquiry of 1804. There were exemptions. No levy was made at Gibraltar, Mahon, or in ports within the limits of the charter of the East India Company. Then no payment was made for apprentices of less than eighteen years of age. When the Sixpenny Office was asked to deduct the number of men from the amount collected, it divided the total number of shillings received by six. Six shillings was the sum each man would have paid in a year if he had been in constant employment—a wild supposition. Figures obtained from this source were of little value.

Other means of getting at the truth were not wholly lacking. By the Act officially known as the 2nd and 3rd Annæ, cap. 6, Custom-house officials were required to enter " in the Bottom of their cocquets [*i.e.*, cockets]* the number of men and boys on board the respective ships and vessels at their going out of every such Port." Now, if all had been good, that was upcome, if these entries had been made with unfailing accuracy ; if the documents had been preserved, collected, and conscientiously sifted, then it would have been possible to estimate the number employed correctly. These, again, are wild suppositions. We cannot state with security what the total number employed was. The utmost we are entitled to believe is that the various authorities concerned—the Admiralty, the Sixpenny Office, the Custom-house, and the Registrar of Shipping—were able to make an estimate " grosso modo." When Lord Mulgrave told Mr. Luttrell in 1776 that the total number of British seamen was 60,000 ; when in 1804 Mr. Dalley, Assis-

* The certificates given to merchants that their goods had been duly entered.

tant-Registrar of Shipping, told the Commissioners of Naval Inquiry that after years of careful study of the subject he had come to the conclusion that the total number employed in the oversea and coasting trades and in the fisheries was about 88,000 men and boys, they were not more than a few thousand out. Of the fishermen he could be sure, for they were registered, and they numbered 14,000. Now in 1802 100,000 seamen and 30,000 marines were voted for the fleet. Mr. Dalley did not include the Irish seamen, but as Ireland possessed only 1,000 vessels averaging 50 tons each her contribution cannot have been large.

We have now looked at most of the essential facts to be taken into account when considering how impressment worked in Great Britain, and how it affected the merchant seamen. But before returning to the place whence I started at the beginning of this chapter, I linger for a moment by the 2nd and 3rd Annæ, cap. 6. Everyone has seen the plate in Hogarth's history of the "Idle Apprentice," in which that predestined gallows' bird is seen in a boat and on his way to a ship in the offing. Now the idle apprentice was being carried to that ship under this Act of Queen Anne for "The Increase of Seamen and Better Encouragement of Navigation.' The Act not only empowered the parish authorities to send all pauper boys of above the age of ten to sea and bind them till the age of twenty-one, it also authorized any master or mistress of an apprentice, and their heirs or executors, to send him to sea, provided that they could obtain the consent of two justices of the county, or of any mayor, alderman, bailiff, or other chief officer or magistrate of any city, borough, or town corporate.

It is true that the apprentice must originally have been a poor parish boy. How far this limitation was observed would depend on the boy's power to defend himself, or the capacity of his relations to defend him, or the honesty of masters and mistresses, heirs, and executors, or of the justices and so forth. The poor parish boy had no defence, and in his case the Act provided not only a rod in pickle for the idle apprentice, but an easy way of relieving those who found the obligation to feed and clothe a lad inconvenient. Thousands of boys of from ten years and upwards must have been sent to sea and to the tender mercies of merchant skippers by virtue of this Act. And that mercy was often but little. When the skipper was a humane man, his apprentice would be well treated, and would have a fair chance of one day commanding a ship himself. But ten years of good opportunity to observe the merchant skippers who frequented a great Mediterranean port showed me that even in our more humane time the percentage of bullies and ruffians among them is not small. I have a vivid recollection of one story of the savage misusage of a wretched ship's boy by a partially crazed and wholly brutal Scotch skipper. Who shall judge how many such stories of bullying cruelty and filthy vice ran their course in the small merchant ships of old days?

The right to send the parish boys to sea had, as its necessary complement, the obligation on the part of the ship to take these apprentices. This condition was duly provided by the Act. Masters and owners of all ships of from 30 to 50 tons were required to take one " such apprentice [*i.e.*, poor parish boy], one for the next 50, and one for every 100 tons above 100." The master or owner could, with the consent of the justices, etc., transfer the services of an apprentice until the age of twenty-one to another master or owner. For the encouragement of the apprentice he was exempted from the Greenwich Hospital tax of sixpence a month up to the age of eighteen. But as he was entitled to just as little as the master or owner was pleased to give him, this relief was slight. He was also protected against impressment up to the same age if he had signed his indentures voluntarily. The proviso appears to have reference only to apprentices other than those sent of the parish authorities, and to imply that involuntary signing was recognized as common.

In plain English, the apprenticeship system regulated by the Act of Queen Anne was on a level with the kind of slavery known by the same plausible name as practised in the Plantations on criminals or kidnapped men and women. Neither differed materially from the serfdom of salt-pan workers and miners in Scotland, or the predial serfdom of Continental peoples—to which our ancestors pointed with

REEFING TOPSAILS.

From an aquatint after W. J. Huggins, engraved by E. Duncan. Kindly lent by Messrs. T. H. Parker, Printsellers, 45, Whitcomb Street, W.C.

pride as being so very different from the liberty of the subject prevailing in our own free country. There was small risk that the Act of Queen Anne would not be enforced. The application was left in the hands of the very persons who were most interested in seeing that it was applied. The justices, mayors, aldermen, portreeves, etc., whose consent was required to the compulsory apprenticing of poor parish boys and burdensome apprentices, were all, directly or indirectly, interested in the shipping business all round the coast. A supply of cheap labour was greatly to their advantage, and they were not at all likely to put obstacles in the way either of the Guardians of the Poor, or of masters and mistresses, heirs and executors. All apprentices were not originally poor parish boys. The sea offered a natural career to the sons of the coast population. They followed it from generation to generation—the son perhaps going to sea as the apprentice of his father, and looking forward to the day when he, too, would be a skipper and have apprentices of his own.

Now, whether he went to sea, as Captain Cook did, because he was the son of poor, but not pauper, people living in a small coast town (in his case Staithes in Yorkshire), and because his natural career was to be a seaman, or whether he went because the guardians sent him, the apprentice, from the day he passed the age of eighteen and was a grown man who had served his time, was the most valued game of the pressgangs. Those who had served their time were the skilled artificers, the regular bred seamen, prime seamen, sailormen whose art and services were indispensable. They had done all the work that is to be done in a ship from stem to stern, from truck to keel. They could hand, reef, and steer. They could rig a ship or repair damaged rigging. The sailors who could not find a ship, or who did not wish to go to sea immediately after a return home, could work as riggers in the dockyards. They had the seaman's foot and eye. They could be trusted aloft " in a storm and in the dark.' Among the sailors of the old sailing navy a great distinction was made between the man-of-war's-man, who was a sailor simply because he was rated as one, who had never served except in a man-of-war, who knew the work of his station and that only, and the real seaman who had been bred to the sea, whose proper title was the sailorman. When Captain Hays saved his ship in the Pertuis d'Antioche by a miracle of seamanship and nerve, he picked the men to whom the critical work was left. When a warship was clawing off a leeshore under double-reefed topsails and courses, when to miss stays would have meant nearly certain destruction, then only the highly trained men could be trusted.* Now, except at the close of a long war, the navy had no trained seamen of its own. In 1815 there were men-of-war's-men who were indeed bred to the sea, and sailormen. The navy had received them as boys, and had given them a thorough training, but twenty years of warfare were the dreadful price at which they were bought. Nor did such men as these ever form the majority of a crew. When one-third of a ship's company was made of men bred to the sea, she was well manned. Marines formed between a fifth and a fourth of the whole, and then there were landsmen, waisters, men who worked below under the mate of the hold, a subordinate element of " sea labourers."

Let us take a last year of peace, when war was visibly at hand, and see what was the case of our friend the merchant sailor.†

The navy, having been for some years on a peace footing of eight or ten thousand, of whom some three thousand were genuine sailors, had been able to recruit by voluntary enlistment. There is no established corps of navy sailors, and there is not to be any till the middle of the nineteenth century. When a ship was commissioned, at which time she was lying unrigged in the dockyards, her captain put out bills calling for volunteers. There were men who pre-

* My father, who served as a cadet in the Syrian War, 1840, could remember such a crisis as this. The ship he then served in—the *Cambridge*—was taken in a heavy gale while on a leeshore. Her Captain, Barnard, sent below all boys, ordinary seamen, marines who had not served a full commission at sea, and the younger midshipmen. Then he and the senior officers and the fully trained men fought it out for thirty-six hours, taking snatches of rest under cover of the booms in the intervals of tacking.

† It is unnecessary to give a date, for the story was ever the same; but if the reader wishes for a typical example, he can take the years 1776-77.

ferred the navy, and there were men who liked to try it. They served for the commission, and when the ship was paid off they went where they pleased, no man saying them nay so long as peace lasted. But when war was coming Parliament voted forty, fifty, sixty thousand men for the navy, of whom about a fifth were to be marines. If the other elements were to be all drawn from the merchant service the trading ships will be unmanned. You cannot deduct thirty, and still less forty, thousand men from sixty thousand without depriving the trading ships of their full crews. The State knew that very well. It did not suppose that all the men it must have over and above the marines were to be prime seamen, but about a third of them ought to be. Even they would make a great gap in the merchant ship crews. So the State suspended the manning clauses of the Navigation Acts, and promised that foreigners who would serve in any British ship of trade, or of war, for two years should be entitled to take out letters of denization. We make our wars for the sake of our trade, and our trade paid our navy. Therefore it must of necessity go on. The State would obtain its men by volunteer enlistment if it could. So it offered bounties of thirty shillings or two pounds to mere landsmen, and of as much as twelve guineas to prime seamen. The difference fairly represented their respective value to the navy. But the State knew very well that it would not secure all the men it needed by voluntary enlistment. It knew in particular that it would not obtain the needful number of prime seamen in that way. Therefore it issued its press warrants, and then began the chase of the rogues and vagabonds and the prime seamen.

The hot press, which is now in full swing, works in three ways—one indirect, the others direct. When the Seven Years' War began, Captain Cook was a sailor in the employment of a Whitby firm, with which he had served his time. His ship was in the Thames. The press being hot, and the chance of escaping it not great, Cook thought it better to take the bounty and volunteer. One volunteer was more thought of than three pressed men. Moreover Cook knew that his late employers had influence with their Member of

Parliament, and could rely on them to speak for him. They did, and he was rated masters' mate. So he put his foot on the ladder of promotion which he was to climb till he became one of the most famous Englishmen of his time. Others of less fame acted in the same way. Yet they certainly were but a minority.

The bulk of the prime seamen were brought into the navy by the direct action of the press, exercised in big drives at the ports or on the ships at sea. Of these two methods the first made the most noise and was by far the less productive. When it was decided to make a clear sweep in this or that port, the local authorities were called upon to co-operate, soldiers were employed, the exits were stopped, pressgangs of trustworthy men were sent under the command of commissioned officers to overhaul all imaginable hiding-places. A great haul was made, and a multitude of men collected in the receiving ships. Then they were to be mustered and reported on. The next part of the story was the discovery that many of the men seized must be released, either because, being neither vagabonds without visible means of subsistence, nor sailors, they were not subject to impressment, or because they were physically unfit. Then the naval officers began to complain that, though hundreds of stout seamen were known to be in the town, very few had been secured. The local authorities professed deep concern, and the public laughed. The naval officers were quite right. The men were in the town, and yet could not be found, though half the population knew where they were.

In fact, the pressgangs worked at a great disadvantage in these drives. Englishmen were as illogical as to impressment as they were about many other things. They supported it as necessary for the defence of the country, and yet they sympathized with the individual hunted sailors. Government offered rewards to informers, but the fate of the informer had been always the same. He has been encouraged, paid—and kicked for informing. Decent people would not betray the sailor. As the object of the press was to obtain men capable of work, no firearms could be used. The weapon of the pressmen was a cudgel. But the sailors could use cudgels, and public opinion would not condemn them for making a fight. So long as they did not do anything so un-English as draw a knife or use a pistol, they were held to be within their right. It was a game in which the pressgang played for pay and head-money, and the sailor for his freedom. If the pressgang won, well and good. If the sailor escaped, well and good also. If the pressgang broke the sailor's head, or the sailors beat the pressgang to a jelly, why people who play at bowls must look out for rubbers.

Then impressment was necessarily worked by means of local authorities. When they were Vice-Admirals of the counties who were peers, or justices of the peace who were country gentlemen, they worked for the State as zealously as their gentlemanly leisure allowed. But these dignified persons gave directions from above. The execution was left to mayors, aldermen, portreeves. Now these were all more or less connected with the shipping business, if not as owners, still as friends, customers, tradesmen. It was not their interest to make the stout seaman too scarce. Whenever we hear the voice of the naval officer on the subject of impressment he is generally heard complaining of the insufficient numbers and the bad quality of the men sent him by the port authorities. It is the same story under Elizabeth, the Commonwealth, Charles II., or the Georges. When we hear these complaints, when we know that the marines and the sea-labourer element were obtained without the use of the press, when we are told on excellent authority that during the last years of the Napoleonic War only about twenty-four thousand men were obtained by the press on shore, that nearly all of them deserted, and that to obtain this negative result two thousand men of the navy and a staff of officers were maintained at a considerable cost, we are tempted to wonder why it was thought worth while to make use of the impressment at all.

It was maintained in order to secure the prime seamen, and the vast majority of them were obtained in the way shown by the story of the *Mortar*, the *Bremen Factor*, Broadfoot, and the man he killed. They were taken out of merchant ships at sea. There were certain limits to the power of a naval officer who had a press warrant to execute. If he pressed men near home, he was bound to put a crew of his trustworthy men into the ship, and see her safe to harbour. If he pressed them at sea, he was forbidden to take so many as to leave the ship dangerously undermanned. Masters, first mates, and apprentices under eighteen were exempt. Whalers were privileged for the encouragement of the trade. After 1810—very late in the day—the East India Company secured exemption for twenty-one men in its smaller vessels, and from forty to forty-eight in the 800, 1,200, and 1,500 ton ships. It obtained this privilege on the ground that naval officers had often impressed so many men out of Indiamen that they were left undermanned and unable to resist attack by privateers. But this was the exceptional case of a privilege obtained by a powerful corporation. When the naval officer abused his powers, he had little to fear unless a shipowner brought an action against him. When the case was very clear—as, for instance, with the whaling ships—he might be cast in damages. But the individual sailor had no remedy. The degree of severity with which they were swept into the navy depended on the length of the war and the navy's need for men. At the end of the great war, when all trade was by law conducted under convoy and there were few opportunities of evasion, it came to be an understood thing that lads were swept into the navy so soon as they were over eighteeen and had served a three years' apprenticeship. The crew of an average trading vessel would consist of her master, one mate, one boatswain and second mate, and a number of boys under eighteen. If she had more grown men, they were pretty sure to be foreigners, and not seldom even the master and mates were foreign.

How came it that, since they were a leading element in the crews, the men who were necessarily chosen to be petty officers—since, as the example of Captain Cook, of Admiral Campbell, who served with Hawke at Quiberon, and of many others, shows, a man might rise from before the mast to high rank—that the prime seamen were so reluctant to enter the navy? Always in theory, and often in practice, the road to promotion was open to them. Anyone who had served five years in the navy, whether before the mast or not, who could do the work of an able seaman, hand, reef, and steer, and knew a little practical navigation, was qualified to hold a commission as Lieutenant. As Lieutenant he was sure of pay or half-pay for life, and his foot was on the ladder which led to flag rank. Why, then, did the prime seaman hate the navy? Because of the pay, the system of pay, and his dislike to the life itself.

Some writers of to-day who are more influenced by sentiment and "aspirations" than qualified by reason and knowledge, endeavour to explain this dislike by the cruelty of the navy discipline and the abuse of the cat. But it is to be observed that all navy captains were not as Pigot, Corbet, and Carden; that many merchant skippers were every whit as brutal as they; that if the cat was used in the navy the rope's end was used in the merchant ship, for the right of the captain "to inflict paternal chastisement on the delinquent mariner"* was recognized by law; and that marines and landsmen were under the same discipline as seamen bred to the sea, and yet they came voluntarily. We must not yield to the tempting fallacy which attributes our own sentiments to our ancestors. Because flogging has come to be regarded, even by those who think it legitimate at all, as appropriate only to boys or to very vile adult offenders, and is by many considered as always a degradation to humanity and a torture, we are not to assume that men thought so in the eighteenth century. They most assuredly did not. The very leaders of mutinies kept discipline with the cat. There is nothing to show that the seamen thought flogging an improper punishment in itself, though of course they resented its excessive and unfair application. If the seamen disliked service in the navy, it was not because of the severity of the discipline, which did not frighten away the marine or the landsman. It was because, whereas these two elements of the crew lost nothing by going into the navy, the regular bred seaman did.

They lost in mere amount. The East India Company, from the end of the seventeenth century, paid an able seaman £1 15s. a month. The navy paid him £1 3s. War tended

* I think I quote Lord Stowell, and hope I quote him correctly, but my reference is lost.

to send up the pay of the able seamen in the merchant ships. When his services were needed and risks of capture were serious, a man might earn £7 for a trip from Newcastle to London with coal, or £4 or £5 a month for a voyage to the West Indies. And the merchant sailor received advances before and during the voyage. When it was over he was sure of his balance. But in the navy he might have to serve a whole commission without being paid, and at the best of times he was paid only when his ship reached a home port, where there was a commissioner for the payment of navy wages. Even then he was paid only to within six months of the date of arrival. And even that was not the worst. There was no limit to the servitude of a pressed man. He might be shifted from ship to ship on a foreign station, for the length of two or three commissions. If an outcoming ship reached a station badly manned, and the vessel she was to relieve had a good crew, the Admiral, who could not wish to have badly-manned ships in his squadron, simply took the best men out of the homeward-bound ship, and put them into the new-comer, who discharged the worst of her crew into the departing vessel. The better a man was, the worse was his servitude, for he was the man whom the officers wished to keep. When he did get home, he had to present a sheaf of pay-notes, and wait till the formalities of red-tape were fulfilled before he received his money. Very often he sold them at a great discount to the traders, whom he called Jews.

Even if he had been better and more fairly paid, the merchant sailor would still have resented the long confinement to one ship, when no leave was granted, lest men should desert. Here, again, the best man suffered most. The sailor who came of decent people in his native port, and who looked forward to one day being himself a skipper, would not willingly incur the stigma of desertion, which laid him open to be criminally punished. The worst of the men-of-war crews deserted in troops. The best sailormen would not desert, and suffered accordingly.

* There are things which are "tacenda," and of them I do not speak. But if it is indecent to insist on those things, it is dishonest to ignore them to the point of giving the impression that they did not exist. I refer to the awful undercurrent of bestiality in vice which meets all who have turned over the mouldering pages of the minutes of court-

It is not to be wondered at that, if the prime seamen were indispensable to the navy, they could also be a danger. They were the ringleaders of the mutiny at Spithead. They brought about the mutiny of the *Donegal* on the coast of Ireland, when, upon the signing of the Peace of Amiens, they discovered that, after years of service and confinement, they were not to be discharged, but to sail on another and an indefinite period of service in America.

This hatred of theirs for the King's service had been notorious from of old, and the reasons for it were patent. In 1701 an anonymous writer, who signed himself " An Officer of the Honble East India Co.," published a pamphlet, which he called " Piracy Destroyed." He had to point out the reason why the pirate ships of the time were recruited, and that led him into a survey of the general condition of the seaman. Speaking of the grievances of the men-of-war sailors, he says : " Another great complaint is their lying out of their pay, and being turned over into other ships, and made run, etc.* These are grievances with a witness, for how can their families be maintained when they are kept on board three, four, or five years without their pay? Both suffered severely, the men forced to subsist upon the ship's salt provisions, and their families upon the small credit they had, and begging. This occasioned many of them, upon the offer of a good merchant voyage, to leave twenty or thirty months' pay, rather than run the risk of waiting for the King's pay."

To whose advantage was it that sailors should be kept waiting for five or more years ? It was very much to the advantage of the Treasurer of the Navy. Money assigned for the support of ships in commission was paid to him by the Exchequer, and was by him placed to his account at his bank. The banker paid him interest on it. When he went out of office his accounts were not transferred to his successor. They remained in his hands to be settled, and so did the balance of the money given him for the service of the navy. Therefore it was clearly to his interest that pay-

---

martial. They will show, whoever consults them, one reason why service in the navy was hateful to those who came to it with a natural cleanness of nature.

* Written off as deserters without just cause, and so subject to forfeiture of wages due.

ments should be delayed, and, if possible, never made at all. The accounts of the Viscount Falkland, who was Treasurer of the Navy in the reign of James II., from March, 1685, to October, 1688, were not closed when the Commission of Naval Inquiry was set to work in 1804. During all those 116 years a sum of £27,611 6s. 5¼d. had been lying to the account of Lord Falkland, his heirs and assigns. At 5 per cent. this would mean that they had drawn a little income of £1,350 on money of which sailors had been defrauded.

If the purblind stupidity of mankind, the offspring of a mole-eyed selfishness, were at any time a just cause of surprise, we have a good excuse for being amazed that the grievances of the sailors were not dealt with earlier. They were not deniable nor denied. It was notorious that they bred discontent, which was manifested by wholesale desertion and a long series of isolated mutinies culminating in the great outbreaks at Spithead and the Nore. Impressment was, by the consent of all, costly, and, except in the case of ships overhauled at sea, not effective. A string of proposed reforms may be followed up all through the eighteenth century, only to discover that they were all of an unspeakable futility. The officer of the Honourable East India Company already quoted gravely proposed that " our Seamen ought to be made a Corporation, and have their Hall with their Governors yearly chosen, and every man's name registered, with his age and complexion, place of abode, etc.' Other registration schemes were of the same calibre. All were intended to make the sailor's obligation to serve less erratic, but more easily enforced. Meanwhile nobody proposed to remove the grievances which made the service hateful : to pay the navy sailors at least as well as the men of the East India Company—£1 15s. a month—to give them their wages at regular intervals, and to allow a reasonable amount of leave. Of course the sailors refused to register themselves when the chance was offered. They avoided the navy as much as they could, and when the establishment of the independence of the United States gave them a refuge in an English-speaking country, they took to emigrating in swarms.

CHAPTER XII

THE SLAVER

> FIRST PIRATE. Hold, villain!
> SECOND PIRATE. A prize! a prize!
> THIRD PIRATE. Half-part, mates, half-part! Come, let's have her aboard suddenly. [*Exeunt* PIRATES *with* MARINA.
> *Pericles, Prince of Tyre*, Act IV.

WHEN the insulted (and intoxicated) actor told the people of Bristol that there was no brick in their town which had not been " cemented with the blood of a nigger," he came as near to the truth as could be expected of an infuriated rhetorician. Bristol had been a great slave-trading port. But Mr. G. F. Cooke was uttering a charge which applied quite as much to many other ports as to Bristol, and he need not have limited his definition of the victim to niggers. The slave-trade is the oldest of all.* It has gone on by land and by sea—not only in ships on the water, but by caravans, or " cáfilas " (the " coffles " of the West Coast of Africa). Slaves have been swept together by mighty " razzias," carried out by Assyrians and Romans in the ancient world, and by the African slave hunters of our own time. They have also been obtained by the arts of the recruiting sergeant. The rascals who went by the name of " spirits," whose business it was to entrap " apprentices " for American and West Indian plantations in the seventeenth century, had their predecessors from of old, and their successors in

* And it is not extinct now. A very strict vigilance is needed to keep the recruiting of coolies and " Kanaka " labour from becoming slavery. All slaves have not been made so by capture. Some have at all times sold themselves into slavery. Highly respectable shareholders of shipping companies trading with South America make part of their dividends by that trade to-day, and are not too scrupulous to take the money of the " caften," who is just a slave merchant who supplies the brothels of Rio and Buenos Ayres.

the black traders who filled up the Bristol or Liverpool slave ships on the Bonny River. The English countrywomen of the reign of King James I., who ran to the woods in a panic because they feared they were to be swept off to plant Virginia, were not absurd in their fears. In the middle of the eighteenth century the Royal Government of France provided settlers for Louisiana by a process which differed only in scale from the slave-hunting raids which Leon de Laborde saw in Africa in the nineteenth—and not he only, but many others.

A general history of slavery would be a very large subject—and a very monotonous one. Here, if anywhere, similar manners were produced by similar conditions. The depot for "apprentices" kept by the English "spirits" of the seventeenth century on the island of Lundy was by the nature of the case just a "barracoon" such as the Rev. John Newton saw on the West Coast of Africa. Free men who are to be reduced to slavery must be "rounded up" like cattle on the Pampas, confined in pens and sold in the market—like cattle—or taken in traps. They have often been branded like cattle. The Spaniards exercised a jocular fancy in branding theirs. They invented a rebus composed of a capital "S" with a nail ("clavo"), to stand for the word "esclavo," and burnt it on the cheek of the slave.* Of course they were at all times driven to work by the whip and the goad. We may be quite confident that the African slave-trade was essentially the same thing as the slave-trade of all periods. We know it better because it was studied by hostile witnesses. I speak of the trade, of the process by which the slaves were collected, transported, sold, distributed—and by sea. I do not assert that slavery was always the same thing. The servitude of Jew to Assyrian, Greek or Syrian to Roman, Slav to Teuton, or of the unfree men of all races to free among their own people, was not exactly the same thing as the slavery of the black

* And this was not done only to the negroes, but to the Morisco slaves in Spanish households at home. The heroine of Lope de Vega's play, "La Esclava de Su Galan," who passes herself off as the slave of her lover (in the literal sense), paints the rebus on her face. The Moriscoes were the more or less forcibly converted "Moors," and were, in fact, commonly identical in race with other Spaniards.

men to the white. Emancipation made it possible for them, or at least for their children, to become identified with their masters. There can be very few of us of whatever rank who, if we could know the whole of our pedigree, would not find unfree persons among our ancestors. Even for the black there was a difference between being carried in a Liverpool slaver to Jamaica or in a dhow from Eastern Africa to Turkey, Persia, or Arabia. If he became a Mohammedan he was accepted in Islam, and identified with his masters when once he was free. Among Christian nations —as far as my knowledge goes—only the Portuguese have acted on the principle that race is a small matter, and that religion is much.* And if this is to the honour of their humanity, it has been disastrous to the race, both in Portugal herself and in the Colonies.

And now let us see the slaver at work. We can look at him through the eyes of Mr. Alexander Falconbridge, Surgeon, who " had been driven by his necessities to earn his living in a branch of British Commerce which ever since its existence has been held in detestation by all good men, but at this time [*i.e.*, in 1788] more particularly engages the attention of the nation, and is become the object of general reprobation." Mr. Falconbridge promises, and keeps his promise, to confine himself to a recital of facts. He arranges them in simple direct narrative under five heads : " Proceedings during the Voyage "; " The Manner in which the Slaves are produced "; " Treatment of the Slaves "; " Sale of the Slaves "; and, not the least shocking part of his story, the " Treatment of the Sailors." The reader will not omit

* I do not profess to have read more than a small part of the books which deal with the African slave-trade from the west or from the east coasts; but I am not the less assured of my understanding of what the wicked thing was. It could not vary because its character was dictated by varying conditions. I bow to the authority of the more learned, and write subject to correction ; and then I submit that the whole mass of material collected by societies and independent authorities could be no other than an amplification of, and extended commentary on, the fifty-five pages of " An account of the Slave-Trade on the Coast of Africa," by Alexander Falconbridge, late Surgeon in the African Trade, London, 1788. He saw it closely during years, and reports what he saw with an admirable brevity, and in plain words, all the more impressive because of their sobriety. But nobody ought to neglect " The African Slave-Trade and its Remedy," by Sir Thomas Fowell Buxton, London, 1840.

to note that Falconbridge's " account " was written while the trade was still lawful—twenty years or so before it was suppressed in the British Dominions in 1807. So long was it before " general reprobation " could conquer " vested interest."

The slaver would be a vessel of from 200 to 250 tons. From other sources we know that the trader estimated a full cargo at five blacks for every 2 tons ; but he could not always obtain a complete load.* When the ship had reached her port of loading in the Bonny River, or on the Gold Coast, or the Windward Coast, the first thing to be done was to propitiate any native potentate whose help was desired by presents of finery and strong drink. Then the crew set to work to make a " house." " The sailors first lash the booms and yards from mast to mast, in order to form a ridge pole. About 10 feet above the deck several spars, equal in length to the ridge pole, are next lashed to the standing rigging, and form a wall plate. Across the ridge pole and wall plate several other spars or rafters are afterwards laid, and lashed at the distance of about 6 inches from each other. On these other rafters or spars are laid lengthwise, equal in extent to the ridge pole, so as to form a kind of lattice or network, with interstices of 6 inches square." The whole was then tiled with mats, which were supposed to complete the roof. They were, of course, of no

* When the movement for the suppression of the trade was in its first flush, before the threatened interests had rallied, and the country had been frightened by the Jacobins of France and the negro revolt in Hayti, two regulating Acts were passed. It was hoped that they would serve to render the trade as humane as such a thing could be till the time—then supposed to be at hand—when it was to be suppressed. These Acts were passed in 1788-89. They declared that negroes were in future to be shipped in the proportion of 5 to 3 tons (about as tight as soldiers were packed in transports) up to a tonnage of 201. Beyond that the proportion was to be one per ton. If the blacks were males of 5 feet 4 inches and upwards, they were to be taken at one per ton up to 201 tons, and at three to five beyond that tonnage. If two-thirds of the cargo were young blacks of less than 5 feet 4 inches in height, then all other young blacks beyond the proportion of two-thirds were to be counted as five to four adults. Even if these Acts had been carried out, the overcrowding was gross for vessels making a long tropical voyage. But there was no inspection in Africa, and, though one was ordered to be made in the West Indies, it was to be carried out by officials who were under the influence, corrupt or violent, of the infuriated West Indian planters. What effect could they produce ?

use as a protection against heavy tropical rains. What they did was to prevent ventilation, to reduce the between-decks of the ship to a fœtid state, and to confine the smoke of the galley fire, fed with mangrove wood. The fumes produced inflammation of the eyes, which frequently ended in blindness. This was a known fact so long as the trade lasted. In the Spanish Asientos it was always stipulated that negroes suffering from ophthalmia would not be received. The space between the wall plate and the deck was closed by lattice-work. In fact, all exits and entrances were stopped, and a barricade was built across the deck to separate the male from the female negroes; and it was loopholed to allow the crew to fire from under cover on the men in case of a mutiny.

The "house" having been prepared, the occupants were next to be provided. If the ship was at Bonny, she lay about a mile below the town, and began by landing the goods which were to be swopped for "ebony." The trade was settled by the King of Bonny in council with his "Parliament Boys." A price was fixed, an export fee was charged, and the King of Bonny placed an "Officer Boy" on board the ship to receive the royal dues. The slaves were provided by native traders, who went up the river in large canoes capable of holding from thirty to forty persons, and either raided and kidnapped themselves, or dealt with the raiders and kidnappers of the interior. On the Gold and Windward Coasts there were differences. The sailors had to go "boating"—*i.e.*, had to go up the rivers themselves in search of blacks—a kind of work fatal to the health of the white man. But with variations in detail it all came to the same thing. The native trader was the go-between, who played broker to the robber of the interior, and the Christian receiver, of stolen men, women, and children. To the trader the intercourse was indispensable. When it was stopped, as it was while the market of the plantations was closed by the American War of Independence, he was reduced " to digging and planting yams," as he complained to Mr. Falconbridge. The blacks naturally endeavoured to escape as often as they could, and from time to time they broke out in mutiny, not always without success.

Cases did occur in which the white crew was overpowered, and their captives took a more or less adequate revenge.

When the desired number, or as near an approach to the desired number as was possible, had been secured, the "house" was pulled down, the vessel rerigged, and she went on her way. The black men were allowed on deck from 8 a.m. to 4 p.m. on fine days, during which interval of ease they were fastened on a chain, which was itself made fast to a ringbolt on the deck. The women were not chained. To keep them in good spirits the blacks were "allowed" to dance, with the alternative of doing it freely, or being flogged till they did not do it. They were also required to sing to the music of a drum, or, failing a drum, of a tub, which was turned upside down and thumped. Mr. Falconbridge bears testimony that their chants were but melancholy howls. The greater part of the passage was spent below, and a few figures will do more than much rhetorical description to show what confinement below must have meant. Falconbridge gives the dimensions of one vessel, which by the confession of her officers once shipped 600 negroes for transport to the West Indies. The traders at the port assured him that the number taken was 700. She was of 235 tons, and her lower deck was 25 feet wide at the beam, and 92 feet long. The storeroom, in which the horse-beans, oil, and flower—the provisions for the blacks—were carried, was to be deducted from this space. There remained a compartment of 45 feet long for the men, one of 10 feet for the women, and one of 22 feet for the boys. They were divided longitudinally by platforms intended to provide sleeping-room, which left a height of $3\frac{1}{2}$ feet. Into such a space hundreds of human beings were crowded. At the best, they were allowed the minimum of room in which to lie at full length. In the case of the overcrowded vessel, he quotes, they had to lie upon one another. The greed of her Captain overreached itself. Fever and dysentery broke out in her, and more than half the blacks died.

This was an exceptionally bad example of overcrowding. But in all times the number carried was excessive. Our ancestors had but little humanity even to their own countrymen. Soldiers were crowded into transports in the propor-

(A) THE HOLD OF A SLAVER.

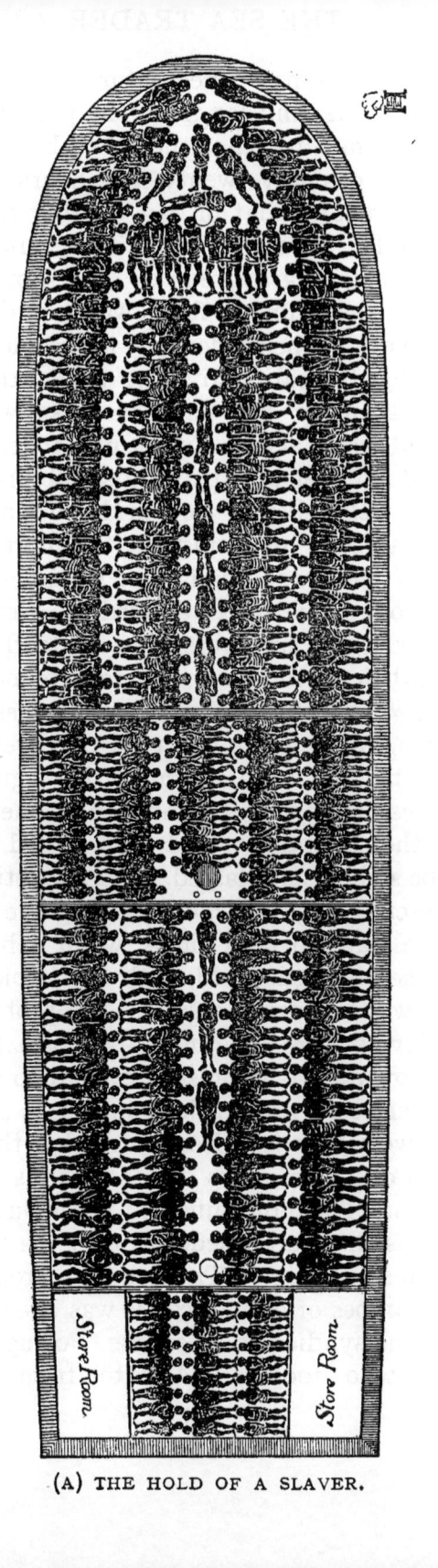

tion of three to two tons. They naturally showed even less regard to the blacks, and for them the proportion was five to two tons. Remember that the miserable captives spent the greater part of every twenty-four hours in these overcrowded quarters, and that in bad weather they were confined to them for days together. They suffered horribly from sea-sickness, aggravated by the horse-beans and " slabber " sauce of palm-oil, flour, water, and pepper, they were forced to eat. The reader who needs the details given by Falconbridge to realize to what a condition of stench, heat, and lack of air the between-decks were regularly reduced would need actual experience to enlighten him. Most ships did not even set up a windsail to provide ventilation. We can well believe Falconbridge when he says that the surgeon on going his rounds in the morning generally found some of the cargo dead, that the average loss on a voyage was from a quarter to a third of every cargo, and that a number of the survivors were at death's door when they reached their destination. There were men of business in the Indies who made a trade of buying these sick blacks for small sums, and tending them till they were sufficiently recovered to be sold at a remunerative figure. Most of their purchases died on their hands, and sometimes all did.

Such was the slave-trade, and such it had always been, and was to be so long as it lasted. It is sometimes assumed that the overcrowding, which constituted one of the worst horrors of the trade in later times, when it had been condemned by the civilized world, and was forbidden by laws and treaties, was the direct result of the prohibition. The smuggling slavers were, so their apologists have argued, compelled to overcrowd because they had to employ small vessels in order to be able to lurk in creeks and to escape notice. But we see from Falconbridge that the evil was as bad as it well could be in his day, and he is borne out by other witnesses. The quite sufficient testimony to the truth of his picture is the established fact that the mortality was always high in slave ships. The immense proportion of the loss in these cargoes of human cattle was one of the reasons why the various syndicates—Genoese, Portuguese, French, and English—who took an Asiento from the Spanish

Government for the supply of slaves, failed to make the profits they expected. Observers who looked at the trade as a mere matter of business were tempted to wonder why the traders did not employ larger and better ships; why they did not content themselves with carrying a less number

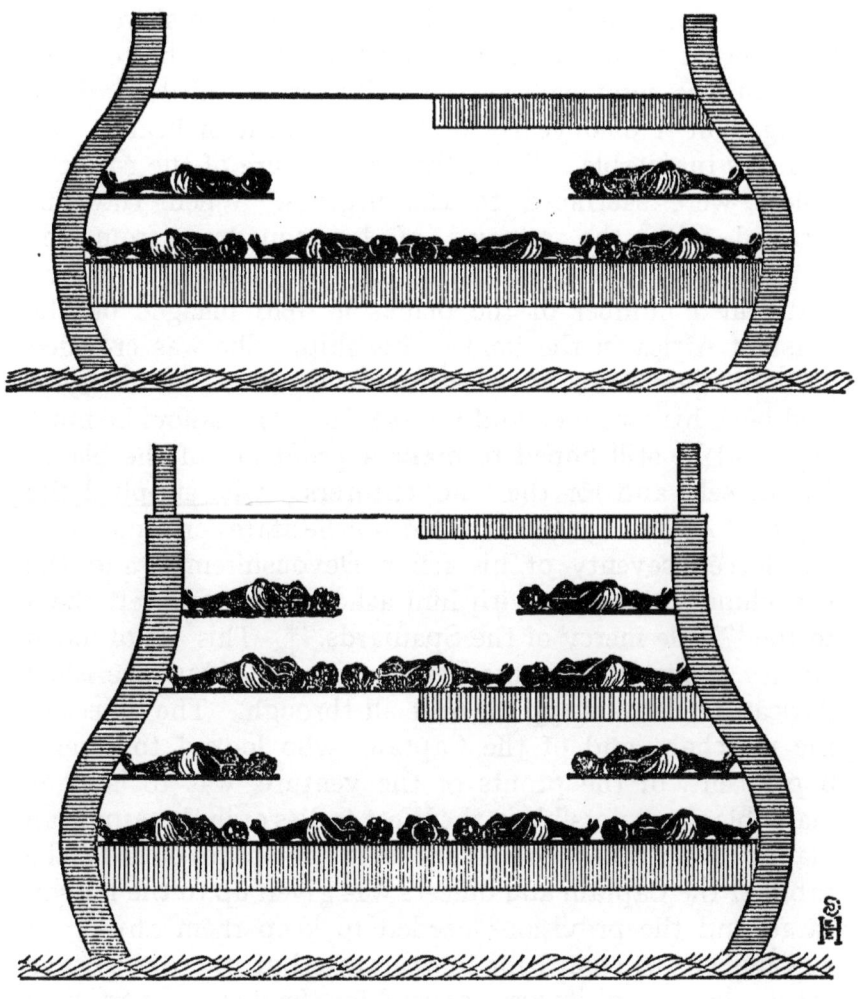

(B) THE HOLD OF A SLAVER.

of blacks, and look to make their profit by delivering them in good health. As it was, the trader had to discount not only the negroes who died, but the sickly survivors, whom he was forced to sell at a loss. It would have paid him better to be more humane. The answer was that men engaged in what by the very nature of it was a speculative and cruel business were certain to be reckless and inhumane. Slavery has always been wasteful of life so long as slaves could be easily procured. Falconbridge, who saw the trade for years, says deliberately that he never knew but one Captain who was humane to his captives or to his crew. The best kind of men would not go into such a trade at all, and those who followed it were brutalized by the life.

For it is not the least horrible fact about the slave-trade that the lot of the sailors was but little, if at all, better than that of the wretched negroes. Nearly a third of those engaged in it died yearly or were wrecked in health, and this was inevitable. From the very nature of the case the sailors were sacrificed to the negroes. When Hawkins escaped with the remains of his squadron from the "treachery" of the Spaniards at San Juan de Ulloa, he had still a number of the blacks he had pillaged on the coast of Africa in the hold of his ship. She was crowded with refugees from the destroyed vessels. He could not feed both his own men and the blacks. The sailors he must pay, and he still hoped to make a profit out of the blacks for himself, and for the "adventurers" who supplied the capital for the voyage. He did not hesitate for a moment, but forced seventy of his fellow Devonshiremen and the Frenchmen who were with him ashore, where he left them to the "little mercy of the Spaniards."* This act of mean cruelty, committed in the very beginning of our cherished African trade, was typical of it all through. The object of the merchant and of the Captain, who looked to receive 6 per cent. of the profits of the venture, was to land as many blacks as possible in the West Indies or in the American plantations. Therefore every inch of space outside the cabin of the Captain and officers was given up to the human cargo and the provisions needed to keep them alive. It was not out of regard for temperance, but in order to save space, that no spirits were carried for the men. Every inch of the space between decks was needed for the blacks, the horse-beans, the flour, and the water served out to them in

* The Spaniards, who were glad enough to have their labour, treated them kindly till the Inquisition, then just established in Mexico, got its eye on some of them for heresy, and on others for bigamy.

strictly limited quantities. Therefore the crew were compelled to spend the whole " middle passage " from Africa to the West Indies on the deck, where their only cover when off watch was a tarpaulin stretched across the boats in the booms. Of course they suffered from being perpetually wet in the tropical rains. The deck was, it is true, the only refuge from the heat and foul smells of the hold. The Captain himself was often driven from his cabin by the stench rising from the festering mass of dirt and disease below, and compelled to sling his cot on deck. But he had his choice. His men had none. They were frequently tainted before the voyage began by bad water or by fevers contracted while boating up the rivers. Falconbridge records that, of forty-six men who, in addition to the Captain and mates, formed the crew of one of the vessels he sailed in, only fifteen returned home with the ship. It was not unusual for a slaver to lose so many men that she could not sail when the blacks were collected. As an all-round voyage to Bonny or New or Old Calabar lasted for ten months, and one by the Gold or Windward Coast from fifteen to eighteen, there was ample time for the unwholesome conditions to work their full effect. Falconbridge knew of one case in which a vessel belonging to Miles, Barber and Co. lost all hands from coast fevers while they were boating up the rivers.

It is only consistent with the morality produced by a trade of legalized meanness and cruelty that the sailors were cheated and ill-used, and were ill-used in order that they might be cheated. The mere fact that they received no allowance of spirits told against them, and gave an opening for fraud. While they were collecting the captives on the coast they would sell their very clothes to the local traders for drink. But they were not confined to the longshore trader as a vendor of alcohol. The officers had their private stores, and supplied the men at a stiff figure, which was then debited against their wages. Even if a man did remain by the ship, he would have little or nothing to receive when the voyage was over. And yet the sailor who indebted himself to the full extent of his wages was, perhaps, more prudent than his messmate who allowed them to accumulate, since it was not equally to the interest of the Captain to drive him to desert when the ship, having reached the West Indies and landed her blacks, was waiting for her homeward-bound cargo. Vessels engaged in the African trade carried crews twice as numerous as those employed in other lines. They were needed to meet the loss of life on the coast and to overawe the negroes. But when the port of delivery was reached, a large crew became a cause of expense. The movements of commerce were then leisurely. A vessel loading at a West Indian island might lie at anchor for months while her cargo was being brought to her in driblets by carts from the interior or in small craft along the coast. It was an addition to expenses to pay wages for this interval. Therefore the owners would approve of the Captain who worried his men into desertion, and the greater the amount of wages due to the deserter the greater would be the satisfaction of the owners. As for the means by which desertion was provoked, they were of the simplest. They may be summed up by the one word—the lash, which was as brutally used and misused in slavers as ever it was in a man-of-war commanded by a " tyrant Captain." This practice of forcing desertion was so notorious that after 1790 it was made obligatory by Act of Parliament on the owners to pay the balance of wages of deserters to Greenwich and to Seamen's Hospitals, so that they themselves should derive no benefit from the desertion. A survey of the African trade shows at once and clearly why it was that the pirates who haunted the African coast found it so easy to recruit men from the merchant ships they met on the coast. The whole atmosphere reeked of crime, and the sailors could rationally calculate that whatever life in a pirate might be, it could not be worse than life in a slaver. The Rev. John Newton, friend of the poet Cowper, who spent his youth in the African trade, and commanded a ship himself in three voyages, notes quite calmly, and as if it were a matter of course, that the crew of his vessel was once plotting to seize her and go on a piratical cruise.*

* The Acts of George III., drafted to prevent the desertion of seamen in the West Indies, can have had but little effect. The amount paid to Greenwich Hospital as its third of the wages of " run

The question how men were found to engage themselves for so miserable a life may be put by those who do not know the recklessness and helplessness of the sailor, and by them only. A part of the crew had sufficient reasons for preferring the slave-trade. If it was necessary to carry a large crew in order to coerce the blacks, it was no less advisable to carry a large proportion of officers in order to control the sailors. The fighting mate and boatswain were needful members of the slaver's crew, and their services were no doubt duly rewarded. To such men as these the absolute command they had over the enslaved women would be no inconsiderable attraction.* As for the bulk of the sailors, the habits of the class account for their presence. They earned their money like horses, and spent it like asses, by their own confession. The sailor who landed at Liverpool with a balance of wages to draw was only too likely to squander every penny, and run into debt with his lodging-house keeper. All the members of that class were not dishonest. There were some who kept the sailor's money for him, treated him fairly, and protected him from his own natural tendency to get into mischief on shore. But there were many who were crimps. It was their business to supply him with drink while his money lasted, and when it was spent also—up to the point at which the two months' advance paid to him when he shipped would repay them with a large profit. When that point had been reached they provided him with a ship. They were in league with the slaver Captains, and to them they delivered the sailor, sober and reckless, or helpless and drunk. The whole system was a circle of fraud and violence. That negroes might be kidnapped into slavery the sailors were degraded and wasted. We cannot know how many prime seamen were sacrificed in this odious traffic, but it must have surpassed the number of men who fell in battle in the

---

men" rose from £16 18s. 2d. in 1790 to £2,530 8s. in 1802. And it was shown, to the satisfaction of the Commissioners of Naval Inquiry of 1803, that the Hospital never received the full sum to which it was entitled. There were causes other than those given in the text why men deserted.

* For light on that side of the life the reader can consult "A Mariner of England."

navy very largely. The South Sea Company, which, as we have seen, was mainly a slave-trading company, calculated that it would employ 3,000 sailors. Many others were engaged in the same trade. The total number of men employed must have exceeded 3,000 a year throughout the seventeenth and eighteenth centuries on an average one year with another. As the recognized loss was from a quarter to a third in each all-round voyage from home to the coast of Africa, from Africa to the West Indies, and so back to Great Britain, it is a safe calculation that every year cost a greater loss than the total list of killed and wounded at Trafalgar. Between the day when Sir John Hawkins, reflecting that negroes found a good sale in the Spanish Colonies, set out, with the help of eminent persons, on his career of kidnapping, murder, and smuggling, down to the suppression of the trade in 1807—a period of two centuries and a half—the slaver must have cost England the loss of 250,000 men at least. All the killed and wounded in all our naval wars did not reach that figure.

It is not without a certain hesitation that a decent man will say anything which is capable of bearing the appearance of an excuse for an industry of such essential bestiality as the slave-trade. To say that all who were concerned in it were not necessarily ruffians may seem to be a palliation of its abominable character; but the fact that an honest man might be drawn into the life, and might see no wickedness in it, does not palliate its vices. On the contrary, it only goes to prove that the toleration of what is in itself vile helps to spread the corruption. Who can say how far the mere fact that the slave-trade, which by its very nature could not but be cruel, worked to perpetuate, perhaps to intensify the brutality, which persisted alongside of the effusive " sensibility " of the eighteenth century?

The sea life certainly grew worse because of the slave-trade. No one who turns from the narratives published by Hakluyt, or the letters of the East India Company's Captains, to equally authentic testimony for the later times, can help becoming conscious of a different atmosphere. The earlier men could be fierce, but they did not continually flog and drive. They had no scruple in using the whip as a punishment, nor did the men who were so punished think it an outrage ; but I have not found evidence that they took a pleasure in inflicting the lash. That there were many among the later Captains who did is manifest. Other causes than the slave-trade were at work to remove restraint from the brute who delighted in exercising his power in the most direct of all ways, and in watching the infliction of torture. The example of the navy had a share in promoting the evil. The age was an industrial one, and to the industrial spirit man is a mere instrument to be used for the production of wealth, and to be used up without scruple when large profits will repay the expenditure ; and negro slavery had the most powerful possible tendency to develop the worst of that spirit. It was cheaper to expend gangs of savages kidnapped in Africa than to preserve them. The sailor who brought the human cattle was but a tool to be employed, and to be himself expended rapidly when there was any profit to be found in using him up. The slaver had the lash continually in his hands to force the captive blacks to obey. Unless he could be restrained by fear of revenge, he used it on the sailor. It was there always, and was for ever being used. Flogging became something other than a punishment ; it became an excitement, an indulgence, a source of pleasure to the man who commanded. In the eighteenth century the fear of revenge was not the check it could be in earlier times. The sailors who rebelled against a ruffianly Captain knew that rebellion would be punished as if it were piracy ; that there were Admiralty Courts everywhere ; and that behind the tyrant there were warships, and judges and juries of merchants and planters ashore, whose sympathies would be against them. The ways of the slave-trade became a model. The spirit it generated spread far and wide.*

* Here, as in all places, it is well to be on watch against the invasion of cant. There never was a time when all men saw no harm in the African trade. It was always condemned by somebody, and was defended on the ground that it was profitable. The British Government gave money, and used its authority to promote the slave-trade during generations, on no other ground. On many occasions the settlers in the British plantations in North America grew frightened at the importation of savage negroes in large num-

So long as the trade remained legal, it was, of course, just possible for an honest man to follow it, without being forced to confess to himself that he was earning his livelihood ignobly. Such a man as the surgeon Falconbridge could practise his profession in a slaver with repugnance, but also with a reasonable belief that he was supporting himself by honest industry. We have seen that he met one Captain who was a just, humane man. We have the direct testimony of one who was a slaver Captain, and was also, in the opinion of many, a saint—John Newton, the curate of Olney, who was the friend of Cowper, and who was afterwards Vicar of St. Mary Woolnoth, in the City of London, and a famous evangelical preacher.

Newton is a particularly valuable witness to the sea life of the eighteenth century, and not only to the African trade, in which he spent most of his time. He was the son of a merchant skipper, trading to the Mediterranean. The father had, curiously enough, been educated in a Jesuit house near Seville, and appears, from the glimpses we get of him in his son's autobiography (or, rather, fragment of autobiography in epistolary form) to have been a man of parts and character, who kept himself to himself, and held all about him at the pikestaff's end. Fortunately for John Newton, the elder man had good friends in Liverpool. The boy served his time in the Mediterranean trade with his father, from the age of eleven, and after some very summary schooling. The father was a man whom a son could learn to respect at a distance, but it is plain that there could be no friendship or confidence between the two. The father was cold and distant; the son eager, passionate, restless,

---

bers. They endeavoured to stop the dangerous nuisance by laws, or by imposing prohibitive import duties. The laws were always disallowed, and the duties taken away by the Royal Government to the utmost extent of its effective power. The relations of the British Government to slavery have been divided between the strenuous advancement and the passionate condemnation of the trade. From the reign of Charles II., who was himself, in his capacity of shareholder in the Guinea Company, a slave-trader, down to far into the reign of George III., the British Government was the greatest promoter of the slave-trade in the world. After the abolition of 1807 it became indefatigable in its efforts to suppress the trade entirely. But the period during which it promoted slavery was far longer than that in which it wrought for the suppression, and its exertions were incomparably more successful.

with something, he knew not what, fermenting in his head. In later days, when the Rev. John Newton looked back on his boyhood, he seemed to himself to have been truly reprobate. All "these convertites" see their own early sins magnified in the mist of memory. There was nothing wrong with the boy, except one thing, which he never came to recognize as having existed, still less as a sin. He had a colossal, but absolutely unconscious, estimate of the importance of John Newton. If he did not see visions, he dreamt dreams. When at anchor in Venice, he saw himself on night watch, and all the powers of heaven and hell contending for his soul. When he was awake he was—always excepting the ferment within—just like other lads of vehement spirit, till they find their way.

He groans to think how, when his father placed him in an office at Alicante, he made himself impossible in a counting-house and on a high stool. His father had to take him back to sea. Then an accident happened to him —a very common accident in the life of a sailor of his day. The War of the Austrian Succession had begun, and there was a hot press. Young Newton was so rash as to wear " a checked shirt." This visible sign of the seafaring man attracted the eye of a zealous Lieutenant armed with a press warrant, and Newton was sent to serve the King. If he had been born to run in a curricle, his prospects would have been good. His father's friends exerted themselves for him, and on their recommendation he was placed on the quarterdeck. He had only to stick to the service, and the same interest would in due time have helped him to a Lieutenant's commission. The Rev. John Newton, D.D., Curate of Olney, and Vicar of St. Mary Woolnoth, might have died Sir John Newton, Admiral of the White; but he was meant for other things. Moreover, he had just met the girl who was, after years of adventure and sorrow, to be Mrs. Newton. He, so he tells us, often forgot his God, but the girl never, not for an hour. At that period he also forgot the discipline of the navy. He would break his leave to go from Chatham to her father's house in Kent, just to see her. After several escapades of this kind the patience of his Captain was worn out. Newton was arrested as a deserter, turned off the quarterdeck, flogged, and sent forrard.

In later days he allowed that he got no more than he deserved, and, so little was there then of the sensitiveness of our age, he shows no squeamishness about the flogging. At the time he was sore and wroth, and dwelt on thoughts of revenge ; but another change was to come. When his ship was on the coast of Africa, he found a chance to exchange into a trading vessel. The whole incident throws a curious light on the discipline and organization of the navy of the time. Newton quotes it as one of many proofs of Divine intervention on his behalf, and almost the only one which is not rather disagreeable to a reader who does not share his grim cold theology. When Divine Providence interfered to help him, it was generally by causing somebody else to be drowned in his place. He records these deaths of others with a complacency which is positively nasty. His religion made a man of him, no doubt, but it did not make him tender nor humble. On the contrary, it filled him with a repellent spiritual pride because he was a brand plucked from the burning by the hand of the Almighty. The immediate example was innocent enough ; though he had been disgraced, he was still on friendly terms with his late messmates in the gunroom. One morning he was sleeping in (the discipline of the ship would hardly have satisfied a smart First Lieutenant of later times), when a friend from the gunroom came down and urged him to turn out. He refused, and his friend playfully cut him down. He was spilt on the deck, and picked himself up in a bad temper ; but Providence was watching over him. When he went on deck, he found that two men had volunteered from an African trader, and that the Captain had given orders that two of his ship's company should be discharged into her to take their places. The sailor of that day belonged to his ship only, not to the navy. The Captain probably acted on the well-worn maxim that a volunteer is worth three pressed men. Newton says that he had a wish to see the African trade. We can very well believe that he had no wish to remain in a ship where he had been disrated and flogged. He applied to two of the officers to be allowed to go, and, though he was not on better terms with them than with others, they spoke for him. The Captain had formerly declined to discharge him at the request of Admiral Medley (a further proof that he had good interest), but now he let him go, a most undeniable sign of Divine intervention.

His adventures on the coast need not be told in chronological order. With one Captain, who was not on a slaving voyage, but in search of gold dust, ivory, palm oil, and dyewood, he quarrelled, because, having (he tries to look regretful as he says so) a share of the thing called " wit," he composed verses to ridicule the skipper, his person, ship, and voyage. It is difficult to forgive him for not preserving the verses. They would have borne testimony to the life of the time. He passed into the service of a trader on the coast who had " turned black." By turning black, he gravely explains, a man did not change his colour ; he only took to living like a black. This one bought slaves from up-country traders, and resold them to passing ships. He had married a black woman, a person of " some consequence in her own country." The woman took a dislike to Newton, who led almost as wretched a life as any of her slaves. In time he bettered his case, worked with other men, went " boating,' and wrote to his father in England, by whose help he was taken off in a Liverpool ship. We need say nothing of the spiritual experiences he went through till he reached the conviction of sin and the assurance of grace. It is plain enough that, if he fell deeper and remained more imprisoned in the " sins of the devil "—of which spiritual pride is one—than he was ever brought to confess, he was free from the sins of men. He did not drink and he did work. He struggled with Euclid, drawing the diagrams with a stick on the African sands, and he laid the foundation of as much Latin as helped him to qualify for orders in the Church of England. It is characteristic of the type of man he was that his sinfulness took the form of profanity, which he carried to such a pitch as to shock one of his Captains, himself notorious for swearing and cursing. If he is to be fully trusted, he found both in the navy and among merchant sailors many who were so far concerned with religion as to be blasphemous free-thinkers. One suspects that they were but echoes of himself. His Liverpool friends remained firm, and at last he obtained command of a ship for three voyages. The rest of his biography belongs to the Church of England and the evangelical movement.

In his later years he joined the Abolitionists, and provided Wilberforce with part of the evidence for his case against the slave-trade ; but while he was engaged in the trade he had no doubt of its lawfulness. He did, indeed, strive to pursue it as cleanly as might be. When he became Captain, and reflected that he was carrying women who were wholly at his mercy, he made it a rule to mortify the flesh by abstaining from wine, spirits, and meat during the voyage from Africa to the West Indies. We see, therefore, that it was possible to be a very " serious " man, to be deep in religious thought and emotion, and yet to be a kidnapper, and to share in the abominations of the slave-trade. We do not know whether he imposed his own regimen for the middle passage on his mates and crew. As he was never actually sent adrift by mutiny—though his crew once talked of going on a piratical voyage—it is probable that he did not. Nor do we know how he reconciled the obligation not to run deliberately into temptation with the continued pursuit of a trade which compelled him to seek in semi-starvation the means to resist the use of his undoubted power to force his women captives to prostitution by the lash if nothing else would suffice. Newton's virtue is not the least damning piece of evidence against the slave-trade.

The African trade as pursued by Europeans and Christians in late ages makes but a small part of the maritime slave-trade. It is the best to study because it was the worst, and therefore showed the thing in its perfection. Essentially it must always have been the same. When free men and women in the Ancient World were swept off by pirates, they must needs have suffered acutely. The episode of the capture of Marina, which Shakespeare found in the story of Pericles, Prince of Tyre, was common form in ancient romances, but it was so because it was common in life. Great and grave historians do not dwell on such

details. But an event which is lost in general wars and the fall of empires might stand out in the records of a small town. One did seem of sufficient importance to the people of Amorgos—the modern Amorgo or Morgo, one of the Sporades in the Ægean—to be recorded by an inscription :*
" Pirates having landed in the country by night, and taken girls, women, and others to the number of more than thirty, Hegesippos and Antipappos, who were themselves among the captives, persuaded the pirate chief to restore the freemen, and some of the freed men and slaves, offering themselves as a guarantee [by paying their ransoms ?], and showing an extreme zeal that none of the citizens, men or women, should be divided as booty or sold, or suffer aught unbecoming to their condition." It was fortunate for the thirty natives of Amorgos that Hegesippos and Antipappos were men of good-will, and perhaps that the pirate chief was a moderate man—perhaps also that none of the women were exceptionally good-looking. Other captives taken in thousands of these raids were swept away to slavery.

They were, however, not chained in a between-deck, with a height of 3 feet or so, and carried across a tropical ocean. We must not go to the West Coast of Africa and to Christian traders—British, French, Dutch, or Portuguese—for the equivalent of the maritime slave-trade of the ancient world. It is represented by the trade of the East Coast and the dhows which carry negro slaves to Arabia, Persia, and Turkey. Admiral Colomb† has put the difference between the two into a nutshell. The sign that a vessel overhauled on the West Coast was fitted for the slave-trade was that she carried chains and shackles. And there was a tradition that a naval officer once found a pair of shackles in a dhow. The dhow, which is simply a slightly modified survival of the ships of Hatshepsitu, is but a ramshackle craft, poorly constructed and only partically decked. The Arabs who command them and fit them out are the most casual of men. Nobody could be comfortable in a dhow, but Captain, crew, and slaves shared alike. If the provisions were

* Quoted by M. Wallon, " Histoire de l'Esclavage dans l'Antiquité," from Bæckh, " Corpus Inscriptionum," Sup. 2,263, c.
† See his " Slave-Catching in the Indian Ocean," 1873, *passim*.

scanty, it was because the trader had miscalculated and there was not enough. The captive black might become and remain part of the crew. He showed small or no disposition to desert. That slavery was not cruel among Oriental nations would be an absurd proposition. I have a lively recollection of hideous stories of passionate ferocity and long-drawn-out barbarism told me by H.B.M. Consul at São Paulo, Mr. O'Sullivan Beare, from his own experience in Zanzibar. But it was not so universally cruel as it was

A SLAVE DHOW.

in the New World, while the trade, which is my proper business, was humane and enlightened in comparison.

Apologists for the trade have maintained that it grew notably worse after it had been condemned by the public opinion of civilized nations and forbidden by law. Authorities who despised and condemned it have been known to express the same opinion. We may be very sure that it did not grow less barbarous when it passed entirely into the hands of men who knew that they were rendering themselves liable to punishment, and were engaged in a particularly bad form of smuggling. Yet there are reasons of considerable force for doubting whether those who thought it grew worse were not arguing too much from what was in reality only a plausible assumption. Was the comparison ever fairly made between the old legal and the later illegal states of the trade ? And were not certain very important considerations overlooked ?

It is said, for instance, that when the slaver was forced to become wholly a smuggler (we have seen that, even when he was not only tolerated but encouraged by his own country, he had always smuggled blacks into the Spanish Colonies) he was forced to pack his captives more closely. It is difficult to believe that any slaver in any time was more shamefully overloaded than the vessel quoted by Falconbridge. The recognized scale of 5 to 2 tons represented a maximum. The enormous proportion of loss from disease which had marked the trade from the beginning proves that the ships had always been overcrowded. The utmost we can assert with confidence is that such inhuman crushing of excessive numbers into small spaces as Falconbridge quoted may have become rather more common. Yet it must have produced the same results, which cannot have been profitable to the smuggling trader. When the price of slaves had risen, as it did in the nineteenth century, to a figure which allowed of 600 per cent. profit on a successful run, the trader could afford to carry fewer. It was his interest to land the blacks in good condition, and to obtain an immediate sale. What interest had the trader in incurring the certainty of the loss of great part of his cargo ? There is, so far as I can discover, little reason to suppose that the vessels employed by the illicit modern trader were on an average smaller than those sent out by the lawful trader of early times.

Down to the close of the first quarter of the nineteenth century the merchant ships of all nations were small. Mr. John Dalley, the Assistant-Registrar of Shipping, gave the figures for 1799 to the Commissioners of Naval Inquiry of 1803. They show that the total merchant shipping—oversea and coasting—belonging to Great Britain at the close of the eighteenth century amounted to 13,518 vessels of

1,485,291 tons. The average was therefore about 110 tons.
This average was obtained by taking in at one end the
two score or so vessels of 800, 1,200, or 1,400 tons, employed
by the East India Company in the trade to the Bay of
Bengal and to China, and at the other the diminutive craft
of 20 tons or so used in the coast trade. The figures for
Ireland are 1,004 vessels of 54,291 tons. Their average
was therefore 50 tons. The merchant shipping of other
peoples did not exceed the British Standard. It tended
rather to approximate to the Irish. And these figures meet
us everywhere. In 1760 the number of vessels employed
in the African trade was 163 of 18,000 tons. The average,
again, in round figures, is 110 tons. And many vessels
engaged in the slave-trade were of smaller size. Let us
take, for instance, the brigantine *Sanderson*, of Newport,
Rhode Island, which began her voyage in 1752.* The size
of her crew—Captain, two mates, and six men—shows that
she was a very small craft, and her voyage was an example
of a multitude of others, whether made from Europe or
from the New England States, which did not encourage
slavery among themselves, but were very ready to make a
profit by providing the West Indies and the southern
plantations. She sailed in March, 1752, with " a cargo of
8,220 gallons of rum, together with ' African ' iron, flour,
pots, tar, sugar, and provisions, shackles, shirts, and
water." I do not find that the quantity of iron, etc., carried
is specified. The 8,220 gallons probably represented the
greatest weight in the brigantine *Sanderson* in 1752. The
slave-trade was largely conducted by exchange of coarse
spirits for negroes. If a gallon of rum at Newport, Rhode
Island, in the year 1752, distilled for consumption by black
slave hunters, was equal in volume to " ten imperial
standard pounds' weight of distilled water weighed against
brass weights, with the water and air at the temperature
of 62° Fahrenheit, and the barometer at 30 inches," we
could make a plausible guess at the tons displacement
of the *Sanderson*. But did they ? And if they did, what

* " American Historical Record," vol. i., 315-319, 338-342, quoted
by Dr. W. E. Burghardt du Bois in " The Suppression of the Slave-
Trade to the United States of America," 1896.

would that fact tell us as to her tons register?* She probably paid light and harbour dues as a vessel of 35 or 40 tons. Be that as it may, her Captain, Lindsay, made his voyage to the satisfaction of his masters. He sailed to the coast of Africa, and there exchanged his rum for negroes—not, it appears, without difficulty. By June, 1753, he was at Barbadoes with his African cargo, 40 ounces of gold dust, 8 or 9 hundredweight of pepper, and fifty-six slaves " all in helth and fatt." The good condition of the negroes was all the more to his credit because the voyage had been stormy and dangerous. Whether those fifty-six healthy and fat blacks represented the whole number shipped by the *Sanderson*, or only the survivors, does not appear. If the *Sanderson* was of 40 tons, and had loaded up to the standard of 5 to 2 tons, she would have started from the coast of Africa with a hundred. At Barbadoes either the Captain or his consignees were decidedly unfortunate. Negroes were then selling at from £33 to £56 per head in lots. At the lower rate, fifty-six healthy and fat blacks would have brought in £1,848. But the net proceeds of the sale of his whole cargo—gold dust, and pepper, as it would seem, included—was only £1,324 0s. 3d. The difference of more than £500 cannot be accounted for by expenses. Neither is it probable that a particularly fine consignment of blacks would be sold at the lowest prevailing market price. It is to be feared that the consignees quoted by Dr. du Bois' authority were not strictly truthful, and that some at least of the fifty-six belonged to the class of damaged blacks who were sold for very much less than £33 a head to speculators who fed them up—or the minority of them who survived—and resold them at a profit.

We can for our own instruction follow Captain Lindsay to the completion of his voyage. He shipped molasses and sugar to the value of £911 17s. 2½d., received bills on Liverpool for the balance, and returned in safety to Rhodes Island.

* While making these calculations, it is well not to forget that the measurements of ships were untrustworthy until very recent times. But when every allowances is made, I still see no reason to believe that the lawful slavers were larger, or notably less overcrowded than the smuggling craft of the age of the unlawful trade. After all, Falconbridge gives measurements of the holds by length, breadth, and height.

Of course the molasses and sugar were in due time turned into more rum, to be exported in its turn to Africa, and laid out in slaves. Captain Lindsay may have carried it himself, for he had done so well that " he was immediately given a new ship and sent to Africa again.' And that was the " carrera de Indias " of New England and Old. The rum made out of the sugar-canes of the Sugar Islands was sent to produce drunkenness in Africa, and Africa paid it with kidnapped labour, which was to grow more sugar-cane, to be worked into more rum, which was to buy more slaves. And the bills on Liverpool represented the profit. When the great Chatham thundered his high appreciation of " Shugger Islands " (so he pronounced it), this was what he had in his mind—the manufacture of delirium tremens, with which to purchase dysentery, fever, filth, and cheap labour, which could be rapidly used up at hand-worked sugar-mills to produce more molassses, to be sent through the same round. The slave-trading industry and Africa lived by exchanging beastlinesses. Rum making for the African trade was the " chief manufacture " of Massachusetts. Trading Captains in other lines who wished to provision their ships with the materials for grog found that it was all bought up by the slavers.

Apologists of the slave-trade and of slavery have been much in the habit of maintaining that the necessity for concealment weighed hard on the slaves in transit. They were confined still more closely, deprived still more cruelly of air and space, in order that they might escape the notice of an inspecting naval officer. It is difficult to see how the most determined smuggler of slaves could do more than force them into spaces in which they could just lie on their sides, or confine them in less than a height of 3 feet 6 inches between decks. While a visit was actually being made aboard the Brazilian slaver, who spread a layer of innocent cargo over the concealed slave-hold " por Ingléz ver " (for the Englishman) to see, the concealed blacks were very possibly brought rather nearer asphyxiation than usual. But that would be the case only during the search which was to be feared at the point of departure or at the landfall, and not during the passage. And in one

H.M. SCHOONER PICKLE.

Lieut. J. B. B. McHardy defeating the notorious slaver the Boladora, June 6th, 1829. From an Aquatint after W. J. Huggins engraved by E. Duncan. Kindly lent by Messrs. T. H. Parker, Bookseller.

Of course the molasses and sugar were in due time turned into more rum, to be exported in its turn to Africa, and laid out in slaves. Captain Lindsay may have carried it himself, for he had done so well that " he was immediately given a new ship and sent to Africa again." And that was the " carrera de Indias " of New England and Old. The rum made out of the sugar-canes of the Sugar Islands was sent to produce drunkenness in Africa, and Africa paid it with kidnapped labour, which was to grow more sugar-cane, to be worked into more rum, which was to buy more slaves. And the bills on Liverpool represented the profit. When the great Chatham thundered his high appreciation of " Shugger Islands " (so he pronounced it), this was what he had in his mind—the manufacture of delirium tremens, with which to purchase dysentery, fever, filth, and cheap labour, which could be rapidly used up at hand-worked sugar-mills to produce more molassses, to be sent through the same round. The slave-trading industry and Africa lived by exchanging beastlinesses. Rum making for the African trade was the " chief manufacture " of Massachusetts. Trading Captains in other lines who wished to provision their ships with the materials for grog found that it was all bought up by the slavers.

Apologists of the slave-trade and of slavery have been much in the habit of maintaining that the necessity for concealment weighed hard on the slaves in transit. They were confined still more closely, deprived still more cruelly of air and space, in order that they might escape the notice of an inspecting naval officer. It is difficult to see how the most determined smuggler of slaves could do more than force them into spaces in which they could just lie on their sides, or confine them in less than a height of 3 feet 6 inches between decks. While a visit was actually being made aboard the Brazilian slaver, who spread a layer of innocent cargo over the concealed slave-hold " por Ingléz ver " (for the Englishman) to see, the concealed blacks were very possibly brought rather nearer asphyxiation than usual. But that would be the case only during the search which was to be feared at the point of departure or at the landfall, and not during the passage. And in one

H.M. SCHOONER PICKLE.

Lieut. J. B. B. M'Hardy defeating the notorious slaver the Boladora, June 6th, 1829.
From an Aquatint after W. H. adins engraved by E. Duncan.

way the wish to avoid capture led to a certain alleviation in the miseries of the captives. The slaver was driven to employ a swifter vessel than the square-bowed, wall-sided, flat-bottomed tub of the eighteenth century. One of the fine American clippers, bought, if not actually built, for the slave-trade in the nineteenth century could make the passage in a third less time than the brigantine *Sanderson* or her like. If ever there was a case for applying the Spanish proverbial phrase, " De lo mal lo menos " (Of evil the least), it was this. The less time the slave was on the middle passage the better for him.

It is, too, very possible to exaggerate the danger of capture and the influence it had on the slaves. The truth is that no Power except Great Britain exerted itself seriously to stop the trade, and Great Britain was hampered by the obligation to respect the flag of other nations and to confine herself strictly to the exercise of her treaty rights. Now, until France abolished slavery in her own Colonies, her flag was constantly employed by the connivance of colonial officials, if not of the Home Government, to cover the slave-trade. And the flag of the United States was used for the same purpose during all the predominance of the slave power in the Union—that is to say, from the immense development of the cotton industry, about 1820, down to the outbreak of the Civil War in 1861. Search treaties might be made, but they were limited, and they could have been worked only by the honest co-operation of both parties. The first Right of Search Treaties were made with Portugal in 1815, and with Spain in 1817 (two small Powers which, owing to their peculiar position as clients of Great Britain in the Napoleonic War, and their pecuniary obligations to her, could not say her nay as boldly as they would like to have done), confined the right of search to the north of the Equator. If the chase began north of the line, it could be continued to the south, but it could not begin in the south. Arrangements for joint cruising were not made with the United States till 1842, nor with France till 1845 ; and it is notorious that neither of those Powers was zealous in carrying out the search. The United States sent few ships to the African coast, and the slave interest, which was predominant in the Union, took care that they should be both ill-adapted for the work to be done, and stationed where they could see little or nothing.

At its strongest the American squadron was composed of from two to six vessels of from thirty to ninety-eight guns, and the use made of it was accurately stated by Lord Napier to Mr. Secretary Cass in 1857. "The force habitually and actively engaged in cruising on the ground frequented by slavers has probably been less by one-fourth, if we consider the size of the ships employed and their withdrawal for purposes of recreation and health, and the movements of the reliefs, whose arrival does not correspond exactly with the departure of the vessels whose term of service has expired." In fact, so long as the Government of the United States had to be conducted with the co-operation of the slave-holding States, the suppression of the slave-trade was a sham as far as America was concerned. All Americans, too, had a dislike to a general right of search—that having been the point on which they had fought England in the war of 1812. They were afraid of committing themselves to toleration of the accursed thing. For one reason or another nothing was done to suppress the participation of Americans in the slave-trade. The instructions given to naval officers of the Union appear to have been framed for the express purpose of encouraging the slaver. Commodore Perry was told in 1843 that—"(1) You are charged with the protection of legitimate commerce. (2) While the United States wishes to suppress the slave-trade, she will not admit a right of search by foreign vessels. (3) You are to arrest slavers. (4) You are to allow in no case an exercise of the Right of Search, or any great interruption of legitimate commerce." Wash the skin, but don't make it wet. The American naval officer could arrest an American slaver only when she was actually carrying slaves, and would not exercise a right of search of vessels under other flags. The course to be followed by the slaver from the Union was marked out to him by his own Government. He came out under the American flag, and till his slaves were aboard he had no reason to avoid the navy of his country. He slipped into some port in

Africa, hoisted the Spanish flag by collusive arrangement, and had brought Spanish papers with him. Unless a British man-of-war caught him there and then, he went off, and could safely sail past the whole navy of the United States with his cargo of " ebony." Nothing could be more simple, nor, if hypocrisy is discreditable, more discreditable.*

The conclusion of the whole matter is that Sir Henry Manwaring's maxim holds good for slavery as for piracy. The only effective way of clearing out the foxes was to stop the holes. The exits might have been stopped by Great Britain herself, and very easily too. If she had declared at the time when the Peace of Paris was signed that she proposed to take possession of the whole coast of Africa from which the slaves were shipped, nobody could have said her nay, and it may be added that the subsequent partition of Africa would have been notably simplified. A hundred or two of the thousands of naval and military officers of all ranks—commissioned, warrant, petty, and non-commissioned—who were turned off on half-pay, which was really quarter-pay and less, to vegetate or to go ranging down the wind to peck at fortune under the flag of Simon Bolivar in South America, to win the Battle of Carabobo for the behalf of a rabble of half-breeds, and to die miserably, could have done a great work for their country and for humanity. But Great Britain would not take the Slave Coast, and could not control the importers in their own countries.

Their method was uniform. It was practised with more seamanship, more dash, by the slave smugglers of the United States, but the difference was only in the degree of spirit and skill shown. That the trade was conducted mainly under the Spanish flag, that the slavers sailed by the dozen and the score from Havannah, was due to the fact that those colours afforded protection against search by a United

* See Dr. Burghardt du Bois, " The Suppression of the Slave-Trade," pp. 158 *et seq.*, for these and other illustrations ; and also remember that what the United States did was being done by everybody except Great Britain and Holland. The Dutch, with a business faculty and direct simplicity of method characteristic of them, " hired " black coolies from the King of Dahomey and potentates of his kidney. They left money with the negro King for " the support of the free hired men's families." Then they sailed with their coolies unchained under the very noses of the British naval officers, who could do nothing because they could not find shackles !

States warship. There were Spaniards in the trade, but they were not the most skilful at it, nor were they the most numerous.

I can draw on my own recollection—not for confirmation, which is unnecessary—but for a small illustration of an acknowledged fact. Between 1868 and 1879 I was generally resident in the port of Barcelona. There were then several men of business and ship Captains who had been engaged in the trade, and who made no concealment of the fact, though they did not parade it. If taxed on the subject, they had no scruple in defending the slave-trade, and they dismissed the abolitionist activity of Englishmen as another example of British cant. They compared our condemnation of the slave-trade to our disapproval of the bull-fight. " A ' corrida,' " said they, " is not nearly so barbarous as your own prize-fights. Bulls and negroes are not ' Christians.' You say you are Christians, and yet you allow your brother-Christians to batter one another for your amusement. You are worse than we, quite as inhuman, and you cant into the bargain." I have seen the statement of that point of view cause considerable irritation to Englishmen. But demonstration that it was wrong-headed is not so easy as persons who prefer to assert what they ought to prove may be inclined to think.* The Spaniards did not approve of slave trading as virtuous. They assimilated the " negrero " to the " torero,' the professional bull-fighter, whom we will persist in calling a " toreador." These men were useful or entertaining, but respectable people did not frequent their society or desire them as sons-in-law—very much as we regard the professional pugilist. Though they considered that the activity of Great Britain in suppressing their slave-trade was a harsh abuse of her strength, they looked down on the " negrero."

Among those whom I knew, or knew of, there was one

* What are our obligations as " Christians " ? Do they include abstention from all encouragement for our profit or amusement, of acts which may barbarize, or cause pain or death ? If they do, how do we reconcile Christianity with approval of a sport which frequently causes death on the spot from fracture of the skull by a knock-out blow under the chin, or, later on, through the disease which is started by the " heart knock-out," or " the kidney punch " ? I am not writing a treatise on morals, and ask " for information."

who, by his personality and his fate, was illuminative to me. He was a small, wizened man of the lean, sallow, Spanish type—who looked a regular bred seaman, and capable of anything. In circumstances unknown to me he had married an Englishwoman of very motherly and pleasing appearance. They were the parents of two beautiful girls. The man lived in easy circumstances on the product of (it was said) three successful runs from the Slave Coast to Cuba. He was subject to fits, accompanied by agony of pain in the head, and while they lasted he screamed in a dreadful way. It was generally asserted by his countrymen that these fits came when he was haunted by the ghosts of a cargo of blacks whom he had drowned by scuttling his ship when he was chased by a British cruiser on his last voyage. They did not condemn him for having been a slaver, nor blame him for the death of such blacks as were sacrificed in the ordinary course of trade, but for the wholesale murder which he perpetrated to suppress evidence against himself. He was avoided, but nobody proposed to prove the truth of the story (which in itself is not incredible, for such things were done) by bringing him to trial, and when he died he ended like a "Cristiano," having taken the Sacrament and received the Viaticum. I may add, with no controversial purpose, but simply to illustrate the moral atmosphere of a community which tolerated slavery, that, though the trade was condemned by the Pope, I never heard that any of the persons whose connection with it was notorious was ever called in question by the Church.

The Spaniards are to answer for their share of the common sin. They did all they could, but, left to themselves, they could have done but little. The capital, the skill, the swift-sailing clippers of the slave-smuggling trade, came from the United States, supplied by the abolitionist North, and paid for by the slave-holding South. They supplied themselves, and the Spaniards and Portuguese communities of America also. There were cases of slavers captured under the Spanish flag which did not contain more than two or three Spaniards in the crews, and they were kept only "por Ingléz ver," to make a show when the nationality of the vessel had to be proved. The American who disputes the fact only proves that "le cant Britannique" crossed the Atlantic together with the principles of the British Constitution.

Let us hear what the *New York Herald* of August 5th, 1860, said :*

" To have boldly ventured into New Orleans, with negroes freshly imported from Africa, would not only have brought down upon the head of the importer the vengeance of our very philanthropic Uncle Sam, but also the anathemas of the whole sect of philanthropists and negrophilists everywhere. To import them for years, however, into quiet places, evading with impunity the penalty of the law, and the ranting of the thin-skinned sympathizers with Africa, was gradually to popularize the traffic by creating a demand for labourers, and thus to pave the way for the *gradual revival of the slave-trade*. To this end a few men, bold and energetic, determined, ten or twelve years ago [1848 or 1850] to commence the business of importing negroes, slowly at first, but surely; and for this purpose they selected places on the coasts of Florida, Georgia, and Texas for the purpose of concealing their stock until it could be sold out. Without specifying other places, let me draw your attention to a deep and abrupt pocket or indentation in the coast of Texas, about thirty miles from Brazos Santiago. Into this pocket a slaver could run at any hour of the night, because there was no hindrance at the entrance, and here she could discharge her cargo of movables upon the projecting bluff, and again proceed to sea inside of three hours. The live stock thus landed could be marched a short distance across the main island, over a porous soil which refuses to retain the recent footprints, until they were again placed in boats, and were concealed upon some of the innumerable little islands which thicken on the waters of the Laguna in the rear. These islands, being covered with a thick growth of bushes and grass, offer an inscrutable hiding-place for the ' black diamonds.' "

There is the whole process of all smuggling, and when

* The passage from the *Herald* is quoted in Dr. Du Bois' "Suppression of the Slave-Trade," pp. 180, 181. Dr. Du Bois took it from the Introduction to the " Revelations of a Slave Smuggler," by Richard Drake. I have not been able to find the book, but Dr. Du Bois quotes it more than once as authentic.

the authorities on shore were in connivance with the smuggler, it was easy, and was not dangerous. In the case of the slave smuggler who was sure of connivance on the American side, whether it was English, Spanish, or Portuguese speaking American, the process was particularly easy. The only serious danger belt was on the coast of Africa, where the British naval officer was active. In that region the slaver might be overtaken and captured, if he had not time to run ashore, or fire, or scuttle his vessel, and escape in the boats. Even there he had a resource which was not seldom successful. When a British cruiser was on the watch a dummy slaver was sent to draw her off, and while she was chasing the decoy the real sinner slipped off with her cargo of negroes. When he found he was deceived, all the British officer could do was to unbend all the decoy's sails, drop all her anchors, run the cables out to their full length, and leave her crew with twenty-four hours' hard work to be done before she could get back to port. On the whole, it is not at all surprising that, in spite of the exertions of the British Government, and the promises of others, the smuggling of slaves went on increasing till the very outbreak of the Civil War in America. It was stopped altogether only by the abolition of slavery in Cuba and Brazil, though it diminished to a small matter after the closing of the American market, and the withdrawal of American capital, energy, and skill.

If there is little reason to suppose that the blacks were worse treated by the illicit than by the lawful trader, there is a certainty that the sailors were much better off in the smuggling trade. When the crew could mutiny and carry the slaver into port, not only with safety, but with applause (the thing did happen), no Captain could well dare to misuse his men. When their evidence might ruin him, an employer would have to take good care to see that they were well and punctually paid. There were cases when the blacks mutinied and obtained possession of the vessel—more cases, no doubt, than we know of. When a slaver sailed and was never heard of again, the reason may have been that the blacks mastered and killed her crew, which they had a good right to do, and then perished themselves in the first gale, or drifted about till they died of starvation in the doldrums.

When the vessel ran ashore or was picked up by an English or American cruiser, as happened more than once, the difficulty of discovering how the thing was done was considerable. The crew would have been despatched, and the blacks were unintelligible.

My chapter, which is, I fear, but an insufficient sketch of a huge barbarism, cannot end better than by the story of a particular voyage performed while the trade was lawful, and therefore the better evidence for its real character at its best.*

Our witness is Adriaen Blaes, of the Veer, skipper of the Dutch African trader *St. John*, who appeared before the authorities of the Dutch island Curaçoa, and deposed to this effect: He was commissioned by the Governor of Elmina, the Dutch post on the Slave Coast, to go to Calabar and collect a cargo of blacks. He was to sail to Curaçoa, then governed by the Dutch West India Company, to which the *St. John* belonged. The blacks were, no doubt, to be smuggled into the Spanish Colonies. The Dutch islands Curaçoa, Buen Ayre, and Oruba, were noted depots of the contraband trade with Spanish America. We are not told what the size of the *St. John* was, but as her whole crew could be packed into one boat, and make, as we shall see, a run of some length in it, though somewhat overcrowded, we may safely conclude that she did not exceed 100 tons. Adriaen Blaes, who was to all seeming an honest man enough, and who, at any rate, professed much zeal for the company's interests, went to Calabar, and there collected 219 blacks, " big and little,' of both sexes. But he had also to collect provisions, and that, he found, was not to be done at Calabar. So he went to " the Highland of Ambosius," where also there was no food to be obtained. At the Cameroons River he did purchase a little, and so, after taking in wood and water at " Capo de Lopo Gonsalves," he went farther, though suffering much misery, to Anabona, where he secured as much food as justified him in striking across the Atlantic to Tobago, at that time also in possession of the Dutch West India Company.

* " Voyage of the slavers *St. John* and *Arms of Amsterdam*, 1659-1663," translated from the Dutch by E. B. O'Callaghan, Albany, 1867, vol. iii. of " New York Colonial Tracts."

A list of the slaves who died on the passage is preserved with the summary log kept by Skipper Blaes. It shows that the blacks died in batches. The 219 were reduced to 90. From Tobago the *St. John* pursued her voyage to Curaçoa, but she ran on Los Roques, a patch of rocks lying directly between Tobago and Buen Ayre, but rather nearer the second island. The vessel was fixed on the rocks, and there was nothing for it but to send to the Honourable Director of the Company at Curaçoa for another craft to take the blacks off. Blaes and all his crew took their boat and went off, leaving the blacks in the wreck. They reached Buen Ayre, where part of them landed, for the boat was dangerously overladen. Blaes, with the others, reached Curaçoa, and reported to the Company's Honourable Director Mynheer Beck.

The director was full of zeal, but he was hampered by the fact that the only vessels he had at command had been sent the day before to Oruba, farther to the west. As soon as might be, Blaes was sent to recover the blacks, with the company's ship, whereof Hans Marcussen Stuyve was Captain, and the *Young Brindled Cow*, commanded by Jan Rickertsen. Blaes was plainly no witch at a narrative, and loses his head among the relative pronouns as he goes on. But the drift of the story is clear enough. He and the company's ships were met and seized by a Jamaica "privateer"—*i.e.*, buccaneer, and, when occasion served, pirate—sailing with a commission from the English Governor of Jamaica, according to the custom of the lawless West Indies. Blaes and the other servants of the company were close, and said not a word about the shipwrecked blacks in Los Roques. There was peace at that time between England and Holland; but there was no peace beyond the line—only combinations to plunder. It was better not to put temptation in the way of the Jamaica privateer.

Unfortunately for the company, the privateer took the vessels to Buen Ayre. The men Blaes had left there, suspecting no harm, hailed the new-comers with inquiries after their Captain, and whether he was come to take off the blacks. The privateer pricked up his ears. Blacks were a welcome commodity on the Spanish Main, and the

Jamaica man, a worthy successor of John Hawkins, knew that to plunder the blacks whom somebody else had been at the trouble of collecting, and vend them by a contraband trade to the Spaniards, was a profitable business. Blaes did not quote Puffendorff and Grotius, for good reasons, but he did appeal to first principles, his own hard case and the rights of the honourable company. The Jamaica man cared as much for these things as Blaes would have cared for the same appeal from one of the kidnapped blacks he shipped at Calabar. It is not easy, and it is hardly worth while, to disentangle the subsequent movements of all the vessels concerned, as told in the involved sentences of the Dutch skipper's deposition. The long and short of it was that the Jamaica privateer put Blaes into the *Castle Frigate*, of four guns and thirty men, commanded by Jan Pietersen, a Dane, called in his Lieutenant, who was cruising in a " periauger " (*i.e.*, piragua, or big canoe), near Curaçoa, enforced the aid of the company's ships, and took off the survivors of the blacks—eighty two and two " sucklings " miserable little morsels of black flesh born in the midst of death, disease, and shipwreck. It was no easy task to bring them off, for the weather was bad, and the blacks were frantic with terror. They were brought under control by Blaes's mate, whose voice they knew. The Jamaica privateer sailed away with them, after warning the Dutchmen not to follow him, and he, no doubt, traded his booty on the Spanish Main, and did a good stroke of business. Adriaen Blaes came back to Curaçoa to tell his tale. It is sweet to learn from certain accompanying documents of the high moral indignation of Mynheer Beck, whose function it was to direct kidnapping and armed smuggling, when he was presented with this outrageous instance of the unscrupulous ways of Jamaica privateers.

CHAPTER XIII

THE SEA TRADER IN WAR-TIME

THERE is a big book still to be written on the conduct of maritime commerce in war-time. The statement may appear rash, in view of the fact that whole libraries are full of treatises on International Law, Orders in Council, Milan and Berlin Decrees, Continental Blockade, and so forth. But my reference is not to what was legislated, speculated upon, threatened, thundered, and published in proclamations. It is to what was done, which was apt to differ very materially from what was ordered to be done. In so far as law-makers and other exalted persons were concerned, a treatise on " The Conduct of Maritime Commerce in War " would have to take note, not only of what they would have achieved if they could, but of what the necessities of the case compelled them to wink at, or even to license. And that was a great deal.

There is a dominating fact which even learned writers on International Law, and still more demonstrators of sea power, seem commonly to forget. It is that a country may stand in absolute need of the produce of its enemy. When that is the case, it cannot stop the trade except by injuring itself. In the extremely improbable case that Great Britain were at war with the Argentine Republic, the fact that five-sevenths of the chilled and frozen meat sold at Smithfield is drawn from this South American State would produce certain infallible consequences. If the trade were stopped, the price of meat would rise enormously in the London market, and, as the industry is largely promoted by British Capital, the loss would fall most severely on British investors. The Argentines would lose, but they would keep the food to eat. Some means would be found for permitting the importation of a supply Great Britain could not afford to lose. But in that case it would be necessary to pay the Argentine producer a remunerative price, and the payment might have to be made in bullion. The supposition is not an arbitrary one. The case actually arose in the heat of the struggle with Napoleon. While Berlin Decrees and Orders in Council were being hurled with much stage thunder, Great Britain found herself menaced, through the failure of harvests, with famine. She had to obtain wheat from the Continent, and could secure it only by the consent of Napoleon. He gave the necessary leave, partly because he wished to obtain the bullion paid for the breadstuff, and partly because he hoped to destroy the credit of British paper money by depleting the metallic reserve. Great Britain had to pay her enemy for the means of preserving her own existence.

Nor is this a solitary case. When did English men and women who wished for French wines, silks, and laces, find it impossible to buy them because the two countries were at war? During the French revolutionary war the Parisian women who exhibited themselves in " Greek "— *i.e.*, transparent — dresses wore English muslins. They might rise in price because they came by a roundabout route, and through neutral hands, or by smuggling, or with a licence, but they came—and the French producer was paid for them by English money, or *vice versa*. And these were luxuries. A people can do without champagne, brandy, claret, burgundy, silks, laces, and muslins. But if it is a manufacturing people, it cannot do without raw material, and, whatever it be, it cannot do without food. During our wars with Spain trade never ceased. There were two things which we were under a peremptory obligation to obtain from the Spaniards—certain qualities of wool needed for our cloth manufactures, and the silver of American mines, which was absolutely necessary for the East India trade. And both were obtained by the simple process of paying for them. Licensed traders went to Santander for wool, carrying the price with them in goods. A declaration of war was promptly followed by the appearance of vessels under the Prussian flag, which went with English manufactures and came back with Spanish wool. The war of 1739 was begun in the hope that the Spanish Colonies would be conquered and the silver mines pass into British hands. When conquest proved impossible, the old tolerated trade came up again. The necessities of great communities of men have a force of penetration far beyond the resisting power of such porous barriers as paper decrees and ordinances. The sea power of a people who must import food and raw material is not limited only by the sufficiently obvious consideration that its ships cannot go where they cannot float, but also by the no less obvious, though much neglected, consideration that they cannot be used to stop the export of supplies indispensable to itself from countries with which it may be at war. Could Great Britain, even if it had the necessary naval supremacy, put a stop to the export of cotton and food from America, without at the same time condemning herself to starve behind her impenetrable cuirass ? She would inflict loss of wealth on her enemy—mere temporary loss—but on herself death. The last war against a nation which provided her with raw material on an important scale waged by Great Britain—that is to say, the Crimean War—supplied a singularly good example. Russian tallow, hemp, and timber were indispensable to British industry. When the Russian ports on the Baltic were blockaded, direct export was stopped. But the things must be obtained, and they were—through neutral ports, and after they had been transported by land over the Russian frontier. So it came to this : the Russian producer sold as much as before, and was paid as much ; the neutral carrier was paid for transporting the goods, and his revenue benefited by the dues paid at his frontier ; the British purchaser had to give a price which covered transport and dues. Who lost ? Well, in so far as the goods were consumed in Great Britain, the British consumer lost. In so far as they were re-exported, some third party helped to pay. Who gained ? Obviously, the neutral middle-man. As for the Russian, against whom the sea power of Britain had been triumphantly directed, he neither gained nor lost. He was paid as before. Most of his produce had been shipped in British vessels, and therefore he lost little freight. What he did lose was compensated by the stimulus given, at the expense of the British purchaser, to his land-transport business. In the meantime the British taxpayer was paying for the maintenance of his navy on a war footing, which was doing all the harm. The loss in this case was not too severe to be borne, but if Great Britain had been called to pay an enormously enhanced price for food and cotton, the strain might have become intolerable, and the Power which possessed an overwhelming superiority at sea might have been compelled to sue for peace.

The " licensed trade," which arose out of the peremptory necessity weighing on Great Britain to find a vent for her goods, and to obtain food and raw material from her enemies, and out of their pressing need to acquire what she had to give in exchange, is no doubt mentioned by all serious writers. I have not the ignorant conceit to suppose that I am revealing a secret unknown to learned authorities. But I do submit respectfully that the scope and the importance of the thing have been rarely recognized, and have been habitually disregarded by those who applied themselves to the military side of naval wars. I shall try to give reasons for believing that the licensed trade always modified the commerce-destroying operations of our fleets, and that when the mutual efforts of Great Britain and her enemy Napoleon to annihilate one another's commerce came to a height, after 1806, it developed to such a point that it reduced their avowed policy to a farce—and that farce one played with a cynical hypocrisy and a positive spilth of perjury, forgery, and make-believe which would be incredible if the evidence did not impose belief.

The words " licensed trade " are easily written, but they do not enlighten us as to the nature of the thing. The Navigation Laws forbade the importation into the country of foreign goods by a third party. They must be brought either in British bottoms or in vessels belonging to the country which produced them, and the colonial trade was a rigid monopoly. This policy was carried farther by Great Britain than by most other nations, but it was a pretty general rule. When war came, the case might, and did, arise that the importing nation stood in need of the produce of its enemy, or could not conduct its colonial trade in safety. The second condition did not apply to Great Britain, but the first did. We have seen that the Manning Clauses of the Navigation Laws were habitually suspended in war. The clauses which regulated the carriage of cargoes were also suspended by the use of " licences." Permits were issued by Government to British merchants authorizing them to make use of foreign ships other than those of the country with which we were at war, or, in the West Indies, even of our enemy Spain, in order that they might vend their own goods and receive bullion, or mules, horses, and the food required for the negroes. These permits protected the vessel from molestation by our cruisers. It is true that after 1756 Great Britain laid it down as part of her maritime rights that a neutral must not be allowed to enjoy in war a trade from which he was debarred in peace; that, for instance, a Danish vessel, which was excluded from the colonial trade of France before hostilities began, was not to carry goods between the French West Indian Islands and France in war. He was, in fact, not to do for our enemy what we invited him to do for us. There was no exclusive " cant britannique" in this, nor any double dose of original sin. We did it more than others because we were stronger. They would have done it if they could. In the American War of Independence Great Britain was not so much superior at sea as she had been in the Seven Years' War. She was faced by the armed neutrality of the Northern Powers, at a time when colonial supplies were cut off, and naval stores could be obtained only from the Baltic. She drew in her horns, moaning more in sorrow than in anger over this immoral disregard of her " rights," which were, in fact, her pretensions of a kind highly injurious to neutrals. The capacity of the human countenance to remain grave in circumstances of quintessential absurdity is great.*

* The armed neutrality is sometimes said to have produced no effect, apparently because Catharine II., who loved her jest, described it as as an " Armed Nullity." But Catharine cared little for the trade, and a great deal for a free hand in dealing with the Turk. She meant that the British Government might have all the maritime " rights " it pleased if she could have her way in the Near

The licensed trade, which had been a palliative and a resource in particular cases during the seventeenth and eighteenth centuries, rose to its altitudes when Napoleon on the one hand, and Great Britain on the other, began to try to annihilate each the trade of the other in real earnest. The Emperor dominated all Europe, from the Baltic to the Adriatic, in 1806. Great Britain commanded the sea. Napoleon said, British trade shall not reach the Continent at all. Great Britain said, that no trade shall reach it except through me and by paying toll. If anybody pays you toll, said the Emperor, I will confiscate his ship and goods so soon as they are within my reach. The neutral was to be ground between the upper and the nether millstones. The only true neutral was the United States. The New England States had the immense advantage of possessing a command of good ships' timber near their ports at a time when the price of wood was rising in Europe. They had excellent seamen, who were not numerous enough to supply more than a third or so of their crews, but who did provide the leadership and brains. They had bulky outward freights of cotton, wheat, and timber. With these advantages they profited hugely by their position as neutrals. The spectacle was disturbing to many in Great Britain, who began to fear that the " Yankees " would capture the carrying trade of the world. Self-defence against Napoleon, combined with aggression against America to produce the famous Orders in Council, which were just so many dictatorial decrees issued by Great Britain to the world at large. There was nothing new in the ideas on either side. The Jacobins, who had the example of the Dutch of the seventeenth century to guide them, had endeavoured to destroy British trade by paper decrees which they could not even begin to enforce. The policy of the Orders in Council had

---

East. She would have thrown over her northern allies as readily as Great Britain threw over Prussia at the end of the Seven Years' War when it had secured what it wanted for itself, and as Frederick the Great threw over France in the War of the Austrian Succession when he had pocketed his share. Treaties hold good, said Bismarck, "rebus sic stantibus," and the "res" to be considered is the good the treaty owes you. The armed neutrality forced Great Britain to swallow a good deal.

been urged on Pitt, and rejected by him because he foresaw its consequences.*

Those consequences became manifest from the very moment the " fell incensed enemies " began to carry out their policy of " thorough." They were simply that each found he was cutting off his own nose in his effort to damage his enemy's face. The loss of revenue and the disturbance was so great that each began to cast about for palliatives. Napoleon set the example, and Great Britain followed. The " licence " provided a ready means, and it promptly came to this—that Napoleon sold permission to escape the oppression of his decreees at a stiff figure, and Great Britain gave, for reasonable fees, permission to her merchants to make use of the ships of countries at war with her. It had to be done for a reason very well stated, not by an enemy of the policy of the Orders in Council, but by a member of the very Ministry which was engaged in promulgating them and suspending them at one and the same time—Mr. George Rose, Vice-President of the Board of Trade and Treasurer of the Navy. The honourable gentleman " put it to the House, he put it to the hon. and learned gentleman opposite, whether it was possible to stand by in cold blood and see the manufacturers of the country starving rather than permit the produce of the country to be exported in foreign ships."† By " manufacturers " Mr. Rose meant the workmen who were rioting from distress in many parts of the country. "Manufacturer" had not yet lost its proper meaning—the man who shapes with his hand—and was not applied to the capitalist who pays those who do. It was under

---

* For the large, or even commanding share which jealousy of American shipping had in producing the Orders in Council, see " War in Disguise ; or, The Frauds of the Neutral Flags," by James Stephen, 1805. The American " Answer " of Gouverneur Morris, 1806, and the " Inquiry into the Causes and Consequences of the Orders in Council," by Alexander Baring (Lord Ashburton), 1808.

† " Parliamentary Debates, 1,119, vol. xxi., Report of Debate on Brougham's motion relating to the Orders in Council and the Licence Trade. Mr. Stephen, who spoke in the debate, agreed with Rose. He was credited with having inspired the Orders in Council. There was, however, nothing inconsistent in his support of the licences. He was consistent enough in approving of the use of the ships of nations whom he did not fear as maritime rivals, so long as we continued to injure the Americans whom he did fear.

pressure of these riots, this distress, and not only at the request of mill-owners and merchants, that licences were issued. Here is a model licence. The document is long, but the thing was important enough to be worth looking at :*

" To all commanders of His Majesty's ships of War and Privateers, and all others whom it may concern, greeting.

" I, the undersigned, one of His Majesty's principal Secretaries of State, in pursuance of the authority given to me by His Majesty's Order of Council under and by virtue of powers given to His Majesty by an Act passed in the forty-eighth year of His Majesty's reign [here follows the title of the Act several lines long, and not necessary to be repeated], and in pursuance of an Order of Council specially authorising the grant of this licence, a duplicate of which Order of Council is hereunto annexed, do hereby grant this licence for the purposes set forth in the said Order of Council to Messrs. —— of London, and other merchants, and do hereby permit a vessel, bearing any flag (except the French), and that [*i.e.*, the French flag] subject to the conditions hereinafter expressed, to proceed with a cargo of grain, meal, or flour (if importable according to the provisions of the Corn Laws), and bare stores from any port of France, between Brest and Bayonne, both inclusive, to any port of the United Kingdom ; the Master to be permitted to receive his freight, and depart with his vessel and crew to any port not blockaded, notwithstanding all the documents which accompany ship and cargo, may represent the same to be destined to any other neutral or hostile port, and to whomsoever such property may appear to belong ; provided that the name of the vessel and the name of the Master, and the time of clearance from her port of lading shall be endorsed on this licence, that the vessel shall be permitted to bear the French flag only till she is two leagues distant from her foreign port of clearance, or the neighbouring coast ; provided always that this licence shall not be understood to protect any vessel navigated by French seamen or any vessel that shall appear to be French built, save and except French built vessels, which may have been transferred into foreign possession, prior to the operation of the order of the 11th of November, 1807, or which may have been taken as prizes from the French, and shall not have returned again into French possession."

The licence was to be good for three months. The length of the period of protection, nature of cargo, destination of

* Quoted from the appendix to " Reflections on the Nature and Extent of the License Trade," by Joseph Phillimore, LL.D., 1812.

ship, and names of persons varied, but this was the standard model of a licence. It will be seen that the use of false papers was actually enjoined. The "simulation and dissimulation" which, as Lord Stowell said, were encouraged by the whole system of licences were of course unavoidable. Armed with this protection, the British merchant went to Holland, Denmark, and Norway for his ship, and employed it to import and export from and to French ports. We were at war with those countries, and the Danes, exasperated by the seizure of their fleet in 1807, carried on an active and often destructive warfare against our trade in the Baltic. Yet we went to the "dirty little ports of Denmark," as Brougham called them rudely, in search of ships in which to carry on our trade. There was no real check on the use which could be made of licences when once obtained, since the use of false papers was allowed, and our naval officers were commanded to let the ships pass. The number of licences granted was immense, and increased by leaps and bounds. It rose from 1,600 to over 18,000 in three years. The ships employed came from Holland, Denmark, Sweden, and the old Hanse towns, Kniphausen, Pappenburg (wherever that is, said Brougham with a snort), Emden, and so on. They are in East Friesland.

The merchants, shipowners, and other inhabitants of Hull, whose petition against the grant of licences was presented by Mr. Staniford on February 3rd, 1812, had their axe to grind, and were somewhat greedy. They were doing excellent business in supplying transports for the Government, and had lately raised their freights, but many of the facts they quoted were allowed to be true. They were right in asserting that large numbers of foreign ships had been employed of late years at three times the freight prevailing in times of unrestricted trade, and by British capital. They were not wrong when they said "that numbers of British licences have been publicly sold on the Continent, and that by means of those licences, and even under the protection of British convoys, our enemies have been supplied to a great extent by naval stores conveyed directly into their own harbours from different ports of the Baltic." They grew pathetic, but were entitled to be believed when they said they had been "eyewitnesses of the rapid and astonishing improvement in the appearance and skill of these men during the last few years." When they begged that no more licences should be granted, they were asking for what they were not likely to obtain, and when they proposed that the British Government should seize Bornholm and Eastholm (as they did in a memorial), and there establish a smuggling depot, to be filled and emptied by British ships alone, they were asking for what had been tried and found insufficient. The Hull men held fast to the faith that the possession of ships and sailors by any other nation was an invasion of the sacred maritime "rights" of England. But the licences were used because we could not do without them till the disasters of the Russian campaign brought about the ruin of Napoleon's Empire. And the fact that we could not do without them should be borne in mind by people who say that we drove all flags off the sea except our own in the Napoleonic War. We had to pay treble freights to foreign flags—not to neutral, but to hostile flags—in order that we might carry our goods out and bring our food in. The amount paid in freight by 1812 was put at £10,000,000.

That the licence trade, which unavoidably employed falsity, encouraged fraud does not need demonstration. A regular industry arose on the Continent and in Great Britain which was devoted to the fabrication of licences and papers of all kinds, with forged seals and signatures, even that of "Nap" himself. The shipowners of Hull—honest men who thought smuggling wrong unless it was conducted wholly by Englishmen and for their advantage—veiled their faces at the horrid spectacle. Lord Stowell reprobated it. Dr. Joseph Phillimore sighed deeply over it. Brougham thundered against the degrading practices which were besmirching the spotless integrity of the British merchant. The business of an Opposition is to oppose, and Brougham would have done the same thing if he had been in office, and for the same reason—because he just must. Meanwhile British merchants were besieging the doors of the Board of Trade for licences. Meanwhile, also, Americans could observe that while their neutral trade was to be crushed in defence of British maritime rights, British capital was employed in paying freights to the shipowners of her enemies to carry her trade—which helps to explain how they got into the state of mind which ended in the war of 1812. The war had been very lucrative to the United States. Their ships had, for instance, made a great business of carrying colonial produce from the West Indies to Europe. War had a peculiar effect on the Spanish Colonies. It freed them largely from the monopoly and control of the Mother-Country. The royal officials became less able to coerce the colonists, and they were, if possible, more open to bribes. Therefore the colonists traded briskly with whomsoever came along, and the neutral could be more easily dealt with than a smuggling belligerent. So the Americans bought Cuban sugar, carried it home, and reshipped it from the States to Europe. The export of sugar from Cuba went up in a few years from 90,000 to 250,000 tons, to the benefit of the Cubans and their carriers from the States, but not to the advantage of the British Sugar Islands. The Orders in Council were designed to stop that.

How did the existence of a state of war directly affect the seafaring man ? It acted in one way already dealt with. It rendered him liable to be pressed for service in the navy of his country, and whatever his country might be the consequences of this obligation were the same in kind. The most grievous of them all to him was that compulsory service in the navy shut him off from the chance of making far more money in his own line than he could earn in peace. The evil was not equally great in all countries. It was, for instance, far worse in France than in England, and worse in Spain than in France. If the British Government paid only twenty-three shillings a month for the month of four weeks, of which there are thirteen in the year, and if it held back the pay, its credit was good, and it paid in the end. A man could sell his pay-tickets, and at least he was abundantly, though, no doubt, coarsely, fed. The rations were not so chosen as to keep off scurvy, from which the officers suffered as well as the men. But, then, that was the case in the merchant service, and was not a main grievance. In France, where even the officers were left unpaid, and in Spain, where the King's management of his navy was at once beggarly and pretentious, the case of the men was far worse. But it was quite bad enough for the Englishman.

Let us listen to Captain George St. Lo, writing at the close of the seventeenth century.* He speaks of men impressed as their ships returned home, and so compelled to lose their " little ventures "—a point we will return to. And he expounds : " The seamen for the lucre of such great wages in merchant ships do lurk and hide themselves from their Majesties' service [their Majesties William and Mary] whereby it becomes so difficult to get men for the King's ships; whereas if their wages were alike their Majesties would never want Seamen in their fleet. A seaman's wages, in a merchantman in time of peace, is usually about 25s. a month, and in a collier 30s. or 40s. a voyage, which now is come to £6, £7, and £8 a voyage: and 50s. and £3 a month in a merchantman, which while they can have they will leave their Majesties' ships and abscond themselves from being impressed rather than serve for the usual rate of the Navy which is 23s. at 28 days in a month, which is 25s. a month at twelve months in the year—and till such their extraordinary wages be brought down, it is not to be thought it will be otherwise, though it is not evident they are ever the richer at the year's end for any such larger wages."

The words of St. Lo call for no lengthy commentary. We have to thank him for the information that in his day the sailor was still a trader as he had been in the Middle Ages. From a casual remark in the same pamphlet we get an indication that the status of the sailor had fallen. St. Lo was proposing that an impressment was both erratic and costly (he puts the yearly cost at £60,000); it would be advisable to classify merchant ships, and compel them to contribute men " pro rata." It would, he considered, be

* " England's Safety ; or, A bridle to the French King," reprinted in " Somers Tracts," vol. xi., p. 57 ; and " Reasons humbly offer'd by Captain Saint Lo for bringing down the Exorbitant Rates of Seamen's Wages from 50s. and £3 a Month to 30s. and 35s. a Month "— a pamphlet not, so far as I know, reprinted in any collection.

impossible to register the men, because " not one in ten was a householder," and therefore there was no security that they could be found when needed. Would this have been truly said of the seamen of the fourteenth and fifteenth centuries who sailed from their native towns? In the conditions of modern industry the sailor had become an unhoused vagabond man. Observe that St. Lo does not for a moment think of so improving the case of the navy sailor that men should not flee from service in the warship. His one resource was a good sharp " assize of labourers " for the seafaring man, which should fix his wages at some rate not so exorbitant as to compete with the twenty-three shillings a month for the month of twenty-eight days of the navy. It will be noted that the pay of the navy was not lower than that of the merchant service in peace, and that it was possible to obtain the small number of men needed for the peace establishment without the use of the press. When war came, when the establishment of the navy bounded up from being counted by the thousand to being counted by the ten thousand; when freights rose to meet war risks and insurance against them; when the shipowner could well pay more and the competition of the State made the sailor more valuable, why, then, the case was altered, and his wages rose to " exorbitant rates." That he was generally none the better for such great wages at the end of the year may well have been true. The class was not thrifty, nor was a wandering, houseless life calculated to breed habits of thrift. But he appreciated good wages when he could get them, and if he drank them it was because he liked drink, and increased earnings made it possible for him to purchase larger quantities.

As it was when Captain St. Lo wrote his pamphlets, so it continued to be while the Old World lasted, which may be taken to be till the end of the Napoleonic Wars. The men kept up a perpetual struggle to profit by the enhanced value of the services of such of them as escaped impressment. One learns with satisfaction that they were frequently aided by the enlightened self-interest of shipowners, who would pay high wages to attract the men they needed to sail their ships when freights had run up to fancy figures.

Of course it would happen that the self-interest of one owner would lead him to bribe men to desert from the ship of another, and, in fact, this practice, which I do not undertake to excuse, led to the passing of the Act entitled : " An Act for preventing the Desertion of Seamen from British Merchant Ships trading to His Majesty's Colonies and Plantations in the West Indies." It was passed in the thirty-seventh year of the reign of King George III., and its purpose is sufficiently stated in the Preamble :

" Whereas Seamen and Mariners, after entering into Articles to serve on board British merchant ships, during the voyages from Great Britain to His Majesty's Colonies and Plantations in the West Indies, and back to Great Britain, do frequently desert from such ships on their arrival at or in such Colonies and Plantations, on account of the exorbitant wages given by Masters and Commanders of other British merchant ships, by the Run or Gross, to Seamen and Mariners when in such Colonies or Plantations, to induce them to enter on board their ships, and whereas such seamen and mariners upon entering for articles for such voyages from Great Britain usually receive large sums of money in advance for the purpose of their outfit, and monthly allowances are frequently paid to their families towards their support and maintenance during the absence of such seamen and mariners, and whereas such desertions have been the means of depriving many merchant ships of a sufficient number of seamen and mariners to navigate them back to Great Britain, and thereby occasioned great losses to the merchants trading to such colonies and plantations. For the Remedy thereof," etc., etc. It could all have been said in a quarter of the words, and one wonders at the disinterested love of pleonasm which made it impossible for the persons who drafted the Act to name " seaman " without adding " mariner," or say " support " without going on to " maintenance," or think of " colony " without automatically putting down " plantation." But the mere profusion of the language serves to make us realize the copious anger of the shipowner or skipper who was deprived of his crew by the unscrupulous bidding of a rival for his seamen.

This tendency of the sailor to desert is by no means one

of the good features of the type. It indicates a certain moral laxity which is not in itself praiseworthy. But it had some excuses. In the first place, stability was not fairly to be expected from men who were houseless, and invited by the very conditions of their trade to be restless. It was calculated that the sailor was out of employment for a third of every year. During that period he must make shift as he could. He might help to take in the harvest when the season suited. He might get a job in the private dockyards as a rigger, and then he might earn on piecework ten shillings a day. The State yards he would avoid. In peace they afforded no opening, and in war they would have been traps where the press could find him. In England, too, it was the vicious rule of the yards to hold back part of the pay as a guarantee that the men would remain. The sailor liked to be paid quickly—as other men do. And then it was too much the custom of shipowners and merchant Captains who had no more foresight than the sailor, to encourage him or even drive him by worry and ill-usage to desert, when the ship was lying for weeks, or perhaps months, in some colonial or foreign port waiting for her cargo. It is obvious that this practice did not tend to give the sailors a strong sense of the iniquity of desertion. And common it was, and so remained. Then men who were liable to be taken out of a ship by an officer with a press warrant in war must have felt the uncertainty of their position. It may be, though the truth of the opinion is by no means self-evident, that the sea life would have rendered the sailor a wanderer and reckless. What is certain is that the conditions on which he was employed had a most undeniable tendency to strengthen whatever influence of that nature came from the sea. It is not at all wonderful if he came to rely on living by a succession of odd jobs, or, as Dugald Dalgetty would have said, " caduacs " (flukes of luck). He would quite naturally be prepared to leave his ship when a big wage was to be obtained elsewhere, because it was a piece of luck, because he knew that the skipper might worry him into desertion if anything was to be gained by cutting off his wages, and he would not be troubled by a thought of the advance he had received, and had, perhaps, not quite worked out. The advance had often gone into the pocket of the crimping lodging-house keeper who preyed on his weakness, and had carried him on board drunk—if not " hocussed."

The inclination he had that way was not likely to be counteracted by the Act of George III. It simply said that he was to lose the wages due to him—which he knew he had lost already, and it forbade the ship's Captain to pay more than double wages when he hired a man in the West Indies. Double wages were quite temptation enough, and " assizes of labourers " are waste paper when the employer must have the services of the man, and the man will have the money. No doubt it did happen, and not seldom, that a sailor, who had lived with an honest lodging-house keeper, shipped at Liverpool or elsewhere freely, took his advance, completed his kit, left his ship in the West Indies, and in debt to her, and came home at double wages, or for a lump sum the " run ' or " gross "—that is to say, an amount arranged between them for the voyage, whatever its length might be. In war-time, when the navy was seizing every man it could lay hands on, and if fever was busy, a laden ship ready to return was very likely to be undermanned, and prepared to pay high. Then he had money in hand if he escaped the press waiting for him at the other end. Considering how the sailor was treated, I am glad to have reason to believe that he did meet these occasional " bonanzas." It would be inaccurate and unjust to say that nothing was done to protect the sailor. Very creditable laws were passed to secure him a contract and the due payment of his wages.* But nothing was done to make the conditions of his life more stable, or to protect him from sharks on shore. And when war broke out he was hunted pitilessly. The British sailor had to find himself swept into the navy, where wages never rose above thirty shillings a month, and that only towards the end of the Napoleonic Wars, where he was paid at the end of the commission, or up to within six calendar months (not sea months of twenty-eight days), when his ship came home to a port at which there was a

* An Act was passed in the reign of George II. in 1747, establishing a fund for the benefit of seamen injured in the Merchant Service.

commissioner authorized to pay wages. In the meantime the suspension of the Manning Clauses of the Navigation Acts had opened the merchant navy with its " exorbitant wages,' month, run, or gross, to the foreigner. When the merchants and shipowners of Hull complained, with patriotic indignation, that the " Licences " were allowing swarms of foreigners to learn their business in our school, they were canting. Our merchant ships had been full of foreigners from the beginning of the war, and in all our wars. If the rivalry of foreigners was dangerous, and if our training made them more dangerous, we gave it with both hands, and we did it because we needs must, because it was matter of life and death to Great Britain that its trade should go on ; because we had not men enough for both our navy and our merchant ships.

Then it followed, as the night the day, that war subjected the merchant sailor to the risk of capture by the enemy, and the danger was very serious. It hung over the British seaman, though the navy of his country was generally predominant. It menaced the merchant sailor more than the man-of-war's-man. History takes little notice of the fate of obscure men, and there is a difficulty in following the fortunes of individuals. But family traditions linger on, growing more vague till they perish. I have heard the tantalizing story of one merchant Captain who had been taken prisoner by the French in the Napoleonic War. For five years he remained a prisoner, and went through adventures. One night he startled his family, who did not know whether he was alive or dead, by knocking at his own door after midnight. He had escaped, and had tramped home. Through all his fortunes he had preserved one guinea as a last resource. It was concealed in the sole of a boot, and was piously preserved, after being honourably set in the bowl of a punch ladle. I would cheerfully sacrifice a good dozen accounts of gallant affairs in boats and frigate actions which tend to be the same thing told in nearly the same words, for a good narrative of his wanderings. No doubt he told them all, with pardonable embellishments, but he never wrote them down. We hear constantly that such and such a number of merchant vessels has been taken by war-ships or privateers, and the crews carried off as prisoners. But we can rarely follow the men, nor see what their captivity meant to their families.

Therefore we are grateful to Robert Stevenson, builder of the Bell Rock Lighthouse, and the admirable historian of his own achievement, when he tells the case of one of these families, which were assuredly numerous. A man who worked under him was drowned by accident. The engineer stops to record that his loss was the greater disaster to his mother, because his father had been for three years a prisoner of war in France. Stevenson praised the courageous spirit of the woman who allowed her one remaining son to take his brother's place. No doubt she was a woman of resolution, but she was also a woman of sense. In the employment of the Commissioners of Northern Lights, her son would at least be a "protected man." The press was worse than the dangers of work on the Inchcape Rock. Capture did not threaten the sea trader only in open and distant seas. It might and did happen to him on the coast of his own country, and that when the supremacy of his own navy was most assured. In 1810 Mr. Wilberforce, being for his health's sake at Brighton, was the pained and indignant witness of a proof of this fact, and he records it in a letter to Lord Muncaster. He actually saw two scrubby French privateers, mere open or half-decked boats, capture three English merchant ships, and carry them off. One was taken within a mile of the pier while running for the protection of the batteries.*

It is a truth to be realized by an easy experience that the largest navy, and the most numerous merchant shipping, become scattered into minute points on the surface of the sea. No piece of water outside actual harbours is more

* There is much matter in this episode. Brighton was then fortified. It had become, said Mr. Wilberforce, "an iron coast." Yet all the King's guns and all the King's gunners could not save those three poor coasters from being snapped up before the eyes of the fashionable visitors by two scrubby privateers—a pretty good example of the little value of fortifications on shore as a protection to that very vital part of England which is afloat. Marryat, in "Poor Jack," gives an account based on realities well known to Englishmen of the time, of the capture of a British merchant ship close to the mouth of the Thames.

frequented than the British Channel. Yet it is quite possible to cross it half a dozen times, coming and going between Dieppe and Newhaven, and to see not as much as a fishing boat. At the harbour mouth, or at such points as the *Royal Sovereign* Lightship, which the trade " picks up " as sea marks on the route, there is a perpetual coming and going. A few miles to either side the horizon is empty. It is as if ships were swallowed, and lost when once they have steered out into the sea. The trade route down the east side of South America carries an immense commerce. But you can make a voyage from Monte Video to Madeira, and from the time when the steamer turns up between Punta de Este and the Isla de Lobos, till she stops for coal at Funchal, you may not sight more than two or three vessels, and then only at Cape Frio when the coast turns in to Rio de Janeiro. When the sails of the British navy " covered the ocean," as a particularly pinchbeck piece of rhetoric has it, there were hundreds of thousands of square miles of sea on which they were never seen, where the British merchant ship was beyond protection, where the foreigner passed out of sight, and the privateer might prowl at little risk except that of barren solitude—and that not in the Pacific, but in the most frequented seas.

The solitary merchant ship was always in some danger, but she had far less to fear on the open ocean than as she neared port. For it was just at the approaches to ports that the commerce destroyer cruised. He had the best chance of meeting his prey there, and the shorter distance to carry his prize into port. The protecting ships were there also, no doubt, but if they were just under the horizon line on the clearest day they were too far off to give help, and the days on which there is a clear view to the horizon are the minority in many seas. Merchantmen did, it is true, go armed. It was even their universal custom when they were sailing on long voyages and were vessels of any considerable size—that is to say, of 200 to 500 tons. Until after the close of the seventeenth century the ship which sailed to the Eastern Seas knew that she must protect herself, and she was, in fact, a quasi-war-ship. So the ships of the East India Company remained to the end—that is to say, till the last of the Company's privileges, the monopoly of the China trade, was lost in 1834. This partly military character of theirs was recognized. When the obligation to sail in convoy was imposed on all merchant ships in the reign of George III. by the Acts passed during the Revolutionary War and renewed in 1803, special exemption was granted to the East India and Hudson Bay companies. But we need not make too much of this exemption, or of the value of the armaments even of these exceptionally strong vessels.

Convoy was a very familiar word to the merchants and sailors of the ages of insecurity on the sea and of the great naval wars. The term is not altogether free from ambiguity. Strictly speaking, the "convoy" was the armed ship which accompanied the merchant craft. They constituted the "trade." A naval officer was properly said "to give convoy to the trade." But for convenience, and for the avoiding of the use of many words, it became the custom to speak of the whole, composed of protecting man-of-war and protected merchantmen, as a "convoy." In that sense, and with this warning, we will use the term, and it must be understood that the presence of a war-ship was not indispensable to constitute a convoy. When the traders sailed together for mutual support and defence, they were going "in convoy." So when the East India Company's Commodore, Nathaniel Dance, was attacked by the French Admiral Linois at Pulo Aor, he was sailing in convoy. The heavy 1,400 tonners which were bringing tea and silks to Europe were accompanied by a swarm of the traders from port to port in the East—small craft incapable of defending themselves. Therefore he commanded a convoy in the full sense of the term, though no man-of-war was present. Still, these collections of merchant ships into associations for mutual defence—into what was known to the medieval Venetians as a "mudna" (a mutual)—were exceptional. The regular convoy was composed of traders and an armed guard, which might be privateers hired by the merchants or men-of-war told off to perform the duty.

The trade was carried in convoys from pure necessity and to escape worse. They were not only a protection, but an unavoidable evil—one, and perhaps not the least vexatious, of the evils of war. In certain circumstances they were not even a protection, but on the contrary an aggravation of danger. That the merchant ships must collect in the needful number at a given rendezvous was an evil. The vessels which were first ready might have to lie for weeks in some roadstead, paying wages and expending provisions till the laggards had come in. And this delay might be aggravated by the fact that the State, having many calls on its navy to meet, might not be able to tell off the protecting ships at once. During the American War of Independence heavy loss was inflicted on the British Baltic trade for these reasons. In 1781 the Baltic trade rendezvoused in the Firth of Forth. Two hundred ships collected in the spring. The war was then rising to its height. The British Government had to face the privateers of the insurgent Americans, which infested even the route of the linen trade between Belfast and Liverpool, and the navies of France, Spain, and Holland. The North Sea was swarming with privateers. Hard pressed as it was, the Admiralty could not spare ships for more than one convoy. Therefore the traders were compelled to wait until the whole of the Baltic trade had been collected, and could sail under the protection of the squadron commanded by Sir Hyde Parker. The Admiral came along the east coast of England, stopping off every port to collect the trade, and did not reach the Firth of Forth till June 10th. In the meantime the ships waiting for him there had consumed all their provisions, and were compelled to lay in fresh stores. Even after the whole trade of 500 sail had been collected, the convoy did not leave till the 27th of the month. And this was only an extreme example of a common case.

And if convoy delayed the whole trade, the necessity for keeping together imposed a restriction, often of a highly injurious kind, on the best appointed vessels. Since the whole must be kept together, it followed that the convoy was condemned to sail at the rate of speed (if speed can be predicated of vessels which went on the average at the rate of 3 miles an hour) of the slowest among them. A quick sailing ship (as quick sailing went in those days) lost the whole advantage of her superiority. She could neither obtain the advantage of being early in the market, nor make prompt arrangements to unload and reload. She was brought down to the level of the most lumbering tub. It is therefore easily to be understood that, though shipowners and merchants and merchant skippers were forced, by fear of capture by an enemy's war-ships and privateers, or by law, to sail in convoy, it was much the habit of those of them who could trust the sailing of their vessel, or who were of an adventurous disposition, to strike out for themselves when the great, unwieldy swarm of traders was approaching its destination. There was danger in the enterprise, because the enemy's commerce destroyers would naturally cruise as near as they well could to the ports of departure and the landfalls of their booty, since it was at these points that the traders were most easily found. But the owners protected themselves by insurance against loss by capture till the passing of the Acts for the Protection of Trade in the reign of George III. These Acts imposed fines on skippers whose ships wilfully left the convoy, and debarred the owners from recovering their insurances. But from the facts that it was found necessary to increase the fines from £200 and £300 to £1,000 and £1,500, and also to fine brokers who paid in spite of the law, this legislation does not appear to have been effective. The lesser fines were levied when the cargo was composed of private property, and the higher when they carried naval and military stores. If convoy had not been nearly as much a grievance as a protection, it would not have been shirked by owners who covered themselves by insurance, and by skippers because they were tempted by rewards.

The conditions in which convoy was given, taken, and carried out, or disregarded, can almost all be seen from one example. At the close of 1780 Sir Samuel Hood was appointed second in command to Sir George Rodney in the West Indies. He was to take out reinforcements, and it was a matter of course that he should take the trade with him. In the eighteenth century and in war-time—that is to say, in nearly half the years between 1700 and 1815—the British Admiral, whether outward or homeward bound, took the trade with him. In the lawless West Indies he might do it even in peace. Hood's charge included not only the traders, but three regiments which were to be carried in the West Indiamen. His convoy was to be formed at Spithead, and the vessels composing it were to be gathered from various ports. On November 1st only six out of twenty-eight he was to take under his charge were with him. On the 11th "a pretty large convoy" was in sight coming from the Downs. It included the ships which were to carry the troops. Hood, who was at St. Helens, prepared to put to sea at once with his war-ships. Their anchors had been buried so deep by a gale that they were not got up without great difficulty and breakage of tackle. To get the men-of-war out was one thing. To bring the merchant ships from behind the Motherbank was another. On the 17th they were still inside, and when the Admiral made the signal to unmoor the tide was running to leeward, and none of them could come. Then the weather fell calm and nobody could move. On the 19th Hood hears that other " very valuable West India ships now in the Downs " are waiting for a fair wind to join him, and he is asked to delay or to leave part of his men-of-war to protect them. He points out that he cannot bring out all the vessels now collected to St. Helens within twenty-four hours. The merchant captains will not come out from the Motherbank and anchor at St. Helens to be ready to start at any moment. They protest that they do not fail to come out of dirsespect to the Admiral's orders, but because they cannot renew their water at St. Helens. If they have to lie there they would use up their store, and they must start with a full supply. On the 29th the very valuable ships from the Downs have come in, and the wind is at last favourable for a start. But when the Admiral gives the order to unmoor, the ships inside the Motherbank cannot come because, though the wind is favourable, it is not strong enough to enable them to stem the tide. Finally Hood had to sail with the ships from the Downs, leaving three men-of-war " to hasten the trade out." More than a month had been spent in making a beginning of the voyage from St. Helens.

When the whole of Hood's " trade " was collected, it amounted to 118 sail of 31,471 tons, carrying 801 guns and 2,159 men, including, no doubt, the apprentices, of whom there would be, if all laws were obeyed, two for the first 100 tons and one for each 100 above the first. On December 11th, when Hood was well out in the Atlantic, in latitude 46° 14′ N. and longitude 27° 53′ W., he found means to send a letter reporting progress to the Admiralty. On December 10th " it blew as hard at south and south-south-west as ever I knew it," wrote the Admiral. " Happily the gale was of short duration. At daylight the men-of-war and convoy were much scattered, and one ship of the line was seen far to leeward, with only a foremast standing, which I bore down to and found it to be the *Monarca*." The crippled *Monarca* brought home the letter, for it was of no use to take a ship in her state to the West Indies. Though the gale had blown over, the sea was still so high that no boat could go to the *Monarca*, and Hood was not sure that he could send his letter by the crippled ship. Sent it was, and it told the Admiralty of the condition of the convoy. Hood had heard from Captain Hope of the *Crescent*, who joined him at sea, that a powerful force of the enemy—guessed to be twenty-six sail of war-ships with the trade in charge, one hundred vessels as far as could be counted—had been sighted west of Finisterre, and to all appearance bound for America. Sir Samuel, whose force, including the *Monarca*, was but ten sail, was not desirous of falling across a superior enemy. So he laid his plans to take a northerly course, though it would lengthen his voyage. When he had reached so far west as to feel safe, he proposed to push on with five sail of the line and join Rodney. Two men-of-war would be left to protect the slow trade.

It was fortunate for the convoy that the gale of the 10th was as brief as it was violent. If it had lasted for two or three days the whole convoy might have been scattered beyond hope of complete reunion. In that case a large part of it might have fallen into the hands of any hostile force which was also being blown about in the storm. If, again, an enemy had been within striking distance, it would have been well for the merchant ships that the whole of

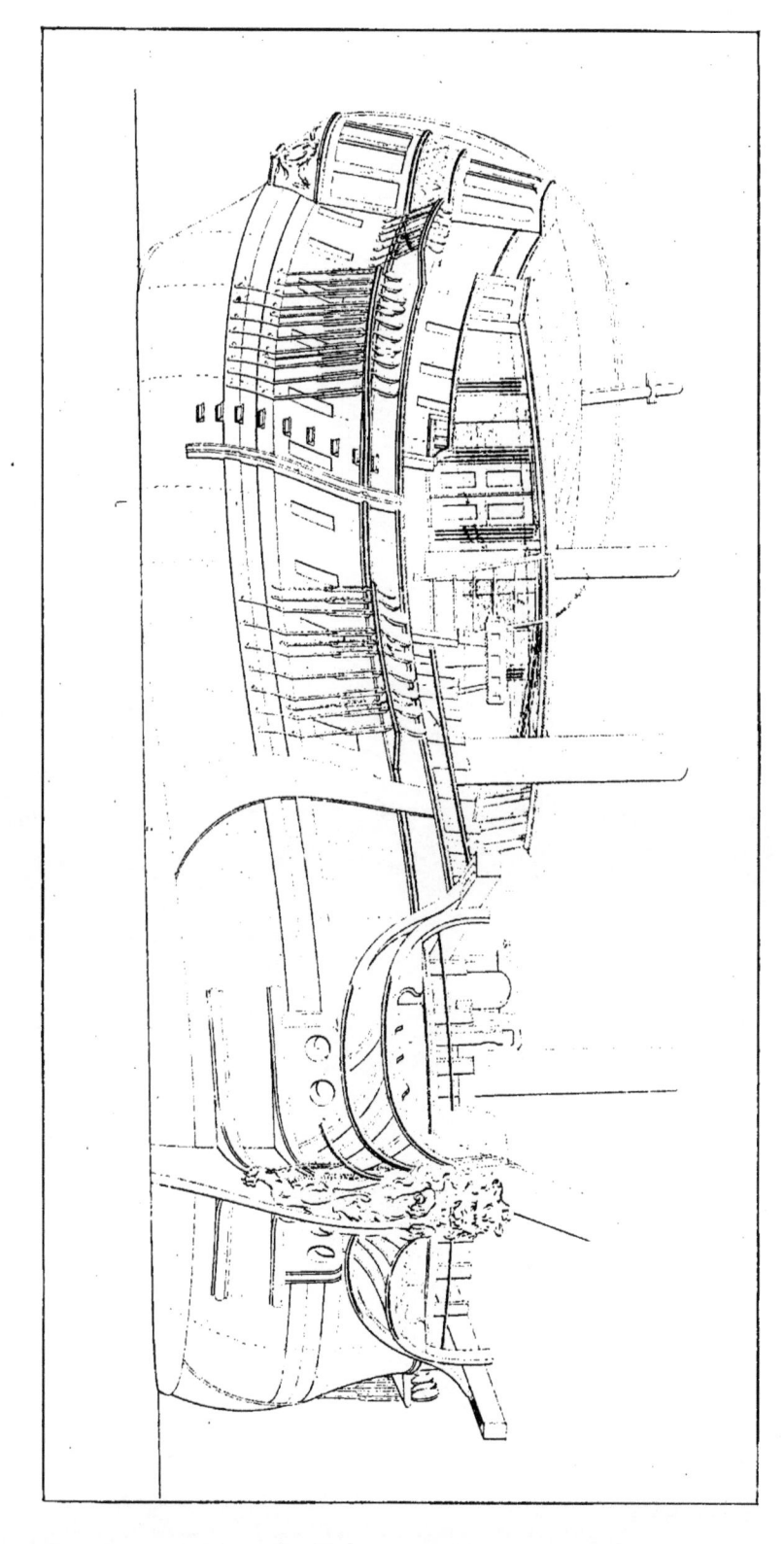

MERCHANT SHIP.
From Chapman's "Architectura Navalis Mercatoria."

To face page 352.

Sir Samuel's squadron was near. They might very well have been protected only by one line-of-battle ship, and she might have suffered the misfortune of the *Monarca*. " All her ironwork of the main channel gave way, and the mast went by the board. The mizzenmast and foretopmast soon followed."* In that helpless state she could have protected none of her charge from even a " scrubby " privateer. Such accidents did occasionally render convoy of no avail.

The end of Hood's convoy is illuminative.† The telling may be begun by Beatson, who in his " Naval and Military Memoirs " (vol. v., p. 160) writes thus : " When the Admiral drew near to the West Indies he missed in one night no less than twelve of his convoy. It was given out that they considered themselves as out of danger from the enemy, and had proceeded to the various British islands to which they were destined. But when the island of St. Eustatius was taken, Sir Samuel Hood there found his missing ships, busily employed in landing their cargoes to the agents of the British merchants. The masters, mates, and crews of

* These words, taken with Sir Samuel's previous statement that the " foremast " of the *Monarca* was standing when she was seen after the gale may excuse a note. It is only necessary to read Sir Samuel to see that the word " mast " is ambiguous. It is used by him, as by others, in two senses. Sometimes it means the whole structure made up of mast proper, topmast, and topgallantmast. Sometimes it is used for the mast proper—that is to say, the lowest of the three divisions of the total mast—the part which started from the foot, and ended at the top. Sir Samuel uses it in both senses. He means the mast proper when he speaks of the foremast of the *Monarca* as standing after her topmast—which, of course, carried the topgallantmast with it—had gone over her side, or had come down in ruin on the deck. He means the whole structure when he says that the mizzen was dragged down in the wreck of the main. He also means the whole structure when he says that the giving way of the ironwork of the main channel caused the corresponding mast —*i.e.*, the main, which was supported by the shrouds made fast at the channel—to go by the board. The total mast "went by the board " when the mast proper broke below the top and above the deck. It is easy enough to account for the rise of the ambiguity. The earliest form of mast was a single spar ending in a top. The addition of topmast and topgallantmast came late in the development of the ship's rigging. When the simple single spar grew into the elaborate combination of three—the lowest fixed, the middle, and the highest movable—language proved unequal to the task of begetting a new term for the whole.

† Its history, up to the writing of the letter quoted in the text, is told in the " Letters written by Sir Samuel Hood in 1781-2-3," printed for the Navy Record Society, 1895.

these ships were immediately pressed, and put on board the ships-of-war." Here is a passage no less instructive than misleading. We see the merchant ships taking advantage of the dark to slip away and push for port. It was not a difficult thing to do. The men-of-war would be to windward of the convoy. An enemy would come down before the wind, and would not beat up against it, a slow process when his object was to slip into a convoy and drag one of the ships out. When darkness had fallen, the skipper who meant to be off would extinguish all lights and run to leeward. In the easterly trade-wind, which was bringing the convoy along, his easy game would be to go off on the wind to north or south of the route to the west. His course would make a good wide angle with that of the convoy, and by daylight he would be out of sight. It is true that he might be running into sight of a French or American cruiser or privateer. But his owner was insured against loss by capture, and as for himself and his men, they took the risk as they did others. But there is more in Beatson's words than an example of a common practice.

The patriotic man wishes us to understand that these masters, mates, and crews who ran for St. Eustatius were basely aiding the enemy. Let us look at the facts, just to see what the iniquity amounted to. St. Eustatius belonged to the Dutch, who were not at war with Great Britain until November, 1780. In normal times trade was not permitted between the British West Indies and a foreign State, except that tolerated trade with the Spaniards which has already been mentioned. But 1780 was not a normal year. The revolt of the American plantations had threatened to deprive the British West Indies of the supplies of Indian corn and bacon, which formed the regular rations of the blacks. If the British Government had enforced the prohibition of all trade with rebels to the full, it would have done so at the cost of the total ruin of the Sugar Islands.

The West India interest, at that time the strongest of all, was more than strong enough to avert such a disaster. The British Government did what it had always done, and was to do again on a larger scale. It licensed a trade through St. Eustatius in order that Indian corn and bacon might be obtained in exchange for British manufactures, so that the blacks might be kept alive to grow sugar for the West Indian planters, who spent their profits on other British produce, and who paid freight to British ships. There are few finer proofs of how much pinchbeck and loud assertive make-believe there is in the tall talk about the destruction of an enemy's commerce—when that commerce is indispensable to the self-styled destroyer. Of course St. Eustatius became a depot of a trade which was unlawful in so far as it contravened the general prohibition to carry on commerce with enemies and rebels, but was perfectly legal in so far as it was licensed by the British Government. The merchants who fitted out the vessels found at St. Eustatius when it was taken by Rodney in February, 1781, had so far done nothing unlawful, though they stretched a point if they sent their ships to the island after the declaration of war.

Yet it was not so easy to say how and at what point they overstepped the line, as Rodney was to discover to his cost. When he took the island he laid hands on all he found there as prize, whereby he brought down upon himself lawsuits and orders to pay damages to merchants who were trading with licence of the British Government. There is an end to the end. The seizure of St. Eustatius did stop the "treasonable" intercourse with the rebels for a time, and the consequence of the stoppage was a lesson. Fifteen thousand negroes died of starvation in our islands, and the planters were rendered so savage that they imbibed much "rebel" sentiment, and in some cases, notably at St. Kitts, positively refused to take any part in defending their homes against the French on behalf of a Government which had distressed all and ruined some of them.*

Cases in which a storm, such as that which fell on Hood's convoy on December 10th, 1780, proved disastrous are not

* Prize-money is an interesting theme. Given for the encouragement of seamen, it has commonly served to encourage something else—namely, neglect of duty, the subordination of the service to the lucre of gain, and ignominious squabbles between rival claimants to plunder. Some encouragement it did give, no doubt, to honest zeal, but, on the whole, it has tended to promote a spirit which, to me at least, appears utterly incompatible with the character of the "noble cavaliers who follow the honourable profession of arms."

lacking. There is, for instance, the story of the "small fleet" of five Indiamen which sailed from the Sand-heads of the Hooghly on May 2nd, 1809. The story makes it necessary to name three vessels only—the *Streatham*, Captain John Dale; the *Europa*, Captain William Gelston; and the *Lord Keith*, Captain Peter Campbell. This trade was under the protection of the ship-rigged sloop *Victor* of 18 guns, Captain Edward Stopford. The company's ships were not bound to take convoy, but a series of losses in the Bay of Bengal had brought the authorities in India to see the necessity for seeking the protection of a war-ship. The fate of the three named will serve to show what were the limits set to the force of the best-appointed armed merchant ships when left to themselves. The *Streatham* and the *Europa* were vessels of 800 tons register. Each was armed with twenty medium guns—pieces not so long and heavy as the real gun, nor so light as the carronade, and had also ten of these. The *Lord Keith* was of 600 tons, and was armed with ten or twelve guns. The constitution of the crews shows how the ships of the company were manned. The *Streatham* complement was 137 strong, of whom 60 were British and other European seamen, and the balance were Lascars. In the *Europa* there were 56 Lascars, and 72 British and other European seamen. How the crew of the *Lord Keith* was divided is not stated, but some of her 30 or 40 were assuredly Lascars.*

On the 24th the *Victor* lost sight of her charge in dark and squally weather, and on the 30th two of the Indiamen composing the small fleet of five parted company in a gale. On the 31st the *Streatham*, *Europa*, and *Lord Keith* were left together. They were then between Ceylon and the Nicobar Islands. On that day they being on the starboard, tack heading to south-south-east in a south-westerly wind, were aware of a big ship steering towards them from the south. She was the *Caroline* of 46 guns, commanded by the Lieutenant de Vaisseau Feretier. The *Caroline* was one of the French frigates which till nearly the end of the war eluded the blockade of their ports in Europe, and carried a harassing commerce-destroying activity into the

* See James's "Naval History," vol. v., pp. 92 *et seq.*, ed. 1837.

Eastern Seas. She had just been cruising off the Sandheads, without notable success, and had come to the Nicobar Islands to renew her supply of water. When a ship had no need of coal, she was very independent of a basis of operations. He heard of the convoy at the islands from an American who had sailed for a time with it.

When the sails of the *Caroline* were seen, the Indiamen had hopes that she was their friend the *Victor*. As she drew nearer this hope was utterly destroyed. It was plain that, whatever she was, she was not the British ship-sloop. Captain Dale, as the company's senior officer, hoisted the private signal, and when he obtained no answer saw that the new-comer was beyond peradventure an enemy. There was no equality between the Indiamen and the French frigate. She could have blown the *Lord Keith* out of the water. The betwixt and between medium guns of the *Europa* and *Streatham* were no match for the long guns on the *Caroline's* maindeck. Their 18-pound carronades were far inferior to her 36-pounders, and she was full of men. Even if the *Streatham* and *Europa* had engaged the Frenchman together, which they could only have done if he mishandled his ship, still they would have been outmatched. Though they must have known as much, the company's Captains formed a line, the *Lord Keith* leading, the *Streatham* in the middle, the *Europa* closing the rear, and prepared to offer as stout a resistance as they could. M. Feretier made no mistakes. He swept down before the wind, hauled up on the weather quarter of the *Europa*, ran up the Tricolour, and opened fire. In half and hour the *Europa's* rigging was cut to pieces, her hull badly pounded, and her carronades dismounted. The *Streatham* shortened sail to get into position to help her friend. There was nothing else Captain Dale could do. If he had turned, it must have been by tacking or wearing. As the Frenchman had engaged the *Europa* on the weather side, if Captain Dale wore his ship he must have passed to leeward of his friend, and could not have fired through him. If he tacked, nothing compelled Feretier to wait till the English ships were one on one side and the other on the other of him. He could always have shot ahead, making full use of the superior speed of his fine frigate over the heavily laden *Europa*, could have crossed her bows, raking her as he passed, and could then have come round on her lee side. That, in fact, was what in the end he did. When he saw that the *Europa* was crippled, he shot ahead, passed between her and the *Streatham*, giving her a broadside as he went, and then engaged Captain Dale on the lceside. The *Streatham* made as long and as good a fight as she could, considering that neither threats nor persuasion could keep the Portuguese, who formed a large part of her European sailors, or the Lascars, to the guns. Then, after another half-hour or so of fire, the *Streatham* surrendered. Feretier now proceeded to make an end of the *Europa*. Captain Gelston renewed the fight. The *Lord Keith* made an attempt to support her companions, but was not of sufficient force to make an impression on the *Caroline*. At last the *Europa* tried to escape before the wind, but was overtaken and compelled to surrender. The *Lord Keith* got away. Feretier, one is pleased to record, behaved like a gentleman and a good fellow to his prisoners.

It would not have been difficult to tell cases in which the company's ships did beat off enemies. There was the leading case of Commodore Dance's encounter with Linois near Pulo Aor in 1804. Now, that Dance and his brother Captains showed themselves both shrewd and valiant men is true. But it is also true that they won because Linois let them win. He was frightened because two of the biggest of the Indiamen, which were painted to look like two-decked ships, hoisted the man-of-war pennant. When they boldly tacked in succession, and bore down to engage him, he would not stay to put his unscientific hypothesis to the test. The company's Captains could not know that the Frenchman, with his "74" the *Marengo* and his fine frigates, would make himself a laughing-stock. They deserved all the praise and the reward they received. But because Linois ran from a shoal of armed traders, whom he ought to have taken one after the other, it would be sheer folly, and even very mischievous folly, to suppose that a merchant ship with guns can ever be a match for a real fighting ship. When an Indiaman was attacked by a resolute opponent, whether she was a heavy privateer like the *Confiance* of Robert Surcouf, who took the *Kent*, or the frigate *Piémontaise*, which took the *Warren Hastings*, the victory rested with the vessel built, armed, and manned for war. Captain Rivington of the *Kent* fought his ship with admirable courage till he was killed. Captain Larkins of the *Warren Hastings* made all the defence that judgment and courage could make. All was done that man could do, and all was done in vain.

The misfortunes of the *Streatham* and the *Europa* show that to sail under protection of a man-of-war did not necessarily imply that the voyage would be continued with her. But there was worse among the things which might happen to a convoy. One of them was that the mere fact of being in convoy was the direct cause of total capture. And that this could happen was proved in August, 1780, when Moutray's convoy fell bodily into the hands of a combined French and Spanish fleet in latitude 36° 40′ N. and longitude 15° W. The convoy consisted of fifty-three East and West Indiamen and transports carrying troops. It sailed from Spithead on July 9th, under protection of the *Ramillies*, 74, Captain Moutray, and two frigates. Captain Moutray was to see the whole well clear of European waters, to the point where the East and West Indiamen would separate, in the latitude of the Canary Islands. He was escorted for 340 miles of his way by the Channel or Grand Fleet. Now, the formation of such a convoy as this was not a thing to be done quickly, nor in a corner. Newspapers were eager to find out what was going on. And of what use is it to a newspaper to know if its readers do not know it knows? There was no lack of smugglers and licensed traders ready to turn an honest penny by importing welcome information. Somehow or other, news of the sailing of the convoy and its route reached the Spanish Prime Minister in time to allow him to send the Spanish and French ships then at Cadiz under the command of Don Luis de Côrdoba and the Chef d'Escadre Bausset, to intercept it. On the evening of August 8th, when the convoy was almost on a level with the Straits of Gibraltar, the topsails of the allies were seen on the horizon to the south. It did not at first occur to Captain Moutray that the sails belonged to an enemy. But after dark the number of lights seen ahead warned him that there was something serious there. He ordered his convoy by gunfire to lie to, with their heads to the west, and then, again by gunfire, to continue on their course. The order was ambiguous, for it might either mean that they were to continue in the direction in which their heads were then pointing, or that they were to resume the course of their voyage. Moutray meant the first; the skippers understood the second. So; while he went west, they went south, and at daybreak next morning they all sailed right into the arms of the Spaniards and French. They were all carried into Cadiz, to the huge delight of the Gaditans, who had never been at such a feast, and the proportionate wrath of the English, who were not accustomed to have such tricks played on them by the Spaniards. On this occasion the fact that they were all in one body, with a weak guard, was the cause of their total capture. If the merchant-ships and transports had been allowed to scatter after leaving Admiral Geary, some of them—in all probability the majority—would have passed out of sight of the allies.

When a convoy was not powerfully protected, and was strongly attacked, then it was nothing more than a way of putting a whole flock of prizes into the enemy's hands at once. That, perhaps, is one of the reasons why shipowners had a hankering for sending their ships alone, and why it was necessary to pass Acts of Parliament to force them to take convoy. A strong protecting force, even when assailed by superior numbers, might fight long enough to enable the merchant ships to escape. But then they went off in a scattered condition, and became liable to capture in detail. So when, in 1747, M. Desherbiers de l'Etanduère made a gallant fight in the Bay of Biscay against Hawke's superior numbers, he gave the trade he was protecting time to escape. But his ships were bound to the West Indies, and most of them were captured as they neared their destination. Not much worse could have happened to them if they had sailed, each ship for herself, from different ports at different times by varying routes, without beat of drum. One weakness of convoy was that it could not be managed without beat of drum. A rendezvous must be appointed, and be known to thousands. Spies, smugglers, licensed traders, brought the news. The British Government was warned of the sailing of L'Etanduère's convoy in ample time to send Hawke to intercept it, just as the Spanish Premier, Floridablanca, was told of the coming of Moutray's. There is no advantage but

SHARE IN A PRIVATEER.

has its countering drawback, and the drawback to convoy was that it could not help being the "secret of Punch" and of the housetops.

War brought one opening to the merchant seaman. He might go into a privateer, and beyond all question he was tempted so to do, and he frequently yielded to the temptation. But what did privateering do for him? The answer which first presents itself is that it gave him a chance of winning booty in a life of exhilarating adventure. There is an air of verisimilitude about this which secures general acceptance, but, like many other easy answers, it has the misfortune not to be accurate. When Lord Clarendon, in the course of his years of exile, passed through the noted corsair town Dunkerque, he was assured by local authorities that no owner of privateers was ever known to die rich. And the experience of Dunkerque was confirmed by the no less famous corsair town St. Malo, and by the American privateer owners of the war of 1812. Privateering was essentially a gambling business, in which, by its very nature, the occasional stroke of luck was more than counterbalanced by recurring runs of bad fortune. Few, indeed, were the owners and captains of privateers who were content to stop when they had made a good haul. Some did deliberately, and some were saved from the risk that they would waste their gains in unsuccessful attempts to make other and better hauls by the return of peace. Woodes Rogers, Dr. Dover, and Stephen Courtney, kept the £70,000 apiece they made by the voyage of the *Duke* and *Duchess*. But that is not all the story. When Shelvocke made his voyage a few years later, his crew, with or without his instigation, mutinied, and declared that they would revise the articles of their agreement, for they would not be treated as Woodes Rogers's men had been. Now the *Duke* and *Duchess* had been taken into Amsterdam, and the spoil had been divided there. The belief of the sailors was that they had been carried to a foreign port in order that they might be the more safely and effectually cheated.*

* Privateering is, properly speaking, a part of the history of war, and does not belong to my subject directly. Books on what may be defined as the banner-waving and gaseous aspects of it are numerous. The reader who may wish for a more serious knowledge of the thing may be advised to consult " An Essay on Privateers," etc., by M. de Martens, in French, but translated into English by T. Hartwell Horne, 1801 ; the statutes at large for a long series of Acts passed between the reigns of Queen Anne and George III. ; and the pamphlet which I quote in the text, " A Full and Faithful Account of the Life of James Bather, late Boatswain of the *Nightingale* Brig, Thomas Benson, Esq., Owner." The main purpose of the boatswain's story is to give an account of a common crime—an attempt to defraud the insurers by the wilful loss of a ship. The offence was common, and all the more common because the owners ran comparatively little risk. The offence was committed within

The sober fact is that privateering was always a half-criminal and disorderly business. The crews were out " on the plundering account," and were not much more disposed to fight than were the pirates. The reader whose leisure and curiosity may combine to take him to the Record Office may find significant examples of the privateer at work in the Minutes of Court Martial. The years of the War of the Austrian Succession, when privateering was exceptionally active, will provide him with stories of crews who declared that on no condition would they fight, who locked the Captain in his cabin, drank his liquor, and finally ran the ship close to the shore and deserted her in the boats. Mr. James Bather, late boatswain of the *Nightingale* brig, will give him a privateersman's reminiscences. Here is one of them. After telling how the *Benson* galley, in which he was then serving under Captain Richard Vernon, allowed a big Dutch snow to pass her unquestioned, he goes on :

"The same evening that we parted with the snow, as we were cruising in the Bay, we saw a large Spanish ship. It being then dark, we kept close under her stern all that night, and in the morning we shot just abreast of her, but not near enough to hail her. We had not lain long in that situation, before she fired three small shot at us, her Spanish colours flying at the same time. We returned the compliment with our English colours flying. It was my opinion then, and is so still, that on our firing the Spaniard struck to us ; for at the time when our Captain ordered our helm a-weather, they hauled down their ensign, doubtless in order to strike. But Captain Vernon averred that was only a decoy to fetch us within reach of their great guns. But though some of our people pretended to be highly incensed because our Captain would not fight the Spaniard,

---

the jurisdiction of the Lord High Admiral, and was capital ; but the owners, who played their part in their offices, and not within the jurisdiction of the Admiral, by plotting and instigating, were safe from the rope. For a case in point, see " State Trials " (Howell), vol. xxviii. : " The Trial of William Codling, Mariner ; John Reid, Mariner ; William Macfarlane, Merchant ; and Geo. Easterby, Merchant ; for wilfully and feloniously destroying and casting away the Brig *Adventure* on the High Seas, within the Jurisdiction of the Admiralty of England, A.D. 1802." Codling, an incredibly stupid rogue, was hanged for scuttling the brig off Brighton ; Messrs. Macfarlane and Easterby, who were conclusively shown to have laid the whole plot in the office in the City of London, escaped.

and so give us an opportunity of making our fortunes at once, yet I am certain that had the Captain been willing to engage, the ship's company would have failed him, for the time the enemy fired I believe there were between twenty and thirty of our people upon deck, who instantly fell flat down for fear the shot should take the buttons from their shoulders. Among these lion-hearted souls it must be acknowledged that I was one, for when I saw the rest fall I thrust my head against the end of the windlass (near which I just then happened to stand), believing the shot would not pass through it to hurt me. However, there was a great squabble among us when all was over, each laying the blame one on the other that we did not fight."

The *Benson* galley was a "regular built privateer,' to use the contemptuous phrase of the naval officers for a disorderly, ill-handled ship. Bather's account of her subsequent fortunes throws a very unpleasing light on the ways and morality of the privateer world. The *Benson* galley took a number of French "bankers"—*i.e.*, fishing vessels on the banks of Newfoundland. She transferred the dried fish of some of them to her own hold. While her crew were at this work they took off the red and blue "favours"—*i.e.*, bunches of ribbons—they wore in their hats to show that they were men-of-war, though not regular navy seamen, and put small fishes there instead. The prizes were brought home. On a later cruise the *Benson* galley was hired to give convoy to some merchant vessels. They were all taken by French warships. Bather asserts that they were deliberately steered to where it was known they would be captured. The purpose was to defraud the insurers. The owners had insured them heavily against war risks. We will finish with Mr. Bather by noting that, having shipped with one Prance for a voyage to South Carolina, he discovered that his skipper was an insufferable bully. To escape his violence Bather volunteered into H.M.S. *Aldborough*. All the tyrant Captains were not naval officers, and the navy could be a refuge for the ill-used merchant seaman.

There were no doubt privateers which differed widely from the *Benson* galley, but on the whole the life was a bad one, and its influence was degrading. The unfailing tendency of the privateer to become a pirate was notorious.

Privateering encouraged that brutal side of the seafaring life to which the Provost of Edinburgh referred when he was called in question for not making a better defence of the town against the Jacobites in 1745. When Mr. Archibald Stewart, the Provost, was asked by citizens eager to display zeal to bring sailors from Leith to help in a defence, he said that none should be brought into Edinburgh while he was Provost. He was asked why, and retorted " with some heat ": " My reason, sir, is plain. If they should be admitted here, it would be, ' Damn your blood, Jack! fire away, and be damned!' and so they would fire upon and murder the inhabitants ; and it is my duty to protect the lives of the inhabitants as well as to defend the town against the rebels." Mr. Archibald Stewart was a nervous man, and perhaps his heart was not in the work of resisting Prince Charlie and his loyal Highlanders. But his excuse would have been devoid of plausibility if the sailor had not suffered from a reputation for violence.

CHAPTER XIV

CONCLUSION

WHEN Napoleon sailed for St. Helena in 1815 an old world was ending on the sea, and the new was beginning. Three years, or thereabouts, are still lacking to make up the century since Sir George Cockburn sailed with his prisoner. But in that time the life of the seafaring man has changed more than it had done in all the centuries since the ships of Hatshepsitu made their voyage to the Land of Punt. The instruments he handles, from his vessel to his compass, have altered from truck to keel, from figure-head to taffrail. A new power drives the ship, requiring new arts and making a new life. The old never gives way to the new on one day and altogether. There are still vessels on the sea which would not have surprised the seamen who brought the corn tribute to Rome. But they are survivals and are dying. They remain to show what the sea life once was for all seafaring men, and that is all. The large sailing ships which survive, and will in all probability not disappear wholly till the wind is more costly than coal, are in reality a new thing. They have one quality, and one only, in common with the sailing ship of old—that they depend on the wind. But they are made not of wood, but of metal; their rigging is in part of metal, their sails are different in arrangement, their very masts, which were laboriously composed of pieces of wood, are hollow cylinders of iron which can be used to ventilate the between decks. And these changes in the mere machinery have come along with a complete alteration of life.

The new was already at work before 1815, and it came from whence it might have been expected to come—from the United States. Sea commerce had at all times been based, in so far as men could attain their wish, on monopoly. It had moved amid regulation which was also restriction. You could not sail to this or that sea without paying toll to this or that company and submitting to its rules—at least after a sort. There were seas to which you could not go at all save as member or servant of a corporation, or at the best after obtaining its leave. The British sailor who went to the East, and who did not go in the pay of the company, had to apply and pay for its leave to follow his trade as a " free mariner." And what England did was done by others. The spirit of commerce chafed in the bonds. It struggled to reach a compromise, if it could not attain to freedom. Sometimes it defied the law. It could never quite shake off the check. Until the great settlement of the world by the Treaty of Paris in 1815 sea trade had always gone on under shadow of war, actual, or impending, or probable. Therefore safety was a first consideration, and if the private trader was ready to take risks, the anxious State was always at hand, intent on averting diminution of the national wealth, to force him to go in the flock called a "convoy."

Monopoly and convoy worked together to favour stupidity, routine, and timidity. When the shipowner and merchant had no foreign rival to fear, why should they spend energy and ingenuity, to say nothing of hazarding their capital, in improving the speed of their ships and in seeking for shorter and better routes ? When all went slow, speed was of but subordinate value. Large profits could be made without its help. When the old beaten routes would do, why risk the perils of a new passage ? It was not until the middle of the eighteenth century that the Captains of the East India Company began to try whether they could not find out a better route from India to China than the way first discovered by the Portuguese. And then the innovators were frowned on. Captain Wilson might be praised for having discovered Pitt's Passage, between Xulla and Beroe in the Banda Sea, in 1759, whereby he " pointed out to admiring nations a new track to China founded on philosophic principles." But read the melancholy story of

Mr. Alexander Dalrymple, and admire the angry anguish with which men resent every demonstration that they can do better than follow the old familiar way, the method that would just do. So long as monopoly lasted the shipbuilder was asked for a ship which would carry a great deal. She need not be well-proportioned, but she must have a roomy hold. The ship Captain was not asked to go rapidly but to go safe, by the beaten track, reducing sail or lying to at night. And whatever influence monopoly had, convoy intensified. It had gone all through the eighteenth century, and it had been imposed for over twenty years together at the end. Now, convoy was dominated by the slowest ships. Of what use was it to build for speed, to be alert, to seek for better ways, when the law passed by Governments naturally, even laudably, intent on preventing loss, stood over you, fine and imprisonment in hand, to make you go slow, to force you to follow the known road? Monopoly may have helped sea commerce to grow, convoy certainly helped it to exist, but the two together did more than tolerate routine and stupidity. There were the old ways, and men knew them. They would have remained in them if some stimulus had not been administered from without.

> " Des Menschens thätigkeit kann allzuleicht erschlaffen
>   Er liebt sich bald die unbedingte Ruh :
>   Drum geb 'ich gern ihm den Gesellen zu,
>   Der reizt und wirkt, und muss, als Teufel schaffen."

It was the function of the " Yankee " sailors to play the part of the fiend who stung, worked, and shaped on the sound and vigorous body of the Old World sea commerce when it was in danger of becoming more than a little torpid. They came to the work with every motive for exerting themselves and a fine training. The United States had the natural human liking for a monopoly. They have shown it by keeping their coasting trade to themselves, and by interpreting coasting trade so freely as to make it include a voyage round the Horn between the Atlantic and Pacific coasts of the Union. But then they had no oversea dominion to keep as a preserve on the Spanish, Dutch, English, and French model. Therefore it was their interest to trade with all the world. The Navigation Laws had always fretted New England, and had been constantly evaded. Generations of practice had developed in the Yankee seamen a faculty for astute evasion, a sense of the importance of time, a habit of calculating chances, and making speed serve as a concealment. "For when things are once come to the execution, there is no secrecy comparable to celerity. Like the motion of a bullet in the air, which flieth so swift as it outruns the eye." It was not at all necessary that Yankee ships should be wholly manned by Yankee sailors. They were to their own merchant navy what the men bred to the sea were to the man-of-war, the dominative element, the skilled leaders. They saw no need to be jealous of the foreigner. On the contrary they invited recruits, who came from all nations. Naturally enough they came in the largest numbers from the Mother-Country.

The effect which the existence of another English-speaking country had on the British sailor does not require demonstration. The mere fact that another English-speaking country where their labour was in demand had come into existence altered the world for them. There is no need to go once more into the angry and confused dispute of the years before 1812. The population of America was being recruited by immigration on a large scale, and the seafaring element with the rest. The case quoted by Lord Ashburton may have been exceptional, or the American skipper may have exaggerated for effect. He says that a certain American ship was searched by a British naval officer with a press warrant, who came to take her British-born seamen out. The doctrine that a man could renounce his allegiance was not accepted by the British or any other European Government. The officer found that all the members of the crew were protected by certificates declaring them to be American born, except one. Him he took. When he had left the side the American skipper said with a laugh that the officer had taken a man who had never been out of Philadelphia in his life, and who had not imagined that he needed a certificate. All the others were British born and for that very reason had provided themselves with the document. That naturalization and certificates of American birth were readily granted is undeniable, even if it is not strictly true that a friendly and unscrupulous old dame in New York gained an easy subsistence by swearing that candidates for a certificate were to her knowledge American born, at the rate of a dollar per perjury. These stories are told with embellishments, but not without foundation. The existence of a refuge for seamen across the Atlantic was one of the reasons which convinced the British Government that it must renounce the use of impressment. The seamen could elude it by emigration, and they could not be reclaimed except at the risk of a renewal of the war of 1812. and that, too, in all probability when it would be a far greater misfortune, a far greater strain, than it was when it did occur.

The history of the successive steps by which the Navigation Laws of Great Britain, which dominated the commerce of Europe, were broken down is a long one—not because it lasted for many years. The edifice was fairly beaten to ruins in about a generation. But the work was accompanied by an immense amount of diplomacy and legislation, to say nothing of makeshift and make-believe. The essence of the dispute was that England had aimed at forcing all the trade of the world to reach Europe through her, that other peoples grew impatient of this pretension, and that the United States aimed steadily at making themselves the carriers and the channel of universal commerce. England's instruments were monopoly and restriction. The weapons used by the States were enterprise and the clipper ship.

The question what particular shape and qualities constituted the kind of vessel called a clipper may be put to books and men without eliciting a short and satisfactory answer. The term is in reality not a definition, but a rhetorical epithet of praise. It was no fixed place of greatest breadth nor settled proportion of beam to length, or of beam to draught, which constituted the clipper. A ship was a clipper when she was not a tub. The word indicated an effort to obtain speed, smartness in method, and something of grace. What the origin of the term was, and how it came to be applied to a ship, are questions of some obscurity.

THE CLIPPER SHIP DUNCAN DUNBAR.

From a Lithograph by T. G. Dutton. Kindly lent by Messrs. T. H. Parker, Printsellers, 45, Whitcomb Street, W.C.

document. That naturalization and certificates of American birth were readily granted is undeniable, even if it is not strictly true that a friendly and unscrupulous old dame in New York gained an easy subsistence by swearing that candidates for a certificate were to her knowledge American born, at the rate of a dollar per perjury. These stories are told with embellishments, but not without foundation. The existence of a refuge for seamen across the Atlantic was one of the reasons which convinced the British Government that it must renounce the use of impressment. The seamen could elude it by emigration, and they could not be reclaimed except at the risk of a renewal of the war of 1812, and that, too, in all probability when it would be a far greater misfortune, a far greater strain, than it was when it did occur.

The history of the successive steps by which the Navigation Laws of Great Britain, which dominated the commerce of Europe, were broken down is a long one—not because it lasted for many years. The edifice was fairly beaten to ruins in about a generation. But the work was accompanied by an immense amount of diplomacy and legislation, to say nothing of makeshift and make-believe. The essence of the dispute was that England had aimed at forcing all the trade of the world to reach Europe through her, that other peoples grew impatient of this pretension, and that the United States aimed steadily at making themselves the carriers and the channel of universal commerce. England's instruments were monopoly and restriction. The weapons used by the States were enterprise and the clipper ship.

The question what particular shape and qualities constituted the kind of vessel called a clipper may be put to books and men without eliciting a short and satisfactory answer. The term is in reality not a definition, but a rhetorical epithet of praise. It was no fixed place of greatest breadth nor settled proportion of beam to length, or of beam to draught, which constituted the clipper. A ship was a clipper when she was not a tub. The word indicated an effort to obtain speed, smartness in method, and something of grace. What the origin of the term was, and how it came to be applied to a ship, are questions of some obscurity.

THE CLIPPER SHIP DUNCAN DUNBAR.

From a Lithograph by T. G. Dutton. Kindly lent by Messrs. T. H. Parker, Printsellers, 45, Whitcomb Street, W.C.

CONCLUSION

The first appearance of the word was as the name of the criminal who " clipped " the King's coin by paring off the edges. Yet the name was given to small, quick-sailing boats used as packets on the British Coast, and it very probably emigrated from Liverpool to New England. Be all that as it may, the clipper ship known to fame was a creation of New England, and the nearest approach to a strict definition of her is that she was built to carry cargo as quickly as might be, and was not so built as to sacrifice every other quality a ship can have to the capacity for stowing a great deal of cargo.

The conditions of trade had tended to make mere capacity to hold cargo the first of virtues in a ship. As far as Great Britain was concerned, they had been aggravated by the practice which levied harbour and light dues on tonnage estimated by multiplying the length of the keel by the beam, multiplying the product by half the beam, and dividing by ninety-four. The rule was established in the eighteenth century on the assumption that the depth of the hold would be half the beam. But it was obvious to those who had to pay the dues that if the vessel was built with a greater depth of hold she would carry more goods, and would continue to be taxed at below her real carrying capacity. She was not a good ship, nor a safe one, but she carried a big load, and that was all she was asked to do. The American clippers were evolved to beat her, and they did.*

The clippers were the fine flower and last development of the sailing ship. While they were fighting out their rivalry the enemy who was to sweep them, if not quite away, certainly into subordination, was advancing apace. The steamer was just beginning in the dawn of the nineteenth century. At the close it had conquered river and ocean. The use of iron was beginning to be imposed on the shipbuilder of Europe in the first quarter of the century. At the close the art of building wooden ships was dying.

* The history of the clipper has been so often and so recently told that there would be superfluity in going over the ground again. Mr. W. P. Lindsay's " History of Merchant Shipping," and Mr. A. H. Clarke's " The Clipper Era," are new and at hand. Both rather tell what the clipper did than what she was. But even technical books do not explain that to the non-technical reader.

A French proverb says that new men are needed for new things—" À des nouvelles choses il faut des nouveaux hommes." Between the opening of the ocean routes and the victory of the steamship the sailor was a man who vanished away from his people for months, perhaps years. The Indiaman looked to spend eighteen months going and coming, and that when the length of a voyage had been much shortened from what it had been. He was once the " man who went aloft." He is becoming one who simply steers and directs on deck. He went in peril of pirates even when the nations were at peace. Now, the sea is so thoroughly policed that the pirate hardly lingers in remote and barbarous coasts. In the shape of the European sea-robber and rover he has vanished altogether. The very Red Sea has been purged of him in the shape of the Arab plunderer, and he only makes an occasional appearance mostly at the expense of his countrymen, among the Malay Islands or in the China coasts and rivers. It has become a matter of some difficulty to realize that the lighthouse was once a rare and feeble help. Antiquity knew it, and there perhaps never was an age so barbarous that some form of guiding light was quite unknown. But they were few— so few that they could be counted on the fingers, and they were mere beacon fires. The use of oil lamps and reflectors began with the close of the eighteenth century. Now the way is lighted through the " passages " of the Indian Ocean and down the coast of Brazil. Once the sailor was separated, solitary, condemned to go in danger, and to grope in the dark. Danger there always is and will be on the sea, but to-day the means of avoiding it are so abundant that, with the exercise of care and foresight, the life of the sailor is not more perilous than the miner's. The greatest change of all is that the sailor, the man who could reef and steer, is ceasing to be the prominent type on the sea. Seamanship, if not giving place to engineering, has to share with it, and the management of furnaces and engines afloat is but a variant, and not a very great one, of the same work on land.

In the first half of the nineteenth century a curious but withal a characteristic thing happened both to and concerning the British seaman. When the old era of war and monopoly

CONCLUSION

was drawing to its close, the British ship and seamen were recognized as the first of their kinds on the sea. The vessels and the men of New England were compelling attention and respect as rivals, but the old-established masters of the sea had not quite got beyond the point of considering the pretensions of New England as impertinent. In good-humoured moments they patronized the "Yankee" and his ships as chips of the old block still marked by the sauciness of youth and inexperience. Within a generation there was a great change in tone. Shipowners were dismally pleading that if they were cruelly deprived of protection they were ruined men. Thoughtful persons were coming to the conclusion that the once unrivalled British seaman was drunken, ignorant, careless, dishonest, and that unless he was forced to mend his ways he would soon be driven off the sea, not only by the Yankee, who was a recognized master, but by the very Prussians and Italians. The clamour and lamentations were at their height between 1840 and 1850, the years which saw the final sweeping away of the Navigation Laws. In the shipowners' Press there was one long howl. In 1843 the Foreign Office called upon its Consuls not to report what evidence there might be for all this melancholy stuff, but to give all the evidence they could possibly rake together of the decadence of the British seaman.*

There was the usual proportion of exaggeration in all this, but there was happily also the usual element of saving good sense in the country. The shipbuilding and shipowning interests were loud for Free Trade when they understood it to mean freedom to import at remunerative rates in their ships. They were made to understand that their principle held good when the demand was for free trade in freights. After 1849 they had to fight in the open market—with the common results. When their backs were to the ropes they hit out, and soon found that they were not nearly so decrepit as they thought they were. The shipbuilders set themselves to show that they could build against New

* See "Foreign Office Circular," July 1, 1843, and the Consular Returns. The whole is well summarized in the "History of Merchant Shipping" of Mr. W. P. Lindsay, himself a seaman bred and a shipowner.

England and win, and they did. The exhaustion of the forests helped them, for Great Britain had many advantages for working in metal; but they might have made that discovery before, and they would have delayed making it if they had lacked the needful stimulus. The vast extension of British shipping followed the repeal of the Navigation Laws—a pretty clear proof that the laws were not necessary to its growth, and never had been so beneficent as their admirers supposed.

What was done for the men is, or ought to be, more interesting than the history of the ship. The question what basis of truth there was for all the outcry of 1843 and thereabouts is worth putting and answering. I have said that the charge was sweeping. Drunkenness, ignorance, carelessness, dishonesty, were alleged to be the growing vices of the British seaman, and he was unfavourably compared with rivals. The comparison was not made only by His Majesty's Consuls, who by the very nature of their work in foreign ports were brought into contact daily with the worst. When Marryat was writing " Snarley Yow," he more than once forgot that the date of his story was put at the close of the seventeenth century. He did overlook that fact when he described the sailors' eating and drinking house in Holland, and spoke of the clean, sober, and self-respecting American seamen, and the contrast they afforded to the men about them. The American seaman had hardly become a known type in the reign of William III. But Marryat spoke of what he had seen, and for that he was a good witness. We have quite sufficient evidence to show that when the nineteenth century was half through there was serious reason why the human, which is the vital, part of the merchant shipping of Great Britain should be taken in hand.

How came this to be the case in the nation which of all others had flourished by the help of its seamen, which not only professed to love and admire them, but did so honestly ? Let us allow that there was a great deal of exaggeration, and that the relative proportions of bad and good were absurdly misestimated. They commonly are. Mr. Burke, putting good sense into lofty English, exhorted a reader of his " Reflections on the Revolution in France " not to

CONCLUSION

suppose that, because half a dozen crickets under a fern fill the field with their importunate chink, they were the only inhabitants, or the most important. Still, their importunate noise forces itself on your attention, and so does the riotous person who smashes a shop window, though he (or, in our times, it is she) is of infinitely small importance when compared to the hundreds who are going about the street on their lawful occasions. In 1843 and thereabouts the mass of British sea-borne commerce was going successfully all over the world. Nevertheless it was the case that it was infected, and that in face of a growing rivalry it must rid itself of the infection or be outstripped.

The causes of the evil are easily found. They were two. The first was that if the country loved the sailor, it did not love him in the right way. The second was, that while it allowed a freedom from internal control which gave opportunity to the best elements, it did nothing to keep down the worst.

Whoever has looked at what the eighteenth century wrote about the sailor, or how it drew him, must have been struck by one thing. Fielding has summed it all up in a few sentences as only the master of style can. The sailor was the finest fellow in the world when he was at sea and at his work, but on shore he was a nuisance. He was expected, he was even actually encouraged, to be a drunken fool. To make his money like a horse, to spend it like an ass, was the note of the sailor. The crew of the man-of-war which had taken a rich Spanish prize made haste to throw away their prize-money on gold lace for hats, gold watches, which they then fried, liquor, and the rest. It was thought quite natural—in fact, gallant and admirable. And that incident was typical of the life and nonsense of the time. It was thought to be so like sailors that the majority of the men forced the minority to be as great fools as themselves. The majority, for their part, did it largely because they had been told that this was the correct behaviour for a sailor. To make the picture complete it is necessary to take an incident of another character. This also is part of the records of the navy, but the seaman and the sea life were the same from whichever side we look at them. Early in the nineteenth century a Lieutenant Tyrwhitt was sent from his ship at St. Helens with a boat to bring off stores from Portsmouth. While the boat was being laden some of the men succeeded in obtaining drink, and when she was to return to the ship with her lading several of them were too much intoxicated to row. They were told to lie down in the bottom of the boat. One of them was in that stage of drunkenness in which a man is firmly, even fiercely convinced of his sobriety. He insisted on pulling an oar, though he was manifestly unfit for the work. Lieutenant Tyrwhitt ordered him to leave the oar and lie down on the bottom of the boat. The sailor was too tipsy to be manageable. He refused to obey. The officer took the tiller, and struck him with it on the hand. The man was insensible to the blow, and Tyrwhitt struck again. This time the blow fell on the man's head, and with such force that he dropped senseless. When the boat reached the side of the ship she was unloaded, and the intoxicated men removed, except that one of them who had been struck by Lieutenant Tyrwhitt. He remained where he was till the attention of some of the men of the ship was called to him. Then his fellow-seamen lifted him on board, laid him on the forecastle, and left him there till next morning. He was found lying motionless and apparently dead. The doctor of the ship was called, and certified that he was dying of apoplexy brought on by drink. He was taken to the hospital, and there the doctors discovered that his skull was slightly fractured.

The naval authorities took no steps in the matter, but the blow had been given in sight of a crowd on Portsmouth Hard. When the death of the man became known there was an outcry. Tyrwhitt behaved with spirit and good sense. He took the full responsibility for what he had done, came boldly forward, and stood his trial at the Assizes. He pleaded that he had not struck the man on the head expressly, but by accident, and when he was aiming at his hands. The drunken man had thrust his head forward, and had, in fact, put it in the way of the tiller. Proof that the sailor died only of the blow was not forthcoming, and the Lieutenant was acquitted. I do not say that the verdict was wrong. Tyrwhitt does not appear to have behaved with gratuitous brutality. The drunken obstinacy of the man was dangerous to a heavily laden boat. The rights and wrongs of an obscure homicide may be left alone now. But the story of bestial drunkenness, of violence, and of callous indifference is illuminative for the real meaning of that love of his " flip " and his " can " which all the world tolerated in the sailor. Work was ill done; danger was incurred because of it; brutal measures were taken against it; and the victim was just a drunken sailor to be thrown on the deck with his broken head to recover his debauch and the blow if he could, and to die if he could not.

About the year 1840 the cant of joviality which had been talked about it all was beginning to be found nauseous. The pressure of competition was growing close. Rivals had arisen on both sides of the Atlantic, and there were signs that the superiority of the British sailor would go, not perhaps because he was getting worse, but because his rivals were steadily growing better, and resolute efforts were being made to improve them. We have seen that foreign sailors had always been employed in British ships even in peace, and that in war they had been numerous. Whatever arts we possessed the foreigner could learn from us, and he did. If the best of the British sailors, of whom the Americans were a variant, were at the head of their kind, only the best could make that boast with truth. It was coming to be thought that the best no longer bore the proportion to the whole they once had borne. This may have been an error, and there was very probably much exaggeration. But error and exaggeration were salutary for once. The nation turned to the "Condition of the British Seamen" question, and soon found that there was much to be done.

It soon found, for one thing, that the surroundings of the sailor in port were all calculated to promote the recklessness which ceased to look picturesque when it was threatening to become ruinous. All through the eighteenth century British harbours, and the " London River " not less than any other, had been pestered by dishonesty and excess in drink.* The waste caused by pilfering and smuggling was

* For London we have the invaluable picture of Mr. Colquhoun's "Treatise on the Commerce and Police of the River Thames," 1800. If things were worse in London than elsewhere, which is not proved, the reason was that the opportunities were greater.

enormous, and the necessary agents were the sailors, not only the men before the mast, but the mates and masters. A whole population of receivers and tempters swarmed by wharfs and docks. The lower officials of the Customs, numerous and ill-paid, were active offenders. The "lumpers" and "holders," who set up the rigging and unstowed the cargo, who were often themselves seamen; the "coal-heavers," the coopers, the lightermen, the "mud-larks," who prowled in the mud beside ships in the Pool and were equally ready to steal and to act as go-betweens; the labourers, who were called "scuffle hunters," who were loafers and casuals, and the more regular men employed in the warehouses, all supplied a quota to the army which served certain notorious receivers who were well known on the river. This army of dishonesty had for allies other and more open offenders, who did not even pretend to follow an honest trade—the river pirates, heavy horsemen and light horsemen, who pillaged ships and lighters, either by connivance with the crews and watchmen or by undisguised force. All this robbery went on practically unchecked. The only punishment for fraudulent offences was by fine, and the vermin who preyed on the trade of the Pool formed a union, paid two shillings a month subscription, and so established a fund which served to buy them out when they did have a "misfortune." Open violence was unchecked because there was no river police. High import duties by raising the price of commodities made it well worth the while of the receiver to encourage the thief. He could afford to give a third of the wholesale price of the stolen goods to sell them to tradesmen at a third below that figure, and to leave himself a handsome margin of profit. The evil reached a pitch at which the community was driven to deal with it by the construction of docks and the establishment of the river police. The reduction, or the repeal, of import duties came to make smuggling unprofitable, and the river grew as honest as human nature allowed.

In the meantime, this long prosperity and impunity of fraud had not been without its effect on the morality of the sailor, and it was largely aided by his knowledge of the fact that he was himself fleeced and victimized by the riverside population. The lodging-houses to which he must needs go when he was paid off were—not always—but too often no better than low brothels and receptacles of stolen goods. Dr. Johnson's famous taunt to the waterman, " Your wife, under pretence of keeping a brothel, is a receiver of stolen goods," may very well have been a literal statement of truth. A population of harpies and ruffians—in the strict sense of the word, which was to begin with the exact equivalent of the French " souteneur "— battened on the sailor. Even after the middle of the nineteenth century the sailor, who had been paid off from his ship, found a mob, male and female, waiting for him in the streets, and he had the choice between fighting his way through, or allowing himself to be plucked. Tempted, bullied, unprotected, is it wonderful that the sailor too often failed ?*

Much of the evil could be accounted for by a condition which in Europe, at any rate, was peculiarly British. No measures were taken to provide that the officers should either have a competent knowledge of their business, or should possess a status which they could not afford to lose. The owner was left to find competent men at his own risk. There was no examination, no certificate, for mates or masters. The utmost that even custom demanded was that the officers should be regular bred seamen who had served their apprenticeship. The self-interest of the owner was trusted to make him select the persons to whom he must needs trust his property with care. We have seen

* The conditions as to health in which he went to his work after a period of unemployment on shore make a very shocking subject, and one which need not be followed up. But I will allow myself to give one illustration from my own knowledge. It happened to me once to be called upon to take the notes of a consular court of inquiry into the wreck of a British barque on the Mediterranean coast of Spain. She had run ashore in fine clear moonlight, simply because there was nobody on the watch, and nobody at the helm. And that was the case because everyone in her, except her skipper and part-owner, an old man, but including the boy, was suffering from bad forms of venereal disease. And this happened long after much had been done to improve the condition of the merchant service. In earlier days such cases were less uncommon. When we bear them in mind, we can understand that Consuls could truthfully report in 1843 that almost any flag was preferred to the British by merchants with cargoes to ship.

from the case of John Newton that the owner could take any man whom he trusted, without being subject to the obligation to select one who had been certified as competent. No doubt the self-interest of the owner did in a great majority of cases cause him to exercise some care in the choice of his officers. The self-interest of the man who hoped one day to command a ship led him to qualify himself. The East India Company insisted on proofs of competence from its mates, from among whom it took its Captains. British trade could not have flourished as it undeniably did if the great majority of the seamen of all classes had not been competent.

Self-interest is not always enlightened. There were owners who distrusted an educated Captain because they thought him more able and therefore more likely to cheat them. There were men who trusted to something other than their competence to obtain commands; they were relatives of owners, or they had a little money, or they were prepared to serve the dishonesty of the owner. And it must have been the case that so long as the mate or master was not subject to be deprived of the right to follow his trade by the forfeiture of his qualifying certificate, one great motive for care and honesty must have been lacking. Mr. Colquhoun had suggested in 1800 that no man should be allowed to act as mate without a certificate, and should be punishable by the withdrawal of his qualification if he was detected in the dishonest practices then rampant on the river. It is highly characteristic of British ways that half a century passed before Mr. Colquhoun's recommendation was acted on, and the Merchant Shipping Act was carried. What was no less characteristic was that we were driven to attend to the education of merchant skippers and mates, by the discovery that foreign nations were setting us the example, and were threatening to establish a better level of competence. Yet, if the Trinity House had been used for the purpose Henry VIII. designed it to fulfil, the examination of mates and the granting of certificates would have been the rule from the sixteenth century; but there grew up in England a kind of hatred of regulation and police —part, no doubt, of the general fight for freedom. Much experience was needed to convince us that freedom for ignorance, incompetence, and dishonesty, is a pestilent evil.

Yet the lesson was learnt, and has borne fruit. The last half-century has seen a whole harvest of legislation designed to enforce competence on those who command, and to secure for the sailor protection against inhuman conditions of life ashore or afloat. The abominable dens of vice and fraud which once were the necessary lodging-houses of the sailor are no longer free to fleece him as they did. Some security is afforded that he shall have habitable quarters and wholesome food at sea. Modern England has put herself on a level with medieval Venice by restraining the unscrupulous owner who overloads his ship, and sends an unseaworthy ship to sea. What is even more to the purpose is that a great voluntary effort is being made to provide the sailor with some home, or even some house of call, on shore, where he can escape compulsory squalor and vice. Not only in British ports, but wherever British commerce has a footing—in Bilbao or Rio Janeiro, in Buenos Ayres or San Francisco, or Shanghai, there is such a place set up by the British community for the seafaring man. He cannot be restrained from ruining himself if he is unable to abstain from a rabid indulgence in drink, or if a vagabond element in his blood makes it possible for him to sink into a beachcomber ; but, at least, he is no longer driven to live in conditions unfit for a beast.

INDEX

ABOUSAID KHOSCH KADAM, Sultan of Egypt, 80, 81
Adams, Captain Robert, executes Roan, 131
Adams, Robert, reports on *Madre de Dios*, 95, 96
Aden, English plundered by Governor of, 148
Alexander VI., Pope, his Bull, 163 *et seq.*
Alsedo, Don Dionisio, Spanish officer, suppresses smugglers at Coclé, 232
Amboina, surrendered to Dutch, 144; conspiracy, 145
Amorgos, slave-hunting raid on, 313
Anna, Egyptian official. See Ship
Apollo, first fitted with necklace, 4
Apprentices, 281 *et seq.*
Arlington, Lord, on trade in West Indies, 231
Armour, 38 *et seq.*
Arms of Amsterdam, Dutch slaver, 326 *et seq.*
Ascension, 141
Ashburner, Mr., Rhodian Law quoted, 26
Asiento Treaty, 200 *et seq.*; terms of, 219, 220; end of, 233
Astrolabe, use of, 31, 53
Augereau, Jean, French pirate in West Indies, 260
Avery, Henry, *alias* Bridgeman, pirate, 246 *et seq.*
Avery, Mr., murdered by John Johnson, 131

Balboa, Vasco Nuñez de, discovers South Sea, 91; gives the name to South Sea, 209
Ball, 130
Barret, sailing-master with Hawkins, 195
Batavia, capital of Dutch East Indies, 112
Bather, James, boatswain of *Nightingale*, his adventures, 363 *et seq.*

Beauchesne, M. de, his voyage, 215 *et seq.*
Beck, Director of Dutch West India Company, 327-328
Belon, his account of Levant piracy quoted, 257-258
Bennet, Mr., plundered by Raja of Karwar, 135
" Berlin Decrees," 334 *et seq.*
Blaes, Adriaen, Dutch skipper, his account of slaving voyage, 362 *et seq.*
Blond, French corsair with Hawkins, 197
Borburata, Hawkins at, 179 *et seq.*
Bott, Pieter, Dutch Colonial Governor, quoted, 70; Governor of Dutch East India Company, 112
Bowles, Mr., his musical instruments, 123
" Breaking ground," what means, 141
Brethren of the Coast. See Buccaneer.
Broadfoot, Alexander, trial of for murder of pressmen, 266
Buenos Ayres, trade at, 207
Buccaneers, their origin, 203

Cabral, Pedro Alvarez, discovers Brazil, 167
Cæsar, action with pirates, 251
Calhoun, murdered by Broadfoot, 266
Capello, Jacomo, Captain of Flanders Galleys, 80
Carrack. See Ship
Carrera de Indias, what was, 103, 104, 106
Carwar. See Karwar
Cazeneuve, Guillaume de. See Coulomb
Cecil, Robert, Lord Salisbury, regulates trade with Spain, 109
Census of Seamen, 279-281

Chanty, Spanish, 107
Charles I., King of Great Britain, and East India Company, 113
Charts, origin of, 52 et seq.
Chiourmes, chusmas, ciurme, meaning of, 35 and *note*
Christie, Colonel, his description of pirate in West Indies, 259 et seq.
Chronometers, early efforts to make, 53 et seq.
Cinco Chagas, Portuguese carrack, burnt, 153
Clipper. See Ship
Cock, Captain Richard, Factor in Japan, 130
Cockeram, Martin, first Englishman in Brazil, 170
Coclé, River, smugglers' port at, 225
Colomb, Admiral, his account of slave-trade in Indian Ocean quoted, 313 et seq.
Columbus, Christopher, his first voyage, 90
Commerce, maritime, in war, 338 et seq.
Companies, Chartered, 109 et seq.
Compass, mariners', development of, 45 et seq.
Consent, 124
Conserva (convoy), 62
Consolato del Mare, Catalan maritime codes, quoted, 27 et seq.
Contratacion, Casa de la, Spanish Board of Trade, 93
Convoy: Acts to enforce, 350; advantages and disadvantages, 348 et seq.; East Indian taken, 356; in Firth of Forth in 1781, 349; Moutray's taken by French and Spaniards, 359
Cooke, G. F., his taunt to people of Bristol, 293
Coullon. See Coulombo
Coulombo or Coullon, French pirate, attacks Venetians, 24
Crew, treatment and divisions of in medical ships, 30 et seq.
Culliford, Captain, pirate, 251

Dalley, Mr., "Assistant-Registrar of Shipping," gives number of sailors, 280, 281
Dance, Nathaniel, 358; action with Zinois at Pulo Aor, 348
Darling, 148
Dashur, undertakers' boats, Egyptian. See Ship
Debbo, 67; fair at, 8
Deir-el Bahari, pictures of ships, and inscription on, 1, 9

Del Cano or De Elcano, Sebastian, first circumnavigator, 91
Delgadillo, Captain of Port Vera Cruz, 193 et seq.
Downing, Clement, quoted, 134, 135 and *note*
Downton, Nicholas: his victory at Surat, and death, 157; his voyage in *Peppercorn*, 126 et seq.; with Middleton in Red Sea, 152 et seq.
Dragon, 124
Drury, Robert, his "Journal" quoted, 159-161
Duro, Don Cesareo, quoted, 192

East India Company, Dutch, 110 et seq
East India Company, English, 112 et seq.
East India Company, French, 114
Edgecombe, Captain, murdered by pirates, 251
Edward III., King of England, attacks barques, 72
Elizabeth, 130
Elizabeth, Queen, her share in West Indian voyages, 174, 175
England. See Seager
Essex, South Sea Company's ship, 220 et seq.

Faber, Brother Felix, 29; quoted, 41; his account of the Pilgrim galleys of Venice, 56-60
Falconbridge, Alexander, surgeon, account of the slave-trade, 259 et seq.
Falkland Islands, why occupied, 199
Fandino, "the infamous," 227, 229
Pawk, Captain, taken by pirates, 263
Femmel, Mr., merchant, with Sir Henry Middleton, 148; poisoned, 155
Feretier, in *Caroline* frigate takes East India Convoy, 356
Field, Captain, killed, 178
Flanders Galleys. See Ship
Flota. See Carrera de Indias
Foster, Sir Michael, on impressment, 266-267
Prezier, M., his voyage, 214

Galleon, Spanish. See Ship
Galley slaves. See Chiourme, etc.
Galleys. See Ship
"Gallivats," what were, 136
Gama, Vasco da, reaches India, 91
Garcie, Pierre, *alias* Ferrande, quoted, 64-66

INDEX

Gibson, Captain, and Avery, 246
Gilbaudière. See Jouhan de la
Godolphin, Lord, his arbitration, 113
Gordon, Captain, wounded, 136
Grimaldi, Reniero, takes *Saint Nicholas*, 29

Hacha, Rio de la, Hawkins at, 183 et seq.
Hancock, Richard, drunken cook, his negligence and death, 127
Hansa, or Hanseatic League, 69 et seq.
Hanway, Captain, of *Mortar*, serves press warrant, 265
Hatshepsitu, Egyptian Queen, her tomb at Deir-el-Bahari, 1
Hawkins, Sir John, his voyages to West Indies, 171-198
Hawkins, Sir Richard, quoted, 122
Hawkins, William, his voyages to Brazil, 169, 170
Hector, 124, 141
Henry the Navigator, Portuguese Prince, his explorations, 89 et seq.
Henry VII., King of England, favours the Venetians, 80
Hereditary bottoms, what were, 119
Herrera, Spanish historian, quoted, 192
Hood, Sir Samuel, Admiral, account of his convoy, 350 et seq.
Hortop, Job, quoted, 187, 189
Houtman, Cornelius, voyage to East, 111
Hues, Robert, author of "Tractatus de Globlis," quoted, 54
Huguenot adventurers in West Indies, 171
Hypozoma. See Ship

Ibn Batuta quoted for Chinese ships, 24
Impressment, 265-292; causes of discontent with navy, 289, 290; alternatives proposed, why unsuccessful, 291, 292; in France, 268-272; a general press, 284 et seq.; exemption from, 288
Indiaman. See Ship
Inscription, maritime. See Impressment in France

Jacatra. See Batava
Jaffier Pasha at Sena'a, 149 et seq.
James I., King of Great Britain, and East India Company, 113
"Jenkins's Ear," story of, 226 et seq.
Jenkins, Hercules, Captain of packet taken by pirates, 259

Jesus of Lübeck, 174
Johnson, Captain Charles, his "History of the Pirates" quoted, 255
Johnson, Dr.: quoted, 144, 145, 199; his taunt to waterman, 379
Johnson, John, Dutch sailor, beheaded for murder of Mr. Avery, 131
John II., King of Portugal, helps plundered Venetians, 85
Jonah, 172
Jouhan de la Gilbaudière, French buccaneer, 215
Judith, Drake's vessel, 186

Karwar, Raja of, quarrels with East India Company, 134 et seq.
Keeling, "General," his voyage, 124 et seq.
Kelly, James, pirate, his confession, 256, 257
Keno, capture of, 359
Keno then Broke, ally of the Vitalians, 75
Kidd, Captain, pirate, 248 and note
Knowles, Sir Charles, Admiral, in West Indies, 232 and note
Koen, Jan Pieterz, Governor of Dutch East India Company, 112

Lancaster, Sir James: his first voyage, iii; plunders Portuguese carrack, 140; precautions against scurvy, 122; speaks the cattle language, 143
Lascars, 276-277; employment of, 120
Lasinby, Richard, prisoner among pirates, 261 et seq.
Laudonnière, Réné, relieved by Hawkins, 184
Lawes, Abraham, his delusions and death, 128
Lemaire, Jacob, Dutch merchant, 208 et seq.
Lewis XIV., King of France, and the South Sea voyages, 211
Lexington, Lord, British Ambassador in Spain, quoted, 218
Lezo, Blas de, Spanish officer, threatens to hang English Captain, 224
Licence, a trading, 336
Licensed trade, 332 et seq.; at St. Eustatius, 354 et seq.
Lighthouses, old, 55
Lindsay, Captain of *Sanderson*, 317
Line, the, what was, 167
Linois, French Admiral, at Palo Aor, 348

386 THE SEA TRADER

Linschoten, Jan Huyghen, Dutch adventurer, quoted, 97-98, 101
Lockyer, Charles, " Account of the Trade in India," quoted, 121
Longitude, difficulty of finding, 53 et seq.
Lujan, Francisco, and Hawkins, 192 et seq.

Macrae, Captain, and the pirates, 261 et seq.
Madagascar. See Drury, Robert
Madre de Dios, Portuguese carrack, taken, 95
Magellan enters Pacific, 91
Malipiero, Pietro, Captain of Flanders galleys, attacked by English, 83
Manwaring, Sir Henry, his treatise on " Piracy " quoted, 235 et seq.
Marco Polo: account of Chinese ships, 24 ; quoted, 6
Mare Scourge, or Malice Scourge, 116
Marine interest, what was, 117, 118
Marisma, guild of Basque seamen, 72 ; for Indian trade, 107
" Mast, made," parts of, 4
Melendez de Aviles, Pedro, his ferocity to French, 171
Melo, Gaspar. de, Portuguese Governor of Amboina, 145
Merchant Shipping Act, purpose and influence of, 388
Middleton, Sir Henry: " General " of East India Company, 115 ; his voyages, 141 et seq.; his death, 157
Minio, Bartolomeo, Captain of Venetian galleys, attacked in Colombo, 84
Minion, 176, 177
Mississippi Company, 211
Mocha, English at, 149 et seq.
Moluccas Islands, conflict in, 144 et seq.
Monclova, Count of, Viceroy of Peru, his treasure, 216-217
Monte Video, port of call, 207
Moon, 130
Motta, Aleixo de, Portuguese pilot, quoted, 95
Mudue, Venetian convoy, 61 ; number of, 72
Mulatto, the, pirate in Gulf of Florida, 234

Narborough, Sir John, his voyage to South Seas, 210
Navigation Laws and seamen, 273, 278
Neck, Jacob van, voyage to East, 111

Negroni, Giovanni Ambrosio de, Florentine, hires English ship for piracy, 82
Newton, John: his crew plot to run away with ship, 304 ; his life at sea, 308-312
Nicholas V., Pope, his grant to Portuguese, 164

Officers. See Ship
Oleron, Laws of, quoted, 26 et seq.
Orders in Council, 332 et seq.
Orleans, Duke of, suppresses French trade in Pacific, 217
Ormond, Earl of, warrant of, for arrest of Downton, 130
Ormuz occupied by Portuguese, 138
Oruba, Dutch island, centre of smuggling trade, 225
Oviedo, Gonzalo Fernandez de, his " History of the Indies " quoted, 162-163

Palsgrave, 130
Parker, Sir Hyde, Admiral, and North Sea Convoy, 249
Pasqualiga, Venetian vessel, 83
Paul of Plymouth, 170
Payment of medieval crews, 33 et seq.
Pemberton, Mr., merchant, his escape, 151
Peppercorn, 117 148 ; voyage home, 126 et seq.
Periploi. See Sailing directions
Peru, French trade with, 211
Peterson, John, murdered by Roan, 130
Piebald Cow, ship of Simon of Utrecht, 75
Pieza de Indias, meaning of, 201 note
Pindar, Francis, mutineer, 129
Piracy: Act of Henry VIII. against, 239, 240 ; Act of William III. against, 248-250 ; in the Mediterranean, 252 et seq.; on Irish coast, 238 et seq.; the great piratical round, 243 et seq.
Pirate, the, 234, 264
Portuguese : their disorders in India, 137 et seq.; voyages, 90, 91
Prau. See Ship
Privateers, 361 et seq, 362 note
Puente, Pedro, and Hawkins, 176
Punt, land of, Egyptian voyage to, 1

Ramalho, Jão, his story, 204
Red Dragon, 141
Regib Aga, Governor of Mocha, 149 et seq.

INDEX

Rhodes, Knights of St. John at, assail the Venetians, 80 *et seq.*
Ribault, Jean, killed by Spaniards, 171
Rigging. See Ship
Roan, John : executed for murder, 130 ; dying speech and confession, 131
Roberts, A., his adventures in pirate, 252 *et seq.*
Rodney, Lord, Admiral, at St. Eustatius, 355
Roncière, M. Charles de la, quoted, 29
Rosenfeld, headsman, decapitates the Vitalians, 75
Rudder. See Ship
Rumis, name for Turks, 138
Rutters. See Sailing directions

Sailing directions, old, 48 *et seq.*
St. Eustatius, British licensed trade at, 354 *et seq.*
St. John, Dutch slaver, 326 *et seq.*
St. Lo, Captain, his pamphlets on pay and impressment, 340 *et seq.*
St. Malo trades with South Seas, 212
St. Mark, galleys of. See Ship
Saint Nicholas taken, 29 *et seq.*
Salazar, Eugenio de, quoted, 107
Saldania, original name of Table Bay, 142
Salisbury, Lord. See Cecil, Robert
Sanderson, of Newport, her slaving voyage, 316 *et seq.*
Santa Maria. See Linschoten
Saris, Captain : picture in his cabin, 123 ; meets Middleton in Red Sea, 156
Schmid, Felix. See Faber
Schouten, William, Dutch seaman, 208 *et seq.*
Scuttling, story of, 362 *note*
Scylax of Caryanda. See Sailing directions
Seager, *alias* England, pirate, 261
Seamen: Act for preventing desertion of in West Indies, 342 *et seq.*; complaints of decline of British, 373 *et seq.*; element of truth in, 375 *et seq.*; effect of state of war on, 339 *et seq.*; treatment of, in slave-trade, 302 *et seq.*
Sena'a, English prisoners at, 151
Seville, headquarters of Spanish trade, 93
Ship : the ancient, Malay prau, 6 ; how rigged, 7 ; how manned and officered, 8 ; antique galleys, doubts concerning, 11, 13, and

note ; Venetian, 12, 13 ; Egyptian, at Kau-el-Kebir, 15 ; Una's vessels, 16 ; Anna, 16 *et seq.;* undertakers' boats, Egyptian, 19 ; prau, how constructed, *ibid. ;* weakness of ancient ships, how corrected, 20 ; "Hypozoma," "Tormentum," "swifter," *ibid. ;* steering by oar or rudder, 21 ; proportions of ship, *ibid. ;* rigging, *ibid. ;* speed of ancient, 22 ; size of, *ibid. et seq. ;* Norse ship at Gokstad, 25 ; "exercitor," "merchant," "nauclerokubernetes," "nochiero," "notxer," "nauxer," "naucher," "kubernetes," "pistikos," "gubernator," what were, 29 ; "capitaneus," 33 ; crews of medieval ships, 34 *et seq. ;* pay, allowances, and rations, 36 *et seq. ;* equipment, 38 *et seq. ;* galleys of St. Mark, 59-60 ; rules for lading and ballast, 61-62 ; Flanders galleys, 76-83 ; plundered by French, 84-87 ; Portuguese carracks, 95-96 ; Spanish galleons, 106 ; how manned, 107, 108 ; Indiaman, 115-116 ; life of, 118-119 ; how manned, 119, 121, 123 ; bad health of crews, 121, 122 ; Surat, native ships of, 139 ; clippers, their character and influence, 370-371 ; steamships, first appearance of, 371
Simon of Utrecht defeats Vitalians 75
Sixpenny office, 279-280
Slaver, the, 293, 328
Slave-trade, suppression of, 319 *et seq.*
Smith, Nathaniel, Captain of *Essex*, instructions to, from South Sea Company, 220 *et seq.*
Smith, Sir Thomas, Governor of East India Company, his piety, 148
Solomon, 172, 175, 178
Sorie, Jacques de, plunders Havannah, 171
South Sea Company, 219, 220
South Sea, meaning of, 209
Spanish voyages, 102, 103
Speult, van, Dutch Governor of Amboina, kills English, 146 and *note*
Spirits, the, slave traders, 293
Steelyard. See Hansa
Stent, Captain, pirate, 251
Stewart, Mr. Archibald, Lord Provost of Edinburgh, on moral character of sailors, 365

Stewart, Rear-Admiral Charles, or state of West Indies, 228-230
Stortebeker, Klaus, Vitalian chief, 74
Stuart, Mr. Villiers: his "Nile Gleanings" quoted, 15
Surat, native ships of, 139
Surcouf, French privateer, 359
Susan, 116, 141
Swallow, 172
Swifter. See Ship

Talikoot, Battle of, 112
Tarbutt, Captain of *Apollo*, East India Company, improvement in rigging, 4
Ternate. See Moluccas
Terville, M., attacked by Spaniards at Valdivia, 215-216
Thames, disorder and crime on, 378, 379
Tidoré. See Moluccas
Tiger, 175
Topassies, what were, 135
Tormentum. See Ship
Towerson, Captain: at Amboina, 146 *note*; in Red Sea with Middleton, 156
Trade's Increase, 115, 148
Trenails, or trennels, what are, 126 *note*
Trumpett provisions, pirates', 264
Tyrwhitt, Lieutenant, story of, 375, 376

Ulloa, San Juan de, Hawkins at, 190 *et seq.*
Ulysses, his adventure, 68
Una, Egyptian official, his vessels. See Ship
United States, British sailors in, 369 *et seq.*
Urdaneta, Andres de, Spanish navigator, in North Pacific, 210

Valle, Pietro delle, his criticism of the Portuguese, 99
Venice opposes Portuguese in India, 138
Vespucci, Amerigo, 209
Vitalians, piratical league, 73-75
Vizyanagar, Hindoo kingdom, 112

Wallace, Alfred Russel, quoted, 6 and *passim*
Warren Hastings, capture of, 359
Wilberforce, Mr., witnesses capture of merchant ships off Brighton, 346
Winchelsea, fight off, 72
Winter, ships laid up in, 61
Wreckers, 63 *et seq.*

"Yankee" sailors, their character and influence, 368 *et seq.*
Yule, Sir Henry, quoted, 24

Zacosta, Pedro Raimundo, Grand Master of Knights of St. John, 81

THE END

Date Due

Demco 293-5

HE571F12 BOSTON UNIVERSITY BOSS
The sea trader,

1 1719 00216 2560

**FREDERICK S. PARDEE
MANAGEMENT LIBRARY
BOSTON UNIVERSITY LIBRARIES
595 COMMONWEALTH AVENUE
BOSTON, MA 02215**